THE SECRET HISTORY OF THE

FIVE EYES

Richard Kerbaj is a BAFTA-winning and twice Emmy-nominated filmmaker and writer who has specialised in investigating matters of national security for more than fifteen years. He has written extensively about the impact of counterterrorism and counterespionage on intelligence agencies.

Richard is also a multi-award-winning journalist who was the security correspondent for the *Sunday Times* between 2010 and 2020. Prior to that, he worked for *The Times* as an investigative reporter and foreign correspondent, and for *The Australian*. He has written and produced international award-winning documentaries, including *My Son the Jihadi*, *Hunting the KGB Killers*, about the murder of Russian dissident Alexander Litvinenko, and *Unmasking Jihadi John: Anatomy of a Terrorist*.

The Secret History of the Five Eyes is his first book.

THE SECRET HISTORY OF THE

FIVE
EYES

THE UNTOLD STORY OF THE
INTERNATIONAL SPY NETWORK

RICHARD KERBAJ

BLINK
bringing you closer

First published in the UK by Blink Publishing
an imprint of Bonnier Books UK
4th Floor, Victoria House
Bloomsbury Square
London WC1B 4DA
England

Owned by Bonnier Books
Sveavägen 56, Stockholm, Sweden

www.facebook.com/blinkpublishing
twitter.com/BlinkPublishing

First published in hardback and trade paperback in 2022

Hardback ISBN: 978-1-78946-503-7
Trade paperback ISBN: 978-1-78946-555-6
Ebook ISBN: 978-1-78946-556-3
Audiobook ISBN: 978-1-78946-557-0

British Library Cataloguing-in-Publication Data:
A CIP catalogue record for this book is available from the British Library.

Design by www.envydesign.co.uk

Printed and bound in Great Britain by Clays Ltd, Elcograf S.p.A

1 3 5 7 9 10 8 6 4 2

Text copyright © Richard Kerbaj 2022

Blink Publishing is an imprint of Bonnier Books UK
www.bonnierbooks.co.uk

To Marine, Leo, Dom – and to either Margaux or Nate.
And also to John, my great friend and mentor

CONTENTS

PART THREE: THE WAR ON TERROR

PART FOUR: UNCONVENTIONAL BATTLEFIELDS

INTRODUCTION

THE BEDROCK OF THE Five Eyes intelligence alliance was gradually formed by British and American officials without them realising it. But in their attempt to save their countries from Nazi Germany in the lead up to, and during, World War II, they unknowingly helped build the foundational blocks of the biggest espionage alliance in history.

During that time, Britain's intelligence agencies, MI5, Bletchley Park, and MI6, united with their American cousins – the FBI, Arlington Hall, and the OSS, predecessor to the CIA – out of necessity and self-interest. There were written and unwritten rules of engagement between them which were generally observed but occasionally disregarded. The agencies swapped secrets, pooled resources and exchanged tradecraft – and while they did not completely trust one another, they shared a common purpose in destroying the enemy.

After defeating Adolf Hitler, the United States and Britain suddenly faced a new threat from an old ally of whom they had been suspicious – Joseph Stalin. Yet by the time the two nations figured out what to do about him, Kremlin spies had already stolen British and American nuclear secrets to further the Soviet leader's pursuit of global supremacy. In early 1946, London and Washington quickly repurposed their signals intelligence arrangement, known as the UKUSA Agreement, to widen their global reach and industrialise their espionage missions at the beginning of the Cold War. In a push for greater intelligence coverage, Britain and America expanded the agreement a decade later to include Canada, Australia, and New Zealand, which were geographically well-positioned to plug surveillance gaps worldwide and around the clock. They became the Five Eyes.

Steeped in secrecy, the partnership transformed spy warfare by evolving beyond its signals-sharing heritage to form a parallel – and yet unwritten – pact between its human-intelligence and law-enforcement agencies, including the CIA, MI5, the Australian Security Intelligence Organisation (ASIO), and the Royal Canadian Mounted Police (RCMP). The partnerships among some of the human-intelligence (HUMINT) agencies pre-dated the signals-intelligence (SIGINT) agreements within the alliance, but it is when the two sides started working more closely together that some of the greatest operational achievements were realised.

Together, the Five Eyes have weaponised hacking and agent-running in an intelligence arms race which has spanned the Cold War, rendition and torture of Guantanamo detainees, the battle against Isis, the attempt to disrupt Moscow and Beijing's meddling in western democracies, and supporting Ukraine in its fights against the 2022 Russian invasion. At the heart of this alliance are complex and, at times, flawed personalities whose achievements and failures have helped guarantee the Five Eyes's evolution since its formation. And it is through such personalities that this book is defined; I wanted to explore the stories of the people, rather than the policies which are still largely classified.

My starting point is in the late 1930s when a British detective-turned-spymaster helped form the first exchanges between MI5 and the FBI. But I was also fascinated by the stories of the former home economics teacher from a rural village in Virginia, south eastern United States, who helped create one of the most effective counter-Soviet programmes; the CIA's only officer in Budapest during the Hungarian Revolution; and the Australian politician-turned-diplomat whose tip-off to the FBI helped instigate an investigation into Russia's meddling in the US presidential elections in 2016. And there are dozens of other compelling personalities whose stories appear in this book.

On the one hand, the Five Eyes is equivalent to a band of brothers and sisters drawn together by common values, language and cause, whose historical achievements include the defeat of the Soviet Union, combating Islamist terrorism, and exposing Russian interference in Donald Trump's presidential campaign. But on the other hand, the alliance is a non-binding marriage of convenience riddled with distrust, competing intelligence agendas, and a massive imbalance of power that predominantly favours the United States – despite all the talk of a flat hierarchical structure among alliance members.

While it has played a vital role in episodes that defined the second half of the twentieth century, the existence of the Five Eyes was only publicly declared in 2010 – almost sixty years after its creation – in a heavily redacted document with about two-thirds of its pages blank. I have spent the past decade exploring how it functions, initially through conversations with agent-handlers and spymasters during my career as an investigative reporter – followed by a two-year deep dive into historical records and interviews with more than a hundred current and former intelligence officials, diplomats, and detectives – and some of the family members of legendary code breakers and undercover agents. I also interviewed world leaders, including former British Prime Ministers Theresa May and David Cameron, and former Australian Prime Ministers Julia Gillard and Malcolm Turnbull. I wanted to explore how the collision of intelligence, diplomacy, technology, and geopolitics in an unpredictable world impacts an increasingly crucial pillar in our daily lives – national security. I was also intrigued by the impact political leaders have had on compromising the integrity and independence of agencies in the Five Eyes as they sought to weaponise their intelligence-gathering for personal gain – as President Trump repeatedly showed in his siding with the Kremlin against the FBI and CIA.

As an alliance of autonomous organisations, the Five Eyes does not always agree on everything. It has been repeatedly hindered by the policy, legal, and political idiosyncrasies of each country. New Zealand was partially cut from the alliance for more than two decades after it opposed the US's nuclear policies. Britain defied the US in expelling Soviet spies from the UK during the Cold War, which eventually resulted in a temporary freeze on intelligence-sharing by Washington. The CIA was accused of plotting to depose Australian prime minister Gough Whitlam in 1975. Canada refused to join the US-led invasion of Iraq and, in a separate case, compromised the intelligence of all alliance members after a Canadian naval officer became a Russian spy. And Australia teamed up with the US to pressure Britain into severing its ties with Chinese telecommunications firm Huawei. Despite all of this, the Five Eyes has survived and outlived governments and administrations of all political parties.

The reader may notice an imbalance in the focus of the stories that form this book. That is because material relating to intelligence cooperation between Britain and the US is more readily available than information about the workings of the other three Five Eyes member countries. The spy organisations (and especially the HUMINT agencies) of the two founding members of the Five Eyes pre-date the creation of their counterparts in Australia, Canada and New Zealand (and the clue is in the title of the foundational document of the alliance – UKUSA Agreement). I found the least amount of information relating to the role of New Zealand in the alliance, and that is partly due to the fact that Wellington is the smallest contributor to the Five Eyes – even though it plays an important part in terms of its geographical positioning.

Most of the key intelligence agencies in the Five Eyes have had detailed histories written about them. To devote as much attention to each member agency in a book about the Five Eyes would require volumes. Instead, I had to be selective – to focus on a number of individuals and intelligence agencies who, in my opinion, have enormously contributed, either knowingly or unknowingly, to the overall legacy of the Five Eyes.

RICHARD KERBAJ
JULY 2022

PART ONE: ORIGINS

CHAPTER ONE

A CRUCIAL TIPOFF

THOUSANDS OF PEOPLE EMBARKED and disembarked freight and passenger vessels at the port of Hamburg in the winter of 1937, greeted by a frenetic atmosphere of docking boats, blaring ship horns, and wafts of fuel-laced sea water. As a local, Jessie Jordan had become familiar with the atmosphere of the twelfth-century seaport, central Europe's most important transatlantic hub for trade and tourism. But it was a familiarity that she wanted to escape in preparation for a new life away from Germany, the country she had made her home for 30 years. She farewelled her daughter, Marga, and her granddaughter who carried her namesake, and arrived at the harbour unaccompanied on 2 February, in time for a vessel bound for Scotland, her country of birth. The events that followed that day would only ever be known through Jessie's inconsistent, and often unreliable, recollection. In one version, Jessie said she had left the port to stay the night with a close friend after being told by the ship's steward that the steamer would be delayed by a day. In the other version, she claimed to have been intercepted on her way to the docks by officers of the Gestapo, the feared German secret police, known for their brutality. In any case, her delayed journey to Scotland resulted in her recruitment by the Abwehr, the intelligence arm of the German armed forces responsible for Adolf Hitler's counterintelligence and sabotage campaigns. As a heavyset, 49-year-old grandmother with a cloud of thick, ash-blonde hair, Jessie appeared unassuming – and that was an advantage. It gave her a sense of anonymity that is desirable for espionage work. Another obvious advantage that the Abwehr would have spotted in Jessie was her British heritage and somewhat uncertain identity.

Even before her birth in December 1887, Jessie had been abandoned by her father, William Ferguson – and upon being discharged from Glasgow maternity hospital, had been left in the care of her maternal grandmother for five years before her mother, Elizabeth Wallace, was able to take her in. By then, Jessie's mother had become Mrs Haddow, following her marriage to a widower, John Haddow, who had children of his own. Jessie had initially been given her mother's last name – rather than her absent father's – at birth. But following her mother's marriage, Jessie Wallace would become Jessie Haddow. The uncertainty around her own shifting sense of identity accompanied her through her early adult years – even after she had run away from home to escape her mother's physical beatings, which were the expressions of an unhappy marriage.

Jessie's life took yet another turn after she met a German waiter, Karl Friedrich Jordan, while she was working as a chambermaid in Dundee in 1907. They fell in love and she followed him to Germany where they married five years later. Jordan, whose last name and nationality Jessie adopted, died on the Western Front in July 1918, leaving her and their four-year-old daughter, Marga, to fend for themselves. Within two years, Jessie had built a successful hairdressing career and found new love. But her marriage to Baur Baumgarten, another German man whose last name she would adopt, only lasted three years – and she reverted to being Jessie Jordan, the name she would maintain for the rest of her life.

Unlike the four different surnames by which she was known at varying stages in her life, Jessie's willingness to become a spy was a complete identity makeover; a complete shift of allegiance that not only betrayed the country of her birth but also the Jewish community – which both her former husbands were from – and on which she relied for her livelihood, and success, as a hairdresser. It was predominantly Jewish women who had attended the three salons she had operated in Hamburg. For a woman who once told her daughter she would 'die for Germany', Jessie also claimed that she never felt at home in her adopted country. She felt like a foreigner, part exposed by her inability to fluently speak the local language, but chiefly because of the anti-British sentiment whipped up after World War I. Jessie claimed that the experience of people going 'out of their way to be nasty' to her, were reminders of the rejection she had become accustomed to in her life. She merely wanted to 'live in peace and bring up my little Marga better than I had been brought up myself.'

Whether the Abwehr had known of the extent of Jessie's turbulent past before her recruitment is unknown, but, over eight days in early February 1937, she was taught the basic tradecraft of spying at their offices in Harvestehude, 13 kilometres north of the port of Hamburg. She was trained in how to collect basic information about British military facilities without arousing suspicion and told that she would be paid by the Abwehr for her efforts. The money was not the main attraction, however – Jessie was largely driven by the adventure of spying because it appealed to her obsession with thriller novels. And her declared motive for wanting to relocate to Scotland provided her with the best cover story. Jessie's intended relocation was for family reasons: she wanted to become a housekeeper for her half-brother, William Haddow, who lived in Perth, central Scotland, and whose wife had passed away. By the time she arrived in Scotland in late February to live with him, Jessie had the perfect cover: she was someone in search of a new start in the country she had spent three decades away from. Neither William, nor her daughter, Marga, were aware that the country Jessie had once associated with all the pitfalls of her childhood and early teen years was to become her testing ground for spying.

Eager to use her profession as a hairdresser in lieu of a legend – a cover story used by spies to conduct espionage work to avoid suspicion – Jessie travelled to Dundee, on the east coast of Scotland, in the summer of that year to inspect a hairdressing salon. She had spotted a newspaper advertisement for Jolly's Saloon, 1 Kinloch Street, and had arrived with ambitions for expanding the local business to also offer massage and beauty therapy. The salon was located 40 miles north of naval installations at the Firth of Forth, an estuary where warships sheltered and docked for repairs. Among the installations Jessie was interested in was Fife Ness, a coastguard station.

Even on the eve of her 50th birthday, Jessie appeared to possess the energy of a young entrepreneur, willing to take a risk on an unremarkable salon in a 'working-class locality' for the sake of beginning a new adventure in Scotland. She was effectively sold on the salon the minute she walked in to meet with Patrick Robbins, who had been entrusted to sell the business on behalf of its owner. The shop fittings and goodwill were merely valued at £25 – but instead of negotiating, she offered twice the value. She appeared 'unusually keen to get the shop', according to Robbins, and so he did what any shrewd businessman would do: held out for an even better offer. After further conversations with Robbins, Jessie finally paid the owner £75 – in £5 notes – after claiming to have borrowed the money from her aunt in Wales.

She took ownership of the salon on 7 September 1937, seven months after her relocation to Scotland, and commuted by bus back and forth to the shop from Perth most days – a forty-mile round trip which seemingly illustrated her passion and commitment to hairdressing. To conceal her espionage missions, she hired assistants to manage the salon in her absence, including Mary Curran, the previous owner's sister-in-law, who had been familiar with the customers. Unbeknown to Curran, Jessie travelled between Scotland, England and Wales to sketch and photograph defence force facilities for her Abwehr handlers.

Curran admired Jessie's quirks, including her addiction to coffee and fish suppers. But the middle-aged assistant was puzzled by Jessie's grasp of the English language, which became self-evident during a conversation around her intention to rename the business Saloon Jordan. Curran suggested that Jordan's Saloon would be a better way to phrase it – and Jessie agreed. But her habit of 'putting remarks the other way around', coupled with scraps of paper misplaced around the store –

including one with the word 'Zeppelin' written on it – raised Curran's curiosity. For a fashion-conscious hairdresser, often dressed in fur coats and plumed hats, Jessie's fascination with the military, and, in particular, army barracks, bemused Curran, who was entrusted to manage the salon each time the owner left on her travels. It was Jesse's trip to Hamburg in October that tipped Curran's interest from curiosity into suspicion. Jessie had returned from several days in Germany with her daughter, Marga, who by then was a 23-year-old trained soprano whose ambitions to perform at the Hamburg Opera House had been crushed by Hitler's anti-Jewish campaign. Like her mother, Marga had been unlucky with men: she had divorced her first husband – a Jewish man – shortly after their daughter was born in 1934. Marga then remarried another Jewish man, reinforcing a suspicion held by the Nazi authorities that she had 'Jewish blood in her veins'. Hoping to allay these suspicions, Marga had arrived in Scotland to obtain paperwork relating to her Scottish grandfather – the man who had abandoned her mother before birth. Jessie's upbringing and difficult life were all the more reason she wanted to ensure her own daughter's success.

However, Jessie's return-trip to Germany was not solely to help Marga. Curran suspected as much when she discovered that Jessie had brought 'a fairly large amount of money' for a 'redecoration' that was estimated to cost £300 – four times the amount she had paid for the salon. The salon owner even boasted to her assistant of successfully smuggling hair products past Customs officials, saying that 'things were easily done if one had a head'. But the light heartedness with which Jessie recounted her trip turned to rage when she discovered that Curran had told a customer about her trip to Germany. She warned Curran that 'no person must know' of her travel plans. It was one of several tradecraft blunders by Jessie which contradicted everything she had been taught by her handlers about not arousing any suspicion.

As Jessie arranged yet another trip to Germany the following month, again leaving Curran in charge, it seemed increasingly odd to the salon assistant that a woman who had effectively severed her ties with Germany was keen to revisit so regularly. Curran informed Patrick Robbins –

who had negotiated the sale of the salon – of Jessie's trip and he in turn passed the information to Dundee Police. Could Jessie be a German spy? The police were sceptical about Curran's information but nonetheless attempted to get closer to Jessie by deploying an undercover agent. 'To test this information, a policewoman was sent to make an appointment for hair-waving,' the chief constable of Dundee City Police noted in his investigation file. 'She saw Mrs Jordan, who was willing to take her on 19 November 1937, but on the policewoman saying that was unsuitable, Mrs Jordan said that she could not take her until Monday, 29 November, as she was fully booked. This was untrue as no bookings had been made.'

On the evening of 7 December 1937, Curran acted on a hunch, and went through Jessie's bag in the salon. Inside the bag, she discovered a clue to Jessie's fascination with army barracks – a map of Scotland and England, on which military installations including Fife Ness, a coast guard station, and Montrose, an army barracks, had been marked up in pencil. The map seemed too detailed and annotated to belong to a military hobbyist. Curran smuggled the map out of the salon by tucking it under her clothes and gave it to Robbins, who then passed it on to Dundee Police. Jessie neither suspected Curran nor did she seem to miss the map – and by the time Curran returned the map to her handbag, the police had informed MI5, Britain's domestic security service, which was in charge of investigating counterespionage.

MI5 had its origins in the Secret Service Bureau (SSB), created in 1909 in response to Germany's threat to Britain's national security and economy. Germany's aspiration under its ruler Kaiser Wilhelm II had been to become a world power through economic and military domination, which threatened peace and stability on the continent. The English Channel separating the United Kingdom from mainland Europe was hardly a buffer against the threat and so it fell to the 'domestic arm' of the Security Service Bureau – later named MI5 – to investigate German espionage in the lead up to and during World War I. Under its founding director, Major General Sir Vernon Kell, MI5 had a proven track record in hunting spies – and on the eve of Britain going to war in

August 1914, its officers orchestrated the arrests of 22 suspected agents of the Nachrichten-Abteilung, Germany's naval intelligence department. Among them was Karl Gustav Ernst, known as the 'Kaiser's postman' for handling all correspondence between the head of Germany's intelligence service and its British-based agents. As part of his cover, Ernst had worked as a hairdresser at a barbershop in north London in the lead up to his arrest.

In the immediate aftermath of WWI, with the German threat largely diminished, MI5 had another fight on its hands, which threatened its very existence: a proposed merger with Britain's foreign intelligence organisation, MI6, for the sake of cost-cutting. Although it survived the bureaucratic battle, MI5 remained severely underfunded, with only 26 officers on its books in the late 1930s. Among them was Guy Liddell, the deputy head of the agency's 'B-branch', which specialised in rounding up, and sometimes recruiting, Nazi and Soviet spies. Liddell's division was the investigative heart of the security service: it ran operations involving informants, telephone and postal interceptions and physical surveillance.

Liddell's personal accomplishments included a Military Cross for his distinguished service as an officer in the Royal Field Artillery (RFA) during the Great War. He had then spent 12 years at the Metropolitan Police Service, Scotland Yard, investigating Soviet-Communist subversion at the organisation's Special Branch which majored in national security. In 1933, two years into his career at MI5, Liddell anticipated a growing threat to Britain from Germany's military- intelligence agency, the Abwehr, as it evolved from a counterespionage service to an aggressive foreign intelligence force following Adolf Hitler's rise to power. Liddell suspected that the Abwehr had been attempting to recruit and run agents in Britain – a suspicion confirmed when MI5 intercepted a letter in the summer of 1937 addressed to 'Sanders' at Post Box Office 629, Hamburg. MI5 had been alerted to the German address a year earlier by a British double agent, who informed Liddell's team that the post box had been used by Nazi spies to communicate with their handlers in Hamburg. Acting on the intelligence, MI5 sought a Home Office Warrant to place all mail deliveries to the address under surveillance, and intercepted, read and photographed all letters intended for 'Sanders'. The author of an unsigned letter intercepted in June 1937 had described the barracks and officers' mess of Aldershot Garrison, a military town in southeast England. Colonel William Edward Hinchley-Cooke, a fluent German speaker who worked in Liddell's department, considered the letter, postmarked from Talgarth, Wales, a 'feeble attempt at espionage'. Hinchley-Cooke allowed the intercepted letter to go through to its intended destination in Hamburg.

'Approximately a month later, a further communication sent to the same address gave a clue to the writer of the first letter,' an MI5 memorandum concluded. The clue that had given the writer away had been a secondary envelope inside of the main envelope. The secondary envelope contained a letter outlining a series of instructions about an upcoming meeting between Nazi agents. Yet more compelling were the traces of an address on the secondary envelope which had been badly erased. Hinchley-Cooke's team identified the address as 16 Breadalbane Terrace, Perth – the house in which Jessie Jordan had been living with her half-brother, William Haddow.

In spite of MI5's concerns about German espionage in Britain, there was no political will by the Conservative government of the day to take an aggressive approach against it. And although MI5 had warned Neville Chamberlain about the Nazi threat before he had succeeded Stanley Baldwin as Prime Minister in May 1937, Chamberlain was determined to avoid military confrontation with Hitler, following the loss of a generation of young men in World War I and the economic devastation of the Great Depression in 1930, from which the country was still reeling. Despite opposition from some cabinet members, including Foreign Secretary Anthony Eden, who ultimately resigned in protest over Chamberlain's appeasement of Hitler, the prime minister maintained that position until Britain finally declared war against the German Reich in September 1939.

MI5 continued its investigations of Nazi spies despite Chamberlain's appeasement, and coordinated its surveillance of Jessie with the help of the police, tracking her pattern of movements, including her train journeys back and forth from Leith, the port from which the SS *Courland* ship would sail to Hamburg. MI5 also began monitoring the frequency with which Jessie was sending and receiving mail. Her mail was intercepted, steamed open, and its contents were photographed. Over the course of the investigation in late 1937, MI5 discovered letters and packages addressed to Jessie from a range of countries, including France, Holland, South America and the United States. With the exception of a letter containing £5, which had been delivered to her home in 16 Breadalbane Terrace, Perth, MI5's investigation found that 'all material documents were found at Mrs Jordan's hairdressing establishment at 1 Kinloch Street, Dundee.' However, none of the letters and packages seemed to be intended for her. She was merely a conduit, or as MI5 described her, 'a letter box', who forwarded the post to the German intelligence agency and its intelligence agents in other parts of the world. The Abwehr had used this mode of communication to diminish the risk of their agents being caught. MI5 worried that Jessie was part of a 'German 'shadow' scheme to be brought into operations in the event of hostilities breaking out'.

Among the dozens of messages that had been sent by German spies via Jessie were a series of letters from 'Crown', including one dated 17 January 1938, which seemed to outline a sinister, but overambitious, plot to steal US military secrets. The plot aimed to target the 'secret plans relating to the defence of the Atlantic coast of the USA' held at the office of Colonel Eglin, the commander of Fort Totten military facility in New York. 'Crown' proposed to set up an 'emergency staff meeting' at a hotel in Manhattan, inviting the Colonel to bring the defence plans, at which point 'Crown' would 'overpower' the Colonel and steal his defence plans 'by force'. Guy Liddell had been briefed on the plot by his MI5 investigators, and while he deemed it 'extremely crude', it was too important to dismiss. He carefully mulled over the impact it would have on MI5's ongoing investigation. A tipoff to American authorities through the US embassy in London could compromise MI5's case against Jessie without even ensuring the arrest of Crown, whose real identity was unknown to the agency. However, Liddell and his team made a decision almost a fortnight later that would step up and reform the basis of intelligence-sharing between British and US authorities, unknowingly contributing to the foundation of what would become the world's most powerful spy network – the Five Eyes.

Guenther Rumrich had become a seasoned traveller by the time he joined the US Army, aged 18. The young serviceman had benefited from his father's diplomatic postings to countries including Hungary, Russia, and Italy. Having spent the majority of his early life around Europe with his Austrian parents, in late 1929, Rumrich returned to the United States, his country of birth, and enlisted in the army. Surviving on a US$30-a-month salary was a major change of lifestyle to the one he had been used to, and eight months into his new career, he fell into debt and temporarily deserted the army before turning himself into his superiors in August 1930. Following a court martial and a six-month jail sentence, Rumrich was determined to take his role as a serviceman more seriously. His change in attitude was noticed by his commanders and he was promoted to the rank of sergeant shortly after his release from prison.

Rumrich was an ordinary soldier in both ability and stature, described in one of his files as having a 'medium build, dark brown hair, brown eyes' and 'ruddy' complexion. He served at Governors Island and the station hospital at Fort Hamilton, Brooklyn, and was also assigned to the station hospital at Fort Clayton in the Panama Canal Zone and Fort Missoula, Montana. During the six years that he served at such medical facilities, Rumrich became very aware of the importance placed by the military on medical information and the extent to which it sought to protect it. The medical records of personnel elicited a far broader picture than the ailments, blood results and fitness assessment filings that they contained. They symbolised the military's deployable manpower – or the preparedness and availability of its combat troops, versus the overall number of soldiers the army had.

In late 1937, Rumrich needed to obtain statistics relating to the prevalence of venereal disease in the US Army ahead of a conference on military readiness being held in New York City. The sexually transmitted diseases – including gonorrhoea and syphilis, which caused health complications including sterility, heart disease and even blindness and paralysis – had been a scourge on the army in the previous decade and had incapacitated many soldiers. At the time, it was the second highest health problem resulting in hospitalisation, after respiratory illnesses. Rumrich contacted the medical section at Fort Hamilton in Brooklyn and told the duty officer on the other end of the telephone that he had forgotten the statistics on venereal disease at his Washington, DC, office. Having identified himself as a specialist with the US Army Medical Corps, Rumrich pulled rank over the duty officer, and before long the documents he had requested were delivered to him by a soldier at the Hotel Taft in Manhattan ahead of the supposed conference. Neither the courier who delivered the documents nor the duty officer who sent them had any idea that Rumrich was no longer a member of the US military. In fact, he had deserted the army – for the second time – almost two years earlier and had started working for the Abwehr.

As a US citizen with a military background, Rumrich was a dream target for Abwehr recruiters eager to expand their espionage operations in America. The German espionage assault on the USA had been dealt a huge blow with the capture of their most valued agent, Wilhelm Lonkowski, in 1935. A former aircraft mechanic in World War I, Lonkowski had been recruited by the Abwehr and deployed to the US in 1927 under a fake passport to obtain information about airplane engines and other new technology being developed and tested by Westinghouse Corporation. His mission was to fulfil Hitler's ambition of shortcutting the technological advancement gap between Germany and America; a chance to attain military superiority through the theft and duplication of US defence secrets and product designs. Lonkowski's previous experience in the aviation industry gained him employment at the Ireland Aircraft Corporation in Long Island, New York, and over the subsequent five years, he began running two other Abwehr agents, alongside his day job. Under Lonkowski's direction, his agents Otto Voss and Werner Gundenberg stole sensitive technical secrets, including the designs for a fireproof plane and the world's most advanced air-cooled engine. Undetected for several years, Lonkowski sent secret material to Berlin, until he was detained by US customs officials in New York while trying to return to Germany in 1935 with blueprints for an experimental bomber and other sensitive material in his possession. Fortunately for Lonkowski, the customs authorities deemed the material inconsequential and released him, allowing him to flee the country, through Canada, to Europe.

Unlike Lonkowski, who was talent-spotted and subsequently recruited by the Abwehr, Rumrich had not waited to be approached by the organisation, but volunteered his services in 1936. By then, Rumrich had been married to Guiri Blomquist, a teenage girl from Montana, for less than a year, and the pair were expecting their first child. His ambitions beyond family life had been inspired by the memoirs of Colonel Walter Nicolai, an intelligence chief in the German Army, which detailed the spymaster's daring missions during the Great War. Rumrich reached Colonel Nicolai by writing to him through a Berlin-based newspaper, *Völkischer Beobachter*, in early April 1936. In his correspondence to the Hitler-owned newspaper, which had been a mouthpiece for the Nazi Party, Rumrich pretended to be a senior US army official with access to sensitive information. Instead of providing his contact details, he appealed to the Abwehr's sense of intrigue and asked to be contacted through an advertisement in the public notices section of the *New York Times*, with the words: 'Theodore Kerner – Letter received, please send reply and address to Sanders, Hamburg 1, Postbox 629, Germany.' The Abwehr received Rumrich's letter and subsequently set up a meeting between him and one of its agents at a restaurant in New York on 3 May. It would have seemed obvious to the Abwehr agent that Rumrich was slightly unconventional, a risk taker, and eager to prove himself as a spy. And he did.

Rumrich obtained information for German intelligence that varied in sensitivity. By acquainting himself with unsuspecting sailors and merchant seamen at bars along the port of New York City, he had been able to glean information relating to the movement of cargo and warships and report it back to Germany. He even obtained information relating to the planned installation of anti-aircraft weapons in New York and tried his hand at becoming a recruiter. Rumrich managed to corrupt Erich Glaser, a private in the Army Air Corps at Mitchel Field in New York. Through this newly found fellow traitor, Rumrich was able to obtain army, air force, and navy codes and ciphers, reporting his findings back to Germany by post, or in other cases, through Johanna Hoffmann. Hoffman was an undercover agent working as a hairdresser on the Europa cruise liner, which crossed the Atlantic Ocean weekly. She was the Abwehr's courier and transferred messages, money, and military secrets between the Nazi spy ring in America and Germany. All members of the Nazi cell in New York, including Rumrich, reported to Ignatz Griebl, a regional spy chief who doubled as an obstetrician with a medical practice on the upper east side of Manhattan.

Almost two years into his career as a Nazi spy, Rumrich was overcome by his own confidence and success, especially after managing to get his hands on the medical documents relating to the scale of venereal diseases among military personnel. Instead of merely replicating the successful ploy, he upped the ante. He adopted a much more elevated persona than the senior army official he had previously impersonated. On 14 February 1938, Rumrich dialled the number for the Passport Office in New York from a phone booth at Grand Central Station. When his call was answered, he adjusted his voice to impersonate Cordell Hull, the US Secretary of State. If it were not a stretch of his ambitions, it certainly was beyond his acting abilities – even to the junior clerk on the other end of the line whom Rumrich had ordered to deliver 35 blank passports to the McAlpin Hotel in Manhattan. There were numerous flaws in Rumrich's approach, but among them was that Hull, the man he had purported to be, was in Washington, DC – and not in New York – at the time of the call. It did not take long for the junior clerk to come to that conclusion.

The package Rumrich had ordered was sent, but with a slight variation. Instead of blank passports, the package contained blank passport applications – not exactly useful for Nazi intelligence bosses who wanted

US passports for their spies in Europe and Asia to help them operate under false identities. Worse still for Rumrich, was that the men who delivered the package were investigators from the State Department and detectives from the New York Police Department (NYPD). Rumrich was arrested but he protested that obtaining blank passport applications was by no means a crime. His only crime was impersonating Hull, which, although enough to secure a conviction, was deemed by officials to be slightly too embarrassing and inconveniencing for the US Secretary of State. One available option for the officials, while Rumrich was awaiting his fate in a holding cell, was to notify the Army that the deserter was in their custody. The other option was to release him.

Major Joe Dalton, Assistant Chief of Staff at G2, the US Army's intelligence division, interrogated Rumrich at a military facility on Governors Island, located between Lower Manhattan and the Brooklyn waterfront. Dalton had been one of the first people to read a missive sent by Colonel Raymond E. Lee, the military attaché at the US Embassy in London, outlining a conspiracy against Colonel Eglin, commander of the Fort Totten military facility on the north shore of Long Island. Lee had relayed intelligence from MI5 regarding the plot; information contained in a letter intercepted in Scotland by the British intelligence agency around two weeks earlier. The letter, written by an agent using the codename 'Crown', detailed the plan to lure Eglin on the basis of a 'bogus message, purporting to come from the aide-de-camp of the commanding general [...] ordering him to appear before a supposed emergency staff meeting to be held in the McAlpin Hotel' – the very location used by Rumrich when he had sought delivery of the blank passports. The letter had also revealed that 'every effort will be made to leave clues which will point to communistic perpetrators'.

MI5 had sought one assurance regarding the intelligence it had provided Colonel Lee: 'It is of the utmost importance that in any action which is taken on this information, no indication whatsoever should be given of the fact that it was obtained in Great Britain.' Although unaware of the true identity of its author, MI5 suspected it had been written by 'a German espionage agent (he may be of any nationality: he had good knowledge of the English language) whose identity is unknown'. Details of the same plot outlined by 'Crown' had been scrawled on a paper found in Rumrich's briefcase after he was arrested. When Major Dalton confronted him about it, Rumrich admitted his part in the plot. Crown had been one of ten aliases that Rumrich operated under.

In 1935, three years before Rumrich's arrest, a national crime-fighting body under the auspices of the US Department of Justice had changed its name to the Federal Bureau of Investigation. The FBI traced its lineage to the Bureau of Investigation, created in 1908 during Theodore Roosevelt's administration to probe criminal activities, including land fraud, forced labour, and copyright violations. It also investigated Anarchist violence which had resulted in the assassination of President William McKinley in 1901. The bureau's mission expanded over time and it gained notoriety after spying on leftists extremists, Anarchists, and Communists in 1919, by collecting personal information on them and their affiliated groups. Through its General Intelligence Division, created by a then newly appointed attorney general, Alexander Mitchell Palmer, and run by a former US Department of Justice lawyer, J. Edgar Hoover, the bureau had responded to a growing hysteria around the spread of Communism in America, which became known as the Red Scare. Over one year, and with Palmer's authority, Hoover's special agents oversaw the raids, mass arrests and violent beatings of thousands of suspected radicals and Communists throughout the country. In some cases, suspects had been detained for months without charge, starved, and even tortured. Although the attorney general was publicly criticised by members of congress, civil-rights groups, and the media for the 'Palmer Raids' that had been carried out on his orders, Hoover was left unscathed – and by 1924, had become the bureau's director.

The FBI had gained experience in stamping out domestic threats from subversives and Anarchists, but unlike Britain's MI5, it was focused on crimes such as homicides, bank robberies, and kidnappings rather than on counterespionage. To the US law-enforcement agency, MI5 was like a distant cousin on the other side of the Atlantic, connected merely through their allied nations rather than joint operational work – unlike the Royal Canadian Mounted Police (RCMP) with whom the FBI had collaborated on cross-border criminal investigations since the early 1900s. The RCMP had deployed an officer in Washington, DC, in 1919 to 'initiate a funnel of information sharing and act as an on-site liaison with US agencies'– and some of its officers had even been trained by the FBI academy. The familiarity and common investigative interests between the RCMP and FBI at the time trumped the diplomatic channels, which had operated through embassies, between the US and Britain. However, it was MI5's core business of intelligence-gathering and counterespionage experience and capabilities that distinguished it from the American and Canadian organisations – not its lack of geographic proximity. Nothing like MI5 had ever existed in the United States or Canada.

Up until MI5 provided information about the Nazi plot against Colonel Eglin, intelligence-sharing between the US and UK had been sporadic, and during the Great War, predominantly conducted through MI6's US representative, Sir William Wiseman. The most notable tipoff during that time between London and Washington had come through British Royal Navy's code-breaking department, Room 40, almost two decades earlier. Room 40 had intercepted and decoded a German diplomatic cable, known as the Zimmerman Telegram, revealing the enemy nation's ambition to undermine America's sovereignty by creating a military alliance with Mexico. The British tipoff in 1917 ultimately led the US to join the war.

While Fascist movements, including ones with sympathies to Hitler, existed in both the United States and Canada during the 1930s, they were not yet perceived as serious national security threats by the countries' law-enforcement agencies – until MI5's Rumrich tip emerged in late January 1938.

FBI Director J. Edgar Hoover had been made aware of Rumrich's arrest, but he perceived it to be a jurisdictional headache because of the number of investigative bodies involved: the US Army, NYPD and US State

Department. After initially resisting the call for his agency to take over the case, Hoover relented, and on 19 February 1938, appointed Leon Turrou, an agent from the New York field office, to the case.

Fluent in seven languages, including Russian and German, Turrou had a knack for getting people to open up. With around 3,000 cases to his name, he had tracked down kidnappers and escaped convicts through his nine year career at the FBI. He was brimming with ambition, and at 38, he had 12 years on Rumrich in age. Turrou quickly discovered that Rumrich was far from a bumbling army deserter – he was part of an elaborate Nazi spy ring that exposed Hitler's aggression towards the US at a time when the country was committed to neutrality. The Neutrality Act, ushered in by US Congress in 1935 to avoid what appeared to be a looming military conflict in Europe and Asia, banned the sale of 'arms, ammunitions and implements of war' by the US to foreign countries at war. However, the discovery of the Nazi spy ring brought the legislation into question and foreshadowed the impact that intelligence would have in shaping foreign policy under the Franklin D. Roosevelt administration in the late 1930s and early 1940s.

With Rumrich in FBI custody, MI5 and the Dundee Police raided Jessie Jordan's hairdressing salon on 2 March 1938. During Jessie's arrest, Colonel Hinchley-Cooke found sketches of military facilities at the shop, which compounded the evidence that MI5 had against her, including the intercepted letters that had been sent to her salon. Three weeks after her arrest, MI5 deployed Guy Liddell to the United States and Canada. His trip was as much about intelligence-gathering as it was about offering help to the FBI on the Rumrich case. The deputy head of MI5's counterespionage unit was not the most senior representative to whom such an important mission could have been entrusted – but he was operationally capable and already a part of the agency's succession planning to lead the B-branch. Several months shy of his forty-sixth birthday, Liddell's success had been shaped as much by his analytical skills and ability to foresee national security threats as his capacity to talent-spot and inspire young intelligence officers.

He was short and unimposing, yet self-assured and unafraid of making witty remarks and impersonating others. Liddell's sense of humour was offset by his more refined and cultured side: he was a gifted musician who could have thrived as much in a career as a professional cellist as he had at dismantling spy rings.

On arriving in the US in the spring of 1938, and with J. Edgar Hoover out of town, Liddell was invited to a meeting at the State Department on the morning of 25 March. After a conversation with its Head of Political Relations, James Dunn, Liddell immediately sized up the power struggle which had long existed between the State Department and the FBI. Both had been vying for funds to create a counterespionage organisation – particularly following Rumrich's arrest in New York the previous month. Dunn was eager to help realise MI5's ambition of creating an intelligence-sharing platform on espionage threats emanating from Nazi spies and Italian Fascists loyal to Prime Minister Benito Mussolini, who was closely aligned with Hitler. 'Mr Dunn was very anxious to have an exchange of information on the subjects,' but the US official wanted to sideline the FBI and military, Liddell later noted in a report about his visit to North America. 'Quite obviously, the [US] State Department wish to keep the strings in their own hands. Their attitude as I sensed it was: "It would be better not to allow those soldiers and policemen to get loose on their own. If we do not exercise a restraining hand they may lead us into deep water politically and there may be awkward repercussions in [the US] Congress."'

Liddell humoured Dunn without giving any assurances, but could foresee future problems in dealing with counterespionage cases through the State Department because its agents were 'not in a position to go very much beyond obtaining passport particulars'. He strongly felt that the FBI and military intelligence were better equipped in dealing with such matters and were less likely to politicise and compromise ongoing investigations. The journey of diplomatic manoeuvring led Liddell to New York next, to meet with Major Dalton at Governor's Island. Dalton, who had interviewed Rumrich, understood the value of Liddell and his organisation. The US military official expressed a 'willingness to cooperate with us in any way in the future', noted Liddell, and perhaps more importantly, acknowledged MI5's crucial role in informing US authorities about the Hotel McAlpin plot. 'It is realised that had it not been for the information supplied from this side of the Atlantic, it is quite possible that the facts as now disclosed would never have been known,' Liddell wrote. The FBI's special agent Leon Turrou, who had identified 'some twenty people' suspected of involvement in the Rumrich spy case, was also eager to win Liddell over, and in the process, had shared his investigation notes with the MI5 officer. 'He also gave me the fullest possible details of the case,' Liddell noted.

After his US trip, Liddell travelled to Canada where Nazi espionage, Italian Fascism, and Communism were also deemed a serious concern, as he discovered upon arriving in Ottawa on 31 March to meet with Royal Canadian Mounted Police officials, including the commissioner, Colonel Stuart Wood. 'The Canadians are very alive to the activities of Nazis and Fascists', and were closely monitoring the groups through RCMP agents. Liddell was told that 50 per cent of the 475,000 Germans living in Canada 'are regarded as at least sympathetic toward the Fatherland', while locally based, Fascist Italians were 'trying to suborn British subjects of Italian origin from their allegiance to the Crown and encouraging them to sign the oath of allegiance to Mussolini'. Liddell's mission in March and April 1938 reinforced a shared vision by the RCMP, MI5, and US officials, including the FBI, that intelligence-sharing was imperative to defeating foreign threats. In the final paragraph of his 12-page report, Liddell wrote: 'We should whenever possible keep up personal contact with Mr Hoover in Washington and his representatives in New York.'

During a court appearance in Edinburgh in the spring of 1938, Jessie Jordan's fate had all but been sealed. Having initially feigned ignorance about any wrongdoing and 'steadfastly and confidently' maintained her innocence, Jessie could no longer keep up the façade. The upbeat smile, which was a key fixture at earlier court hearings – some of which were held behind closed doors – changed to a 'wan crooking of the lips' when she changed her plea. She was described by one reporter as 'so completely ordinary in appearance that no one without foreknowledge would have suspected her espionage. She was not the dark-haired and glamorous beauty of the melodramas, but fair, plump, and over 50.'

With nowhere to go and the evidence stacked against her, Jessie admitted that she had been an intermediary between German spies in the United States and the Abwehr in Hamburg. She had also admitted making the pencil annotations on the map of Scotland that had been discovered by her assistant in her handbag, and later acknowledged that such drawings would be of 'great value' to any pilot of an enemy bomber. She also pleaded guilty to two charges under the Official Secrets Act, including obtaining information 'relative to coastguard stations and coastal defence' on the east coast of Scotland which was 'calculated to be directly or indirectly useful to an enemy'. In spite of claiming that she had been forced by a member of the Gestapo, the German secret police, to spy for the Abwehr after the intelligence agency had become aware that she was relocating to Scotland in February of the previous year, Jessie finally admitted to getting a thrill out of spying. Her daughter, Marga, had been completely oblivious to her mother's double life. Seated at the back of the court during one hearing, she sobbed loudly. But Jessie remained unmoved, 'bare of any expression' without looking over her shoulder to try to offer Marga a comforting glance. She was ashamed of what she had put her daughter through, yet seemed to accept her own fate. 'So far as I can fathom her own attitude, she seems to realise that in view of what occurred, neither this country nor Germany has any place for her except in prison,' Jordan's senior counsel, A.P. Duffess, KC, told the court. 'The position seems to be that, having started as an unwanted child fifty-one years ago, she finds herself now, partly through her own fault and partly through fate, once again an unwanted child as regards her native country and the country in which she has spent the greater part of her life.'

Jessie was sentenced to four years in prison under the Official Secrets Act in May 1938. Following her conviction, she told a newspaper: 'Sitting in my prison cell, I have come to the conclusion that it was sheer unhappiness, coupled with a love of excitement and change, that made me adopt the course I did. And, even admitting that, if I had not missed a boat at Hamburg on a certain faithful occasion, I question whether I would ever have become a spy in the land of my birth [...] How different it all worked out from those dreams. Instead of being an artist working on silks and satins, I shall maybe be making mail bags and cleaning cells.'

In the same month that Jessie was convicted in Edinburgh, Leon Turrou identified 18 Nazi spies in the FBI's first major espionage case. Through interviews with Rumrich and his fellow agents, including Voss and Hoffmann, he had obtained information about how the cell had stolen military and industrial secrets in service of the Abwehr. Yet for all the accolades he had amassed for past investigations, Turrou failed to grasp the nuances of the espionage case: unlike conventional criminals, spies were much more wily. After interviewing the Nazi suspects, Turrou had informed them that they would be subpoenaed to appear at a grand jury scheduled in May. It was an amateurish move which led 14 of the suspects to flee the country. The remaining four, including Rumrich, were the only ones the authorities had held after his confession in February.

The botched FBI investigation exposed Turrou's mishandling of the case and became a public humiliation for Hoover who until then had gained admiration and notoriety as a national law-enforcement czar. With the FBI shown up by the Abwehr, Hoover sought to discredit Turrou as self-serving and incompetent, and ultimately forced him out. The espionage case also revealed the unbridgeable gulf between President Roosevelt's democracy and Hitler's dictatorship. It turned public opinion against the Neutrality Act and put the United States on an ideological war footing against Germany. Voss and Hoffmann, the aviation spy and transatlantic hairdresser, each received a four year prison sentence. Rumrich and Erich Glaser, the US private from the 18th Reconnaissance Squadron, were each sentenced to two years in prison. Three of the four convicted spies were naturalised American citizens, raising questions about how others were willing to betray their adopted country in service of Hitler. The FBI was forced to undergo some soul searching on the home-grown threat it faced and recognised the need to begin training its staff in counterintelligence.

The failure in the Rumrich case became a symbol of the FBI's early inexperience in counter espionage, but heralded the growing influence of William J. Donovan, the former assistant attorney general who had appointed Turrou to the bureau in 1929. Like Hoover, Donovan was a shrewd political mind who recognised the importance of being in Roosevelt's inner circle. Once rivals from opposite political parties, Donovan ultimately gained Roosevelt's trust to create America's first intelligence organisation – one which closely reflected MI5's sister spy agency, MI6. The key person who helped Donovan set up the Office of Strategic Services (OSS) – predecessor to the famously known Central Intelligence Agency (CIA) – was neither American nor British. He was a wealthy Canadian with investments in various entrepreneurial ventures, including pressed steel, which ostensibly had nothing to do with the business of spying.

CHAPTER TWO

BUILT IN LONDON'S IMAGE

WILLIAM SAMUEL STEPHENSON'S EYELINE was barely above the five-foot corner posts each time he stood in the boxing ring waiting for the starting bell to sound. His puny frame was wiry and agile. With no brute force to draw on, Stephenson relied on being evasive and unpredictable, calculating and deceptive, to get the upper hand on his opponents. It was a formula that had accompanied him through amateur boxing bouts during his early teens in Winnipeg, western Canada, where he had grown up – and eventually became a way of life. He temporarily hung up his boxing gloves after the beginning of World War I to join the Canadian military and, by 1916, had been deployed to fight on the Western Front where he suffered two poison-gas attacks on the battlefield. Stephenson was rendered 'disabled for life' by military doctors, but managed to fudge his own medical history and wrangle a transfer to the Royal Flying Corps to become a combat pilot. He won two of the highest military honours during his service, including the Military Cross for bombing enemy troops and aircraft, before his Camel single-seat fighter biplane was gunned down in July 1918 by the French who mistook it for an enemy bomber. He suffered two bullet wounds to his leg and was taken prisoner to Holzminden, a maximum security facility on the River Weser near Brunswick in north central Germany. Stephenson escaped three months later and wrote a detailed report about his experience at the prison camp.

The report was shared by his superiors with Room 40, the Royal Navy's code-breaking department, created at the beginning of the war to intercept and decrypt German communication. After reading Stephenson's report, Admiral William Reginald 'Blinker' Hall, director of naval intelligence who oversaw Room 40, admired the Canadian's bravery. Having returned to Canada after the war, Stephenson migrated back to England in the early 1920s to pursue commercial opportunities. By then, Admiral Hall had temporarily left the intelligence community for a life in politics. The two remained in contact, but at that point, there was nothing in Stephenson's biography to indicate that he was destined to become a spymaster for Britain.

Born in Winnipeg to an Icelandic mother and a Scottish father, Stephenson was named William Samuel Clouston Stanger at birth. His mother could not afford to raise him following his father's death, and aged five, he was adopted by the Stephenson family. Twenty years later, Stephenson arrived in England with more ambition than money to his name and invested in General Radio and Cox-Cavendish – local companies that manufactured electrical receivers – on the eve of a radio boom that followed the creation of the British Broadcasting Corporation in 1922. With the money generated from the sale of thousands of home radios to BBC listeners, he funded scientific research aimed at improving the quality and speed of wireless photography – a venture which turned him into a millionaire by his thirtieth birthday. His business portfolio eventually became global and included a film production company and plastics manufacturer in Britain, coal mines in the Balkans and oil refineries in Romania. But it was his takeover in the mid-1930s of Pressed Steel Company Limited, in Oxfordshire, southeast England, that eventually armed him with information about Nazi Germany's military, which proved useful to British intelligence and brought him closer to Admiral Hall.

Pressed Steel had become a dominant force in the world of motorised vehicles, building car body shells for 90 per cent of the country's brands, including Morris, Austin, Humber, and Hillman. Stephenson travelled back and forth to Germany to source material for the company at around the same time that Admiral Hall had become an adviser on intelligence to a backbench Conservative politician – Winston Churchill. Having previously served in the nation's most senior political posts, including as Secretary of State for War and Chancellor of the Exchequer in the 1920s, Churchill had been overlooked for a ministerial role in 1931, despite his party winning the general election by landslide. The nation was in political and economic turmoil following the Great Depression two years earlier which had slashed its overall exports of steel, textiles and coal by half and forced more than three million people out of their jobs.

With an eye on becoming the country's saviour, Churchill turned his attention to Germany after Hitler came to power in 1933. He repeatedly warned of the threat of Nazism which successive British governments appeased for fear of being drawn into another war. Churchill maintained his public and parliamentary warnings about Hitler, despite being mocked and accused of warmongering by politicians for his hardline views on the Third Reich. Yet with no access to official intelligence to prove his suspicion of Nazis, he turned to the private sector for information relating to the German dictator. His adviser, Admiral Hall, contacted Stephenson, aware of his connections to Germany through Pressed Steel. The timing was fitting. Stephenson had discovered during a visit to the country that the majority of German steel plants had been ordered by Hitler to produce armaments and munitions. It was in contravention of the Treaty of Versailles which prohibited Germany from maintaining any armed forces following World War I and demilitarised the Rhineland, an industrial region in the country's west, bordering France. Hitler's ambition for world conquest arguably revealed itself for the first time in March 1936 after he ordered more than 20,000 of his troops to invade the Rhineland – an aggressive move backed by Italian Fascist leader Benito Mussolini and largely unchallenged by Britain and France.

A month later, Stephenson claimed to have obtained the balance sheets of steel factories in Ruhr, Rhineland, which revealed that the Nazi regime had spent around £800 million on what clearly appeared to be military preparations, including strategic roads. The London-based Canadian businessman passed the information onto Admiral Hall and Churchill in an intelligence exchange that drew Stephenson into the future prime minister's inner circle, and would ultimately transform him into a kingmaker of spies. Canada would have been unaware at the time that through one of its citizens, it had made a contribution to British intelligence almost two decades before the formation of the Five Eyes alliance.

Britain's foreign intelligence service, MI6, had become curious about Stephenson's international business network and knack for obtaining secret information, and it invited him for an interview in the summer of 1939. The spy agency was severely under-resourced, with fewer than 40 intelligence officers at its head office at Broadway Buildings by St James's Park, in central London. But worse still, MI6 had suffered a reputational setback after informing the Foreign and Commonwealth Office (FCO), the ministry to which it is answerable, of Hitler's intention to attack Holland in the spring of 1939. The FCO passed the information on to the United States, in the spirit of continued intelligence-sharing, reinforced a year earlier by MI5 during the Rumrich case. But unlike MI5's tipoff to the FBI, which ultimately disrupted the Abwehr's espionage mission in America, MI6's intelligence through the FCO was 'unfounded' and proved to be 'humiliating and damaging' to the British government. It also stoked an atmosphere of mutual distrust between the UK and Germany at a time when Neville Chamberlain, the British Prime minister, was trying to uphold a policy of appeasement.

The intelligence failure had not been a good look for MI6, and least of all for its director Admiral Hugh Sinclair who had set a high standard for British spying while at the helm of the agency over the previous 16 years. He had succeeded Admiral Hall as the director of naval intelligence in 1919 and founded the Government Code and Cypher School (GC&CS), which replaced Room 40 and became responsible for intercepting and decrypting foreign communication signals. Sinclair maintained his oversight of the signals agency after becoming MI6's chief, or 'C', in 1923. He ran both organisations from the same headquarters at 54, Broadway Buildings in central London, before relocating GC&CS in 1939 to a countryside mansion in southeast England called Bletchley Park. Sinclair had moved the signals agency around fifty miles north of the capital because he feared it could become vulnerable to potential German bombing. The mansion itself was discretely located but deemed too small to house the code breakers. Yet its surrounding fifty-five acres of land provided ample room for prefabricated wooden huts. It was in such huts – known only by their numbers to protect the secrecy of the intelligence work within them – that Britain's code breakers attacked the secret communications of the Axis powers.

Having secured GC&CS's new location at Bletchley Park, Sinclair needed to address MI6's patchy intelligence on Germany, which had also been criticised by Britain's Air Ministry for failing to produce adequate information about the Nazi's aircraft production and armaments. By then, he had formed three new sections at the agency: Section X specialised in intercepting the telephone calls of foreign embassies; Section D plotted sabotage missions; and Section Z focused on penetrating Germany and Italy through the recruitment of agents from the world of academia, journalism, and business. It was through this route that an overseas MI6 unit fashioned on Section Z came across the Business Industrial Secret Service (BISS) – a private business intelligence firm that had been supplying secrets to Churchill through its founder, William Stephenson.

During the interview with Stephenson on 12 July 1939, Sinclair's officials were impressed by the entrepreneur's access to industrial intelligence, but were perhaps a little shocked to discover that some of his sources were MI6 officers moonlighting for the BISS to subsidise their salaries. By the following spring, MI6 officially brought the BISS under its umbrella and personally tasked Stephenson with improving its intelligence links with the United States.

Britain had been at war with Germany for two months when Colonel Stewart Menzies was put in charge of MI6 and GC&CS after Sinclair lost his battle with cancer in November 1939. As the former deputy director of MI6, Menzies was an intelligence veteran, accustomed to talent-spotting – but what he saw in Stephenson had little to do with conventional spying. The 'Quiet Canadian', as Stephenson had at times been known due to his listening skills, was neither a traditionally trained agent handler nor an intelligence analyst – and, aged 43, he would hardly have qualified as a fresh-faced recruit. But his lack of tradecraft skills was counterbalanced with personality, charm, and an unusual access to the White House corridors of power through a former American boxing world champion, Gene Tunney. The pair had formed a friendship around two decades earlier after watching each other box – and with a heavyweight title to his name, Tunney had been elevated to rarefied social circles where he often rubbed shoulders with the high and mighty, including FBI director J. Edgar Hoover.

Aware of Stephenson's closeness to Tunney, Menzies sought to create a backchannel with the FBI that could bypass the US State Department's strict application of the Neutrality Acts. At the time, the State Department had a stranglehold on any communication between America and its allies to avoid a diplomatic fallout with Berlin which could result in war. An additional problem for Menzies was that the US Ambassador to Britain, Joseph P. Kennedy, was an 'appeaser' who could not be trusted for many reasons. The father of future president, John F. Kennedy, had helped convince Prime Minister Neville Chamberlain to trust Hitler and sign the Munich Agreement which, along with approving Germany's annexation of Sudetenland, a part of Czechoslovakia, exposed the UK's weakness. Ambassador Kennedy then publicly declared that the Fuhrer would defeat Britain, triggering a hostile response from the Foreign Office, reversing their previous policy of sharing confidential information with senior US Embassy officials.

To navigate such diplomatic landmines, Menzies could have sought the help of MI5, especially since its newly promoted director of counterespionage, Guy Liddell, had maintained his working relationship with the FBI following the Rumrich case. But that would have placed the power in MI5's hands, which would not have suited MI6's sense of unjustified superiority over its sister agency. Instead, Menzies opted for a 'cleanskin', an operative whose identity is unknown and deniable, to connect his agency to the FBI director. In the greatest test of Stephenson's intelligence credentials, Menzies posted him to Washington, DC, to make good on his anticipated access to Hoover – and he did. Hoover and Stephenson immediately connected during a meeting on 16 April 1940, and with no love lost between the FBI director and the State Department, he agreed to forming a backchannel with MI6, but only with presidential approval.

President Roosevelt sensed the political value of shared intelligence between the two agencies – even if it were a little risky in exposing America's contravention of its own Neutrality Act – and gave it his blessing. With that, Stephenson was suddenly catapulted from his position as a virtually untested intelligence official, to monopolising the information exchange between Menzies and Hoover, and controlling a direct line to Roosevelt through his newfound friendship with the FBI boss. To preserve the secrecy of the new mission, Menzies and Hoover used codenames to communicate – 'Scott' and 'Jones', respectively. Stephenson also adopted a harmless-sounding title to mask his work: 'Principle Passport Control Officer for the USA'. Under that guise, the Canadian took overall control of MI6's operations in the US and Mexico in June 1940, a month after Winston Churchill, his confidant and champion, succeeded Chamberlain as British Prime Minister.

Britain was fighting for its survival, militarily outgunned and out-powered by German troops by almost three-to-one as, nation after nation, Europe fell to Hitler. Churchill was desperate for Roosevelt's help, but the available secret intelligence he could provide the president would not be enough to sway the US Congress – let alone the public – into entering the war. So, MI6 plotted a new mission to overturn public opinion by creating the British Security Coordination (BSC), an organisation run by Stephenson in New York, which would become the largest foreign intelligence operation ever established in America.

The United States had an uneasy relationship with spying in the early twentieth century, made worse by the absence of an agency to coordinate the nation's espionage and counterespionage operations. In 1919, The US Army and State Department jointly created a code-breaking organisation, The Black Chamber, following the disbandment of a cryptographic military-intelligence section, set up at the beginning of the Great War. The Black Chamber, also known as the Cipher Bureau, targeted and decrypted diplomatic communications to give America an edge over foreign states – in effect, fulfilling the duty of a signals intelligence agency. But it was shut down a decade after its formation when the Secretary of State, Henry L. Stimson, withdrew his department's funding because he felt that 'Gentlemen do not read each other's mail'. Stimson's apparent noble and moral superiority naively overlooked the live threats of Communist and Fascist regimes that western democracies, including his nation, faced.

A year later, his bad political judgement was made right when the US Army formed the Signal Intelligence Service (SIS), a division within its Signals Corps, to break foreign government codes. But even then, America's intelligence capabilities remained largely limited to communication interception through the Army's SIS, and FBI detectives who were predominantly focused on domestic security, with virtually no experience in counterespionage – as would become clear eight years later in the 1938 Rumrich spy case.

By contrast, Britain's well-oiled intelligence community was professionalised in the early 1900s, and traced its lineage to Sir Francis Walsingham. As principal secretary and spymaster to Queen Elizabeth I, Walsingham oversaw espionage missions in the sixteenth century, including the physical interception and unsealing of diplomatic letters, deployment of spies around Europe, and infiltration of the Spanish military. Four centuries on, when William Joseph Donovan, President Roosevelt's closest aide on intelligence, aspired to bridge his nation's counterespionage gap – he turned to Britain.

Donovan had been Roosevelt's classmate at Columbia Law School at the early turn of the century. But the pair never interacted then, and became political rivals before being united by a common purpose. After a brief stint as assistant attorney general with the Justice Department in the late 1920s, Donovan made an unsuccessful run against Roosevelt for New

York governor in 1932, before setting off on regular trips around Europe and Asia, ostensibly in pursuit of commercial opportunities. However, Donovan's travels were part of a secretive network of businessmen and lawyers, known as the 'Room', which traded intelligence about the developments on the European continent. He met with senior statesmen, including Benito Mussolini, presenting himself to the Italian prime minister as a Republican envoy keen to further his party's understanding of Italy's war with Ethiopia. However, Donovan's primary focus was to gather intelligence on the military capabilities of potential future enemies.

By 1940, Donovan's sheer determination and ambition had elevated him to the country's elite foreign policy and business circles. It may have seemed a remarkable achievement for the son of a railroad superintendent from an Irish neighbourhood in Buffalo, New York, but Donovan's true path to greatness would begin in June of that year, when Roosevelt appointed Frank Knox, a newspaper publisher and senior member of the Republican Party, to Secretary of the Navy. Along with being a fellow Republican, Knox respected Donovan's judgement and grasp on global affairs and convinced President Roosevelt to draw on the lawyer's knowledge.

Donovan's ascension to an informal presidential adviser that summer coincided with William Stephenson's arrival in New York to set up MI6's US bureau. The two had a lot in common, beyond growing up in tough neighbourhoods and relative poverty. They shared an appetite for risk-taking and had known each other for over two decades, having first met during the Great War in which both had become decorated flying aces. There was something mutually beneficial to the roles they now occupied: Stephenson would double his access to the White House, which had initially been limited to going through FBI director J. Edgar Hoover; and Donovan would develop a direct line to Winston Churchill and the British intelligence community through his Canadian friend.

Stephenson encouraged Roosevelt's new adviser to visit the UK and helped set up a series of meetings with senior officials. By the time Donovan landed in London as Roosevelt's personal envoy on 14 July 1940, the Battle of Britain was underway and Hitler was plotting the kingdom's invasion. Donovan's mission to evaluate the country's war effort on the president's behalf was timely – and also played into Churchill's hands. The prime minister appealed for more help from America, but persuaded the envoy that Britain would remain standing and resolute in the face of Germany's bombardment. Churchill also authorised military officials and spy chiefs, including MI6 chief Stewart Menzies, to brief Donovan on their intelligence, ranging from the country's Spitfire fighter planes to its coastal defences. Donovan even met with King George VI in what appeared to be a complete and unfettered red-carpet service, with access to Britain's most treasured people and secrets. However, one secret Donovan would not have been made aware of at the time was that which had been closely guarded at Bletchley Park – the decryption of the Enigma, Germany's most secret, cypher weapon.

On his return to America from Britain in early August, Donovan convinced the president of Britain's willingness and ability to fight the war but reinforced Churchill's appeal for military support.

The president sympathised with Britain's anxieties about Hitler, whose ultimate vision for world domination through the destruction of western democracy had become increasingly apparent. Roosevelt was not averse to taking calculated political risks, having already approved a secret backchannel between the FBI and MI6 for intelligence cooperation. But with his eyes locked firmly on an unprecedented third re-nomination to the White House, the offer of military support to Britain would require some rather creative manoeuvring. It was in that vein that he tasked Donovan to identify legal loopholes which would allow the US to provide military aid without openly trampling on the Neutrality Acts and triggering the ire of Congress.

Donovan faced numerous challenges from the get-go. The Neutrality Act of 1939, passed by congress two months into World War II, had been amended to allow the sale of arms to belligerent countries. But the military weapons could only be purchased on a 'cash and carry' basis, requiring buyers to pay up front and use their own ships to transport the cargo, and The Johnson Act from five years earlier prohibited credit to nations that had not repaid US loans given during the Great War. Such legislative restrictions were particularly bad for Britain – which, along with being short on hard currency to qualify for 'cash and carry', remained financially indebted to the US from the earlier war. Compounding all of this was an opposition by US Army Chief of Staff General George C. Marshall to arming the UK, because he anticipated its invasion and feared that the provision of American weapons would ultimately end up in German hands.

Yet Donovan's confidence in Churchill's armed forces – which had largely fended off the threat of German invasion during the Battle of Britain military campaign – convinced President Roosevelt to sign the 'Destroyers-for-Bases' agreement on 2 September 1940. The agreement led to the provision of more than 50 navy destroyers to the United Kingdom in exchange for rent-free, 99-year leases on British land in the Atlantic and Caribbean, which would be used for the creation of US air and naval bases. Kindley Field was among the first bases built for the US air force in Bermuda and became an important link for air and sea traffic between America and Europe during the war.

The destroyers deal was a worthwhile trade-off for Britain: it received additional firepower which helped offset the French naval support, lost three months earlier due to the Vichy Government's surrender to Hitler. The deal also reassured Canada, a British dominion, whose small navy had sailed the Atlantic since the beginning of the war, trying to protect Allied convoys of food and other supplies. By then, more than 200 Allied ships had been sunk by German military submarines, U-boats, resulting in the deaths of thousands of seamen on board. For Churchill, the destroyers agreement was a victory that demonstrated Roosevelt's willingness to get alongside Britain and draw his country one step closer to war. But unsurprisingly, Hitler deemed the deal a provocative act and five days later, on 7 September 1940, he commanded Germany's air force, the Luftwaffe, to trigger the Blitz against the UK. The bombing campaign killed more than 43,000 civilians in Britain and destroyed more than a million houses and flats in London alone.

Donovan's pursuit of new measures to help his country defeat Nazi Germany without direct involvement in the war led him on yet another intelligence-gathering journey to Britain in December 1940, this time joined by MI6's established US representative, William Stephenson. The trip was paid for by MI6 in the interest of a much greater goal. The British agency ultimately wanted to help the US create an intelligence service in its image, over which it could have some influence. The intelligence cooperation between the two countries was rapidly developing, but Donovan was not the only official from the other side of the Atlantic who was close to the president and had his mind set on creating an intelligence agency. J. Edgar Hoover had his own ambitions to expand his counterespionage reach – and in the same month Donovan met with MI6 in Britain, Stephenson helped the FBI director separately dispatch two of his detectives to London to meet with British spymasters, including MI5's Guy Liddell.

Liddell made sure the FBI special agents, Hugh Clegg and Clarence Hince, received a series of high-level briefings about 'tactics, techniques, wartime policing' relating to M15's work and even organised for them to meet with MI6, Bletchley Park code breakers, and other authorities, including the fire brigade.

The bilateral intelligence cooperation between Britain and the US was rapidly growing in depth and coverage and had developed a third, and more secret, dimension. The British government had opened up a new frontier to lobby for American support in the summer of 1940 through its ambassador in Washington, DC, Philip Henry Kerr, Marquess of Lothian. Kerr informed the US War Department of his country's proposal for an 'interchange of secret technical information', including gains that had been made by Britain during the previous nine months in penetrating the ultra-wave radio technology of its enemy. Kerr's aide-memoire of 8 July offered Britain's 'fullest cooperation, to be perfectly open with you and to give you full details of any equipment or devices in which you are interested'. However, the offer was intended to be more of a bargaining chip than a cry for help, stating what Britain 'might' include should the deal be agreed to. Among the inclusions that he teased in his correspondence were the 'method of detecting the approach of enemy aircraft at considerable distances, which has proved so successful; the use of short waves to enable our own aircraft to identify enemy aircraft, and the application of such short waves to anti-aircraft gunnery for firing at the aircraft which are concealed by clouds of darkness'.

The British proposal was positively received by General Marshall and President Roosevelt, amid recognition by defence officials of how the ally's developments – and others, including the penetration of encrypted military and diplomatic communication systems used by Germany, Japan and Italy – could benefit America's national security. Correspondence from a Brigadier General from G2, the US Army's military-intelligence department, revealed that Britain's technical advancements could save the US up to two years in research. In a letter dated 4 October 1940, the senior military official highlighted the ways Britain's intelligence may also help 'disclose espionage, sabotage […] and fifth column in this country and its possessions' and provide insights into the 'Axis intentions, plans and operations in the Canal Zone, Caribbean area and Central and South America'. The US Army was conscious of its own limitations, stating that 'without the aid of information expected to be gained by this exchange, the time necessary to obtain such results might extend from half a year to two years'.

However, the US Army and Navy were not in agreement at first about swapping secrets. The Navy had reservations about Britain's intentions and feared becoming a victim of inter-agency spying, according to the same correspondence: 'The Navy Department is opposed to any exchange of information on cryptanalysis of foreign codes and cipher. I understand that this opposition is based on a fear that information we give on our methods of cryptanalysis may aid the British in breaking down our codes and ciphers.'

There was no mention in the correspondence of the success Bletchley Park code breakers had made in breaking the Third Reich's military communication – the supposedly impenetrable Enigma – because that secret had not yet been divulged by Britain. It was such success that gave Bletchley Park the upper hand in its negotiations with Washington at the beginning of the following year, ten months before Japan's attack on Pearl Harbor, which would draw America into the war.

HMS *King George V* had been anchored in the Chesapeake Bay, an estuary off Annapolis, Maryland, when four men dressed in civilian clothing boarded the British battleship on 15 January 1941. It was obvious that the men, aged in their late 20s and early 30s, were travelling together – and equally clear by virtue of their accents that they were not British. Over the duration of their two week voyage, the men pretended to be Canadian for the sake of protecting their real identities from the other passengers on board – even though officials who checked them onto the vessel would have known they were carrying US diplomatic passports.

The cover story adopted by the two US Army officers and their US Navy counterparts was to circumvent their country's Neutrality Acts, which prevented American personnel from boarding the warships of belligerent nations. 'We were all on diplomatic passports, and that was the way they got around this proscription against travel on vessels of a belligerent nation,' recalled Dr Abraham Sinkov, a code breaker with the US Army's Signal Intelligence Service, who led the delegation. What became known as the 'Sinkov Mission' was aimed at kick-starting a signals intelligence exchange between American code breakers and Bletchley Park. Yet it was so secret that even the military attaché at the US Embassy in London, who would otherwise have been briefed on sensitive security matters, was told by an intelligence chief in Washington to stay away from the four officers and 'forget that you have ever seen them'.

Their arrival at Bletchley Park in February was in itself a milestone because they were the first foreigners to visit the wartime code-breaking establishment, from which they could hear the sounds of German bombing raids on England. The American visitors were there to impress Bletchley's director, Commander Alastair Denniston, a fluent German speaker whose experience in code breaking started at Britain's World War I signals agency, Room 40. In 1919, Denniston had been promoted by Admiral Hugh Sinclair to become the first director of the Government Code & Cypher School, which later became known as Bletchley Park following its relocation to the country estate.

Aged fifty-nine, and with more than two decades as spy chief under his belt, he was far more experienced than the members of the Sinkov Mission. But he was nonetheless excited about meeting them – and had even prepared his assistant to serve them an aperitif on their arrival. 'There are going to be four Americans who are coming to see me at 12 o'clock tonight,' Denniston had told his assistant. 'I require you to come in with the sherry. You are not to tell anybody who they are or what they will be doing.' The wartime meeting between the veteran code breaker and his American guests foreshadowed the birth of a bilateral, signals exchange programme between the US and Britain. It also exposed the disparity in Britain's signals capabilities and experience, over its ally, particularly when it came to dominating the Enigma.

Denniston's fascination with the Enigma dated back to its creation in 1925 by a German electrical engineer, Dr Arthur Scherbius, whose invention was capable of transcribing coded information. Intended for commercial use by banks and other companies interested in secure communication, the Enigma, which was produced in a variety of models, was available to anyone willing to pay for it. On the surface, it looked like a cumbersome typewriter, but each time a letter was pressed on its keyboard, rotors would scramble it into another letter. The rotors would move with each keystroke, meaning even if the same letter was tapped twice, two different letters would appear. The only way to decode the letters sent from an Enigma was to know the exact settings of its rotors and apply them to the recipient's machine. It was far from simple because some Enigma models had a theoretical permutation, or possible arrangement of numbers, of 100,000 billion billion. The complexity of its cipher made it an attractive tool for trading secrets and wrongly convinced the German government that it could not be broken. The country's navy, army, air force, and secret services had already been using the Enigma for their communications by the time Hitler became Chancellor in 1933.

The Poles were the first to make a breakthrough and they went on to build a replica of the Enigma, along with an electromechanical machine they named 'bomba' which accelerated the decryption process. When they revealed their findings to Bletchley Park – which had been collaborating with them since the early 1930s to understand Germany's military intentions – Denniston was so impressed with the way they used maths to break the Enigma that he recruited two mathematicians to his agency in 1938, including Alan Turing, to build on Poland's achievements.

Turing had made a breakthrough on a pre-war Enigma at the beginning of 1940, but at the time of the Sinkov Mission, he was still a year away from breaking the Naval Enigma – an even more complex machine with extra code-wheels and more elaborate settings. It was the breaking of the Naval Enigma – through Turing's own creation of a 'bombe', a more advanced version of the Polish replica 'bomba' – that would be credited for arguably shortening the war by two years.

Abraham Sinkov and his American colleagues were told nothing about Bletchley's work on the Enigma during the first few weeks of their visit, despite providing the British code breakers with material relating to their own success in breaking Japanese communications. The American delegation had even gifted Bletchley a replica of a cipher machine, codenamed 'Purple', used by the Japanese to protect its most secret diplomatic communications. Sinkov's organisation had broken the Purple in September 1940 after five months of intense work. According to Sinkov, his team also gave Denniston's code breakers 'material connected with Italian systems, and some general information about cryptanalytic techniques.' Sinkov was hoping to leverage the Purple because at the time the US Army's signals service had little else to demonstrate its capabilities against military systems of the Axis powers. His two colleagues from the US Navy's signals section, OP-20-G, had even less bargaining power: they had made little to no progress against the cryptosystems of the German and Italian navies – and the little success they had made against Japan's system had been limited to low-grade communications, such as those used for weather reports. Bletchley officials were way ahead of their visitors. They had already succeeded in intercepting and reading some Japanese diplomatic traffic and had broken Italian cryptosystems since June 1940. Two months, on, they had made major inroads against the Luftwaffe's Enigma.

While the US Army's signals service was familiar with the commercial history of the Enigma, it was unaware that Germany had adopted the technology, with variants for its different services. Despite Britain's appeal – through its Ambassador in Washington the previous year – for an exchange of information with the US in which it promised to be 'perfectly open' about the 'full details and devices' in its arsenal, the reality was different. The Sinkov Mission was not briefed on the Enigma until shortly before it was due to return to the US in March. 'We were unaware at this time of the special interest that the British had in the Enigma,' Sinkov later said. 'Apparently, what was happening was that discussions on the higher lever were taking place as to whether anything should be told to us about the Enigma and not long before we were due to leave, apparently a decision was made to give us a preliminary briefing and we were taken to one of the particular buildings at Bletchley.'

Despite the briefings on the Enigma, and the bombe – of which Bletchley had six in full operation – Denniston did not provide his American guest with any hardware to reciprocate their gift of the 'Purple', fearing that the technology could be compromised by enemy agents in the US and end up in German hands. And it was not until weeks after their return to the US that he agreed to provide them with detailed documents about the Enigma and Turing's notes on it. Without the Enigma material, the American delegates would have been giving away more than they were getting, Sinkov had noted, 'but when that Enigma information is added in, I think that throws the balance in their direction, because the solution of the Enigma was quite an accomplishment and of extreme importance in the conduct of the war'.

The Sinkov Mission in the winter of 1941 exposed an element of early distrust between Britain and America – a problem that had not been limited to the code-breaking community. Not long after William Stephenson became MI6's head of operations in the United States and Mexico, he lost the trust of J. Edgar Hoover after manipulating the flow of British intelligence to his bureau. The fallout threatened to derail cooperation between their two countries and steeled the FBI director's intelligence overreach: he was no longer happy just being close to MI5 and MI6. He wanted Bletchley's secrets.

Arthur McCaslin Thurston was about 28 years old, with less than five years of experience at the FBI, when he joined the law-enforcement organisation's Special Intelligence Service, located at the Rockefeller Center in New York. Despite his relative inexperience, he had proven himself a few years earlier at the bureau's San Francisco office, during an investigation into a German diplomat suspected of trying to extort military secrets from soldiers. The case led to the diplomat's expulsion and brought Thurston to the attention of J. Edgar Hoover. On a personal, and perhaps more important level, Thurston was appointed as Hoover's driver during the director's visits to the FBI's office on the West Coast. The car journeys to meetings and social outings also included stopovers at the 'Nude Ranch', where a famous burlesque dancer and stripper, Sally Rand, performed. The time spent behind the wheel at Hoover's service elevated Thurston into the boss's circle of trust.

It was trust that Hoover was after when he organised for Thurston to be briefed about the British Security Coordination in November 1942. Thurston's briefing centred on MI6's operations in the US, run by William Stephenson through the BSC. Thurston would no doubt have been familiar with the BSC because its headquarters were located in the Rockefeller Plaza, the same building as his office, and it had been running political warfare operations against the Nazis since its creation the previous year. Among its activities, the BSC had been organising mass propaganda campaigns in the American mainstream media, including the *Herald Tribune* and *New York Post*, by feeding pro-British and anti-German stories to journalists. It had an estimated 1,000 agents and sub-agents working for it, including broadcasters, political activists and operatives who specialised in document forgery, poll manipulation to misrepresent public opinion, and the planting of false news into US media to undermine the Nazis. In some cases, the fake news was also intended to boost the morale of Allied troops through fictitious feature articles that lauded heroic military raids by members of their forces which had never taken place. Although its main mission of pushing the US into war by influencing public and political opinion had effectively been made redundant by Japan's attack on Pearl Harbor in December 1941, the BSC had become Stephenson's lifeblood for continued relevance in intelligence circles and corridors of power, including the White House.

The operations of the British Security Coordination were supposed to be known to Hoover, especially since he had authorised the use of an FBI radio station in Maryland, Virginia, for the BSC to safeguard its communications with British intelligence officials across the Atlantic. As many as 300 encoded messages were sent back and forth each week. Stephenson refused to provide the FBI with full transcripts of the messages despite his prior agreement to do so. The BSC had also been withholding operational information from Hoover, and had even been spying on one of his most senior staff members, Percy Foxworth, director of his Special Intelligence Service.

Hoover had become even more enraged by Stephenson's secondary role at the BSC: Britain's representative was effectively the conduit for all of his country's intelligence exchange with the US and the FBI director suspected him of withholding intelligence between his bureau and MI5. Hoover's suspicion was confirmed in the summer of 1942 following a meeting in Washington, DC, with MI5's head of counterespionage, Guy Liddell. The pair discovered that intelligence they had shared with each other's organisations through the BSC had not been respectively received.

It was Liddell's second major visit to the US to meet with the FBI, following his trip four years earlier to help on matters relating to the Bureau's investigation into the Rumrich case. Liddell wanted, as much as Hoover, a direct intelligence-sharing relationship between their two organisations, outside of the BSC's control which neither of the men trusted. Prior to meeting Hoover, Liddell had spent several days acquainting himself with other officials at the FBI and was given a tour of its training academy in Quantico, Virginia, and its Laboratory Division in Washington where technology was being developed on covert photography, secret inks, and concealment devices. In an act of reciprocity, Liddell briefed FBI officials on his organisation's own secret operations, including the Double Cross System in which Nazi agents had been recruited and used by MI5 to deliver a combination of real and false information to their Nazi controllers. The aim of the system was to hamper the enemy's offensive and military operations.

Liddell wanted MI5's relationship with the FBI to be as 'free and frank in our exchange of information as possible' and wanted to draw Hoover closer, despite considering him to be a 'prima donna type'. But he also noted in his diary entry of 16 June 1942, the day of his meeting with Hoover, that he 'was very cordial and held forth at great length about his organisation and his difficulties. I gave him a sense of our experiences in England whenever he showed signs of drawing breath, which was not often.'

The FBI strongman was also not holding his breath because his nemesis, William Donovan, President Roosevelt's former adviser on intelligence, had received a major promotion three days earlier. Donovan had already served around one year as the US's Coordinator of Information (CoI), leading a team of about 100 civilian officers to collect and analyse intelligence relating to national security for the purposes of keeping Roosevelt fully briefed. On 13 June 1942, the CoI became the Office of Strategic Services – the country's first, primary secret intelligence service with a wide-ranging remit, including sabotage operations in Axis countries and the training and financing of opposition groups there. Donovan's expanded organisation had been set up in the image of MI6 and with the help of William Stephenson who transferred some of his BSC agents to work for it.

Stephenson and Donovan had become so close that they had even become known as 'Little Bill' and 'Big Bill', respectively, because of the disparity in their physical sizes. Their friendship was a threat to Hoover who perceived Donovan as a rival and suspected Stephenson of being disloyal to him. It was clear to Liddell that 'Hoover hates Donovan's guts'. But even more so, Donovan's new high-profile role as OSS director appeared to undermine Hoover's goal of becoming an espionage czar alongside his existing role as the nation's crime-fighter-in-chief – but he refused to be steamrolled out of the intelligence game by Donovan and Stephenson.

Armed with the information from Liddell, along with other tipoffs about the BSC's distrustful behaviour, the FBI director placed the British intelligence community in his sights and appointed Arthur Thurston for the assignment with only a day's notice. It would not have been lost on Thurston that he was to be authorised with the FBI's most important diplomatic mission to date, even though he had never left his country of birth nor even had a passport to his name at the time.

On 15 November, as he boarded a Pan Am flight from Glen Gove, Long Island, with a crisp passport in hand, Thurston had been fully briefed and he was to deliver his boss's message without compromise. He was to initially operate out of the US Embassy in London – America's most important diplomatic mission, at the time employing over 4,000 people at its One Grosvenor Square Building in Mayfair.

Neither MI5's director-general, Sir David Petrie, nor his counterpart at MI6, Stewart Menzies, were pre-warned about Thurston's arrival in London – but their reactions to it differed as much as their characters. At sixty-three, Petrie had held a series of intelligence roles for over four decades, and had taken over MI5 in April of the previous year with the view to repairing its 'poor management and planning which had led to organisational breakdown and confusion'. But unlike his counterpart at MI6, who was close to Prime Minister Winston Churchill and keen to cultivate relationships within his government, Petrie placed more emphasis on forming working bonds in the best interest of MI5 and not for the sake of accumulating political capital.

Petrie invited Thurston to meet with him and MI5 staff at the agency's headquarters in Blenheim Palace, a country house near Oxford. He also gave him access to MI5's files and provided him with office space, reinforcing his agency's eagerness to work directly with the FBI. However, it was not until 7 December, nearly a month after his arrival, that Thurston was invited to meet with Menzies at MI6's head office on Broadway in London. Menzies had already been aware that Stephenson was monopolising his intelligence role, and in some cases disregarding the chain of command. However, the MI6 chief had to play a careful balancing act: he needed to appease Hoover through his young representative, but at the same time keep Stephenson on side because he was indispensable to his agency in the US.

Menzies had not expected Thurston's uncompromising ultimatum: the FBI's future cooperation with MI6 would hinge on his willingness to share all intelligence relating to Bletchley's decryption of Enigma messages. There was no negotiation on that point because it had been at the order of J. Edgar Hoover. Menzies, who also had oversight over Bletchley's operations, had been out-manoeuvred.

At the beginning of January 1943, less than four weeks after issuing Hoover's demands to Menzies, Thurston was invited to Glenalmond, a country manor in a village 20 miles north of London. It was from there that Menzies controlled the distribution of Bletchley's Enigma decrypts, which themselves had been given a codename: Ultra. Thurston mined the Ultra messages over four months for anything that would be of relevance to the FBI's operations, including information about German espionage on US soil and secret Nazi networks in Argentina. He sent his findings back to Washington, DC, for analysis – and to protect the secrecy of Ultra messages, the FBI gave them another codename: Ostrich. The intelligence helped the FBI's Secret Intelligence Service at Rockefeller Plaza to 'control the movements of its double agents and ensure they were successful in penetrating German intelligence' and ultimately became the bureau's 'most significant sources of intelligence in World War II'.

Along with successfully seeing out his boss's demands, Thurston had created the FBI's first bureau in Britain which would play a defining role in strengthening ties between the US law-enforcement organisation and British intelligence agencies until this day. The young Colorado native, who had given up on a scholarship to Harvard Business School in 1938 to join the FBI, had perhaps proven to himself that he had made the right choice. As for Hoover, his organisation's access to Ultra had confirmed that the FBI also belonged in the intelligence game.

Half way through WWII, as tensions continued between British and US intelligence agencies, a handful of American officials wanted to uncover the hidden motives of an unlikely ally.

CHAPTER THREE

THE WAR SPREADS TO THE PACIFIC

GENE GRABEEL FELT TRAPPED in her first job as a home economics teacher. Delivering cooking and housekeeping classes to teenage girls at a school in Madison Heights, Virginia, was far from intellectually fulfilling for her – but Grabeel could not see a way out of it. She became frustrated less than a year into the job and made her feelings known to her parents when she returned to Rose Hill to spend the festive season with them in 1942.

The rural hometown in Lee County, Virginia, was Grabeel's birthplace. She had fond memories of growing up there with her four siblings on the family farm, helping their mother and father raise chickens, pigs, and fowls. A town with a population of 300 people, a post office and a petrol station, was hardly full of job prospects. Yet it was there that Grabeel, aged 22, got an unexpected career break after reuniting with an old family friend, Frank Rowlett, at a Christmas party. To her, Rowlett epitomised the story of a local who had made good, escaping the limitations of Rose Hill to become a federal government employee – but she knew little else about his job.

Since 1930, he had been a senior code breaker at the US Army's

Signal Intelligence Service (SIS). He had also played a role with other members of the SIS, commonly known as Arlington Hall, in breaking the Purple cypher machine, used by Japan for its top-secret diplomatic traffic. Within six months of America's entry into war, its code breakers had become so proficient at intercepting and decrypting Tokyo's communications that, by the summer of 1942, they were able to determine Japan's military strategy in the Battle of Midway in the north pacific. That enabled the US to launch a surprise attack against Japan and turn the tide of the war in the Pacific.

Having once been a teacher himself, Rowlett sympathised with Grabeel's workplace frustrations, and sized her up for a job at Arlington Hall. Of course there was an intellectual leap between code breaking and home economics, but Rowlett was confident in Grabeel's intelligence and ability to learn fast. After all, Rowlett himself had learned on the job, having never heard the word 'cryptanalyst', or code breaker, until he first joined the SIS as a junior mathematician.

Grabeel was a patriot, driven by the Christian values she had been brought up with and an eagerness to help her fellow countrymen and women. The proud southerner regularly attended mass and served her Baptist church through community work and donations, but her religious beliefs had been rather like her political support for the Democratic Party – private matters that she never imposed on people. She had a flair of elegance and magnetism that made her popular among her friends, and during her college years, was voted Homecoming Queen. She was also an elegant and beautiful brunette, her petite frame of five-foot-two barely noticeable if it were not for her radiating smile and brown eyes that brimmed with warmth. 'My aunt was very beautiful and intelligent,' said her niece, Gene Cole Knight, who was named after her. 'She could carry a conversation on any subject. She knew a lot about politics and felt comfortable in any intellectual setting.'

A major part of Grabeel's identity had frustrated her throughout her teen years: she hated her name, felt it was 'kind of plain and ordinary', said Cole Knight. 'Aunt Gene wanted to be different. So she was always complaining to her mum that she wished her name was different and often said, "I wanna change my name." And her momma said, "Well, you can change it but you have to wait till you're the legal age."' Grabeel's impression of her name improved when her sister, Victoria, Cole Knight's mother, named her daughter after her. 'I think she was quite touched that my mum named me after her.'

During the Christmas break of 1942, Grabeel was determined to face a new challenge when Rowlett offered her a job, even though she was unaware it would involve code breaking – a career defined by 'pressure, long hours, and hard work'. Eager to quit teaching, she cut short her festive break in Rose Hill and travelled around 300 miles south to Arlington Hall. She arrived on Sunday, December 28 to find only one common feature between her new workplace and the old one: Arlington Hall had been a junior girls' school before it had been bought by the US War Department six months earlier and converted into the army's code-breaking headquarters. It was there, on the hundred-acre grounds, fenced off to the outside world, that nearly 8,000 code breakers, linguists, and analysts would attack the communications of Axis nations, including Japan and Finland, during World War II. And at a time when intelligence work was generally dominated by men, 90 per cent of the code breakers at the signals base were women – who had earned their roles by outperforming men in standard civil service exams. The recruitment of women eavesdroppers had been championed by William Friedman, the founder of the US Signal Intelligence Service in 1930, who along with his wife, Elizabeth, was a pioneer in the field of cryptanalysis.

Arlington Hall was to the United States what Bletchley Park was to Britain – a wartime secret operational base. Its existence was never to be mentioned outside of its gates for fear of turning it into a target for Axis spies. As part of her induction, Grabeel would have been briefed on such restrictions before starting a crash course in code breaking within hours of arriving at the base. She familiarised herself with the basics of ciphers, the system of concealing words by changing or shuffling the letters within them: where 'A' could be interchanged for 'X', and 'B' could be swapped with '2'. She also learned about codes, a method for converting entire words or sentences to represent something completely different: where 'Boss' could mean 'Mission' and 'Star' could mean 'Danger'.

Over the following two months, Grabeel was promoted by Frank Rowlett, who had become chief of Arlington Hall's cryptanalytic branch. Of the thousands of code breakers at the signals base, she was chosen to head up a new, top-secret mission ordered by one of Rowlett's supervisors, Carter Clarke.

Clarke was a maverick brigadier general, who Rowlett described as a temperamental 'man of considerable moral courage' who distrusted all nations, including allies. He said Clarke was of the opinion that the US should safeguard itself from allies becoming enemies by obtaining as much information as possible about them while they are on side. Clarke ran the G-2 Special Branch, a division of the US Army's military intelligence, focused on analysing intercepted signals. Arlington Hall officials would decrypt and translate enemy communications, intercepted by listening posts in areas as remote as Alaska and Ethiopia, and send them to Clarke's team to analyse and turn them into an 'intelligence product'. The product's distribution was limited to officials with the highest security clearances to protect the source and method by which it had been obtained, amid an ongoing fear that enemy nations would catch on that their communications were being read by the United States. Clarke particularly distrusted the Soviet Union, an ally of the West at the time, partly because Joseph Stalin had agreed to a non-aggression pact with Hitler in August 1939, a month before Britain was drawn into World War II. But Hitler considered the peace deal an opportunity to secretly plot against the Soviet Union and, in June 1941, invaded the Communist nation. The following month, Stalin signed a military agreement with Britain. His nation also qualified for military and food supplies under the US Lend-Lease Act later that year. The Soviet Union's inclusion in the Allied forces did not allay Brigadier General Clarke's continued distrust of its leadership.

Mobilising Arlington Hall's code breakers against Stalin required an added layer of secrecy because President Franklin D. Roosevelt was still of the belief that the US and Russia could peacefully coexist in the wake of an Allied victory. In a masterstroke, defined by his unconventional ways, Clarke made sure that his intention to spy on Russian communications would be kept a top secret – even from Roosevelt himself. And who better to appoint to a new mission than a bright, new recruit who was virtually unknown to the point of invisibility at Arlington Hall: Gene Grabeel.

On Monday, 1 February 1943, Rowlett relocated her to a small room in the main building at Arlington Hall to begin attacking Soviet communications. Her counter-Soviet mission was given a random and meaningless name, the Venona Project, and Grabeel was not to discuss its existence, or her findings, with anyone except a handful of superiors with the highest security clearances.

She was provided with a Russian speaker to help her sort through several filing cabinets, rammed with thousands of encrypted Soviet transmissions. The transmissions had been swept up by the US since the beginning of the war in 1939 as part of a wider effort to intercept the communications of Axis nations. And since Stalin's regime had been in regular contact with Germany for the following two years as a result of their non-aggression pact, the Soviet communications were collected, almost accidentally, in what is known as 'incidental interceptions' in intelligence jargon. The interception of Soviet messages continued after the US entered the war in December 1941, and all the encoded transmissions were stored away in filing cabinets – until Brigadier General Clarke could no longer contain his suspicion of the Communist state.

Grabeel's first major task was to establish a common or distinguishing thread among the Soviet transmissions. The messages had been encoded with apparently random numbers by Soviet cryptologists. They were part of a sophisticated system known as the 'one-time pad' that converted each word or letter into a five-digit code group. The Soviet Union had adopted the one-time pad system after its earlier communications were penetrated by British code breakers. That operation had been partly overseen by Guy Liddell, several years before he joined MI5.

* * *

As one of Scotland Yard's countersubversion experts in the 1920s, Guy Liddell had worked very closely with MI5, the organisation he later joined. His knowledge of the Soviet Union and its suspected spying activities in Britain was unrivalled. For several years, he had collated intelligence files against political extremists and members of the Communist Party of Great Britain whom he thought were willing to serve the Kremlin through its UK-based diplomats.

On the afternoon of 12 May 1927, Liddell coordinated a team of Scotland Yard and MI5 officers during a raid on the London headquarters of ARCOS, the All-Russian Co-operative Society, an organisation set up to promote commerce between Russia and Britain. ARCOS shared the London premises of the Soviet Union's trade delegation to which it belonged and was also entitled to diplomatic immunity – a safe passage it used to conceal its activities as a shop front for Russian espionage while ostensibly buying and selling goods, including textiles, timber, and coal.

When Liddell and his officers stormed ARCOS's headquarters in London's central business district, they disconnected telephone lines, searched employees and seized documents, including telegrams between Moscow and the Soviet chargé d'affaires to Britain, Arkady Pavlovich Rosengoltz. However some documents had already been incinerated by the time police got to them in what Rosengoltz later justified as 'nothing mysterious' but rather 'a well-established practice and rule in all cypher departments to burn the copies of deciphered telegrams'.

The sweep of ARCOS's offices had been authorised by Prime Minister Stanley Baldwin to plug the suspected diplomatic breach, but Liddell and his team found no trace of the stolen signals manual that they had been tipped off about by a former ARCOS staff member, nor any definitive evidence of Soviet espionage. Although it was an investigative setback, it had managed to serve a political purpose: the raid suited Baldwin's Conservative party's agenda to showcase its intolerance of Soviet subversion. Desperate to justify the raid, the prime minister addressed parliament on 26 May and revealed four Russian telegrams between Rosengoltz and Moscow in which the head of mission had assured his superiors that no 'secret material' had been found during the ARCOS raid. The telegrams also exposed Russia's ambition to undermine Baldwin through anti-government campaigns – but they were hardly a smoking gun, even though the prime minister used them to sever diplomatic ties with the Communist state. Baldwin's reliance on the telegrams, and quoting from them to make a political point, would no doubt have infuriated Liddell and MI5 because they were operationally compromising. Baldwin's political miscalculation alerted the Stalin regime that Britain had cracked its secret communication.

The Kremlin may not have been aware at the time that the telegrams had been intercepted and deciphered by Britain's signals intelligence agency, the GC&CS, but the leadership in Moscow knew they needed to change their method of communication – and with that, moved their diplomatic and intelligence traffic to a virtually unbreakable system: the one-time pad. The covert numerical system, convoluted with multiple layers of code, hampered Britain's visibility of Soviet communications for almost two decades – until a code breaker on the other side of the Atlantic made it her mission to crack it.

The pressure on Gene Grabeel to sort through thousands of encrypted Soviet transmissions was compounded by a watchword that her senior manager, Frank Rowlett, lived by: 'Make no mistakes; record all findings; identify source of data for each recovery; keep the team informed.' The avoidance of mistakes was obvious to Grabeel but making a record of her findings was near impossible in the early days of the Venona Project. There were no findings; no obvious ways to break into the five-digit code groups, which were completely meaningless without a 'key'. Such keys were usually contained inside a codebook, or a 'key table' – much like a dictionary which provided the plaintext, or decrypted letters, words and phrases in correlation to their equivalent code. The key tables were contained in a 'one-time pad' – essentially a pad of paper with pages on which five-digit groups of random numbers were printed. Each page was to be used only once to protect the integrity of the encryptions, and both the senders and recipients of the encrypted messages had a codebook to translate them – an item closely guarded by Soviet spies to protect their secret communications.

With no codebook to hand, Grabeel and her Russian-speaking team member, Leonard Zubko, needed to find another way into the Soviet transmissions. Their first major breakthrough emerged through a protracted and unanticipated route – via Finland, which had signed an anti-Communist pact with Germany and Japan against Stalin. In January 1943, Arlington Hall code breakers, who had been monitoring Japan's communications, intercepted correspondence between Tokyo and Helsinki. The two Axis allies had been exchanging information relating to Russian diplomatic codes. The Finns had taken an interest in Soviet codes and had recovered material relating to the one-time pad from Stalin's Red Army following its invasion of their country in November 1939. The material provided clues – or 'indicators' – about how their enemy's code system functioned. When the Finns shared the material in correspondence with Tokyo, Arlington Hall intercepted it and handed it to Rowlett – who secretly passed it onto Grabeel. 'We would read everything the [Japanese] sent in diplomatic traffic and we were right up on top of the Japanese military,' Rowlett would later recall.

Using the intercepted clues, Grabeel began to sort out the Soviet transmission in chronological order and eventually figured out that five different communication circuits were in use between Moscow and its missions overseas. One was specific to diplomatic communications and another related to the US Lend-Lease Act – a trade initiative created by the US in October 1941 to supply material, including ammunition, airplanes and food, to the Allies, including Stalin's regime. The remaining three circuits identified by Grabeel related to the Soviet spy agencies, including the NKVD – forerunner to the KGB – and the GRU, Stalin's military-intelligence agency.

Grabeel was still some time away from making any considerable dent in the transmissions. But there was no option of asking code breakers outside her tiny office for help, for fear of tipping off White House staff whom Brigadier General Clarke had assured that Arlington Hall was not snooping on Russian communications. The White House was aware of the organisation's work on the Japanese, German and Italian communications and had 'presumed that we would do the same on Russian and had taken steps on their initiative to cool the effort', Rowlett later recalled. 'Did we stop? We did not. We kept working and went to work harder and harder.'

Arlington Hall had been sharing intelligence with Bletchley Park for 18 months under an agreement specifying that 'all devices, instruments, or systems in use, developed for use or under development by the War and Navy departments will be offered to the representatives of the British Government'. But since the US code-breaking agency was keeping its greatest secret from President Roosevelt himself, it was not going to disclose it to its British counterpart. Compounding that was the lingering resentment that Arlington Hall felt about Bletchley Park's unwillingness to provide its officials with a sample of the Enigma and Bombe machines two years earlier. To help overcome the resentment, Bletchley dispatched one of its best code breakers – a man better known for his mathematical capabilities than his diplomatic touch: Alan Turing.

Turing had cracked an extra-secure version of the Naval Enigma in 1942. It was not unusual for Germany to change its codes as a measure of safeguarding its communications. However, in the winter of that year, Berlin went a step further by modifying its Naval Enigma, adding an extra rotor to it, further encrypting its messages. It had a deadly impact on Allied food supplies being transported by vessels across the Atlantic. Turing and his team could no longer read the Naval Enigma to help divert unescorted vessels away from Nazi U-boats. Around 500 ships were sunk, and thousands of lives lost, with a fear that Britain may be starved into defeat. Compounding Bletchley's inability to read the German communications was Berlin's penetration of Britain's own codes. In August 1942, Bletchley discovered that Naval Cipher 3, used by the British Navy for trans-Atlantic communications with Allies, had been compromised by Germany. Bletchley officials immediately informed Admiralty, but the British department responsible for the Navy failed to plug the breach for almost another year, compromising many more Allied convoys in the process. Turing's fortunes eventually turned after Royal Navy destroyers attacked an enemy submarine, U-599, on 30 October 1942 in the Mediterranean waters off the Egyptian coast. Two British sailors in their twenties, Tony Fasson and Colin Grazier, entered the sinking submarine and obtained secret documents, including a codebook. The two sailors drowned, but their sacrifice was not in vain. The codebook they recovered was sent to Bletchley Park, providing vital clues to re-cracking the Naval Enigma and rerouting convoys away from U-boats. It became one of Turing's greatest achievements during the war; one that ultimately also benefited American code breakers who had already relied on his expertise and designs to create their own version of the Bombe machine. They wanted more from him when he travelled to the US that autumn, and he was equally keen to gather intelligence for Bletchley about American technology.

Having survived the hazardous journey navigating U-boats across the Atlantic aboard the *Queen Elizabeth* ocean liner, Alan Turing arrived in New York in November 1942 to be confronted with a bureaucratic nightmare. The British mathematician was questioned by 'snooty' US Immigration Authorities at Ellis Island for 'carrying no orders and no evidence' to connect him with the British Foreign Office, his 'official's passport insufficient in itself' to allay concerns about his identity. The port authorities did not know that the fresh-faced 30-year-old was a signals intelligence officer; a celebrity among fellow cryptographers at Bletchley Park, whom he had led in the cracking of Hitler's Naval Enigma, leading to the Allied victory in the Battle of the Atlantic.

Turing's showdown with the port authorities, conveyed in a report he wrote from Washington, DC, to his bosses in London a fortnight later, was just one of several irritations he endured during his trip to America, where he had travelled to lend his expertise and assess the US development of the first two Bombe machines – called 'Adam' and 'Eve' – based on his designs.

Unlike the rather seamless cooperation between their political leaders – Winston Churchill and Franklin D. Roosevelt who had signed the Atlantic Charter several months earlier to outline their shared vision for World War II and beyond – the US and British intelligence communities were still struggling to completely trust each other. In fact, some American officials were strongly of the opinion that British code breakers had been aware of Japan's intention to attack Pearl Harbor, and that Churchill had suppressed the intelligence to force President Roosevelt into the war – a theory which had never been proven. That bit of US suspicion was a hang-up from World War I, which the US had entered in 1917 after Bletchley Park's predecessor, Room 40, decoded the Zimmerman telegram – a diplomatic cable in which Germany sought a military alliance with Mexico in exchange for US territory.

Turing's visit was supposed to improve intelligence cooperation and allay tensions between his agency and its US counterpart – but it had its challenges. US officials initially refused him access to Bell Laboratories in New York, which specialised in the research and development of telecommunications products. Named in honour of Alexander Graham Bell, the British engineer who invented the telephone, Bell Laboratories had been developing a top-secret speech and call scrambling device. The device – known by its cover name 'SIGSALY', written to resemble an acronym even though it was not – had been used to safeguard Allied communications, including calls between Churchill and Roosevelt, from the Axis.

When Turing was denied access to the voice-coding technology, Field Marshal Sir John Greer Dill, chief of the British Joint Staff Mission in Washington, DC, intervened on his behalf with a barely concealed threat. Dill sent a letter to General Marshall, on 7 January 1943, warning about the potential consequences of diminished intelligence-sharing. 'This is […] contrary to the spirit of existing agreements,' said Dill. 'It would seriously disturb our people at home and would of course also involve the US Navy who are very much dependent on free exchange with our people. Dr Turing was sent out from England for this one task as our expert representative, and if he is to return empty handed, it could not fail to have an unfortunate effect. I am sure you will agree with me that it is of the utmost importance in this vital matter not to allow any feelings of mistrust to arise.'

Turing's visit to Bell Laboratory was approved two days later. Yet the US Army had reserved its right to 'refuse to permit the "exploitation" of these secret devices by the British', reinforcing the distrust that continued to unfold between them.

Common interest prevailed over intelligence rivalries in the following months as Britain and the US elevated their cooperation in an agreement to pool cryptographical knowledge and resources. The Britain and United States of America Agreement, commonly known as BRUSA, was signed on 17 May 1943 between the US War Department and the GC&CS. The agreement formalised intelligence-sharing 'between the two countries to support US forces in Europe, exchange personnel and develop joint regulations for the handling and distribution of highly sensitive material'.

BRUSA also guaranteed the exchange of training, and sharing 'completely all information concerning the detection, identification and interception of signals [...] and the solutions of codes and ciphers' used by their enemies. Under the agreement, the US assumed the main responsibility for deciphering Japanese intercepts, while the UK focused on German and Italian codes and ciphers. In the wake of the agreement, Turing used insights obtained about SIGSALY from Bell Laboratories to create his own voice-coding system, which he nicknamed 'Delilah', but it was never put to use during the war.

The cooperation between US and British agencies continued to expand, even outside of BRUSA's signals intelligence, after President Roosevelt authorised the formation of a new spy agency, the OSS – Office of Strategic Services – which by the summer of 1943 had around 5,000 people working for it. The organisation and its director, William Donovan, were much better liked by the British intelligence community than by the US Army and Navy.

It was no surprise to William Donovan that the top brass at the US Army and Navy resented his disregard for military protocol and his organisation's cloak-and-dagger take on warfare. But as far as he was concerned, the relationship between the OSS and the armed forces was mutually beneficial, despite its tensions. His agency provided them with useful intelligence from its officers who were busily recruiting and training thousands of spies around Europe and Asia in the art of stealing secrets, gun-running, blowing up enemy bases and killing Nazis.

He had a global vision for intelligence – far beyond the conventional methods of the US military. He wanted his officers to engage in heroic adventures, to push the boundaries of psychological warfare – and he could think of nowhere better to look for inspiration than Britain. Having created the OSS with the help of William Stephenson in the summer of 1942, Donovan turned to his friend again to train some of his officers. Through his directorship of the British Security Coordination in New York, Stephenson had oversight of a training facility in Ontario, Canada, which had been initially set up by the UK and Canada in 1942 to train members of the Canadian forces. It was there at Camp X, located along the north shore of Lake Ontario, that trainees learnt about explosives, small arms, parachute jumping, withstanding interrogation, faking documents and infiltrating enemy lines while being shot at. Donovan sent around a dozen officers there to become acquainted with subversion, sabotage, and guerrilla operations – before they themselves went on to train many others.

OSS officers had a lot more to prove than their British counterparts, eager to demonstrate that their fledgling agency had the potential to be world-class. Their lack of experience also blunted their risk aversion, and in 1943, helped them seize on an espionage opportunity that had been overlooked by Britain. That summer, three diplomats at the British Embassy in Bern, Switzerland, dismissed an indirect offer from a German official, Fritz Kolbe, who was opposed to the Nazis and wanted to spy for the West. Kolbe had approached them through his associate, Dr Ernest Kocherthaler, a German Jew who had converted to Christianity and was known for his anti-Nazi activism in Switzerland. Kocherthaler informed British diplomats that Kolbe – whom he did not identify by name – was an official responsible for prioritising the most important correspondence between the Third Reich's Foreign Office and its overseas diplomatic missions, with access to sensitive material relating to Hitler's military movements and spying networks. The British diplomats turned the offer down, paranoid about Germany's intention to infiltrate its organisations through double agents.

On the following morning, 18 August, Kolbe provided Kocherthaler with three German Foreign Office documents, including one revealing the Nazi plans to penetrate American and British operations in North Africa. As he had been rebuffed by the British, Kocherthaler showed the documents to US Embassy officials in Bern. Among them was Allen W. Dulles, head of the OSS's field station in Switzerland, who had been pre-warned by MI6 not to trust German officials claiming to be anti-Nazis. However, Dulles had also been under pressure from his boss, Donovan, to produce better quality intelligence – and Kocherthaler's approach was too good to pass up. Several hours later, Dulles met with Kocherthaler's 'source': Kolbe. During the meeting, Kolbe told him he would not accept money, saying he was motivated to spy for patriotic reasons because he believed that defeating the Nazis was an imperative for the sake of peace in his country and the rest of the world.

Over the course of almost 20 months during the war, Kolbe supplied Dulles with more than 1,600 diplomatic cables between Germany's Foreign Office and its overseas missions. They included information about the structure of Germany's spy networks and their espionage operations in Europe and Britain, and the Nazis' attacks on American codes. Some of the intelligence was shared in turn by the OSS with Allied militaries and code breakers, including Bletchley Park. Kolbe's spying contributed to the defeat of the Nazis and also helped Donovan, and his star officer, Dulles, reinforce the imperative for unconventional warfare and prove the OSS's capability as a real player in the spy game.

The war had become a real testing ground for intelligence organisations, not only in the US and Britain, but in Allied nations with fewer resources, including Australia, a dominion of the British Empire. Its armed forces had joined the military battle immediately after Britain had declared war on Germany, but Australia's spying capabilities were largely ineffective – heavily reliant on Bletchley Park for signals intelligence and on MI5 for dealing with counterespionage. Its capabilities took a forward leap three years into the war, however, following the creation of the Central Bureau in Australia, an Allied signals intelligence organisation that brought together Australian and American code breakers, including Major Abraham Sinkov. He had become predominantly focused on understanding Japan's military missions in the South Pacific, including Papua New Guinea.

Abraham Sinkov had become accustomed to working with Allied code breakers since his mission to Bletchley Park in 1941, which had kick-started intelligence-sharing between the British agency and Arlington Hall. His arrival in Australia the following year to run a newly formed Allied signals unit had followed the relocation of US General Douglas MacArthur to Melbourne, Australia's southeast. The five-star general had been the allied commander of the South Pacific region overseeing operations from the Philippines. When the South-East Asian country was attacked by Japan in 1942, MacArthur was forced to relocate his military operations to Australia in March of that year. In a drive to crush Japan's military advance in the Pacific and its Navy's proposed invasion of Australia, he turned to code breakers for support. MacArthur set up the Central Bureau one month after arriving in Melbourne and, soon after, appointed Sinkov to run it.

The bureau became the primary signals organisation for the South Pacific theatre and brought together code breakers from Australia, America, Britain, Canada and New Zealand, along with university academics and mathematicians. By the time it had been relocated to Brisbane, on the country's east coast, later that year, its men and women code breakers had made some progress in penetrating Japanese communications, resulting in intelligence about the 'location of transports that the Japanese were using to transport men and material' in the Southwest Pacific. Attempts made by Sinkov's teams to break Japan's tactical communications had been less successful because Tokyo had predominantly been using the one-time pad system, similar to that relied on by Moscow. 'In the main, we didn't have a great deal of success against the tactical material [...] there was a problem of its one-time chart which made it extremely difficult,' Sinkov later recalled.

That changed on 2 January 1944, almost a year into the Huon Peninsula campaign in Papua New Guinea where the Imperial Japanese Army had sustained heavy losses against Australian troops and US aerial raids. Japanese troops of the 20th Division had been weakened from malnutrition, surviving on reduced rations. Their plans for withdrawal from Sio, on the peninsula's north coast, had also been disrupted by Allied aircrafts overhead. Two days later, in a last bid for survival, the division started retreating west towards Madang, battling torrential rains and uphill mountain trails. The infantrymen tasked with gathering the division's radio equipment were already burdened with too much weight to carry. A steel trunk containing accompanying cryptographic material, including codebooks, was among the heaviest items in their possessions. So they buried it in a stream bed and took off.

When Australian soldiers arrived at the site and swept the area for landmines with a metal detector, they recovered the steel trunk and sent its mud-soaked contents to the Central Bureau's headquarters in Brisbane. There, at the grand hillside estate requisitioned by General MacArthur to house the signals agency, cryptanalysts used any method they could think of to dry out the pages, including hanging some on clothes lines and placing others in front of electric fans.

'The books were water-soaked and practically stuck together,' Sinkov recalled. 'We had to separate the pages one by one and [...] worked out an interesting procedure for swabbing the page with something like alcohol, I guess it was, which would cause the written material on the page to show up briefly but long enough to give us a chance to take a photograph of it and we were able to reconstruct practically all of this material.'

'With this capture we had the whole cryptographic material of the [Japanese] division. Everything that the division was using, and it was early in the period. They used to change the systems about every three months, and this was early in the three-month period so that we were able to read approximately three months' worth of transmission without any problem at all. That was the highlight of some of our work.'

The discovery gave the Australian and American cryptanalysts an edge which accelerated their victory over the Japanese in Papua New Guinea. After a painstaking mission to recover the secrets from the mud-soaked recovered codebooks, the code breakers were able to brief the Allies on the Japanese forces' shortages of food, ammunition, ships, and other military equipment. Sinkov's team photographed each page of the codebooks recovered in Sio and sent them to Arlington Hall. With the material in hand, the Virginia-based agency went from decrypting 1,846 Japanese army messages in the first month of that year to 36,000 messages in March.

In the final throes of World War II, as Sinkov continued to attack Japanese communications with Australian code breakers in Brisbane, his contemporary at Arlington Hall, Frank Rowlett, had expanded Gene Grabeel's team with more linguists and cryptanalysts to deal with the volume of Russian transmissions. Just a few days after the war ended, Grabeel and her Venona colleagues grasped the scale of the Soviet espionage threat against the United States. Their discovery followed the defection of a Soviet diplomat in Canada.

PART TWO:
THE COLD WAR

CHAPTER FOUR

THE IRON CURTAIN FALLS

IN EARLY AUGUST 1945, as the world was preoccupied with the US nuclear attacks on the Japanese cities of Hiroshima and Nagasaki, which had killed more than 200,000 people, a young cipher clerk at the Soviet Embassy in Ottawa was fighting for his own survival. Igor Gouzenko had been reprimanded for leaving secret documents lying around on his desk, instead of locking them away in one of the Embassy's cipher rooms. The mistake, in breach of the security measures under which he should have been operating, cost him his job, yet he was required to continue his official duties for an additional four weeks while awaiting his replacement – encoding and decoding messages for the embassy's military attaché, Colonel Nikolai Zabotin. Part of Gouzenko's role was to ensure that all top-secret documents were temporarily filed or burned after his boss had finished with them. But instead, Gouzenko started saving documents intended for burning – hiding them among filed paperwork after turning over one side of their top corners to identify them more easily at a later date.

Gouzenko focused on accumulating material that revealed the extent of Soviet espionage in Canada, America and Britain: evidence that he had hoped would guarantee his defection to the West. The 26-year-old understood the risks involved in taking that step and had discussed them with his wife Svetlana. They were prepared to gamble their lives and that of their toddler rather than return to live in Moscow under a 'regime of violence and suppression of all freedom'.

Gouzenko left the Embassy for the last time at around 8 p.m. on 5 September, with the dog-eared papers shoved under his coat. He had three dossiers containing 109 documents; enough, he thought, to expose Stalin's 'double-faced politics' and intention to 'deliver a stab in the back of Canada'. Yet the cipher clerk's confidence in the documents was severely diminished in the 24 hours following his heist when his attempt to interest Canadian officials was rebuffed. On being alerted to the stolen documents by his staff, the Canadian Justice Minister, Louis St Laurent, turned them down because there was no political appetite to clash with the Stalin regime, still deemed an ally by the West. Gouzenko could not even interest the Ottawa Journal in publishing the stolen papers.

The only people interested in them at that point were four Soviet officials who, on the evening of 6 September, smashed through Gouzenko's apartment door looking for him, unaware that he and his family had been taken in by their neighbour a few metres down the hallway. The thugs soon left empty-handed after two Ottawa City Police officers arrived at the apartment block at 511 Somerset Street West to investigate the break-in. Gouzenko told the officers that he and his family were in danger and that he had documents that he wanted to provide to the Canadian government.

The officers placed his apartment block under surveillance overnight and alerted the Royal Canadian Mounted Police (RCMP), the national law-enforcement service with the resources to deal with sensitive diplomatic matters. The following morning, after a sleepless night, Gouzenko went to the RCMP's headquarters in Ottawa on their invitation, to meet with the service's intelligence branch, run by a British-born officer, Charles Rivett-Carnac. The Soviet clerk arrived with his documents in hand, 'highly agitated and in a disturbed state', close to 'nervous collapse', one of the interviewing officers noted. 'His speech was rather incoherent, and his train of thought and expression were confused to the point of being extremely difficult to comprehend.' The officers became concerned about his 'mental instability' during his interview and feared that the 'weight of his precarious position would have driven him to the murder of his wife and final suicide' had the RCMP not intervened.

Gouzenko had never aspired to be an intelligence officer: his passions were for art and literature and he had begun studying architecture when the Soviet Union joined the war in 1941. As the Red Army began expanding its recruitment, it turned to the Youth Communist League, of which Gouzenko was a trusted member. He was talent-spotted to study at the Military Intelligence Academy in Moscow, and on graduating as a lieutenant, joined the army's Central Cipher Department to study the coding and decoding of secrets. In June 1943, after passing a five-month vetting procedure by the NKVD, Russia's secret police, Gouzenko was cleared for deployment to the embassy in Ottawa with the official title of 'civilian employee'.

Two years and five months after his clearance, Gouzenko was holed up in a room with RCMP officers, providing details about his background and declaring his intention to defect. When Gouzenko talked them through a series of decoded telegrams which highlighted how the Soviet spying network was operating under the diplomatic protection of the Embassy in Ottawa, the RCMP officers were shocked by the treachery of Stalin's espionage machine. He also had proof that his boss, Colonel Zabotin, was using his diplomatic post to run espionage activities for Soviet military intelligence in Canada. Other documents highlighted 'monies paid, tasks given and results obtained' from a ring of agents, among whom were a British scientist and a Canadian Labour politician, operating under the cover names of 'Alek' and 'Debouz', respectively.

Moscow's demands of its Embassy officials in Ottawa was far reaching. It included the provision of intelligence on 'US troop movements' and the 'mobilisation capacities' of the Canadian air force. The RCMP was convinced that the 'very nature and thoroughness of these demands are sufficient criteria of Moscow's intentions and motive' to spy on its allies. An intelligence assessment of Gouzenko's material noted that the 'structure of this espionage ring in Canada entwines almost the whole structure of the embassy itself'.

The RCMP officers interviewing Gouzenko were less experienced in dealing with espionage and defectors than their British and American colleagues at MI5, or the FBI, or the OSS. But it was obvious to the Canadians that Gouzenko's role as a cipher clerk meant that 'everything in the manner of despatches and messages passes through his hands, and because of this, he would be well informed on the plans and activities developed through arrangements or information transmitted to and from the Embassy.' The RCMP concluded that Gouzenko's information and personal story had been 'amazingly accurate' and they provided him and his family full protection, temporarily relocating them to Camp X, the secluded wartime facility at Lake Ontario where Britain had trained OSS officers in the art of sabotage.

Gouzenko's unannounced defection five days after the end of the war was an untimely political headache for the Canadian Prime Minister Lyon Mackenzie King. He was not inclined to be drawn into a diplomatic showdown with the Stalin regime, which had appealed to his government regarding Gouzenko's whereabouts. Unaware of the defection, the Soviet mission in Ottawa wrote to the Canadian Department of External Affairs on 8 September, seeking the immediate arrest of Gouzenko whom they claimed had 'robbed some money belonging to the Embassy and had hidden himself together with his family'.

King's government gave nothing away to the Soviets, but the prime minister personally discussed the defection with his counterparts in Britain and the United States where the intelligence landscape was changing due to the emergence of two new heads of state. Harry Truman had succeeded Franklin Roosevelt following the president's sudden death from health complications in April 1945, and, five months later, had shut down the OSS and transferred its resources and personnel to the State Department and War Office, sidelining the spy agency's founder, William Donovan. The OSS's closure preceded the discovery that it, too, had been infiltrated by the Soviets. In Britain, not even VE Day in May of that year – the Victory in Europe Day – which saw the surrender of Nazi Germany, could guarantee Winston Churchill support from a public that had grown weary from the war. The British prime minister lost a general election two months later to Clement Attlee, who, like his predecessor, took a personal interest in intelligence matters.

As the Gouzenko crisis unfolded in Ottawa behind closed doors, its reverberations were immediately felt by the intelligence communities in Britain and the US. For Mackenzie King, the intelligence coup that resulted from a Soviet 'walk-in' – a turncoat who voluntarily divulged his secrets to RCMP – would reposition Canada's influence in the spy game. During his discussions with Truman and Attlee, the three leaders agreed to coordinate the arrests of Soviet spies exposed by the Gouzenko affair, and the RCMP shared the defector's intelligence with the FBI, MI5 and MI6. To protect Gouzenko's identity, the RCMP gave him a codename – 'Corby'. It was the name used by the Canadian service and its transatlantic intelligence partners in all early communications relating to the Soviet cipher clerk.

It had not yet dawned on Gouzenko, nor on his RCMP saviours that his defection would trigger an arms race for military and espionage supremacy between the West and the Soviet Union for decades to come – in effect kick starting the Cold War.

All communications relating to the Gouzenko case went through MI6 first, thanks to William Stephenson, still the agency's head of the British Security Coordination in New York, who was overseeing the exchange of all information between Ottawa and London during that period. But on receiving a detailed outline of Gouzenko's secrets, Britain's domestic intelligence service, MI5, started mobilising its officers in preparation for aggressively targeting Soviet espionage. Guy Liddell was an old hand at dealing with Soviet embassy officials leveraging diplomatic cover to spy on their host nations. He had developed his experience around two decades earlier through his investigation into ARCOS – the London-based organisation established to promote commerce between the Soviet Union and Britain – that had been used as a front for Stalin's espionage activities. Some of Liddell's colleagues at his sister agency MI6 had also maintained a degree of suspicion towards the Kremlin despite Stalin's contribution to the defeat of the Nazis. Among those who seemed well versed in the Communist threat was Kim Philby, a former foreign correspondent for *The Times* of London who had joined MI6 in 1940. Philby had served in various roles at the agency, including propaganda training and counterintelligence, and handled all the communications relating to the Gouzenko case on behalf of MI6.

Four days after Gouzenko's defection, Philby met with Liddell to discuss telegrams shared by the RCMP relating to the defector's case. The information, which had been provided via Stephenson, included the identities of western spies being run by Soviet embassy officials in Ottawa. One was a British physicist, Dr Alan Nunn May, who had been given the cover name 'Alek' by his Russian agent handler. The physicist had been living in Canada for almost three years, working on an atomic research programme that was jointly run by Canada, Britain and the US. The collaboration between the three countries was formalised through the Quebec Agreement in August 1943. It merged Tube Alloys – codename for a nuclear development initiative between Canada and Britain – with the US's atomic-bomb programme, codenamed the Manhattan Project. It was thought to be the biggest scientific secret of the twentieth century until Gouzenko revealed that it had been infiltrated by the Soviet Union through the likes of May.

Liddell and Philby discussed the different operational scenarios of dealing with May to ensure his arrest and subsequent conviction. 'Kim came over with a series of telegrams received from the Western Hemisphere on the subject of Russian espionage,' Liddell wrote in his diary entry on 11 September 1945. 'The documents in Ottawa indicate that May is to make contact with some Soviet agent over here.' The British scientist turned spy was returning to London following the completion of his contract with the Montreal Laboratory in Quebec where he had been closely involved in the creation of the world's first nuclear reactor. The MI5 officers weighed up seeking the RCMP's help to arrest May in Canada before his return, or 'whether he should be thoroughly searched and frightened on arrival here'. Liddell also pondered the idea of placing the scientist under surveillance on his return to Britain to help 'unearth a Soviet network in this country'. Liddell and Philby met again two days later to determine the course of action to take against May. Liddell favoured May's arrest in Canada because he was concerned that allowing him to Britain could compromise a case against him unless MI5 'actually caught him passing documents' to a Soviet contact, which he felt was unlikely. However, Philby 'was keen' for the scientist to return to the UK in the hope that he would unintentionally expose other agents by making contact with them. 'We felt on balance that it was better for May to come,' Liddell said. He had aligned himself with Philby's operational approach on the case, unaware that the MI6 officer – who had complete access to all of the communications relating to the Gouzenko case, including the information about Alan Nunn May – was a Soviet spy himself.

On Monday, 17 September 1945, five days after his meeting with Kim Philby, Guy Liddell deployed an undercover officer to Prestwick Airport, southwest of Glasgow, to await the arrival of a flight from Canada. Shortly after the plane landed at 6.15 a.m., the officer took a discreet glance at a picture he had been given of Alan Nunn May. It was recent enough to help identify the physicist as he approached the terminal in a grey coat and a matching suit, his stern face slightly obscured by a 'blue trilby hat' and 'horn-rimmed glasses with gold sidepieces'. The officer noted that while May was 34, he looked 'about 40 years of age', prematurely balding with a 'little more than a fringe of dark brown hair' and a 'rather full dark brown moustache'.

The scientist had breakfast alone before boarding a connecting flight at 1 p.m. to Blackbushe Airport in Camberley, around 30 miles southwest of central London. When May disembarked the flight in the mid afternoon, the surveillance officer was among its eleven passengers. The officer then followed him to Camberley railway station and boarded the same train to Waterloo, central London, at 4.50 p.m.

'At Waterloo, Dr May engaged a taxi, had his luggage put on it, and was driven away,' the undercover officer stated in a surveillance report. 'I had by this time contacted my colleagues, who were awaiting my arrival, and they continued the observation.'

The surveillance officer also noted that 'four other passengers from Canada' who had arrived at Prestwick Airport on the same flight as May had also then taken the same route from Blackbushe Airport into Waterloo station. There was no indication that they knew each other or who May was.

What the surveillance officer did not seem to know, however, was that one of these passengers was a plainclothes official from the RCMP, Sergeant Bayfield, who had travelled to London to improve his organisation's relationship with MI5. The surveillance officer would not have been informed about Bayfield, as his UK mission had apparently been carried out on a need-to-know basis to avoid tipping off the likes of the British Security Coordination in New York. The BSC was still in charge of representing MI5's interests in the US and Canada and had positioned itself as the main point of contact on the Gouzenko affair, becoming yet another point of irritation to Guy Liddell.

Bayfield had arrived with a letter of introduction from his boss, RCMP commissioner Stuart Wood, addressed to Liddell. 'From the text of it and also from what Bayfield says, the RCMP would welcome direct communications with ourselves,' Liddell noted in his diary on 18 September. 'Indeed this seems highly necessary.' Liddell had ultimately grown tired of dealing with the RCMP through William Stephenson because 'everything that he does or does not do is a matter of personal prestige and the organisation [MI5] has to suffer accordingly'.

Liddell was meticulous when gathering evidence against spies. He understood that the legal threshold required for convicting someone of treason needed to go far beyond suspicion. He placed May under round-the-clock surveillance and bugged his telephone line in pursuit of any incriminating evidence against him. On 19 September, Liddell wrote to an MI5 colleague, Roger Hollis – a Soviet expert and future director-general of the British intelligence agency – who was in Canada to interview Gouzenko. He asked Hollis whether the Russian defector had produced anything with May's 'handwriting' or evidence in the way of 'original cyphered versions of cables exchanged between Moscow and Ottawa fixing [May's] rendezvous in London'. Liddell added that the case against the Soviet agent would 'rest solely' on Gouzenko's evidence and 'without corroboration this would not support a charge against [May]'.

As MI5 stepped up its investigation into May, the FBI was itself trying to establish the scale of Soviet penetration in the US. J. Edgar Hoover's organisation had not yet been made aware of Arlington Hall's investigation into Soviet spying through the Venona Project, which had been running for more than two and half years by that point. However, the bureau had been alerted to Soviet spying as early as 1942 by Whittaker Chambers, a former writer and editor of Communist publications in the US. Chambers had defected from the Communist party in 1939 after feeling ideologically betrayed by Stalin's non-aggression pact with Hitler. He then aligned himself with a former Soviet intelligence officer, Walter Krivitsky, who had defected to the US at the beginning of World War II. Krivitsky had already proven himself to be an ally to the West when in September 1939, he had tipped off the UK Embassy in Washington about a British government cipher clerk in London, Captain John Herbert King, who had been selling Foreign Office communication to Moscow. An investigation by MI6 and Guy Liddell's team at MI5 resulted in a ten-year prison sentence for King, whose case was not made public until two decades later.

Krivitsky was eager to expose more Soviet spies, despite being hunted down by the NKVD, which wanted him dead. He travelled to London in January 1940 under the cover name of 'Walter Thomas' to meet with MI5 officers, including Liddell. He was offered £1,000 plus expenses but he pushed for five times that amount. In the end the 'deal finally settled on £2,000 and all parties seemed satisfied'. Krivitsky told MI5 'quite a lot' about the structure of the Soviet's secret police, but the information about other alleged Soviet spies in Britain was not specific enough for the identification and arrest of potential targets.

On his return to the US, Krivitsky continued his public opposition to Stalin through the publication of articles and urged Whittaker Chambers to provide information about the Communist party's activities to US authorities. Krivitsky was found dead in a hotel room in Washington,

DC, in February 1941 with a single bullet in the head, and not one but three suicide notes by his bedside. Chambers suspected that he had been killed by the NKVD and, fearing for his own life, met with the FBI in spring the following year. During interviews with the law-enforcement organisation between May 1942 and June 1945, he exposed the names of US government officials whom he said were also on the Soviet payroll, including Alger Hiss, a senior US State Department official who had worked closely with President Roosevelt.

Chambers' claims were effectively ignored by the FBI in what was deemed an operational failure by its own subsequent assessment of his case. The FBI's lack of urgency to properly investigate Soviet espionage in the US during the war was partly because the Red Army was on side and the American people, like President Roosevelt himself, considered their Soviet allies as comrades-in-arms. Compounding that was a lack of coordination and information sharing between the FBI and other US intelligence agencies, especially the OSS.

Gouzenko's defection forced the FBI to re-evaluate Chamber's information in a new light. But it wasn't until November 1945, when an American woman who feared being killed by Soviet henchmen for turning her back on Communism became an FBI informant, that they took Chambers' claims seriously.

Elizabeth Terrill Bentley had been a Soviet spy for seven years when she divulged her secrets to the FBI. Her affiliation with the Communist party had been known to the US law-enforcement agency, as had her connection to a former NKVD agent, Jacob Golos, who had run a travel firm and a shipping company in New York which doubled as fronts for Soviet espionage. An FBI investigation into Bentley in 1941 failed to uncover any evidence against the former school teacher from Connecticut who had been recruited by Golos three years earlier. It later emerged that Golos had been her handler and lover.

One of her missions was to travel between New York and Washington, DC, as a 'courier' to collect a variety of confidential material from agents, including documents and microfilms containing secrets about US troop deployments, technology relating to Air Force fighter planes, and assessments on the state of economies in Asia and Latin America.

Bentley's spying activities were in line with Moscow's aims for its US-based agents. During the war, Stalin wanted to be informed about American intelligence relating to Hitler's plans against Russia; secret military plans between Washington and London; the potential for Western allies to broker a peace deal with Germany; and American scientific technology, especially in the field of nuclear development.

Bentley helped fulfil such Soviet aims for Golos – for whom she worked until his death from a heart attack in 1943. By helping him recruit spies from within the US Communist party ranks, she had also familiarised herself with the structure of Soviet espionage in America and knew the identities of its agents, including those who were government officials and it was that information that she wanted to trade with the FBI in the autumn of 1945 in return for protection and immunity from prosecution.

At 37, Bentley had survived more than a decade of alcohol abuse and depression. She was less confident, however, about surviving the NKVD, who had questioned her loyalty to Russia, stripped her of her network of agents, and found her irrepressible personality difficult to handle following Golos's death.

During an interview with FBI officers in New York on 7 November 1945, Bentley defected from the Communist party – and over several weeks, provided the authorities with the names of dozens of spies, including Lauchlin Currie, a White House economic adviser, and Duncan Lee, a senior intelligence official at the OSS who had leaked her information about some the agency's top-secret missions in Europe and its internal spy hunt to identify Communist sympathisers. Bentley's information dovetailed with that provided by Whittaker Chambers and Igor Gouzenko regarding the magnitude of Soviet espionage in the US. Her information, which would not be made public for three years, had been shared by the FBI with MI5 because it implicated Britons, including Cedric Belfrage, a film critic and author who had been hired by the British Security Coordination in New York to work in its propaganda division.

Bentley claimed he was providing the Soviets with one of Scotland Yard's instruction manuals for British agents.

The FBI were still in the process of debriefing Bentley when they shared their early findings with Guy Liddell of MI5. 'About 30 agents have been identified but the ramifications of the case have not yet been fully explored,' Liddell wrote in his diary on 20 November. Bentley would ultimately implicate dozens more in their connection to the Soviet espionage network in the US. 'The network follows the usual pattern of Soviet intelligence and extensive penetration of American Government Services has been brought to light,' Liddell noted. 'Reference has been made to Cedric Belfrage. This man is said to have handed over a long report of the training of agents by Scotland Yard.'

Bentley also implicated Canadians during her interviews with the FBI. She claimed that Fred Rose, the Canadian member of Parliament, had also been in regular correspondence with Golos – her former boss and lover – through her. Rose ultimately received a six-year prison sentence for spying, not because of Bentley's claims but because of Gouzenko's testimonies to the RCMP.

Unlike Gouzenko who had provided hard evidence during his defection, Bentley only had her recollections to back up her claims. This hampered the FBI's ability to move fast against the alleged spies she named and resulted in lengthy investigations to gather more evidence against them. By Christmas of 1945, the FBI had its hands full with pursuing leads provided by Bentley; the RCMP was continuing its hunt for spies in North America through Igor Gouzenko's secret documents; and MI5's investigation into Alan Nunn May was ongoing. The counter-Soviet mission by the three services foreshadowed an expansion of their counterespionage cooperation and the increased surveillance of their citizens. It also highlighted the value of pooled resources, human-intelligence sharing, and the importance of coordinating arrests to prevent suspects from getting away.

Five months after Igor Gouzenko's defection, the British and Canadian intelligence authorities believed they had sufficient evidence to swoop on the ring of spies he had identified. On 15 February 1946, as the RCMP arrested the first eleven of 22 alleged Soviet agents in Canada, MI5 brought Alan Nunn May in for questioning. The British physicist had been aware of the spy ring in Ottawa following a news report that had appeared in the US media on 4 February, a day before Canadian prime minister Lyon Mackenzie King initiated a royal commission to investigate Gouzenko's claims.

During his interrogation, May was rattled by Guy Liddell's officers, but remained cagey about his previous work in Canada. It was not until five days later that May admitted he had provided his Soviet handler with information and materials relating to atomic research, including samples of uranium-233 and -235. 'He had supplied him with a report and also with two pieces of uranium,' Liddell noted. 'He had done this because he thought it was in the general interest that the Russians be kept in the picture, and should share experimental work.' May's admission corroborated information provided by the RCMP to MI5 that Colonel Zabotin, Gouzenko's former boss, had notified Moscow the previous year of a report submitted by May containing 'details of the scientific features' of the nuclear bomb dropped on Hiroshima. Zabotin had also mentioned a uranium sample that May had provided. May was charged with breaching the UK's Official Secrets Act in the spring of 1946, at a time when tensions between the West and the Soviet Union were rapidly escalating.

Earlier in the year, Stalin had declared that capitalism was to blame for wars, saying the 'development of world capitalism in our times does not proceed smoothly and evenly, but through crises and catastrophic wars'. Meanwhile, Britain and the United States had taken major post-war steps to reinforce their political and intelligence commitments to each other – a pre-emptive move against the emergence of a Soviet threat to western democracy.

On 5 March of that year, Winston Churchill gave a speech in America's Midwest in which he praised the 'Special Relationship' between the UK and US, popularising a phrase he had coined previously. During his speech at Westminster College in Fulton, Missouri, for which he had been introduced by President Harry Truman, the former British prime minister also said that an 'Iron Curtain' had divided post-war Europe: on one side stood a free and democratic west and on the other, a Communist east under Soviet influence and 'increasing measure of control from Moscow'.

On the same day Churchill gave his speech, another historic, but unrelated event, had taken place. A new secret pact was agreed between Britain and America – the UKUSA Agreement. The new agreement was signed between the London Signals Intelligence Board and the State-Army-Navy Communication Intelligence Board on behalf of their respective nations' signals authorities. UKUSA was an expansion of BRUSA, the wartime framework for intelligence-sharing, and had been under negotiation since the summer of the previous year, shortly before the Japanese surrender. The Truman Administration and Attlee government approved the idea of post-war intelligence-sharing to combat a range of threats, including Soviet espionage, the emergence of a nuclear arms race, and potential surprise attacks by future enemies.

The UKUSA Agreement gave the signals intelligence authorities of both countries, including Bletchley Park, Arlington Hall and the US Navy, 'unrestricted' access to each other's 'procedures, practices and equipment', which meant that they integrated more analysts into each other's headquarters, ran joint operations, annual conferences, and made 'directorate level policy decisions' together. The British Dominions, including Australia, Canada and New Zealand, were not parties to the agreement, but according to its terms, they could still benefit from it, providing their participation was required for certain missions and if they agreed to 'abide by the terms'.

Despite being called an agreement, UKUSA was merely a deniable and non-binding memorandum. It was not defined by the nine pages it was written on, but by the feats and failures of code breakers and other intelligence officials on both sides of the Atlantic throughout World War II. While the UKUSA, like its predecessor, was centred on signals intelligence (SIGINT), it ultimately became a beneficiary of, and benefit to, human-intelligence (HUMINT) and law-enforcement agencies, including MI5, MI6, the FBI, and the Central Intelligence Agency (CIA), which was created in 1947 as a successor to the OSS.

The agreement reinforced the Special Relationship between the intelligence communities in Britain and the United States at a time when members of the public in their countries, and in Canada, had turned against the Soviet Union. The solidarity they felt with their wartime ally had started to rapidly give way to a fear of Communism destabilising western democracies, a fear compounded by the international headlines that followed the conviction of Dr Alan Nunn May, in May 1946. The physicist was sentenced to ten years of hard labour for providing the Soviet Union with nuclear secrets.

At the time, the FBI was still investigating Elizabeth Bentley's claims, and one of its officers, Special Agent Robert Lamphere, had been pursuing the idea of combining his expertise in human intelligence with code breaking. As a counterespionage specialist, he had been familiar with the Gouzenko case and had found out that code breakers at Arlington Hall, including Gene Grabeel, had made some headway in penetrating Soviet communications. Some clues into the Kremlin's one-time pad encryption system had been provided by Gouzenko to Grabeel's boss, Frank Rowlett. Rowlett had debriefed Gouzenko at a secret location in Canada in the autumn of 1945. 'Because Gouzenko worked with communications, Frank Rowlett [...] was invited to interrogate him,' states a declassified NSA document. 'During his sessions, Rowlett learned much about the way the KGB codebooks were put together'. Gouzenko's insights about the Kremlin's use of additional random letters to reinforce the encryption of their one -time-pad communications helped diminish some of the struggles that the Venona team had encountered – but they were not enough to make any major breakthroughs.

Although somewhat aware of the challenges being faced by the Venona team, the FBI's Robert Lamphere knew better than to impose himself onto the Project, which had been shrouded in more secrecy than the wartime Enigma decrypts. Even President Truman did not become aware of Venona's existence until the 1949 espionage trial of US State Department official Alger Hiss.

Lamphere required a strategy to convince the Venona team of his eagerness to work alongside them – to help them uncover at least some of the missing clues in a mutually rewarding hunt for Kremlin spies. So he convinced the FBI's liaison officer to Arlington Hall, Wes Reynolds, to introduce him to Frank Rowlett.

CHAPTER FIVE

HUMINT MEETS SIGINT

GRADUATING AS A SPECIAL agent in the winter of 1941, Robert Joseph Lamphere had been deemed unimpressive in 'appearance' and 'manner' by his assessor at the FBI's training academy. The 23-year-old rookie had also been described as 'average', in need of a 'more colourful personality, and more apparent confidence in himself'– an assessment that could hardly have foreshadowed his glowing future as a star recruit. It took some years for the Idaho native to make a remarkable impression on the FBI. Within 15 months of his deployment as a Special Agent, first to the FBI's office in Birmingham, Alabama, and then to New York City, he had thrown himself into his career, averaging around three hours of overtime each day across a range of criminal cases, including extortion and vehicle theft. But his investigations into Soviet spying after World War II were what transformed him in the eyes of his bosses. Following his transfer to the FBI's Espionage Unit in the summer of 1948, Lamphere was praised by one of his supervisors for his 'winning personality' and consistently displaying 'initiative, resourcefulness and aggressiveness in his work'. By then, he was 30 years old, on to his second marriage and preparing to make an impression on the Venona team.

In October of that year, Lamphere travelled to Arlington Hall to meet with Frank Rowlett, head of the intelligence division at the US Army Security Agency (ASA), successor to the Signal Intelligence Service (SIS). Rowlett had been briefed on Lamphere's investigative abilities, but safeguarding the secrecy of his counter-Soviet programme felt more important than inviting the Special Agent's skills into it. He demanded an assurance that any material supplied by Venona for a future FBI investigation would be cited to 'intelligence sources' rather than the programme or its decrypted cables. It was a major limitation for Lamphere because restricted disclosure in criminal cases is often seized on by defence lawyers to discredit evidence against their clients.

Lamphere had no choice but to respect the ultimatum regarding the sensitivity of Venona and agreed to Rowlett's terms. After all, the Special Agent had been offered privileged access to a programme that had been kept secret, even from the Central Intelligence Agency (CIA), formed in the previous year. He was assigned an investigative partner – Meredith Gardner, the principal translator and analyst on Venona. Gardner was a cryptanalyst and linguist, fluent in six languages, including Russian, German and Japanese, and had been recruited by Rowlett in 1946 to target codes relating to the communications of the KGB, the Soviet intelligence agency that ran the Stalin's spying in foreign countries, often by concealing its espionage operations under diplomatic cover.

Gardner began working his way through a backlog of messages, some dating back to the early 1940s, that had been compiled by Gene Grabeel and her team. By Christmas of 1946, he had made several breakthroughs, including the penetration of a message between the KGB's New York station and Moscow containing the codenames of some scientists on the Manhattan Project. By the following summer, Gardner helped produce a report which revealed that Soviet message traffic featured hundreds of cover names for KGB agents, including 'ANTENNA', 'STANLEY', 'GOMER' and 'REST'.

Lamphere was intrigued by Gardner's discoveries, even though the cryptanalyst had not yet identified the people to whom the cover names referred. As an introvert, Gardner was cagey by nature, preferring working alone, and at 36, he was unlikely to suddenly shake off such habits. He was also reluctant to discuss his methods, but when Lamphere spotted a partially burned KGB codebook on his desk, Gardner opened up for the first time and introduced him to its secrets. The codebook had been recovered by Finnish troops in the summer of 1941, following a raid on the Soviet consulate in Finland. Shortly before their surrender, the Soviets had set the consulate's cipher room ablaze in an attempt to incinerate confidential material. The Finns recovered several items from the fire, including a partially burned KGB codebook.

In September 1944, shortly after Finland signed a peace deal with Moscow and Britain, the US wartime intelligence service, the OSS, had been able to purchase Soviet cipher material from them, including the KGB codebook, a copy of which was sent to Arlington Hall. By the time Gardner got his hands onto the KGB codebook, the Soviet intelligence service had moved to a new version – but the former edition provided Gardner with enough clues to crack some of the KGB's communications. Some of his earliest success against the KGB related to its communications between its station at the Soviet Embassy in Canberra, Australia, and its Moscow headquarters. The Venona decrypts identified numerous cover names, including 'KLOD' – a person who had been obtaining secret information through two officials from the Australian Department of External Affairs, including post-war strategic planning that Britain had communicated to the department through telegrams. 'KLOD' had passed the information to a KGB handler in Canberra, setting off alarm bells in the US about Australia's potentially compromised security.

Compounding Australia's position was that neither its Labor government – suspected of being soft on Communism – nor its amateurish security service had been told of Venona's existence. In contrast, Britain had been brought into the loop by Arlington Hall in 1945, a year before Bletchley Park's Government Code and Cypher School changed its name to the Government Communications Headquarters – GCHQ. In 1947, Gardner briefed his British code breakers on Venona decrypts which revealed that Australia's security had indeed been compromised.

GCHQ passed the information onto MI5, where Guy Liddell had been promoted to deputy director-general. Liddell was determined to reform Australia's intelligence organisation, the Commonwealth Investigation Service (CIS), into which the Commonwealth Investigation Bureau (CIB) and the Commonwealth Security Service (CSS) had been merged in February 1947.

'Some success was achieved over a message from Australia, dated about 1945, indicating that a government document, supplied by us to the Australians, had leaked almost in toto [as a whole],' Liddell noted in a diary entry on 25 November 1947. As Britain was sharing so much intelligence with its ally, Liddell wanted to improve Australia's security standards and considered positioning an MI5 representative at the CIS to get a 'far better idea about Australian security and maybe we could do something about it'. The following year, Liddell and his MI5 colleagues had set the wheels in motion to do exactly that.

When MI5 informed Britain's Prime Minister Clement Attlee of the security breach in Canberra, he wanted to address it urgently as the Cold War ramped up in early 1948. While some of Stalin's spies were preoccupied with stealing secrets from Australia, other elements of the Soviet Union were busy destabilising Europe. In February, Communists had overthrown Czechoslovakia's democratically elected government with the covert backing of the Kremlin. By then, Communist cheerleaders in Greece and China had also been embroiled in civil wars with varying degrees of success. The British-backed Greek government eventually rebuffed a violent attempt by Communists to take over the country, but China was taken over by Communist leader Mao Zedong whose worldview is still adhered to by the nation's rulers to this day.

Attlee wanted to illustrate the magnitude of the Kremlin threat to his Australian counterpart. In February 1948, Attlee dispatched Percy Sillitoe, MI5's director-general, and Roger Hollis, an authority on Soviet counterespionage, to Sydney. The two MI5 officials were hamstrung from the very beginning by the necessity to conceal the origins of the information they wanted to share with Australian Prime Minister Ben Chifley. The nature of shared intelligence typically puts the onus on its recipient to comply with its terms of use – and the Venona secrets had been provided to MI5 on such restricted terms because the Americans did not trust the Australians enough to share it with them directly.

During a meeting in Sydney on 12 February, Sillitoe and Hollis lied to Chifley. They told him that a Russian defector had provided them with information about the KGB's activities in Canberra which had deeply concerned Britain and the United States. They also said that the Soviets had obtained secret material dating back to the autumn of 1945 through a yet unknown Australian government official. The material, including a 'Top Secret'-labelled document 'Security in the Western Mediterranean and the Eastern Atlantic', would have aided Stalin during his negotiations with the Allies over post war plans in Europe.

Chifley was unconvinced by the MI5 cover story and took it as a slight against himself and his Cabinet colleagues. 'Chifley appeared to think that there was some personal accusation,' Liddell noted in his diary, yet the prime minister authorised an investigation into the leaked documents that the British officials had raised with him anyway. The Australian prime minister also introduced his MI5 visitors to Sir Frederick Shedden, secretary of the defence department, responsible for the protection and distribution of secret documents shared by Britain. But once Shedden had appointed Brigadier Fred Chilton, the Controller of Joint Intelligence, to investigate, Sillitoe and Hollis changed their cover story in a further act of paranoia to protect the Venona secrets. They told Chilton that their earlier claim that a Russian defector had provided them with information about the KGB's penetration of the Australian government had not been true. They said the information had in fact been provided by a reliable informant in London who had been told that the Soviet ambassador to Australia had 'boasted that he had a number of informants' in Canberra. Chilton went along with MI5's new cover story, even though he did not believe it either.

Chilton's investigation quickly identified a suspect: Dr Ian Milner, an official at the Department of External Affairs who, between November 1945 and March 1946, had twice requested a copy of the paper 'Security in the Western Mediterranean and the Eastern Atlantic' from the defence department's post-hostilities planning committee. Milner had also been granted access to seven other secret documents provided by Britain to Australia, which were feared to have ended up in Soviet hands. The suspicion around Milner's activities resulted in Australian security officials commencing a broader investigation into the Department of External Affairs. Along with Milner, the investigation focused on Jim Hill, another department official who had been suspected of aiding Moscow. The suspects' identities had become apparent after Venona decrypts linked them to the cover names of BUR and TOURIST, respectively. Hollis remained in Australia until April to assist in the counterespionage investigation against Milner and Hill, meeting regularly with top officials, including Shedden whom he tried to persuade on more than one occasion to establish an MI5-style organisation in the country.

Washington had now become so concerned about Australia's porous security that it started withholding intelligence from Britain. The US Air Force stipulated that it would only share information about its guided weapons with the UK once it had been assured that Australia's security standards had been improved. It was a shock to the British intelligence community, and coincided with further secrets, emerging through Venona intercepts, which evidenced Soviet spying in Canberra.

Clement Attlee ordered Percy Sillitoe to visit Washington in the summer of 1948. He wanted Sillitoe to convince the US Communications Intelligence Board, which facilitated SIGINT cooperation between American agencies, that the only way for Australia to take its own security situation more seriously was through the disclosure of the Venona secrets. While American signals officials agreed for Prime Minister Ben Chifley to be informed by MI5, they refused to approve a wider briefing for other Australian officials, including Herbert Evatt, the attorney general and minister for External Affairs, and John Dedman, the minister for defence.

Unwilling to accept no for an answer, Sillitoe appealed to General Marshall, now Secretary of State, whose fear of Communist expansion was well known. It had resulted in the implementation of his post-war vision, the Marshall Plan, in which the United States financed the redevelopment of western European infrastructure and economies to help diminish the spread of Communism on the continent. Having previously coordinated Allied operations during the war, Marshall would have been well versed in Australia's signals intelligence contributions during World War II through the US-led Cipher Bureau in Brisbane under General MacArthur. Marshall accepted Sillitoe's appeal and ordered the American signals intelligence community to approve a wider briefing for Australian government officials on the Venona secrets, including to those within Prime Minister Ben Chifley's inner circle.

At the end of June 1948, Chifley travelled to London and was personally briefed on the Venona decrypts by his British counterpart. The extent of the briefing had become a sticking point, with the US signals intelligence chiefs demanding that Chifley should be partly kept in the dark about the origin of the information. According to Guy Liddell, the US communications intelligence board wanted Chifley to be told that the information relating to the KGB's activities in his backyard had been revealed through the 'interception of one telegram from Australia to Moscow'. It was a stipulation made by the US body because it feared that revealing the true nature of 'a series of messages would definitely imply a cryptographic break'. Despite this, Attlee referred to multiple telegrams when he briefed Chifley, perhaps to drive home the urgency of the security breach that had been at play. By then, the US had downgraded Australia's security clearance to the lowest category, denying it any intelligence of value, and by late July, a month later, Australia was completely stripped of its partial access to American signals intelligence, a privilege it had enjoyed through the UKUSA Agreement by virtue of being a British dominion. Chifley was outraged by Washington's move because, in his mind, it seemed to disregard his military contribution in Japan, where Australia had deployed troops to back the US-led invasion. Australia had committed around 16 thousand military personnel since 1946, including members of its air force, infantry, and navy, to oversee the demilitarisation of the Japanese.

Chifley was left with no choice but to overhaul his country's intelligence standards for numerous reasons: the inability to access US intelligence undermined Australia's defence; evidence against External Affairs official Ian Milner suggested that he had indeed leaked secret information to the Soviet Embassy in Canberra; and any investment into Australia's Defence Signals Bureau (DSB) and Joint Intelligence Bureau (JIB) would have been a waste of Australian taxpayers' money without access to American secrets.

Chifley's headaches were compounded by local press reports about Australia's predicament with the US, along with a growing number of investigations by the Commonwealth Investigation Service into official leaks. By October 1948, the CIS were juggling ten inquiries into Soviet espionage, which had become known as 'the case'. An experienced counterespionage officer from MI5, Robert Hemblys-Scales, had been approved by the Australian prime minister to assist the CIS, as the Australian agency had been regarded as too incompetent to run its own investigations. MI5 also dispatched two reinforcement officers in January 1949, including Roger Hollis, to provide advice on the creation of a new organisation and to showcase a series of Venona material, including copies of decrypted telegrams relating to Australia. Chifley's plans to strip the CIS of counterintelligence responsibilities in favour of creating a new body had gathered pace. He wanted to allay Washington and London's concerns, despite his initial reluctance to cave in to such external demands. On 2 March 1949, he announced the formation of a new agency which would go on to become the Australian Security Intelligence Organisation – ASIO. His government also informed the FBI, Royal Canadian Mounted Police, and New Zealand's police commissioner of ASIO's creation to kick-start its cooperation with the partner organisations. At its inception, ASIO had 15 officers on its staff, along with an MI5 liaison officer who had been provided to help the agency get on its feet. Its mission, which would expand over time, was to 'undertake intelligence activities for the protection of the Commonwealth against espionage, sabotage and subversion'.

Australia's efforts to bolster its security in early 1949 coincided with the formation of a military treaty in the West to stymie Soviet expansionism. One year after Britain signed the 1948 Brussels Pact, a defence alliance that included European nations such as France and Belgium, Clement Attlee understood that Stalin's threat could only be robustly confronted by a union between western Europe and the United States. In April 1949, twelve nations including Britain, the US, and Canada signed a transatlantic defence pact – the North Atlantic Treaty Organization. NATO ensured collective defence for its member nations: an attack against any of them would be 'considered an attack against all' and could result in a military response.

Beyond NATO, Canada had been eager to shed its status as a secondary partner to the UKUSA Agreement following its enormous intelligence contribution through the Gouzenko Affair in 1945 and the creation of its signals agency, the Communication Security Establishment, a year later. It no longer wanted to be treated as a mere British dominion. Ottawa wanted to exchange intelligence with Washington without the 'requirement for UK approval before sharing signals intelligence bilaterally'. On 29 June 1949, an agreement was signed between the Communications Research Committee of Canada, representing all Canadian Communication Intelligence authorities, and its American counterpart, the United States Communication Intelligence Board. Having lobbied the US for three years, Canada was finally granted an 'equal partnership' in the UKUSA Agreement through its new bilateral deal with Washington. Two months to the day after Canada was ushered into the UKUSA Agreement, the Soviets successfully conducted a nuclear test, illustrating a monumental step-change by the Stalin regime. NATO moved to create a military command structure in response to the heightened threat which had ended the US's nuclear monopoly, forcing the Truman Administration and its allies to re-evaluate their foreign policies towards the Soviet bloc. But it also intrigued US intelligence officials who suspected that the bomb had been created with the help of western spies. Alan Nunn May, the British physicist exposed by Russian defector Igor Gouzenko for leaking nuclear secrets to the Soviets, was still in prison after being convicted three years earlier. But another British physicist had emerged as a suspect during an investigation into the Venona decrypts by FBI Special Agent Robert Lamphere.

Robert Lamphere had been trying to determine the extent to which stolen US secrets had aided Soviet scientific advancement, when Arlington Hall penetrated yet another significant KGB cable in early September 1949. The Venona decrypt related to a message from five years earlier, detailing the methods for enriching uranium for the purposes of building a bomb. It included the summarisation of a scientific paper that had been provided by someone from the British Mission to the wartime Manhattan Project. Armed with these two vital clues, Lamphere requested a copy of the scientific paper from the US Atomic Energy Commission, the authority that had been in charge of the Manhattan Project. He also asked for a list of all British scientists who had been involved in the development of America's nuclear weapon.

Within two days, he identified a suspect – Klaus Emil Julius Fuchs, a British scientist of German origin who had authored the scientific paper leaked to the KGB. Through his investigation, Lamphere learnt that Fuchs had embraced Communism while studying physics and mathematics at the University of Leipzig. His fears of being targeted for his ideological views after Hitler came to power had been reinforced when the Reichstag building, home to the German parliament in Berlin, was set ablaze in late February 1933. The attack, later revealed to be a Nazi plot, had been blamed on Communists. Fuchs had no future under the Third Reich as a Communist, and at 21, he had become so enamoured with Marxist views that he was far too idealistic to renounce them for the sake of appeasing the Nazis. He ultimately fled the country for England via France in the summer of that year. Four years later, he graduated with a PhD in physics from the University of Bristol before going on to earn another doctorate in science from the University of Edinburgh.

He lived in Britain as a Communist, openly opposed to Nazis. But at the outbreak of World War II, around 70,000 Germans and Austrians residing in the UK had been classed by the British government as enemy aliens, amid fears that they could become spies for Hitler or assist his regime in the event of an invasion. Under that classification, Fuchs was among thousands of German residents sent by Britain to an internment camp near Quebec, Canada, in 1940. He was held among predominantly pro-Nazi inmates, but during his six months there, he met Hans Kahle, a fellow German Communist who had also been living in the UK before his internment. Kahle, a suspected Soviet spy, introduced Fuchs to other Communists once the physicist had returned to Britain in January 1941 to pursue scientific research in Edinburgh. In an extraordinary twist of fortune, Fuchs gained British citizenship and a position at Tube Alloys, the nuclear development programme operated by Canada and Britain. Following the merger of Tube Alloys with the Manhattan Project, Fuchs was transferred to New York in December 1943 to contribute to atomic research before being relocated to Los Alamos laboratories, New Mexico, to help build the nuclear bomb. Fuchs had already been secretly cooperating with the NKVD, forerunner to the KGB, for about two years before setting foot on American soil.

Lamphere suspected that Fuchs was a Soviet spy but had no evidence against him except for the circumstantial material that had appeared in the decrypted KGB cable at Arlington Hall. Nonetheless, the FBI special agent informed MI5 on 12 September 1949, hoping to track Fuchs in the UK where he had been working at Britain's Atomic Energy Research Establishment in Harwell, Oxfordshire, for the last three years. In a rather humiliating security blunder, MI5 had vetted Fuchs on three separate occasions because of the sensitive research positions he held – and cleared him on all accounts between 1941 and 1947.

Lamphere's tipoff hamstrung MI5 because, once again, it could not use it as the source of evidence against Fuchs for fear of compromising the Venona Project. So the British agency applied conventional methods against the scientist: it bugged his home and work telephones, intercepted his letters, and placed a surveillance team on him around the clock, prying into every part of his life, including the affair he had been having with his boss's spouse. The investigation was exhaustive but failed to turn up any evidence of espionage against Fuchs. As a last resort, MI5 sent its chief interrogator, William James Skardon to interview Fuchs on 21 December. Skardon had joined the agency three years earlier after a successful career at Scotland Yard where he had risen to the rank of detective inspector. While Skardon was renowned for breaking suspected spies, Fuchs proved to be difficult, categorically denying ever working for the Soviets. However, as a proud ideologue Fuchs was consumed with guilt at the thought of lying to MI5 about what he considered an honourable contribution to Stalin's regime. So he sought another meeting with Skardon several weeks later and voluntarily confessed to leaking atomic secrets to Russia.

During his interview on 24 January 1950, Fuchs admitted to Skardon that he had been an active Soviet agent from the early 1940s to February 1949. Over a series of meetings, including some in New York, Boston and Santa Fe, he had provided his handlers with everything he could, 'including details about the manufacture of the atomic bomb.' Fuchs, who operated under the cover names of 'REST' and 'CHARLES', said he had been driven by 'ideological loyalties' to spy, and had reluctantly accepted around £100 in total for his services 'purely as a token payment and as an indication of a bond between him and the ideas for which the Russians stood'.

MI5 acknowledged its own failure to identify him earlier as a spy and attributed it to placing a disproportionate emphasis on his anti-Nazism and not enough on his Communist links. 'On the counterespionage side, I think there is no doubt that if we had turned the heat on Fuchs when he came back to this country [...] we should undoubtedly have bowled him out,' Guy Liddell noted in his diary a day after Fuchs' confession. 'One of his reasoning for ceasing to pass information was that he had come to the conclusion that he liked the way of life in this country. It will be seen how inconsistent Fuchs is in his reasoning: on the one hand, he sets himself up as a kind of God and talks of ideological laws which transcended all personal loyalties, and on the other he admits his fallibility both in regard to assessing the Russian government and the mode of life for which this country stands.'

Two months after Fuchs was handed a 14-year prison sentence and stripped of his British citizenship for providing secrets to the Soviet Union, MI5 were eager to repay Robert Lamphere for the tipoff on Fuchs by authorising him to interview the physicist in London. British officials from the Home Office and Foreign Office were concerned about the precedent that would be set if a 'representative of a foreign power was allowed to interview one of our prisoners'. But Kim Philby, who had been posted to the US the previous year to become MI6's bureau chief, supported MI5's view on allowing the FBI access to Fuchs and feared that if it could not be agreed, the bureau's director J. Edgar Hoover 'was quite capable of reducing our liaison to a pure formality, regardless of the loss that it might be to his own organisation'. Perhaps Philby, who had secretly been liaising with the Kremlin, wanted to leverage Fuchs to preserve his links to the FBI, including Lamphere. After all, Philby had successfully sought information about the Venona secrets and other FBI investigations from Lamphere who remained completely unaware of his Russian connections.

Following an intervention by Prime Minister Attlee to approve the FBI's interview, Lamphere travelled to Britain, determined to obtain information, corroboration, or clues from Fuchs to help identify Americans suspected of being under Moscow's control. To preserve the secrecy of the mission, MI5 organised for a police van with blacked-out windows to deliver Lamphere and his FBI colleague, Hugh Clegg, to Wormwood Scrubs prison on 20 May. They were joined by Skardon who helped break the ice between the two visitors and Fuchs once the physicist emerged into the meeting room located by the prison's entrance and often used for discussions between lawyers and their inmates. Lamphere was struck by Fuchs' idiosyncrasies when he sat down in front of him: he blinked rapidly and regularly, and swallowed hard and frequently as though he had a nervous tick.

Fuchs was very aware of his value as a former Russian asset and knew that he was not obligated to speak. But he was also afraid of incriminating his sister, Kristen Heinemann, who lived in Cambridge, Massachusetts and who had already been interviewed by the FBI because of a phone call she had received from a suspected Russian spy called 'Raymond' about six years earlier. The FBI had learned after interviewing Heinemann that she had been unwittingly used by her brother to connect with Raymond, a NKVD agent. So, Lamphere assured Fuchs that his sister was in the clear and that the FBI's initial interest in her was to aid in identifying Raymond's true identity. Lamphere's explanation won Fuch's trust – and over the next few hours, the physicist scrutinised a series of surveillance photographs of the man whom Lamphere believed was Raymond; the agent through whom Fuchs passed information to the NKVD.

Fuchs' NKVD handler in London, Ursula Beurton, who like him was a British citizen of German heritage, had connected him with Raymond in 1943, shortly after the physicist's arrival in the US to work on the Manhattan Project. He met with 'Raymond' on at least five occasions the following year at discreet restaurants and in public spaces, including movie theatres, to provide him with secrets. On being asked to identify the man in the surveillance photographs, Fuchs told the FBI that it was very likely to be Raymond – but he could not be certain because he had not seen him for over five years. That was not good enough for Lamphere; he required certainty. He returned to the prison two days later with a surveillance film of Raymond. On seeing the projected footage, Fuchs said it was likely to be Raymond. That, too, was insufficient for Lamphere who then returned to prison for the third time on 24 May with more recent footage and surveillance pictures. Fuchs did not hesitate in that instance; he identified the man in the pictures and footage as Raymond, confirming once and for all the FBI's case against the Soviet spy.

'Raymond' was the cover name that had been used by Harry Gold, an American chemist of Swiss origin, who ultimately pleaded guilty to conspiring with Fuchs and was sentenced to a 30-year prison term in 1951. The information Gold provided during his interrogation led the FBI to a ring of spies which had included Ethel and Julius Rosenberg – a husband and wife duo who were executed in 1953 for spying for the Soviet Union.

The FBI's operational relationship with MI5 had been further cemented by the Fuchs investigation. Lamphere had been satisfied with his work in London, and the icing on the cake came in the form of an admission from Fuchs that the information he had supplied the Soviets had accelerated their creation of the atomic bomb by at least two years.

In the summer of 1950, Lamphere farewelled his MI5 colleagues, and returned to Washington to continue his hunt for enemy spies. Fresh out of this joint-operation with the FBI, MI5 had a new case on its hands: a collaboration with Australia's newly formed intelligence agency – ASIO.

William Skardon was nicknamed 'Jim' by his MI5 colleagues. But his nickname was pretty much all he shared with the alleged Soviet spy, Jim Hill, whom he had been assigned to interrogate at the Australian High Commission in central London. As a Department of External Affairs official, Hill had been posted to the High Commission in January 1950 in what ostensibly appeared to be a promotion. But his diplomatic mission had been concocted by ASIO and MI5 to help expose his Kremlin links after the British authorities had linked him to a cover name, TOURIST, identified from Venona decrypts.

During a three-month surveillance operation, MI5 had tracked his movements, including his social interactions with fellow Australian Communists in London and members of the British Communist Party. Hill had been careful not to meet with Soviet officials or engage in any illegal activities, frustrating MI5's investigation. The agency had been unable to find any incriminating evidence to support the material it had obtained through the cable decrypts which, as in Fuchs' case, could not be relied on in the interest of preserving Venona's secrecy. So Skardon became the agency's final option to try to expose Hill.

At forty-six, Skardon was 14 years older than Hill, with an authority that towered over the Australian diplomat from the minute he started interrogating him on 6 June 1950. Hill appeared visibly shaken but denied links to Soviet officials and claimed that he had never leaked government documents to Stalin's regime. 'He was generally evasive when he had the facts formally put to him by Skardon, and was told that we were quite certain of our information,' Guy Liddell noted in his diary following Hill's interview.

Hill maintained his denial during two more interrogations over the following week, yet walked away with a priceless piece of information that had been inadvertently volunteered by Skardon. In his effort to break

Hill, the interrogator told him that MI5 and ASIO had been aware of his close connection to Ian Milner, the other External Affairs official who had been suspected of spying, and Walter Seddon Clayton, a senior member of the Communist Party of Australia. Milner and Clayton had been identified through Venona by their cover names – 'BUR' and 'KLOD', respectively, although Skardon kept that level of granular detail to himself. Skardon did, however, intimate to Hill that Milner and Clayton were of interest to ASIO and faced the prospect of arrest.

Without knowing it, Skardon had committed the same error that had been made by FBI Special Agent Leon Turrou in the Rumrich spy case in New York 12 years earlier: he had given away operational information, compromising a major counterespionage inquiry. Unsurprisingly, Hill acted on Skardon's warning of the likely arrest of Milner and Clayton and alerted the pair through mutual associates. In July 1950, Milner defected to Czechoslovakia, and while ASIO kept Clayton under surveillance for several decades thereafter, he continued to deny being the Soviet spymaster through whom Milner and Hill had passed information to the KGB.

Hill was recalled to Australia three months following his interrogation by Skardon and resigned from public service shortly afterwards. Overall, MI5's attempt to help ASIO had backfired due to Skardon's mistake. Although yet another embarrassment for the agency, it was eclipsed by the discovery of Soviet spies at the heart of the British intelligence community the following year – a case that brought into question the competence and integrity of MI5 and MI6 and outraged FBI Special Agent Robert Lamphere.

For almost three years, Robert Lamphere had repeatedly asked the representatives of MI5 and MI6 in Washington about an investigation by their respective agencies into a British diplomat suspected of being a Soviet asset. He had a vested interest in the case because the FBI had tipped them off about the spy in the winter of 1948. The tip had emerged from a series of decrypted KGB messages citing three cover names. Meredith Gardner, Venona's chief analyst at Arlington Hall, had determined that the cover names, including GOMER, were all references to the same person – a diplomat who had passed secrets to the KGB between 1944 and 1945 while working for the British Embassy in Washington.

The leaked secrets were specific: they related to highly classified cable traffic between Britain and the US, including information about war planning between Prime Minister Churchill and President Roosevelt and developments on nuclear research. Given the sensitivity of the information, Lamphere had figured that it would only have been accessible to a small number of diplomats at the British Embassy. Surely, he thought, that would have eased the burden on MI5 and MI6 to identify a shortlist of targets to go after. Yet each time he had asked the two agencies for an update into their inquiry, they would inform him that no new developments had emerged.

So it was with a degree of frustration and anger that he greeted the agencies' US representatives at his office in the summer of 1951. He had regularly met with Geoffrey Patterson after the MI5 officer had taken up the role as the British agency's representative to Washington around three years earlier – and even considered him a close friend. But Lamphere was less familiar with MI6's man, Kim Philby, who since his deployment in America in 1949 had appeared more focused on developing his service's links with the CIA rather than with the FBI. Years later Lamphere recalled being underwhelmed by Philby: 'He spoke with a stutter; he was sloppily dressed [...] and most of all, he was not friendly to me, never in the time we knew each other. He spent most of his time with [the] CIA.'

Lamphere's purpose in meeting with Patterson and Philby on 8 June 1951 was to discuss a story that had emerged in the UK press a day earlier about the defection of two British government officials, Donald Maclean and Guy Burgess. Both defectors had been known in Washington, largely because they had served as diplomats at the British Embassy. Maclean had joined the diplomatic service on 11 October 1935, and despite his erratic behaviour, secret gay affairs, and bouts of drinking, had landed a prestigious post in 1944 as first secretary to Lord Halifax, Britain's ambassador to the US. Four years later, after Maclean was promoted to Counsellor at the British Embassy in Cairo, he continued drinking heavily to the detriment of his marriage and his career, and was sent back to England. Instead of being fired, he was made head of the US section at the Foreign Office. At 38, Maclean was two years younger than Burgess, who had been his close friend since their student days at Cambridge University. Unlike Maclean, Burgess's entry into the diplomatic service had been unconventional by any standard: after a stint as a producer for currents affairs programmes at the BBC which started in 1936, he left to work for MI5 and MI6 in 1939 before taking up a mid-ranking diplomatic post in Washington in July 1950. He lasted less than a year in the US because of a series of indiscretions, including drunken antics and three speeding tickets in one day. MI5 had warned the Foreign Office six months before Burgess had been sent to Washington that he was 'untrustworthy and unreliable' but the agency's advice was ignored.

On being recalled to London in May 1951, Burgess had discovered that an MI5 spy investigation had narrowed down its list of suspects for GOMER, zeroing in on Maclean. Suspicion surrounding Maclean would undoubtedly have compromised Burgess, too, because both men had been working as Soviet spies since their recruitment by the NKVD, the KGB's predecessor, in the mid-1930s. To escape interrogation and arrest, the two men fled Britain on Friday, 25 May 1951 in an escape that was hushed up until it was exposed by the *Evening Standard* newspaper in London two weeks later.

Lamphere had known about the escape before the news story had emerged, but he felt betrayed by MI5 and MI6 for not informing him that Maclean had been identified as the suspect, despite his repeated requests for updates into their investigation. He felt that the two services had been so eager to shut him out of the loop that they had even gone over his head to get wider access to Venona decrypts, instead of the limited information they had been provided by the FBI on a need-to-know basis. The two British agencies had made a formal request in 1949 to obtain more information on the KGB cables relating to the GOMER case through a GCHQ representative at Arlington

Hall, who had been able to deliver them under the UKUSA Agreement guidelines, according to Lamphere.

But even more perturbing for Lamphere was the knowledge that Burgess had been a very close friend of Philby's and had lived with him for some time during his Washington posting. Lamphere also knew that Philby had attended the same university as Burgess and Maclean, and that he would undoubtedly have known about MI5's investigation. Could Philby have tipped off Maclean about MI5's investigation either directly or through Burgess? Could Philby have also been a spy? These questions consumed Lamphere during the meeting at his office, but he kept them to himself. Following the meeting, his doubts about Philby were amplified as questions started being asked on the other side of the Atlantic about the MI6 officer's loyalties, and whether he could have been the 'third man' in the Burgess and Maclean spy ring.

MI5 had initially been split about whether or not Philby was a Soviet spy. Guy Liddell, the agency's deputy head, had given him the benefit of the doubt, stating that the paperwork relating to the investigation into Maclean may have been randomly spotted by Burgess while he was in Washington. 'Personally, I think it is not unlikely that the papers relating to [the investigation into] Maclean might have been on Kim's desk and that Burgess strolled into the room while Kim was not there,' Liddell noted in his diary on 12 June, on the same day that Philby was interviewed by Dick White, a future director-general of MI5. Philby had been recalled to Britain and 'denied emphatically that he had ever discussed Maclean with Burgess' during a subsequent interview with White on 14 June. However, it had not been enough to contain the cloud of suspicion over his head at MI5, nor at the CIA which had initiated its own 'enquiries about Philby, whom they regard persona non grata'.

Another issue that intensified MI5's suspicion of Philby had been an incident relating to Konstantin Volkov, the Soviet consul to Istanbul, who wanted to defect to Britain in the winter of 1945. He had asked for asylum and £27,500 in return for providing details about 'some seven people in British intelligence who were in Soviet pay', including a 'CE', or counterespionage officer. Volkov provided a 21-day deadline for his proposal to be taken up and demanded that no mention of it be made in writing to London because he believed the Soviets had penetrated Britain's cypher correspondence system. The British Embassy in Istanbul instead sent Volkov's demands by diplomatic courier to London to the chief of MI6, Sir Stewart Menzies, who appointed Philby to investigate the case. Yet before Volkov could provide the information, the Soviets had been tipped off to his proposed defection and he was 'kidnapped by the Russians, carried on to a Soviet plane and carried back to Moscow'. Volkov was never heard from again. He was presumed dead.

By 7 July 1951, MI5 and MI6 had become 'extremely worried about Philby's position and anxious that his case should be further investigated,' Liddell noted in his diary. There had also been concerns about whether Philby had been the 'CE officer mentioned by Volkov'. Aware that he was no longer trusted, Philby resigned from MI6 that month, but was exonerated in parliament four years later by the British Foreign Secretary and future Prime Minister Harold Macmillan, who said: 'I have no reason to conclude that Mr Philby has at any time betrayed the interests of his country, or to identify him with the so-called 'Third Man', if indeed there was one.' It was not until Philby defected to Moscow in 1963 that the truth emerged about his treachery, including that he had tipped off Burgess and Maclean, and alerted the Russians about Volkov's attempt to defect to protect his own identity as a Soviet spy. In fact, by the time he defected, Philby had been a spy for three decades, having been recruited at Cambridge University by Burgess in the mid-1930s around the same time as Maclean. The spy ring also included Anthony Blunt, who worked for MI5 during World War II before becoming Surveyor of the Queen's Pictures and ultimately confessing to being a Soviet spy in 1964; and John Cairncross, who worked for Bletchley Park and MI6 during the war, before being exposed as a Soviet agent in 1979. None of them were ever prosecuted in what has historically been deemed as a cover-up by British intelligence to conceal its own failings. The spies became known as 'The Cambridge Five', yet even before they were all exposed as traitors, the British intelligence community had been keen to settle the score with Moscow.

Stalin's appetite for advancing Soviet causes through meddling in foreign countries had remained unabated in the winter of 1952. By then, the Korean War, between Soviet-backed troops in the north and armies in the south chiefly led by the US with the support of Britain, Australia, Canada and New Zealand, among other members of the United Nations, had been raging for 18 months. Away from the battlefield, Moscow had slightly restructured its espionage activities in Australia, handing overall responsibility for foreign intelligence work there to a newly promoted diplomat, Vladimir Mikhailovich Petrov. ASIO had sought information about Petrov from MI5 that February, before he had been made Chief Resident of the MGB, an organ of the Soviet espionage machine. But the British agency knew little about him, except that he had been an active intelligence officer who had served for three years at the Soviet Embassy in Stockholm, Sweden, between 1943 and 1947. So, ASIO decided to do some of its own digging into the mystery figure.

CHAPTER SIX

UKUSA BECOMES THE FIVE EYES

VLADIMIR MIKHAILOVICH PETROV WAS panicking, his eyes darting between the road ahead and the rear-view mirror of his Skoda. He accelerated towards the Soviet Embassy in Canberra, treating the streets of Australia's capital like a racetrack in his mission to outpace a police motorcycle on his tail. On reaching his destination, Petrov rushed into the twin-storey building – a fortress separated from the road by a high hedge, out-of-bounds to anyone without an invitation or diplomatic clearance.

Petrov managed to escape questioning, forgoing a confrontation with the police officer for breaking Australian law that could have resulted in a diplomatic headache in July 1952. A subsequent police enquiry into the car chase confirmed that he had been driving 'under the influence of alcohol and had narrowly missed running down a police constable' who had ultimately pursued him on a motorcycle. 'On arrival […] Petrov disappeared into the Embassy, sending another member to placate the constable and drive the Skoda out of sight. The police were unable to take any action in this matter owing to the diplomatic status involved.'

Unlike the police, the Australian Security Intelligence Organisation – ASIO – had not been surprised by Petrov's drunken behaviour. It had been monitoring him since his arrival in the country with his wife, Evdokia, on 5 February of the previous year, ten days before his forty-fourth birthday. By May of 1951, Petrov had become a frequent visitor to Sydney to ostensibly 'meet Diplomatic Couriers arriving from overseas'. But ASIO had known that the real reason behind Petrov's interstate travel had been to meet with Communist party officials and trade unionists, and to engage in 'immoral pursuits, in search of wine [and] women'. The Australian spy agency had also been told by one of its informants that Petrov had boasted about exploiting his diplomatic cover, saying 'one can do some good work here without much danger, if one goes about it quietly'.

In fact, Petrov's assignment in Australia had been wide-ranging. As a longstanding member of the MGB, another predecessor to the KGB, he had been sent to infiltrate and disrupt the activities of Soviet expatriate organisations and had also been instructed by Moscow to identify Kremlin-sympathisers for recruitment, providing they had the right 'political views, station in life, position, occupation, marital status, financial standing, circle of friends and access to information.' His superiors at the MGB had told him that the 'work of recruitment should be carried out boldly, with forethought and inventiveness.'

Moscow's interest in Australia related to its geographical importance to central Asia, home to three-quarters of the Soviet Union's territory, including the nations of Kyrgyzstan and Uzbekistan. For Australia, this Asian region was of strategic interest as it presented a Communist and military threat. Aware of this national security anxiety, the MVD, Moscow's Ministry of Internal Affairs, was determined to improve its understanding of Australia's military capabilities to give the Kremlin an edge in the event of a war. Petrov had been instructed by Moscow that 'strong MVD representation in Australia was necessary because it was realised that Australia would be a supply base in the event of war and the Soviet Union desired to know about the preparations of war bases'.

Despite his sizeable appetite for hedonism, Petrov was a skilled spymaster, capable of operating in the shadows, obtaining and concealing secrets. He was disciplined about his communications with Moscow, to the point of ensuring that each missive he sent his bosses underwent multiple layers of protection. He would draft a message in his own handwriting then give it to wife, Evdokia, who was a cipher assistant at the Embassy, to transcribe. He would then burn the draft, photograph the message transcribed by his wife and send it in the form of an undeveloped film via a diplomatic courier to Moscow. 'Upon receipt of the message in Moscow, it was acknowledged by coded cable and Petrov then burnt the only typewritten copy in his possession.'

While ASIO had no visibility into Petrov's communications at that point, it suspected him of regularly attending functions at the Russian Social Club in Sydney, a community network of left-wing Soviet expats. It had become a popular practice for Soviet officials, including those posted to Britain and Canada, to join clubs as a means of collecting intelligence. On assessing the practice, Guy Liddell noted: 'Soviet officials may well have said that they cannot hope to get information unless they are given greater freedom in making contact with nationals of the country in which they reside.'

ASIO suspected that Petrov had been cultivating sources at the Sydney club, including Dr Michael Bialoguski, a general practitioner of Polish descent who had migrated to Australia in 1941 to pursue his medical studies at the University of Sydney. He had become an Australian citizen six years later but remained close to his roots, connected to the Russian Diaspora through his medical practice and the social club, where he met Petrov in July 1951. Petrov identified Bialoguski as a potential recruit: he was a professional of high social standing, had a wide circle of friends, and at 34, he was on the right side of maturity in political activism. The pair met on more than 20 occasions over the following two years, initially at the social club, but later at restaurants and Bialoguski's harbour-side flat in Point Piper, an eastern suburb of Sydney. Petrov had taken a long-term approach to cultivating Bialoguski, occasionally asking him whether he could help obtain immigration papers and driving licenses, presumably for the purposes of providing covers to conceal the work and identities of Russian intelligence officers. He may well have known that Bialoguski could not deliver on some of his requests, but he seemed to be testing the limitations of his connections and his potential for future work as a spy.

That is what ASIO may have observed each time its officers debriefed Bialoguski – who had been employed as an agent, codenamed 'Diabolo', two years before his first meeting with Petrov. At the time of his recruitment by ASIO, Bialoguski had secretly been working as a spy for the agency's predecessor, the Commonwealth Investigation Service, since 1945 while completing his studies and after beginning medical practice. His CIS handler had tasked him to join the Russian Social Club to report on its pro-Soviet members. Several months after joining ASIO in August 1949, Bialoguski was elected to the club's committee, legitimising his cover. His brief was to collect information on Russian diplomats linked to the club – to gain insights into their behaviour, personalities, and their responsibilities as Embassy officials in Canberra. As well as running Bialoguski, the Australian agency was intercepting the Soviet embassy's phone calls, and ASIO field officers were conducting surveillance on Petrov. ASIO initially found it difficult to corroborate some of Bialoguski's discoveries, including ones relating to Petrov's personality clashes with embassy staff. Several ASIO officials even suspected that Bialoguski may have been a double agent. Their suspicion had been heightened by the circumstances under which he had joined the agency and the CIS: *he* had approached *them* for work, and not the other way around.

Was he merely a thrill-seeker, enamoured with the cloak and dagger nature of espionage and the sense of self-importance it gave him? Was his motive to spy for Australia genuinely based on his opposition to the Kremlin and his resentment toward the NKVD, by whom he had been interrogated and temporarily jailed following the occupation of Poland by the Red Army in 1939? Although some were suspicious of Bialoguski's real agenda, ASIO's regional director in Sydney, George 'Ron' Richards, was determined to keep him on the books. Richards's judgement was vindicated when Bialoguski reported in April 1953 that Petrov had become depressed and was 'suffering from "neurological-retinitis" of both eyes', a swelling of the optic nerve that required 'elaborate treatment, failing which treatment Petrov could go blind'. His depression had been largely brought about by Nikolai Lifanov, the Soviet ambassador in Canberra, who had repeatedly mocked him and criticised his work. Lifanov's hostility toward Petrov was due to unreciprocated sexual advances he had made to the latter's wife, Evdokia.

As Petrov's woes were mounting, back in Moscow enormous upheavals were taking place as a result of the death of Stalin on 5 March 1953. The dictator's 26-year reign of terror had built the Soviet Union into a superpower, largely despised and isolated on the international stage, with its economy in ruins. There was a short-lived air of hope among Stalin's critics domestically and abroad that his successor, Georgy Malenkov, would become a moderating influence. Moscow's one-man dictatorship had given way to a power-share between Malenkov, Nikita Khrushchev, the newly appointed head of the Soviet Union's Communist Party, and Lavrentiy Beria, the First Deputy chairman of the Council of Ministers who was also in charge of the Ministry of Internal Affairs. The new regime appeared united, at least at first, and rallied the population, promising better living conditions, including cheaper food, and a friendlier approach to foreign policy. However, Western nations remained sceptical, despite Moscow's intervention in the release of British civilian prisoners, including the UK's former General Consul to Korea, Vyvyan Holt, who had been detained by North Korea since July 1950. Guy Liddell of MI5 chalked up the Soviet Union's proposed domestic and international policy changes to its fear of potential confrontation with the West. 'The present Russian government wishes to consolidate internally, and probably realises that her aggressive tactics against the West might involve them in a world war for which they are not yet prepared,' he noted in his diary. 'It also shows that there must have been disagreement with Stalin only so long as he was alive no one dared to resist him.'

In Canberra, Petrov sought no inspiration or comfort from the new Soviet leadership, despite its expression of good intentions. He saw through the window-dressing and that made him even more critical of his embassy colleagues. His state of mind and failing health provided the right dose of vulnerability for Bialoguski to exploit, and the ASIO agent was determined to turn the Russian official into a 'Cabin' candidate – a potential defector. Bialoguski continued with his cultivation process, drawing Petrov in and reinforcing the friendship between them through dinners, drinks and other social occasions. He appealed to Petrov's boundless urge for an uninhibited social life, away from his spouse and the curtailed privacy of his role as a Soviet official where he was shackled by Embassy protocols. Petrov had become so trusting of Bialoguski that he had even proposed for the two of them to buy a restaurant in King's Cross, a nightlife hub in central Sydney, in order to run it as a front for Russian espionage.

The ASIO agent gave the impression of entertaining the idea for the sake of keeping Petrov engaged, and by May 1953, Bialoguski had largely disarmed the Russian spymaster. The pair had known each for two years by then, Petrov's better judgement clouded by the familiarity of their friendship. He started disregarding his own security, and instead of staying at a hotel on his visits to Sydney, slept over at the doctor's flat at Point Piper, unwittingly forgoing every sense of his privacy. In such instances, Bialoguski set aside the Hippocratic oath he had taken as medical professional, a rite of passage which includes a doctor's ethical obligation of protecting the confidentiality of a person in their care. He occasionally spiked Petrov's drinks with sleeping pills, and one time even injected him with morphine when his Russian comrade had asked for a jab of penicillin as he feared having caught gonorrhoea. After putting him to sleep, Bialoguski would go about his work, searching the pockets of his clothes for anything that could be of interest to ASIO. He even took a picture of Petrov passed out, naked, and gave it to the agency.

Even when he referred Petrov to Dr Halley Beckett, an eye specialist in Sydney, Bialoguski did so to further his own agenda. He had booked the appointment to disrupt Petrov's planned visit to Moscow with his wife – which Bialoguski feared could spell the end of his diplomatic posting in Australia. He was relieved when Dr Beckett informed Petrov that he required an operation and referred him to Canberra Hospital for a fortnight's treatment. He was discharged on 1 June 1953, several days after ASIO had concluded that with the 'repeated cancellation of Petrov's travel plans […] it seemed reasonable to infer that Petrov was not anxious to return to the USSR'. But as much as ASIO was hoping for Petrov to become a turncoat, it had no evidence that he wanted to betray his nation. It also feared the diplomatic backlash of inciting him to defect through a cold approach in case he were to take offence and report the approach to the Soviet Embassy. In further complication to the Australian agency's dilemma, Bialoguski had abruptly resigned as an agent around the time Petrov was in hospital, after ASIO refused to contribute funds towards his Point Piper flat. The doctor, who had been receiving US$10 per week from the agency for his work, felt entitled to more, particularly because his flat had become a de facto facility for his spy mission against Petrov.

After the agency initially accepted his resignation, ASIO's regional director Ron Richards personally intervened to reinstate Bialoguski as an agent. Yet the relationship between the agency and the doctor was again on the rocks after he discovered that ASIO had gone behind his back to indirectly approach Petrov. Through one of its officers, ASIO had told Dr Beckett, Petrov's eye specialist, that the Russian diplomat wished to remain in the country but that approaching him directly through an official could present a diplomatic incident. Dr Beckett agreed to help, and during a follow-up medical check-up with Petrov, he clumsily sounded out the Russian about whether he had aspirations to one day make Australia his home. The specialist's subtle remarks made no mention of ASIO or government officials, but Petrov felt they had a whiff of intelligence tradecraft about them and mentioned the incident to Bialoguski. Outraged by ASIO's move, which he claimed could have cost him his relationship with Petrov and potentially exposed him as a spy, Bialoguski tried to leverage a pay rise out of the agency. On its refusal to comply with his demand, he resigned and complained to the Australian prime minister's private secretary that he had been badly treated by ASIO. The agency took Bialoguski's move as a major indiscretion and officially severed its ties with him. But instead of teaching him a lesson, ASIO's reaction was a misstep that only strengthened his resolve to keep Petrov in his orbit. Bialoguski increasingly sensed a breakthrough on the horizon in Petrov's hostility toward his embassy colleagues, which all came to a head shortly after the appointment of a new Soviet ambassador to Canberra, Nikolai Generalov, in October 1953. The following month, Generalov fired Petrov's wife, Evdokia – both as his personal secretary and as the Embassy's accountant – showcasing his disdain for her and her husband. Falling out of favour with the head of mission was effectively a death sentence for their diplomatic careers, and while Petrov remained in his job, the distress felt by his wife took its toll on him. They even considered suicide.

Along with offering a shoulder to cry on, Bialoguski played on Petrov's emotional fragility, assuring him that he could help him and his wife should they want to remain in Australia. He had planted the seeds of defection, and 24 hours later, on the afternoon of Monday, 23 November, Bialoguski approached ASIO with an ultimatum: he offered to either provide the Petrovs in return for his reinstatement as an agent, or to expose their defection in the Australian press. This was a gamble, because Bialoguski had no evidence that the Petrovs would defect at that stage, but ASIO did not risk calling his bluff. Three days later, agency officials, including Ron Richards, reinstated Bialoguski – and even back-paid him for the time he had been removed from their books. In doing so, the agency had put in motion an operation that was to change the history of Australia's intelligence standing among its western allies, including the US, Britain, Canada, and New Zealand, for decades to come. The scale of impact and sensitivity of Petrov's likely defection was apparent to Charles Spry, ASIO's director-general, who carefully considered the political dimensions and potential diplomatic pitfalls. De-risking a task of that nature required someone immersed in operational intelligence: a space where allegiances were fluid, and the lines between hyperbole, facts, and lies disappeared in shades of grey. It was a space in which Richards, one of Spry's best officers, thrived.

Ron Richards was an intuitive spy catcher. His fastidious take on counterespionage had been coloured by the 15 years he had spent in policing before joining ASIO's predecessor, the Commonwealth Security

Service, in the early 1940s. In England, his father had worked as a bricklayer to fend for a family of seven children, and Richards inherited his work ethic, spending his late teens as a coal miner before migrating to Australia in 1926. He began working as a labourer but in 1928, aged 23, chose a different career and joined the Western Australia Police Force. He worked his way up the ranks through a series of criminal cases, including investigations into Nazi sympathisers and the Soviet infiltration of Australia's Communist party during the war.

As a founding member of ASIO, he had been handpicked in 1949 to investigate Soviet espionage in Australia. He helped identify Australian government officials who had been suspected of spying for Moscow – including Ian Milner, Jim Hill and Walter Seddon Clayton – by working through Venona decrypts. Richards' collaboration with MI5 on the investigation earned him a secondment to the British agency's headquarters in London three years later. He had shouldered such responsibilities with a degree of integrity and professionalism that reinforced ASIO's trust in him during the Petrov investigation. On Spry's orders, Richards had taken personal charge of the Petrov case in late November 1953, and had immediately stepped up the operation into pursuing the Russian official's defection. Richards' gateway to Petrov was Bialoguski – and although the doctor had proven to be a very useful ASIO agent, he was a blunt instrument who needed to be handled with care. Richards could no longer just rely on Bialoguski's recollection of what Petrov was saying, he required irrefutable evidence, grounded in fact rather than second-hand conjecture and interpretation. Richards provided the ASIO agent with a concealable recording device with specific instruction not to incite Petrov to defect, but instead to guide him towards making the decision on his own. And when Petrov expressed an interest in buying a chicken farm in Castle Hill, northwest Sydney, in December, Richards told Bialoguski to encourage him, conscious that the Russian diplomat's willingness to partake in such a business venture would reassure ASIO of his likelihood to remain in Australia.

Richards needed to determine the perfect timing to be introduced to Petrov: a premature approach risked blowing Bialoguski's cover, and a delayed one threatened to ruin ASIO's hope of realising the defection. But in a twist of fate, Petrov's hatred of his embassy colleagues, coupled with his depression and alcoholism, framed his mindset after he crashed an Embassy-owned car in Canberra on Christmas Eve of 1953. He clambered out of the burning wreck unharmed but was convinced that he had been targeted by a large vehicle and forced off the road. His paranoia was heightened by a lack of sympathy from Embassy colleagues, and on discovery that Petrov's insurance had lapsed before the crash, the Ambassador forced him to pay for the car out of his own pocket.

Five days after the accident, Petrov met with Bialoguski in Sydney and told him that he could no longer cope: he wanted a fresh start, a new life in Australia, even if it meant being apart from his wife who was determined to return to Russia for the sake of her elderly mother. Petrov asked Bialoguski to set up a meeting with Dr Beckett, his eye specialist, whom he had rightly suspected of being linked to the intelligence services. ASIO authorised Beckett to meet with Petrov and Bialoguski on 23 January 1954. As anticipated, Petrov expressed his interest in remaining in Australia and Beckett assured him that he would connect him with the right people to help realise that ambition. A deal was in the making but appeared far from certain, with concerns that the Russian may ultimately be swayed from defection by his wife, Evdokia. Bringing Mrs Petrov into the picture was crucial to provide support for her husband's decision, even if she were unwilling to follow in his footsteps. Bialoguski met with Evdokia in Canberra, at her husband's request, to gauge her willingness to turn her back on Moscow. While she sympathised with Petrov's hatred of embassy colleagues, she was an ideologue, committed to the teachings and principles of Marxism. Evdokia told Bialoguski during the meeting on 31 January that she would rather return to Russia and face a death squad than remain behind.

On learning about Evdokia's reaction, Richards realised that he needed to act with more urgency. His boss, Charles Spry, also favoured that approach, as did MI5 officials who had been notified by ASIO about the Petrov case and had offered help in the event that the Australian agency needed it. Spry kept MI5 briefed through its senior liaison officer to

Australia, Derek Hamblen. The British agency's pedigree in dealing with Russian defectors, including Walter Krivitsky in the late 1930s and Igor Gouzenko in 1945, would have provided a sense of reassurance to ASIO. While Spry wanted his officers to land the coup without any direct help from the British agency, the Australian Department of External Affairs had expressed serious doubts about Petrov's proposed defection. The department had feared that his defection could lead to a retaliation from Moscow against Australian diplomats based there, including framing them for bogus crimes and expropriating their premises. However, Hamblen encouraged Spry to carry on with the Petrov mission, assuring him that there had been no precedent indicating that the Soviet Union would resort to such retaliatory measures. And either way, such risks would be outweighed by the intelligence gathered from a defection of that magnitude, he told Spry.

MI5 was of the view that 'no time should be lost in encouraging Petrov to defect and that possibility of reprisal in Moscow can be disregarded [...] the Cold War and disruption aspect should not be lost sight of although C.E. [counterespionage] interest is obviously paramount.' The British agency's advice to ASIO, whether it was coming from the London head office or through Hamblen, was always packaged as such: advice. MI5 did not want its opinions to be seen or interpreted as official orders, but rather as suggestions. It was cautious not to overplay its hand with ASIO and was convinced that the Australian agency was capable of overseeing its own national security arrangements. ASIO had demonstrated its ability in dealing with sensitive matters, not only in relation to America's Venona Project, but also around Britain's first nuclear weapons test in October 1952, which had been conducted at the Montebello Islands, off the northwest coast of Western Australia.

The test had been a top-secret mission, personally approved by the Australian Prime Minister Robert Menzies, a Liberal politician aggressively opposed to Communism. His accession to office in December 1949 had reassured Britain and the US that Australia would take a much more hardline stance against Soviet espionage than under his Labor predecessor, Ben Chifley. Menzies was keen to cosy up to London and Washington, aware that the two powerful allies were essential to Australia's military protection and to propping up its international standing. As someone who had also served as Prime Minister during the first two years of World War II, he realised the influence intelligence had on political negotiations, particularly as Australia continued to reel from being sidelined by the US in the late 1940s following the uncovering of the Kremlin's spying in Canberra. He would undoubtedly have been thrilled to hear that the Soviet embassy's chief spy in Canberra had been showing all the right signs for a possible defection.

During a meeting on 10 February 1954, Menzies was personally briefed by Spry about the Petrov case and the prime minister agreed that ASIO should provide the Russian with protection. While it was natural for an intelligence agency to discuss a diplomatically sensitive operation with the prime minister of the day, the political events that followed ultimately cast a shadow over ASIO's interactions with the Menzies government for decades to come and exposed the close – and at times unhealthy marriage – between spy agencies and their political masters.

Almost three weeks after Menzies had been informed about Petrov, Ron Richards met the Russian official for the first time. The meeting at Bialoguski's flat had been set up at Petrov's request in February 1954, after he told his eye specialist, Dr Beckett, that he had made up his mind about seeking political asylum. Petrov stressed the importance of discretion around any interactions between him and Australian officials; he wanted to conceal his intentions from Soviet colleagues who were anticipating the imminent completion of his diplomatic posting and expected return to Moscow on 5 April. Richards was always discreet – so much so that on arriving at the Point Piper flat on the evening of 27 February he even introduced himself to Bialoguski as though he had met him for the first time to maintain his agent's cover.

Richards had arrived at the flat prepared, hoping to finalise the long-anticipated defection of Petrov with a document authorising the provision of political asylum. The Russian diplomat assessed the document and seemed reassured, comfortable that he was in good

Top left: Jessie Jordan believed that being a hairdresser in Scotland would provide her with the perfect cover to operate as a Nazi spy. Her intelligence blunders inadvertently kickstarted the cooperation between MI5 and the FBI.

Top right: Guy Liddell, a former Scotland Yard detective who became a spymaster at MI5, played a defining role in establishing the working relationship between his agency and the FBI.

Below: William Stephenson, a Canadian entrepreneur, set up the British Security Coordination in New York and inspired William Donovan to create the Office of Strategic Services in the image of MI6. Here, 'Big Bill' (Donovan) is presenting a medal for merit to his close friend, 'Little Bill' (Stephenson).

© Bettmann / Getty

Left: J. Edgar Hoover, the first and longest-serving FBI director, forced Bletchley Park to share its Enigma secrets with his officers, to reinforce his authority which had been challenged by Stephenson and Donovan.

Right: A mathematician and master codebreaker, Dr Abraham Sinkov led the first US visit to Bletchley Park in 1941 which helped form the basis for signals intelligence sharing between London and Washington. He later established a cipher bureau in Brisbane, Australia, during World War II. *The appearance of U.S. Department of Defense (DoD) visual information does not imply or constitute DoD endorsement.*

© NSA, Department of Defense

© FBI

Left: Arthur Thurston, a one-time designated driver for Hoover, was deployed by the FBI boss to Britain in late 1942, among other things to improve his organisation's relationship with MI5 and set up a London bureau the following year.

Top left: Fed up with her job as a home economics teacher, Gene Grabeel became a codebreaker at Arlington Hall and co-founded the Venona Project – the US decryption programme that identified Soviet spies, including those operating in the USA, Britain and Australia.

Top right: Frank Byron Rowlett was among the founding members of the US Army's Signal Intelligence Service and played a major role in decoding Japanese communications relating to the intentions of Tokyo and Nazi Germany. He recruited Gene Grabeel to Arlington Hall.

The appearance of U.S. Department of Defense (DoD) visual information does not imply or constitute DoD endorsement.

Left: The work of Robert Lamphere (right) as an FBI counterintelligence officer, including his investigations into atomic spies, helped pioneer the cooperation between the disciplines of HUMINT and SIGINT.

Igor Gouzenko's defection in 1945 marked the beginning of the Cold War. The Russian cipher clerk's secrets helped expose atomic spies of British and US origin and led to greater cooperation between MI5, the FBI, and the Royal Canadian Mounted Police.

Above: George Ronald 'Ron' Richards was an Australian spymaster who oversaw the recruitment of his country's greatest human asset against the Soviet Union, and in so doing, transformed the image of ASIO in the eyes of Washington and London.

Left: Vladimir Petrov, responsible for Moscow's intelligence operations in Australia, became an ideal target for ASIO to recruit, thanks in part to his 'immoral pursuits, in search of wine [and] women'. His revelations to the spy agency helped elevate Australia into the Five Eyes.

Right: Geza Andrew Katona, the lone CIA officer in Budapest during the Hungarian Revolution in 1956, was all but ignored by the US intelligence agency when he pleaded for weapons to be given to the revolutionaries in their fight against the Soviet invaders.

Below: Revolutionaries wave a red, white and green national flag from a captured Soviet tank in Budapest's main square, during the Hungarian Revolution of October – November 1956.

Above: After bringing the Australian Labor Party into power following its absence from government for 23 years, Gough Whitlam became suspicious about the CIA's previously undisclosed involvement in a joint US-Australian defence facility.

Left: Alan Dulles made his mark as an agent-handler while serving at the Office of Strategic Service (OSS) during World War II. He took over the CIA in 1953, becoming one its most controversial directors, responsible for multiple intelligence failures.

Above: US National Security Advisor Zbigniew Brzezinski urged President Jimmy Carter to punish Moscow for its invasion of Afghanistan in 1979 and was eager to draw the Kremlin into a 'Soviet Vietnam'.

Right: Julia Gillard, who became a Labor prime minister of Australia in 2010, said the Pertrov affair should not be overstated in the damage it caused her party. 'I think it is overblown to say that kept Labor out of office for 23 years. What keeps a political party out of office for more than two decades is it cannot get enough people to vote for it'.

hands. He trusted the environment and the company he was in: after all, the Point Piper flat had become a familiar setting – a safe space where he had embraced and expressed his vulnerabilities without fear, in return for seemingly selfless support and advice from his friend, Bialoguski. And although he knew that Richards' presence in the flat that evening was predominantly self-serving, Petrov respected the spy game's universal rules of engagement where the aspect of give-and-take was necessary for the cultivation of an asset. Both parties needed to feel a sense of victory, and Petrov knew what Richards wanted from him. He told the ASIO officer that he was prepared to expose Moscow's dealings and said that he was the Third Secretary and Consul of the Soviet Embassy with access to secrets that would be of great use to the Australian government. Petrov had dangled the bait but was not yet ready to give it up. He wanted more assurances and a guarantee that he would be given £5,000 and the chance to write a tell-all biography to expose the Soviet Union's aggression to the world.

It was a reasonable request when set against the intelligence that Richards hoped to reap out of him, and on 19 March, the ASIO official met with Petrov again at Bialoguski's flat and showed him a briefcase containing £5,000 in cash. Richards told him that only two things stood between him and the money: going through with the defection and signing the document seeking political asylum. Showcasing the money, according to ASIO's official historian David Horner, was instrumental in convincing Petrov that Richards was a man of his word. But even then, Petrov wanted more time to plan his escape and met with Richards on at least six more occasions in Sydney and Canberra to discuss the impact the case could have on his wife, whom he had not told of his imminent plan to defect. He also wanted an assurance from Richards that, upon defection, he would be able to bring along his fishing rods, shotgun and, Jack, his Alsatian dog. Amid discussing such arrangements, Petrov had been collating secret documents from the Embassy, smuggling them on a plane from Canberra to Sydney on 2 April.

Richards accompanied him on the flight and subsequently took him to a safe house to go through the documents which included operational instructions Petrov had been sent by Moscow and the identities of Russian spies that had operated in Australia, Britain, and other western countries. He revealed that Soviet operations in Canberra had peaked between 1945 and 1948 – which fitted with the timeline of Venona decrypts investigated by ASIO about four years earlier, and which had led to the identification of Australian government officials spying for Moscow. Petrov's documents required translation and further analysis, but Richards was satisfied with what he had provided. Petrov then voluntarily signed the paperwork that granted him political asylum, before meeting Charles Spry at the safe house that evening. Petrov admitted for the first time that he was an MVD officer. While it was hardly a surprising admission at that point, it reinforced his preparedness for complete transparency.

On the following day, 3 April, Petrov needed to tie up loose ends relating to his embassy work ahead of his and his wife's expected return to Moscow, which was supposed to take place forty-eight hours later. Eager to maintain the impression that he was wrapping up his official duties, Petrov travelled to Sydney Airport to welcome embassy officials and organised their onward flight to Canberra. He then saw off two other Soviet officials who were heading for New Zealand. That afternoon, he returned to the safe house where Richards had been waiting for him: it was the last stop in his planned defection. The drama that had preceded his escape gave way to a series of debriefings by ASIO, promising an intelligence bonanza about the methods used by the Kremlin's sprawling espionage network in western nations, including the US, Britain, Canada and New Zealand. The four countries were ultimately informed by ASIO of Petrov's defection and all were typically desperate to learn about the Soviet infiltration of their own governments and societies. But thanks to MI5's close relationship with Charles Spry, the UK was first in line to benefit from Petrov's defection.

MI5's newly appointed director-general, Dick White, had been regularly updated on the Petrov Case by his agency's senior liaison officer in Canberra. He was a seasoned intelligence official who had almost two decades of counterespionage experience prior to his takeover of the British security service in 1953, including his wartime work of recruiting Nazis and turning them against the Third Reich under MI5's Double Cross system. However, like the rest of MI5's senior leadership, the embarrassment caused by his agency's failure to identify Soviet spies in their midst, namely Guy Burgess and Donald Maclean, still haunted him. White would have hoped that Vladimir Petrov's defection to Australia would help redress the balance in MI5's fortunes against Moscow. The MI5 spymaster was conscious of the 'great burden of work' that ASIO had on its hands in debriefing the Russian defector and did not want to compound it. So it was not until five days after Petrov's defection that he sent a telegram to congratulate his ASIO counterpart, Charles Spry. 'My warmest congratulations on your success in bringing about [the] defection of Petrov,' read the personal message from White, dated 8 April 1954. 'His defection [is] likely to be of most importance and may have profound effect [on] your and my counterespionage work.'

By then, MI5 had become concerned that ASIO was being pressured by the Australian prime minister to deliver a 'full exploitation' of Petrov ahead of an anticipated federal election in late May. Spry had taken a partisan position ahead of the election and had even urged MI5 to stop sharing its secrets with Australia in the event that Herbert Evatt, the Labor leader, won the election. Derek Hamblen, MI5's representative in Australia, told London on 12 April that 'Spry strongly supports PM', and added that 'Until now Spry has been very restrained about the prospect of working for Evatt. He states now that in the event of Evatt becoming PM, UK government should seriously consider withholding important secrets.'

Robert Menzies had feared that if he were to lose to the Labor leader Herbert Evatt, his successor could be inclined to suppress the Petrov documents because they exposed ties between the Soviet Union and some of his current and former allies. Hamblen's assessment was that the prime minister believed that 'everything must be done in national as distinct from political party interest to prevent Evatt becoming Prime Minister'. It was more likely that Menzies wanted to weaponise Petrov's disclosures for his self-interest to secure victory in an election that had been widely expected to be won by Labor. MI5 understood the political dynamics in Australia and hoped that ASIO would do its 'utmost to ensure intelligence benefits [are] not sacrificed for speed'. It also posted one of its fluent Russian speakers to Australia to assist the agency.

On 13 April, Menzies publicly announced Petrov's defection in parliament, and four days later, set up a royal commission on espionage to help expose the Kremlin's penetration of Australia. Amid the chaos of the political circus that unfolded, including public accusations by Evatt that Menzies had seized on the Petrov case to influence the upcoming election, ASIO was hard at work with the help of MI5. Petrov's secrets resulted in a treasure trove of information which was of direct and urgent importance to British intelligence. MI5 was told by Petrov that British Soviet spies, Burgess and Maclean, were highly valued by the Kremlin and had been settled in Kuibyshev, southwestern Russia, following their escape. He said that their escape from Britain in 1951 had been planned by Philip Kislytsin, an MVD officer who had since been transferred to Canberra. MI5 was 'vitally interested' in Kislytsin and wanted ASIO's help in persuading him to defect. However, the Soviet embassy had been on high alert following Petrov's defection, fearful that others may be inspired to do the same.

Kislytsin was expected to make his way back to Moscow on 19 April on the same day Petrov's wife, Evdokia, was scheduled to return. That afternoon, the pair were escorted to Sydney airport by Soviet couriers in a car and arrived to a throng of reporters and photographers, and a crowd of hostile Russian expats who confronted the couriers and repeatedly urged Mrs Petrov to remain in Australia. The Petrov Affair, as it became known in the press, had been dominating news headlines by then and information about its development was constantly being leaked to the media. So it was perhaps unsurprising that such scenes had broken out at the airport.

'When we stopped the car near to the airport entrance, there was a crowd of people there,' Mrs Petrov later recalled. 'The crowd started to shout to me – "Don't go back – if you do you will be killed."' Having spent days crying and in a fragile emotional state following her husband's defection, Mrs Petrov was terrified that the crowd at Sydney Airport would hurt her, especially after a scuffle broke out between them and her two couriers. 'The crowds were pushing us,' she said. 'I lost one of my shoes – my handbag was broken – two buttons were torn from my suit.' Shortly after Mrs Petrov and Kislytsin boarded the British Overseas Airways Corporation flight for Darwin, en route to Moscow, the ambition that ASIO and MI5 had held out for was given a lifeline. Press rumours had started circulating that Mrs Petrov was allegedly overheard saying 'I don't want to go' during the scramble at the airport and a Member of Parliament claimed to have received a signed declaration from her asking for help. To determine the veracity of the claims, Prime Minister Menzies ordered ASIO's director-general, Charles Spry, to contact the aircraft's pilot and direct him to personally ask Mrs Petrov whether she wanted political asylum. There was nothing to suggest that Mrs Petrov had left Sydney against her own volition, but she admitted to the pilot that she wanted to remain in Australia and further informed him through a flight attendant that her two couriers were armed.

The captain relayed the messages to Spry in two radio calls, and upon landing at Darwin Airport just before 5am on 20 April, Mrs Petrov was greeted on the tarmac by the acting administrator of the Northern Territory, Reginald Leydin, who had been asked by Spry on behalf of Menzies to intervene in the case. He had been waiting with police officers who quickly became involved in a scuffle with her Russian couriers. The police stripped them of their loaded pistols on the basis that it was against air navigation laws to carry undeclared weapons on an aircraft. The hostile scene only added to Mrs Petrov distress and angered Kislytsin who sided with the couriers. Through tears, she told Leydin that she wanted to continue her journey to Moscow, dubious about the assurances she had been given about her husband's safety and wellbeing – she feared he was dead. In a last-ditch effort, Leydin organised for Petrov to call his wife at Darwin Airport, and following a brief conversation, she sought political asylum – delivering ASIO its second defection victory and another major blow to Soviet intelligence. While Mrs Petrov was not as senior as her husband in the MVD, she was able to corroborate some of the information he had provided to ASIO and MI5.

Moscow severed its diplomatic ties with Canberra later that month, expelling Australian diplomats from the Soviet Union and recalling its own from Australia. Four weeks later, on 29 May, Menzies went to the polls and secured a victory against Evatt. It was a historic election, not only because Evatt and his supporters attributed its result to a conspiracy between Menzies and ASIO, but because its ongoing repercussions ultimately split the Labor Party – which had been out of power for five years – and kept it out of government for another eighteen.

Julia Gillard, who became a Labor prime minister of Australia in 2010, said the Pertrov affair should not be overstated in the damage it caused her party. 'The weaponising of intelligence, Menzies, manipulation, electoral advantage – I follow all of that,' she said. 'But, I think it is overblown to say that kept Labor out of office for 23 years. What keeps a political party out of office for more than two decades is it cannot get enough people to vote for it [...] Ultimately, you've got to say to yourself "Are we going to chase who did what to who when in the historical narrative or are we going to work out why people don't vote for us?"

'That doesn't mean that it isn't important to write the history of the use and misuse of intelligence [...] That should be done. But how much immediate political weight versus long-term political weight there is, I think is a much more nuanced question.'

Away from the political quagmire, the Petrov defection transformed the identity of Australia's intelligence community. It was no longer the bumbling machine that pre-dated the formation of ASIO, sidelined by the US and urged to pick up its game by Britain. It had become a formidable player in the art of spying. In the words of MI5's senior liaison officer, Derek Hamblen, the 'Petrov case has now definitely put the ASIO on the map'.

Charles Spry embraced the grandeur that the Petrov Affair had brought ASIO and himself. It turned the director-general into the prime minister's golden child and brought him a sense of clout and control that was disproportionate to the size of his young agency. He relished the victory and was reluctant to share it with others, having turned down an offer for help with Petrov's defection from the Australian Secret Intelligence Service (ASIS), which had been set up in 1952 to specialise in foreign espionage operations, much like MI6 in Britain. Spry had too much at stake to relinquish any control. He also wanted the distribution of Petrov's disclosures to be made at ASIO's own pace, despite the repeated requests that had been made through MI5 by allies, including the FBI and Royal Canadian Mounted Police. And to further stamp his authority, Spry prevented MI5 from sharing any information relating to the defectors without his prior approval. While the approach frustrated MI5, it helped establish ASIO's early steps toward more independence from – and a friendly rivalry with – its British counterpart.

In June 1954, two months after Petrov's defection, Spry agreed to share substantive information with the Americans, beyond the basic titbit ASIO had provided about the structure of Russia's intelligence apparatus. He also extended the distribution of intelligence to the Canadians and New Zealanders. The revelations included a directive from Moscow, dated September 1952, which had instructed its MVD operatives to 'make a planned penetration of American intelligence and counter-intelligence organisations' as well as 'information concerning Australian, Canadian, English and New Zealand counter-intelligence activities'. Another directive from Moscow in January 1954 had ordered the 'acquisition of ciphers of countries of the Anglo-American bloc, especially England, USA, France, Australia, Canada'.

Petrov revealed the aggressiveness with which the Soviet Union had been targeting the US. Moscow had demanded systematic collection of information on America's intelligence community, including 'agent personnel, methods of recruitments, and training of clients, equipment, cover story [sic], tasks, documentation of cover stories, places and means of transferring agents, channels of penetration into the Soviet [Union]'.

ASIO shared 52 reports with western agencies, according to its official history, varying from the Kremlin's espionage operations in Sweden, to Soviet activities in the US and Britain. It also passed information to NATO and helped with intelligence inquiries from allies, including the provision of analysis by Petrov and his wife of 5,079 photographs and names of alleged Soviet operatives around the world – of whom they exposed more than 500. The FBI, which had largely been dismissive of ASIO in the past, changed its tone in recognition of its success. J. Edgar Hoover praised Spry in a personal message and posted one of his representatives to Australia in August 1954 to speed up intelligence-sharing between his bureau and ASIO. 'The FBI had previously expressed scepticism about ASIO's ability,' noted MI5's liaison officer in Australia, Derek Hamblen, in a letter to his head office in London. 'There has certainly been a marked change in the FBI attitude to ASIO since the Petrov affair – even the correspondence now marked by personal and friendly tone [...] Mr Hoover was personally concerned in all matters of liaison!' With an eye to bringing ASIO closer to the US, Spry had offered to provide the bureau with 'direct access to the Petrovs' and continued building on his relationship with Washington following a trip in 1955 on which he met with the CIA's director, Allen Dulles. The personal bond between Spry and Dulles shaped their intelligence-sharing in years to come.

Spry may well be accused of being a stooge of the Menzies government, but his political wiliness in exploiting Petrov's disclosures for ASIO's interest put Australia's intelligence community on par with the US and Britain. Petrov's seniority made his defection of greater value than that of Igor Gouzenko, the GRU cipher clerk, who had sought political asylum in Canada in 1945. And much like Ottawa had leveraged its intelligence fortunes to work its way into the UKUSA Agreement in 1949, Australia was on the road to receiving the same treatment. Petrov's defection was a shift in Australia's intelligence history that still resonates to this day, according to ASIO's current director-general, Mike Burgess. 'In our business, especially in the countries that trust each other or are developing trust for each other, there is nothing like an operational gain to actually bring you closer together,' he said. 'Because you can see the potential knowledge, advantage, the capability-win in terms of the information you find when you do damage to someone like the Soviets at the time.

The Petrov case was significant in terms of being a very early win in ASIO's history; it was significant in terms of the information advantage it gave the Allies; and it was significant in the way it helped bring us closer together as international partners. So it played a critical part in the wider Five Eyes story.'

In the early and mid-1950s, as Australia's human-intelligence capabilities rapidly improved through ASIO, the country's post-wartime signals organisation – renamed the Defence Signals Bureau (DSB) – had also been progressing. The DSB received major assistance in the way of technology and personnel from Britain's GCHQ and had been run as a 'joint-UK–Australian–New Zealand organisation', manned by integrated staff'. A little more than a decade into the Cold War, Britain and the US wanted to improve their burden-sharing in the field of intelligence. They needed to enhance the efficiency and capacity to translate and analyse more Soviet material, along with intercepted communication and imagery from other threats in Asia and South America. Along with pooling resources and personnel, Washington and London required a wider global coverage to plug surveillance gaps through electronic eavesdropping in multiple time zones. Between them and Canada, which had been operating as part of UKUSA for seven years, they already had a great head start. Britain had been well-positioned to cover Europe from west of the Urals, and Africa; Canada eavesdropped on Latin America, Eastern Russia, the North Atlantic and Pacific; and the US, which always had the most resources in the way of personnel and technical equipment, had monitored the Caribbean, China, Russia, the Middle East and Africa.

On 10 October 1956, the US and Britain expanded the UKUSA agreement to formally include Australia and New Zealand. Discussions surrounding the inclusion of the two South Pacific nations as full members had been ongoing between Washington and London for about two years. Australia was tasked with focusing on South and East Asian communications, and New Zealand on South Asia and the Southwest Pacific. Their inclusion formed an alliance that could watch the world around the clock, and whose existence would remain secret and not officially acknowledged by its key founders, Britain and the US, for more than 50 years. It became known as the Five Eyes.

The intelligence among the alliance's members was stamped 'AUS/CAN/NZ/UK/US EYES ONLY' and specifically related to signals intelligence. No equivalent agreement had been created for the human-intelligence and law-enforcement agencies within the five member countries even though cooperation between some of them, namely MI5 and the FBI, had pre-dated the foundational signals arrangement between London and Washington during World War II. But the story of the Five Eyes is less about the non-binding, memorandum of understanding between its nations and more about the personalities that helped shape and nurture it. And some of those personalities were from the human-intelligence communities. Guy Liddell of MI5, William Stephenson of MI6, William Donovan of the Office of Strategic Services, Robert Lamphere of the FBI, and Ron Richards of ASIO, could not have imagined how their historical contributions would ultimately underscore the future cooperation between their agencies and evolve the Five Eyes into something much greater than the sum of its signals-intelligence parts.

In the same month that the Five Eyes had been officially formed in 1956, the alliance underwent its first stress test when Britain joined France and Israel in launching Operation Musketeer – a secret invasion to capture the Suez Canal that had been historically pivotal for British and French trade. The invasion outraged US president Dwight D. Eisenhower, whose administration had been concurrently dealing with an anti-Soviet revolution in Hungary where a single CIA officer, Geza Katona, had been left in charge.

CHAPTER SEVEN

CRISES: ONE MAN IN BUDAPEST

AS GEZA ANDREW KATONA made his way through a chanting crowd in Budapest's Stalin Square, he saw people trampling the statue of the former Soviet leader, some pounding it with hammers to disfigure and dismember its body parts. The 26-foot-tall bronze monument that had symbolised Russia's stranglehold on Hungary after World War II, had been toppled from its plinth in a poignant expression of public anger that solidified the beginning of a political uprising on 23 October 1956. As Katona walked around, observing other parts of the capital, he saw state security vehicles overturned and in flames and heard the constant echoes of gunfire.

The chaotic scenes had been a culmination of suppressed hostility towards Stalinism and a push for independence from Soviet rule. Hungarians had been empowered by a political revolution in Poland a few days earlier that had resulted in Warsaw gaining greater autonomy from Moscow. It inspired thousands of people in Hungary. Led by student protesters, they took to the streets of Budapest and on to the Hungarian Parliament building. Some forced their way into the city's radio station to relay a series of demands, including a democratically held election and the evacuation of all the Soviet troops that had remained in the country following World War II. Their act was perceived as a provocation by the Hungarian regime. Security authorities opened fire on the unarmed crowd, but instead of stamping out the disorder, news of those injured and killed sparked a nation-wide revolt.

By then, Katona had been living in Budapest for three years as a US diplomat – a cover for his role as the CIA's 'eyes and ears' in Hungary. His recruitment by the agency had little to do with his degree in education from the University of Pittsburgh or his former job as a secondary school teacher in the late 1930s. Katona's attractiveness to the CIA related to his heritage and language skills: he was born to Hungarian migrants in Munhall, Pennsylvania, who taught him to speak their native tongue. It was a crucial language for the CIA which planned to expand its covert operations in Eastern Europe, its eyes set on Hungary. It was in that corner of the world that the agency aspired to boost anti-Communist sentiment through 'methods short of war', including propaganda, to 'bring about the gradual reduction and eventual elimination of preponderant Soviet power and influence'. The agency needed a Hungarian speaker: that Katona had no experience in spying hardly mattered to the CIA when it deployed him to Budapest in 1953 under the assumed role of 'assistant to the political officer'– a convoluted job title within the State Department's legation in Hungary that had been intended to conceal his role as a CIA official.

Katona was 36, with a wife and three children to support – hardly a youngster. However, even by his own admission, he was of 'low-ranking status' whose reports to the CIA's head office in Langley, Virginia, carried little weight, even when he warned about an emerging sea change in public attitudes towards the regime in Budapest around one year before the Hungarian Revolution kicked off. Beyond Katona's weekly reports, the agency had a pre-existing awareness that Moscow would reinforce its post-war military contingent of 50,000 Red Army troops and 'intervene if an overthrow of the Government appeared imminent', according to a declassified CIA report. Despite its assessment, the CIA had done virtually nothing to implement its planned operations in Hungary and was completely blindsided by the revolution. Katona was its only officer on the ground in Budapest and he had been better equipped for replenishing the stationery cupboards of the US legation than for dealing with a political revolt. He had spent 95 per cent of his time fulfilling cover duties as a State Department official: 'He mailed letters, purchased stamps and stationery' and 'did not engage in any active operations'. So it was little wonder that he 'found himself immediately overburdened' at the outbreak of the revolution on 23 October.

Based on the stories that Katona later shared with his family about his time as the CIA's man in Budapest, he had been sent there totally unprepared, armed with a little more than a year of basic training by the agency. 'He went there by the seat of his pants,' said Susan De Rosa, Katona's daughter. In the absence of any major tradecraft training from the CIA, Katona drew on lessons he had learned from his teen years as a boy scout to 'identify problems and try to find solutions,' his daughter said. 'I feel that he survived mostly by innovating and being aware of the climate of the population.' Katona's ability to keep Langley informed about the unfolding events in Budapest had been seriously curtailed by his inability to access any reliable facts. With no agents to hand, or Hungarian government officials on the CIA's payroll, he predominantly relied on eye-witness accounts from locals who visited the US legation, and on cannibalising press reports. 'From time to time, we would send a digest [...] to Washington, without being able to do much in the way of appending any opinions as the political situation was very confused, and we didn't really have any reliable facts about that,' Katona recalled years later. 'At the Legation, it was hectic, with huge numbers of visitors dropping in, mostly just casually to tell us something – an interesting scrap of news, to report on conditions in some part of town or another – and thus, to set down another small piece of the whole confusing large mosaic before hurrying away.'

Hungary's former leader, Imre Nagy, who had been dismissed from his position by the Communist Party because of his criticism of Stalinist policies, was urged by the revolutionaries to return to power.

He was reappointed as Prime Minister on 24 October in the hope of restoring peace, and emboldened by his new role, repeated the calls of revolutionaries for the withdrawal of Soviet troops from the country. But four days into the crisis, with a rising body count and locals pleading for help from Washington through its legation in Budapest, Katona sent Langley a cable inquiring about its policy on the provision of arms and ammunition to Hungarian revolutionaries. It was a fair request considering the CIA's record of meddling in other countries, including the toppling of the democratically elected government of Iran in 1953 with the help of Britain's MI6. In that instance, the two agencies had feared that the collapse of oil negotiations between their respective countries and Tehran would push the regime closer to Moscow. So they mobilised anti-government protesters in a violent unrest that killed more than 200 people, deposed Prime Minister Mohammad Mosaddegh and placed the reins of power in the hands of Shah Mohammad Reza Pahlavi – a friend of the West. Three years later, in the spring of 1956, the CIA had sought to further undermine Moscow's influence in the Middle East – and again with the help of MI6 – had started plotting a coup against the pro-Soviet regime in Syria.

However, there appeared to be less enthusiasm from CIA headquarters about intervening in the Hungarian Revolution. On 28 October, Katona received an answer to his cable from the previous day in which he was told by his superiors that 'we must restrict ourselves to information collection only [and] not get involved in anything that would reveal US interest or give cause to claim intervention.' The following day, Katona received another message from Langley saying that it was 'not permitted to send US weapons' to Hungary. Its timing coincided with a military confrontation between Israel and Egypt – one that had been foreseen by the CIA, exposed Britain's disloyalty to the US and furthered the Kremlin's policies in the Middle East to the detriment of the Five Eyes. The concurrent conflicts that the CIA was attempting to juggle in Budapest and the Suez Canal presented its director Allen Dulles with a major operational challenge.

*   *   *

Allen Dulles had almost four decades of experience in dealing with issues relating to foreign policy when he became the CIA's director in February 1953. He had been posted as a diplomat to Europe by the US State Department before and after World War I and then had become the Office of Strategic Service's (OSS's) station chief in Bern, Switzerland, in 1942. While there, his recruitment of German Foreign Office official Fritz Kolbe, who provided a crucial insight into Hitler's operations by supplying more than 1,600 Nazi diplomatic cables to the OSS, reinforced Dulles's status as a star officer and cemented his upward trajectory in the intelligence community. He was undoubtedly talented and tirelessly driven to realise career goals that were bolstered by his political connections in Washington, DC. He was from a family line of political heavyweights: his older brother, John Foster Dulles, was the Secretary of State – an office that had been previously held by both his maternal grandfather and his uncle by marriage. Foster Dulles ultimately had an airport named after him in Virginia.

Dulles was two months from turning 60 when he became director of the CIA, but his enthusiasm and energy for covert warfare matched that of a man half his age. He made a rapid impact, becoming President Eisenhower's secret weapon against the Soviet Union's expansionist agenda during some of the most heated periods of the Cold War. In less than a year, Dulles orchestrated the overthrow of the Kremlin-sponsored governments of Iran and Guatemala – and while both coups ultimately stoked anti-US sentiment in the Middle East and Latin America, their success in the eyes of the White House drew Dulles closer to Eisenhower.

In early 1956, Dulles had been overseeing a CIA and MI6 plot to overthrow the government of Syria through a series of conspiracies, including the proposed creation of paramilitary factions in the country and the staging of civil unrest in neighbouring states, including Lebanon and Iraq, with the intention of blaming Damascus. Syria had fallen foul of the US and Britain after refusing to sign up to the Baghdad Pact, a military alliance that included Turkey, Iran, Pakistan and the UK, had been set up a year earlier with the support of Washington to help degrade Moscow's influence in the Middle East. However, the Soviet

Union quickly countered its creation by buying up the loyalties of Egypt and Syria, two of the pact's opponents with whom it had close strategic relations, through multi-million-dollar arms deals. The resulting tensions between the two Middle Eastern regimes and Washington also placed the CIA's sister organisation, the National Security Agency (NSA), on alert. In coordination with its military signals division, the Army Security Agency (ASA), and Langley, the NSA started expanding its visibility of the region where it had been heavily reliant on coverage from Britain's signals intelligence organisation, GCHQ. In the spring of 1956, the NSA tasked more than 40 signals specialists, along with Arabic linguists, to monitor the growing Soviet influence in Egypt and Syria. Moscow's reach into the two countries was a security threat that Dulles had been determined to subvert through unconventional warfare, including the plot to overthrow Syria's regime which he had been finessing in the autumn of that year. During the same period, his agency's newly deployed Lockheed U-2 spy planes, which had revolutionised high-altitude reconnaissance through their ability to obtain imagery from around 70,000 feet above ground, identified French fighter jets in Israel. The 60 Mystere jets were more than twice the number of French fighter bombers that Paris had said it agreed to sell to the country.

That, along with an increase of electronic signals traffic between Paris and Tel Aviv, as well as Paris and London, heightened the CIA's suspicion of a potential crisis in Egypt where France and Britain wanted to reclaim their control over the Suez Canal following a call by the country's leader, Gamal Abdel Nasser, to nationalise it. Nasser's announcement in the summer of 1956 had threatened the strategic interest, trade and oil supply routes of France and Britain and shifted the balance of power in the Middle East. While both countries had a stake in the company that owned and operated the canal, Britain was the major shareholder. Now, however, the influence both nations enjoyed over Egyptian affairs for more than eight decades had been dealt a heavy blow by Nasser. Dwight D. Eisenhower sympathised with the frustration experienced by British Prime Minister Anthony Eden, but the US President felt that going to war with Egypt risked a political and military confrontation with the Kremlin. Instead, he wanted a peaceful resolution to prevent unnecessary domestic headaches ahead of the presidential election the following month, despite the fact that his concern over Nasser's relationship with Moscow had been reinforced in 1955 by an arms deal worth more than US$100 million between Egypt and the Soviet satellite state, Czechoslovakia.

With Eisenhower's blessing, an international conference to deal with the Suez crisis was convened in London in August 1956, attended by delegations from 22 countries, including the US and France. Nasser had unsurprisingly turned down an invitation. During the conference, a plan was hatched that included respect for Egypt's sovereignty and the international supervision of the canal. Australian Prime Minister Robert Menzies was tasked to present the plan to the Egyptian president. At least in his own mind, Menzies had the credentials to step up and become a player on the international stage, not only because of his domestic political success which had resulted in his fourth consecutive term in office in December 1955, but also because of the reputation that ASIO had garnered during the Petrov Affair. Like his US and British counterparts, he was determined to stop the spread of Communism and had joined them in signing up to the Southeast Asia Treaty Organization (SEATO) in 1953 to curtail the spread of Soviet policies in the region. The defence alliance, which also included New Zealand, the Philippines, and Pakistan, reinforced Menzies' closeness to London and Washington. It also helped ASIO to establish itself beyond the shadows of its British sister agency, MI5, through setting up military and aviation courses for Asian security officers in early 1956. The training schemes helped the Australian agency form its own bilateral intelligence contacts in cities including Bangkok and Islamabad. ASIO's move had been intended to maintain its post-Petrov stature, rather than undermine MI5. As for Menzies, the Suez crisis presented an opportune time for him to magnify his own political prestige: to impress Eden and Eisenhower by travelling to Egypt to resolve the matter of international importance with Nasser.

However, Eden had other ideas. The British prime minister's public pursuit of a solution that would placate the White House and honour the

Special Relationship between Britain and the US was merely a ruse. Even before Menzies arrived in Cairo for his mission, Eden appeared to have set him up for failure. The British prime minister had agreed for France to station troops at a British military facility on Cyprus in a move that exposed Menzies as being out of the loop, despite his unwavering, and near blind-loyalty, to Eden. It also further reinforced the CIA's distrust of Anglo-French intentions – the US agency had picked up on the build-up of French troops on the island in the Mediterranean Sea, around six hundred miles from Egypt.

In September, Dulles submitted two intelligence assessments regarding the potentially brewing crisis in Egypt to the National Security Council, which advises the president on matters relating to foreign policy and national security. One of the assessments, cited in a recently declassified NSA document, revealed that 'even without further provocation, Britain and France might resort to force if convinced that negotiations were not going to produce a prompt settlement satisfactory to them.' In such circumstances, the assessment continued, 'London and Paris would attempt to document Nasser's refusal to negotiate such a settlement. The British and French would then dramatise the refusal before the world opinion as justification for the use of force.' The assessment was on point, because even while Britain was involved in public negotiations about a resolution in Egypt, its prime minister was secretly plotting with France and Israel to go to war with Nasser. The plot, designated 'Operation Musketeer', was for Israel to invade Egypt through the Sinai Peninsula, providing Britain and France the pretext to order a ceasefire and deploy troops to the canal zone as part of a 'peacekeeping' mission. The leaders of the three conspiring nations agreed that the success of their plot would rely on secrecy. Eden informed only a handful of people, including British Foreign Secretary Selwyn Lloyd. But he kept the plot secret from both US President Eisenhower and Australian Prime Minister Menzies in a move that undermined the newly formed Five Eyes agreement and devalued the moral solidarity which had shepherded the Allies to victory against the Nazis a decade earlier. Even worse, Eden's duplicity failed to consider the setback failure would cause Britain's intelligence community, which until then had proven to have more pound-for-pound tradecraft expertise than any of its Five Eyes allies.

The timing of the Hungarian Revolution in late October favoured Eden's plot as the White House and the CIA became absorbed by the threat of a Soviet invasion in Budapest. Operation Musketeer was launched on 29 October with an attack by Israel on Egypt that paved the way for an intervention by Britain and France who issued an ultimatum for a ceasefire the following day, in line with their tripartite plot. The conspirators had anticipated Nasser's refusal of the demand, but any hope for the US support that Eden and his plotters had anticipated or hoped for was dashed. Eisenhower was outraged. He condemned the attack on Egypt and expressed deep concerns about the wider impact it could have on further destabilising the region and playing into the hands of the Soviet Union. He also told Britain and France that the US could not be relied on for military aid. President Eisenhower's concern was largely ignored by Eden who seemed hellbent on reversing Britain's declining role on the global stage. On 31 October, the same day the US called for a UN Security Council resolution that London and Paris voted against, Britain launched an aerial attack against Egypt ahead of deploying British and French troops.

Eisenhower and Dulles were seething for different reasons over the Suez Crisis: the president claimed he had been caught unawares by the military attack against Egypt while his CIA director insisted that the agency had repeatedly provided warnings in the lead up to the invasion that had been largely overlooked by the White House.

But who knew what and when was the least of their problems at that stage as the Soviet leader Nikita Khrushchev declared his moral support for Egypt, raising questions in the international community about whether he would go further and offer Nasser military backing. The unfolding events in the Middle East had given the Kremlin a timely cover to conduct its operations in Budapest, where the CIA's man, Geza Katona, had become temporarily buoyed by the apparent success of the Hungarian Revolution and the return of calm to the city streets.

* * *

On 1 November 1956, a little over a week into the revolution, Geza Katona observed that Hungarians were celebrating their supposed victory against Moscow's policies and the apparent end of Soviet control over their country. 'Russians were nowhere to be seen; people were happy; life had started to return to its normal routine,' he recalled years later. 'Shops were even being opened here and there, while in many places food was being distributed in the street [...] Politically, too, the situation was calm; as we saw it then, a general settlement and conciliation could now be in reach. It seemed that under Imre Nagy's leadership a true parliamentary democracy might evolve.' The cheerful mood in Budapest had given Katona 'reason for optimism'. It was a short-lived optimism, however. The following days, Katona discovered through the US legation's military attachés that Russian forces had been massing in the east of Hungary and additional units were on the way through Romania. Reports of the advancing troops were verified to Katona by a colonel at the Hungarian Ministry of Defence on 3 November. During the discussion, the local military official also warned about the real possibility of Moscow preparing an attack against Hungary despite the impression it had given several days earlier that it was withdrawing its troops from the country.

Katona anticipated the worst but found it difficult to 'form a clear-cut view of the situation'. He fell asleep at his desk at the legation that evening, listening to news broadcasts on the radio, desperate for any bit of information that could shed light on what he had been told by the Hungarian colonel. In the small hours of 4 November, the clarity Katona had been seeking about Hungary's state of affairs presented itself in the form of reverberating sounds of cannon rounds and machine gun fire as Russian tanks rolled into Budapest to crush the revolution. Groups of locals, along with American and other western journalists who had been reporting on the revolution, poured into the US legation to avoid the indiscriminate shelling and shooting. The bodies of revolutionaries scattered the streets, many flattened by the steel tracks of armoured vehicles. More than 2500 people were ultimately killed. Hungary's newly appointed premier, Imre Nagy, fled to the Yugoslav Embassy, aware that Russian troops were after his scalp. Katona would years later ask himself what Washington's response would have been had Nagy approached the US legation instead and sought political asylum, wondering whether that could have altered the course of history. That very question, however, betrays Katona's lack of knowledge of what his boss, Allen Dulles, had thought of Nagy at the time.

Shortly after Nagy's brief return to power on the second day of the Hungarian Revolution, Dulles had authorised the broadcast of propaganda, including on the CIA-funded station Radio Free Europe, to accuse Nagy of being a traitor with Communist intentions who could not be trusted. Dulles's objective was to sabotage Nagy's leadership in the hope of replacing him with Cardinal József Mindszenty, the head of the Hungarian Catholic church and a vocal anti-Communist who had been granted asylum by the US legation in Budapest on 4 November. Dulles's vision never materialised, nor did any meaningful American help for the Hungarian resistance fighters who had been emboldened in their opposition to Russian troops by earlier suggestions on Radio Free Europe that the US military would come to their rescue. Instead, the CIA's mishandling of the events was partly responsible for the slaughter of thousands of Hungarians at the hands of Russian troops, and the displacement of around two-hundred-thousand other citizens who fled the country.

A secret CIA assessment of its own role during the Hungarian Revolution stated that 'at no time [...] did we have anything that could or should have been mistaken for an intelligence operation'. Instead, the intelligence obtained by the agency, predominantly sent by Katona, had been largely based on newspaper reports and eye-witness accounts that were 'one-sided', failing to provide any real insights about such things as the movements of Soviet troops. 'We had no composite picture of the states of the Revolution in the period between its first victory and its suppression by the Russians,' the declassified assessment concluded. 'We did not have the kind of information on which quick deft moves of our own could have been based, either in the nature of support to the Revolution or of the improved intelligence coverage.' However, the truth may be somewhere in the middle, because despite Katona's limited intelligence capability, he had informed the CIA of ways it could help – but it chose not to. In the heat of the battle, while the Hungarian insurgents were being gunned down, revolutionaries had repeatedly sought assistance from the US legation, and had been specifically interested in weapons, not soldiers, as Katona later recalled. 'In Germany, there were abundant stocks of American weapons that could have been brought over,' he said. 'I even know of an arsenal in West Germany in which were stockpiled weapons of Russian manufacture that had been captured during the Korean War, so if we had wanted to keep it quiet, we could have brought in some of those.' However, much to Katona's frustration, neither the CIA nor the Eisenhower Administration even considered supplying weapons during the uprising. 'It was an error that this was not even raised as a possibility in Washington,' Katona said. 'They sat idly by as Hungarian blood was being shed, calmly looked on as superior Russian forces trampled the glorious revolution underfoot.' The CIA disregarded its moral obligations to help Hungarian revolutionaries whom it had spurred on, a misjudgement that inadvertently reinforced Soviet dominance in Eastern Europe. The US agency's strategic error highlighted the disparity of intentions between Katona's eagerness to help – despite his lack of expertise and resources – and Dulles's cold-hearted approach of undermining the revolution's political leader, Nagy, and effectively marching freedom fighters to their deaths.

The CIA's unilateral mistakes in Hungary impacted other countries in the Five Eyes, including Canada, Britain, and Australia which were suddenly overwhelmed with displaced Hungarians seeking asylum. The exclusion of Kremlin spies trying to exploit the asylum system would have been among their top priorities. In the case of Australia, ASIO's European-based liaison officers, who had been operating under diplomatic cover out of Australian embassies on the continent, were all required to help process asylum seekers arriving in Vienna. With limited paperwork to verify the backgrounds of applicants, ASIO officers resorted to interviewing the heads of families and single people and then rejected or re-interviewed those whose stories did not add up. Of the 13,177 Hungarian refugees who were ultimately resettled in Australia,

ASIO was aware – and had anticipated – that some undesirables would slip through the screening net.

The US embassy in Vienna was also inundated with Hungarian asylum seekers, but as officials frantically dealt with processing applications, a team of NSA analysts who had been monitoring the invasion of Suez were ordered to investigate the validity of a threat by the Kremlin against the invaders – Britain, France and Israel. In letters addressed to the governments of the invading powers on 5 November, Soviet premier and defence minister, Nikolai Bulganin, declared that Moscow was 'fully resolved to use force to crush the aggressors and to restore peace in the Middle East'.

President Eisenhower had a lot on his in-tray on 6 November – it was the day of the US presidential election. He had one eye on securing a second term in the Oval Office, and another on the Suez Crisis which he feared could escalate into a nuclear attack by Moscow against Britain and France following Bulganin's threat. Although Eisenhower also wanted a ceasefire in the Middle East, he resented the Kremlin's intimidation of Prime Minister Eden and company, whom although he strongly disagreed with, he still regarded as close allies. Eisenhower was assured by the NSA analysts monitoring the conflict in Egypt that Moscow's threats were largely hollow because there was no evidence that it had provided Nasser with anything but verbal support. Eisenhower wanted more certainty, so he ordered the CIA to send two U-2 spy planes over Syria and Israel to investigate whether any Soviet troops had been stationed at Syrian bases. At midday, as American voters cast their ballots, Eisenhower was informed by the CIA that there were no Soviet fighters in Syria. The findings provided, if nothing else, a temporary relief for the White House.

However, the intelligence relating to the Soviet threat looked a lot different across the Atlantic, where GCHQ analysts had bolstered the Suez invasion by penetrating Egypt's diplomatic and military communications. In addition, the agency had been able to intercept the secret telegraphic exchanges between Egypt and its embassy in London, which MI5 had previously bugged in a joint operation with GCHQ.

Among the most important insights about the Kremlin's intentions emerged during a meeting between the Russian foreign minister and Egypt's ambassador in Moscow. The ambassador subsequently briefed his counterpart at the Egyptian embassy in London in a message that was intercepted by GCHQ. It revealed Russia's intention to mobilise aircraft in preparation for a military confrontation with Britain. GCHQ immediately passed the message to Britain's Joint Intelligence Committee, which is responsible for assessing security threats and advising the government about them. Some historians have since argued that the intercepted message forced the British prime minister – who had already been weighed down by White House angst and a UN resolution for an immediate ceasefire – to end the invasion of Egypt on 7 November 1956. It may never be known to what extent that intercepted message played a part in forcing Eden's hand, but years later, it emerged that Moscow's proposed military intentions in the Suez were merely a false flag to spook the UK. The Kremlin had known all along that GCHQ had penetrated the cipher communications of the Egyptian embassy in London and had used the communication channel as a gateway to feed misinformation to British intelligence. On 11 November – four days after the end of hostilities in the Suez which the Kremlin had claimed as a victory of its own making – Moscow declared its victory against the Hungarian revolution in a further humiliation to the west.

The Suez Crisis led to Eden's resignation, but far worse, it diminished western influence in the Middle East, furthered Moscow's credibility and reach among Arab leaders, and turned the region into a stage for ongoing proxy wars between the Kremlin and Washington. It also damaged intelligence operations, costing GCHQ its signals base in Ceylon, modern day Sri Lanka, which had proclaimed its independence from Great Britain eight years earlier. The Ceylonese government forced GCHQ out of its base in Perkar, on the country's northwest coast, after it discovered that Britain had used Ceylonese ports to refuel its ships on the way to invade Egypt. It was the Five Eyes' most crucial SIGINT site in the Indian Ocean. The Suez Crisis also increased hatred for British imperialism in Iraq – and against its ruler, King Faisal II, who was a friend of the United Kingdom. In 1958, the king was murdered during a coup by his army, which then seized control of a British military site in Habbaniya, near Baghdad – a secret signals intelligence base for GCHQ. The British signals analysts who had been effectively kicked out of their bases in Ceylon and Iraq had to retrench and limit themselves to GCHQ's other sites, including those in Cyprus, Malta and Gibraltar and Ascension Island.

Eden's political overreach and misadventure was arguably Britain's first public betrayal of its closest ally, the United States. It compromised the intelligence edge and political capital accrued by the UK during the early days of World War Two, permanently relegating it to junior partner. If there had been any ambiguities about who called the shots in the Special Relationship, the US saw them off following the Suez Crisis and proved to the world that it was in charge. While Suez was not the last time Britain fell foul of an intransigent US, it set an irreversible precedent which put Washington in charge of the Five Eyes.

Britain's imperial ambition to impose its rule on foreign countries through clandestine operations could hardly be criticised by US intelligence agencies, and particularly the CIA. Allen Dulles's joint operation with MI6 to overthrow the government of Syria, which had been delayed because of Suez until 1957, backfired after the regime's intelligence service uncovered the plot. The regime's henchmen arrested and effectively beat a confession out of the CIA's man in Damascus, Rocky Stone, regarding his agency's proposed mission. The regime then exposed the CIA's plot in the press, expelled Stone from the country, and sentenced his Syrian co-conspirators to death. The CIA's botched operation magnified the already growing anti-western sentiment in the Middle East, but it failed to stop Dulles's determination to pursue regime change in other parts of the world, until four years later when the CIA tried to overthrow Fidel Castro in Cuba by secretly arming and financing Cuban exiles with the promise of US aerial support. Similar to the CIA's record during the Hungarian Revolution, its promised support for the Cubans exiles never came. A false-flag operation on 15 April 1961, in which American fighter jets were painted to look like Cuban air-force planes, failed in their mission to destroy Cuban airfields. News of the attack, along with photographs of the repainted planes, exposed America's support for the invasion and led President John F. Kennedy to call off a subsequent air strike. Within 24 hours of the attempted Bay of Pigs invasion on 17 April, around 1,200 deserted Cuban exiles were captured and more than 100 were killed by Castro's armed forces. The botched CIA operation forced Dulles's resignation.

Through all the ups and downs, political shenanigans and wilful deceit at the hand of British political and intelligence officials and their counterparts in the US, the burgeoning Five Eyes alliance remained intact. GCHQ's official history reveals that Suez undermined trust between the UK's signals community and its opposite number in the US, despite the assurances it had given to the NSA that it did not share any intelligence with France during the invasion. However, an NSA history views the episode through a more sober lens, saying the crisis had been regarded as a 'high-level tiff that did not affect day-to-today relationships' between its agency and GCHQ.

The tensions between Britain and the US over Suez were short-lived and overshadowed by the ongoing Soviet threat against the Five Eyes, until the early 1970s when Britain and Australia separately questioned the value of their alliances with the United States. Australian Prime Minister Gough Whitlam clashed with the White House, wanting to sever Australia's intelligence ties with the US and accusing the CIA of interfering in his country's political system. In Britain, newly elected Prime Minister Ted Heath wanted to establish closer ties with Europe and to be less deferential to his counterpart in the Oval Office. Heath put the Special Relationship in jeopardy when he withheld details of an MI5 operation to expel Kremlin spies from Britain with the help of a Soviet defector.

CHAPTER EIGHT

DISSENT

OLEG LYALIN'S EAGERNESS TO come clean about his employment history at the Soviet Embassy in Britain seemed a little suspicious to MI5. The intelligence agency had been alerted to the young Russian official by Hampstead police station in north London on 21 April 1971, where he had strolled in earlier that day and voluntarily revealed that his diplomatic role as a textiles representative with the Soviet Trade Delegation was a cover for his work as a KGB spy. The steps he had taken to submit himself to a debriefing bore the hallmarks of a potential double agent sent to provide disinformation about Moscow's activities. His approach intrigued MI5 officers, who immediately whisked him away to one of the agency's safe houses. He agreed for his disclosures to be tape recorded and made no demands for large amounts of money or protection in return, reinforcing the suspicion held by the two British intelligence officers about his true motives. Was Lyalin there to expose one aspect of the KGB's operations for the sake of concealing another? Was he on a mission to determine MI5's knowledge of the Soviet Trade Delegation – which the agency had long suspected of being a conveyor belt for providing cover to Kremlin intelligence officers?

Although MI5 had become familiar with Soviet spies turning against their nation, including Igor Gouzenko in Canada in the 1940s and Vladimir Petrov in Australia a decade later, they had most often done so for the sake of political asylum. In the early 1960s, the case of Oleg Penkovsky, an officer of the Soviet military-intelligence agency, the GRU, had been no different. The Russian officer wanted to be relocated to the West when he volunteered his services to the CIA and MI6 and provided them with thousands of secrets, including photographs of military documents which exposed the installation of Soviet nuclear-armed missiles in Cuba that could reach the US within minutes in the event of a war. Penkovsky's secrets provoked the Cuban Missile Crisis, a major confrontation between Washington and Moscow, but his promised political asylum never materialised because he was caught by the Soviet regime and subsequently executed for treason.

Lyalin, however, was not after political asylum and nothing that he said during his debriefing by the two MI5 officers would have suggested otherwise. Nor did he seem to be driven by some kind of ideological awakening when he started divulging information about his position at Department V, a KGB unit specialising in sabotage. Lyalin revealed that his posting to London in July 1969 required him to identify areas in the country, including on the North Yorkshire coast, that could be used by Soviet saboteurs as dropping zones for sea and airborne landings. The KGB's sabotage plots, part of its contingency planning in the event of a future war with Britain, also included the destruction of railways, the identification of high profile political targets for assassination, and the infiltration of military sites, including RAF Fylingdales, where an early-warning radar installation had been jointly run by Britain and the US since the early 1960s. Lyalin assured MI5 that the KGB plots had remained largely unfulfilled, and provided a tip about a British local civil servant under his command who had been assisting the Kremlin's counterespionage operations. He said Hussein Hassanally Abdoolcader, an employee at the Greater London Council's motor-licensing department, had been providing him with details relating to the owners of MI5 surveillance vehicles that had been suspected of tailing Soviet spies in London. That was enough for MI5 to begin an investigation into Abdoolcader.

Lyalin's disclosures were accurate, and over subsequent debriefings in the weeks that followed, he helped MI5 identify other Soviet spies, claiming that the Kremlin had penetrated the Ministry of Defence and Foreign Office, Board of Trade, the British armed forces, and the Labour Party. Eventually, as he became more familiar with the debriefing officers, his true motives emerged. They were more personal than professional, home-related and had little to do with his work. Lyalin had a lot of self-inflicted stress: his marriage was on the rocks and he had been having two simultaneous affairs with a married English woman and a Russian lover, Irina Teplyakova, whom he wanted to marry. The KGB officer wanted MI5 to arrange for his expulsion from the UK so he could return to Moscow with Teplyakova and continue working for the British agency from there. It was a strange request, and over time, MI5 became increasingly concerned that his bizarre and unpredictable behaviour, risk-taking personality and inclinations to get drunk and disorderly would make him difficult to keep a handle on in Russia. The agency needed to keep Lyalin put, if only to help build a case against other Soviet spies in the UK who it had been lobbying the British government to expel.

At the time, MI5 suspected that there were more than 100 KGB and GRU intelligence officers in Britain, most of whom were undeclared or had been given the protection of cover roles like Lyalin's at the Soviet trade delegation. The government had at first been unconvinced by MI5's proposition for a mass expulsion, fearing the potential trade and international relations damage it could create with Moscow at the height of the Cold War. Another consideration was the fear of retaliation against British intelligence officers in Moscow. To overcome such hurdles, MI5 provided senior officials at the Home Office and Foreign Office with evidence that the suspects it had identified, undoubtedly with the help of Lyalin's disclosures, were in fact spies who posed a grave danger to Britain's national security. Armed with that, Foreign Secretary Sir Alec Douglas-Home and Home Secretary Reggie Maulding wrote to Prime Minister Edward Heath on 30 July 1971 to express their concerns, paving the way for a mass expulsion.

Heath would have known that an expulsion on that scale could frustrate the detente between Washington and Moscow that had been in place since the late 1960s. The reduction of tensions between the two superpowers did not diminish their mutual distrust, but had been intended to prevent the likelihood of nuclear war and showcase them as peacekeepers, despite them funding opposite sides of proxy conflicts, including the Vietnam War. At the beginning of 1969, President Richard Nixon reinforced the detente during his inaugural speech, inviting US adversaries to a 'peaceful competition – not in conquering territory or extending dominion but in enriching the life of man'. If Nixon's words had been meant to inspire a new era of cooperation and openness, they appeared to have been lost on Heath upon his entry into Downing Street the following year. Heath wanted to reframe the Special Relationship, because unlike his predecessor Harold Wilson, he was unconvinced of its value and was instead looking to strengthen Britain's ties to Europe – a move which did not sit well with the White House. Under Wilson's leadership, Britain had shown its loyal commitment to its closest ally, including to its controversial involvement in the Vietnam War. Although Wilson had not sent British troops to Vietnam, he had authorised the secret deployment of Special Forces soldiers, in addition to GCHQ analysts who were supporting the NSA from SIGINT sites around Asia – an act of friendship that had been admired by Nixon.

The ongoing Vietnam War was already straining Washington's relationships with some of its Five Eyes allies by the time Heath had come to power. Canada had refused to officially engage in the war, despite selling weapons to the US, and New Zealand only reluctantly deployed soldiers in 1964, following repeated pressure from Nixon's predecessor, Lyndon B. Johnson. And while Australia ultimately committed more than 60,000 troops, air force, and naval personnel – including some who served alongside the CIA in the controversial Phoenix Program in which Viet Cong members were tortured, 'turned', or assassinated – the Australian Labor leader Gough Whitlam had already declared his intention to withdraw them were he to be elected Prime Minister.

While the Vietnam War highlighted the political differences

between the Five Eyes, the Soviet threat brought them operationally closer together once again, as they expanded their industrialised intelligence-gathering. The alliance had fast evolved from the early days of intercepting High Frequency radio systems – the most common means of international telecommunications up until the late 1950s – and the penetration of microwave relay systems that had been used by the Soviet regime for telephone communications in the 1960s. The interception of such calls was a jointly run mission by British, American, and later, Canadian technical teams, based at their respective embassies in Moscow. A major breakthrough for the Five Eyes intelligence-gathering capabilities coincided with the advent of commercial satellites including those belonging to the International Telecommunications Satellite Organization, or Intelsat, which became a major part of global communications during the twentieth century. The US and Britain built ground stations for the interception of Intelsat satellites, and the means of bugging ocean cables using submarines.

Communications technology evolved exponentially following the installation and orbit of the first geostationary Intelsat satellites in 1967. Four years later, the fourth generation of Intelsat satellites, capable of 'handling all forms of communications channels simultaneously – telephone, telex, telegraph, television, data and facsimile', according to a study by the European Parliament, were introduced. By then, the US and Britain had built two bases to intercept such communications – one in Yakima, Washington State, that was operated by the NSA, and the other in Morwenstow, near the Cornish coast in the south of England, that was jointly operated by the NSA and GCHQ. The British facility intercepted the Atlantic Ocean Intelsat and the Indian Ocean Intelsat, while its US counterpart spied on communication passing through the Pacific Ocean Intelsat satellite. The success of such bases led to the creation of other interception sites in the subsequent two decades, including in Ontario, Canada, Kojarena in Western Australia, and in Waihopai, New Zealand.

The base in Morwenstow, later renamed GCHQ Bude, was, much like other satellite interception stations within the Five Eyes, funded by the NSA. The US agency funded the infrastructure and the technology on the bases while the host countries paid for some of the running costs. Despite such an arrangement, British Prime Minister Edward Heath questioned the value of US-funded facilities in Britain. His scepticism corresponded with the resentment he held for the idea of deferring to the White House on matters of foreign policy in the way that many of his predecessors had done. His attitude had concerned some of his cabinet members, who felt that it overlooked the value that the US military and intelligence community provided to Britain. It took the intervention of his defence secretary, Lord Carrington, to spell out the benefits reaped by Britain through the UKUSA Agreement on matters relating to military threats and developments in the Soviet Union, China and the Middle East. The prime minister was also told by his advisers that the Special Relationship required nurturing and could not be taken for granted after Britain's loyalty had been brought into question during the Suez Crisis in the 1950s. Lord Carrington's intervention may have improved Heath's appreciation of his country's intelligence ties with the US, but it certainly did not alter his resolve to withhold information from the White House, including the plan to expel Soviet spies from Britain, until he decided the time was right. In the summer of 1971, Heath seemed intent on proving his independence of mind to his counterpart, President Nixon.

During an unanticipated event on 30 August, Oleg Lyalin, who by then had been spying for MI5 for four months, was about to unknowingly present Heath with the perfect opportunity to defy Washington. Lyalin had been arrested in the small hours of the morning for drink-driving and held in a police cell after refusing to provide a blood or urine sample. His arrest led to a brief court appearance and created unwanted attention for him, raising questions among his KGB bosses about his behaviour and state of mind. On being ordered by the KGB to return to Moscow, Lyalin knew that his time was up. So he called his MI5 handlers on 3 September and expressed his intention to defect and to bring his Russian lover, Irina Teplyakova, with him.

The couple arrived at an MI5 safe house that evening with a stack of KGB documents Lyalin had stolen from his office at the Soviet Embassy. His defection offered a timely pretext and official justification for Edward Heath's intended expulsion of Kremlin spies under a government plan codenamed Operation FOOT. The prime minister fast-tracked the existing plan – and on 24 September, 90 KGB and GRU officers based in Britain under the protection of official diplomatic cover were expelled, along with 15 other officers who had been on leave in the Soviet Union. It was the biggest expulsion of Soviet spies by any country in history.

MI5 officers raised celebratory drinks at the agency's headquarters at Leconfield House, central London, in honour of crushing the Kremlin's espionage capabilities and bringing about a major turning point in the Cold War. 'The Soviets were "involved in a hive" of intelligence activities in Britain, which included efforts to obtain military and industrial secrets, including data on supersonic airliner Concorde, and had plans to infiltrate saboteurs into the country,' one news report revealed. MI5 states that Operation FOOT had for the first time turned Britain into a difficult espionage target for Moscow. 'For several years [...] the KGB was forced to ask Soviet Bloc and Cuban agencies to help plug the intelligence gap.'

As MI5 and Downing Street revelled in their victory, the mood in Washington's intelligence community was far less upbeat, especially in the office of Henry Kissinger, US National Security Advisor. The first official notification that Kissinger received about the mass expulsion arrived on the day that it had taken place, despite the fact that Heath had approved the plan two months earlier. A letter to Kissinger from the British Ambassador disingenuously claimed that Heath regretted not being able to inform President Nixon earlier about the move against the Soviet spies, saying a press leak had forced the British government to accelerate the expulsion. Heath's attempt to hoodwink his US counterpart was believed by neither Kissinger nor the White House, setting the stage for intelligence tensions between Britain and the US.

Despite the political rift between Heath and Nixon, MI5 shared intelligence it had obtained from Lyalin with US intelligence and law-enforcement agencies, including the CIA and FBI. The British security service debriefed Lyalin on a series of questions raised by the FBI about suspected Kremlin agents in New York. The Russian defector helped identify 45 'new KGB officers in the NY area' who had been either working at the Soviet Mission of the United Nations or the United Nations Security Council. Other Five Eyes partners also benefited from Lyalin's intelligence. While the Australian intelligence agency, ASIO, found no evidence that the KGB had been plotting any sabotage attacks in the country, it reassessed its security measures around defence sites. The Australian government also publicly stated that a new Soviet trade office which had intended to open in Sydney would be stripped of diplomatic immunity to prevent it being turned into a front for Kremlin spies.

The generosity of intelligence-sharing by Britain did not offset the anger felt by the Oval Office about Downing Street taking a unilateral approach on the Lyalin case. As Anglo-American political relations tumbled, Washington became concerned about its intelligence ties with another member of the Five Eyes – Australia. The antipodean nation had been a close ally of the US during its successive conservative governments over the two previous decades. That changed with the election of Labor Leader, Gough Whitlam, as Prime Minister in December 1972.

On 4 December 1972, two days after Gough Whitlam had been elected to office in Australia, the CIA assured President Richard Nixon that the new prime minister had committed to upholding the alliance with the US as the 'cornerstone of Australian foreign policy'. By then, Canberra's intelligence cooperation with Washington through the Five Eyes had come of age.

The Australian Secret Intelligence Service (ASIS), the country's overseas spy agency, had been conducting covert operations in Chile on behalf of the CIA since the summer of 1971 to help destabilise the socialist government of Salvador Allende. Having set up a base in Santiago at the request of Washington, the Australians ran Chilean agents who had been recruited by the CIA, and provided intelligence reports to the US agency's headquarters in Langley, Virginia. The operation had been in play for about 18 months by the time Whitlam came to power, and soon after learning about it, the new prime minister ordered for it to be disbanded despite initial concerns that such a move would irritate

Washington. ASIS wound up its covert work in July 1973, two months before Allende was ousted in a military coup led by General Augusto Pinochet, whose regime became responsible for the torture or murder of tens of thousands of political opponents.

Around the same time that ASIS had been contributing to the CIA's dirty work in Chile, its sister agency, ASIO, which served as Australia's domestic intelligence service, had maintained its close ties with Britain and the United States. The personal relationships that had been cultivated in Washington over two decades by ASIO's former director-general Charles Spry had been smoothly taken over and maintained by his successor, Peter Barbour, by the time Whitlam came to power.

Of equal importance, at least in the minds of the CIA's top brass at Langley, was that Canberra's inclusion in the Five Eyes had reinforced a separate military treaty with the US and New Zealand, known as ANZUS, which had been signed in 1951 to protect the security of the Pacific. To the CIA, the ANZUS pact was an additional insurance policy to safeguard and cushion Washington's dealings with the new Whitlam government. Langley had become aware of Whitlam's intention to reassess security agreements his predecessors had signed with Washington, which permitted the US to build 'military and scientific installations' in Australia. But the agency hoped, and perhaps even expected, that Whitlam would rise above his left-leaning politics when scrutinising the ostensibly mutually beneficial joint-ventures. Among them was a SIGINT base in Western Australia, known as North West Cape, that had been created in 1963 for the US Navy to communicate with its nuclear-armed submarines in the Indian Ocean. Other agreements between Canberra and Washington included US satellite intelligence facilities: Pine Gap, in Australia's Northern Territory, which had been set up in 1966, and Nurrungar, in the South Australian desert, created three years later by the US Air Force (USAF) to detect Soviet missile launches.

Pine Gap, the most secretive surveillance base in Australia, was part of ECHELON – the codename for a surveillance programme that had been set up by the US and Britain under the banner of the Five Eyes in the 1960s initially to eavesdrop on diplomatic and military signals traffic.

The programme's reach through strategically positioned spy bases in Five Eyes countries was eventually expanded to spy on the telephone, fax, and online communications between both public and private organisations, as well as ordinary citizens worldwide. Of all the bases feeding into ECHELON, Pine Gap was arguably the most important to the CIA. Previously known as the Joint Defence Space Research Facility, but since 1988 officially called Joint Defence Facility Pine Gap (JDFPG), its stated mission was rather generic: to support the national security of both countries. But the unstated and real purpose of Pine Gap, as it became commonly known, was to serve as a ground station for the control of US spy satellites and to intercept a range of targets, including commercial communications, and tests of Soviet intercontinental ballistic missiles designed to carry nuclear weapons.

Covering four square miles of desert outside Alice Springs in central Australia, Pine Gap was one of the most valuable interception platforms in the eastern hemisphere. On paper, it was operated by the Pentagon's Defense Advanced Research Projects Agency, but that was a cover story. Pine Gap was in fact an undeclared CIA project that the US agency was eager to protect from political knowledge, scrutiny, and interference by the Whitlam Government.

Langley was confident enough about its ability to stop Whitlam's interference with the US bases that, on 4 December 1972, it raised the issue in a President's Daily Brief – an intelligence assessment by the CIA specifically intended to inform the US leader on matters of global security. 'It is clear that some party leaders [...] are not well versed on the US facilities,' declared the agency's message to President Richard Nixon. 'Once they become fully informed on the benefits Australia derives from the installations, we believe the new government will conclude that they fit within the framework of the ANZUS treaty.' The CIA was wrong.

Whitlam generally despised US foreign policy. From a military perspective, he had described the Vietnam War as 'disastrous and deluded' during his days as Australia's opposition leader. And a month into his first term as Prime Minister, he condemned the US bombing of North Vietnam that killed about 1,600 civilians, and also brought Australia's involvement in the war to an end after a phased withdrawal that had started three years earlier. His immediate mark on military relations with the US angered the Nixon Administration and reinforced a White House perception that the prime minister was soft on Kremlin policies.

Having picked a fight with the Oval Office, the Labor leader then turned his attention to ASIO, over its close operational connections with its US counterparts. Whitlam was uncomfortable with those ties, but first, he prioritised scrutinising ASIO's domestic operations. His view of the organisation would undoubtedly have been coloured by Labor's suspicion that ASIO had conspired to ensure the re-election of the Liberal prime minister, Robert Menzies, during the Petrov Affair two decades earlier. Labor had blamed the events surrounding that election on keeping the Liberals in power for 23 years. It did not seem to matter to Whitlam that ASIO's leadership had changed since then, with the appointment of Peter Barbour as director-general in 1970. The prime minister wanted to shake up the organisation and make it more accountable. And in March 1973, a forthcoming visit to Australia by the Yugoslav prime minister, Džemal Bijedić, gave Whitlam a timely pretext to go after ASIO.

The Australian prime minister was unsatisfied that the intelligence agency had made the requisite security preparations ahead of the state visit. His concerns had been underscored by a police briefing he had received that month claiming that Australian-based Croatian extremists had been plotting to kill Bijedić, a Serb and signed-up Communist. Since ASIO came under the responsibility of Lionel Murphy, the attorney general, Whitlam leant on him to press the agency for more information about the assassination plot. For Murphy, it was an opportunity to exact his own revenge on the organisation which he regarded as right-leaning and conspiratorial. Within 40 hours of demanding more information from Barbour about the alleged plot against the Yugoslav leader, Murphy was convinced that ASIO was withholding information from him and failing in its duty to properly investigate the threat. Without prior warning, Murphy coordinated with the Commonwealth Police to take action against the intelligence agency.

On the morning of 16 March, 27 police officers stormed ASIO's headquarters in Melbourne, took control of the agency's safes, ordered staff away from their desks as they arrived to work and effectively detained them in the building's auditorium. Murphy also arrived at the scene to assess the agency's files on Croatian extremists. The dramatic mission, known as the 'Murphy Raid', was unprecedented, and its repercussion on ASIO's relationships with intelligence agencies in the Five Eyes was immediately felt. Within hours of the raid, American law-enforcement and spy agencies, including the CIA, were ordered to stop sharing intelligence with the Australian agency. The US National Security Agency refused to share around three-thousand pages of secret material, and the FBI also curtailed its dealing with the Australian organisation, despite assurances from Barbour, ASIO's boss, that no US intelligence was swept up in the raid. The US intelligence community's concern was shared by President Nixon and his national security adviser, Henry Kissinger. The White House, according to ASIO's official history, had been shaken by Murphy's actions, which had been authorised by Whitlam.

The Yugoslav prime minister, whose scheduled visit had led to the Murphy Raid, arrived in Australia on 20 March, without any qualms. During Bijedić's state visit, ASIO liaised with the police to disrupt a potential bomb plot by a Croatian extremist who had stored explosive detonators at his house in Canberra. However, as ASIO went about its work that month, other countries within the Five Eyes started questioning their intelligence relationship with it. Britain's earlier intention to brief Whitlam on the existence of the counter-Soviet Venona Project was placed on hold. And the Royal Canadian Mounted Police recalled intelligence material relating to Soviet penetration that it had shared with ASIO and ordered the destruction of all correspondence relating to it.

The intelligence fallout from the Murphy Raid could not have been foreseen by the Australian attorney general and the prime minister. The raid may have stamped Whitlam's authority on ASIO three months into his tenure, but it was a misjudgement that threatened to set the organisation back several decades, at least temporarily, among its

Five Eyes partners. Historians have long argued that Murphy, in his capacity as attorney general, would have been entitled to visit ASIO's headquarters and seek the information he had been after without creating the sense of theatre that had been brought on by storming the agency's offices. Yet the raid betrayed his, and Whitlam's, resolve to break ASIO and reconstruct it in the new government's image of aspired openness and transparency.

As US intelligence agencies pondered the events in Australia, tensions between the White House and Downing Street in the UK continued to play out. President Richard Nixon and his national security adviser, Henry Kissinger, had become increasingly incensed about the Heath government's increased cooperation on intelligence matters with France. Kissinger's paranoia may have been somewhat warranted because unbeknown to him, Britain's Joint Intelligence Committee had at the time been deliberately withholding from the US most of the information it had obtained from Paris. American officials were beginning to question whether Britain was actively colluding with France to undermine US foreign policy, especially after January 1973, when it joined the European Economic Community, which was later incorporated into the European Union.

By the summer of 1973, the Anglo-American relationship was deteriorating rapidly. Kissinger's patience had run out. The calm and warm façade he had projected earlier in the year to the British authorities, who had been helping him plan an arms control agreement between NATO and the Warsaw Pact nations, came to an abrupt end. In late July, he blasted a British delegation in Washington, accusing it of failing to get a quick response from European countries over the proposed agreement, known as the Mutual and Balanced Force Reduction, for the Soviet Union to reduce troops and armaments in Central Europe, including East Germany.

Kissinger's unpredictability and combustible temperament, which the Heath government had been aware of but had never properly experienced during its preceding three years in power, put itself on display. As Nixon's intelligence czar, he used the flare-up over the arms agreement to exact his revenge against Edward Heath for past misdeeds. Along with his suspicion of Britain's ties to Europe, Kissinger had not forgotten Heath's unwillingness to inform Washington about his intended expulsion of Soviet spies in the Operation Foot case of 1971.

During a telephone conversation with President Nixon on 9 August 1973, Kissinger lamented Heath's closeness to Europe, a relationship which he claimed Britain had been nurturing with the 'same single-mindedness that they pursued the Special Relationship with us before'. The national security adviser was outraged that Britain 'didn't feel obliged to tell us what they discussed with the Europeans' and claimed that the Heath government could not be trusted with US intelligence. 'I mean if they are going to share everything with the Europeans we can't trust them for a Special Relationship.'

Kissinger stipulated his authority during the call, telling the president that he wanted to order US spy chiefs to cut intelligence-sharing with Britain. 'I'm cutting them off from intelligence,' he said. 'I am putting it on the basis that we are reassessing all liaison relations. I'm not doing it from the White House, I'm having the Agency heads do it.' Nixon agreed to Kissinger's plan, and the following day, the constant stream of intelligence that had been flowing from Washington to London for the past 30 years – first through the BRUSA agreement of 1943, then through the Five Eyes the following decade – was shut down without warning. American intelligence agencies, including the CIA and NSA, had been equally shocked about Kissinger's decision as their counterparts across the Atlantic, MI6 and GCHQ, who were suddenly flung out into the cold.

British spy chiefs and their American colleagues wanted to safeguard the dealings of their intelligence communities from the bad political blood between the White House and Downing Street. The NSA informed Kissinger that refusing to share intelligence with GCHQ would hamper its own operations, not only theirs; and the CIA told him that it was concerned that its joint HUMINT investigations with MI6 would be compromised. Despite Kissinger's order, the NSA and CIA continued sharing some information with their British counterparts on the basis of mutual need. Their willingness to partially circumvent Kissinger's wishes was testimony to the deep operational bonds, and friendships, that they had developed with the intelligence community in the UK.

British spy agencies reciprocated by lobbying Prime Minister Heath for a little over a fortnight to help reverse Kissinger's intelligence block. The prime minister eventually wrote a letter to President Nixon in early September to assure him that Britain's commitment and relationship with the US was resolute and that there was no question of the two nations ever becoming adversaries. Heath said his country's bond with Europe, which he had known was a sensitive topic in the White House, would complement British and US relations, rather than threaten them. The extension of an olive branch by Downing Street to the Oval Office did little to diminish the suspicion held by the US National Security Committee about Britain's cosiness to Europe. Heath's attempt to patch up the intelligence fallout had effectively been rebuffed.

To make matters worse, Heath infuriated both Nixon and Kissinger the following month when a coalition of Soviet-backed Arab states, including Egypt and Syria, launched a surprise attack against Israel to regain territory that had been lost during the Six Day War of 1967. The new Middle East crisis was initiated by the Arab states on Yom Kippur, the holiest day in the Jewish calendar, to catch Israel off guard. Washington quickly came to Israel's aid, but London adopted a neutral approach – to the point that it banned the sharing of British intelligence relating to the conflict with its US counterparts. Heath even stopped the operation of the CIA's U-2 flights from Britain's military base in Cyprus in a provocative move that further strained tensions with the White House. And for good measure, the prime minister also placed restrictions on SR-17 Blackbird surveillance planes being flown out of Britain without ministerial approval. As a result, Washington was forced to fly the high-altitude reconnaissance aircraft from an air force base in New York, extending the length of the journey and bloating the associated fuel costs. If Heath's political posturing had been intended to outrage the Oval Office – it did. But it also angered Langley, which had taken the risk of going behind Kissinger's back a month earlier to continue sharing secrets with Britain after the national security adviser had tried to switch off the taps. The CIA immediately cancelled all contact with the UK following Heath's actions around Yom Kippur.

The running tussle between Heath and Nixon was plagued by a testosterone overload. It played out like a battle between two allied Marvel characters who prioritise the preservation of their egos over the collateral damage it has on the people around them. On 25 October, the conflict between Downing Street and the White House intensified when President Nixon placed the US military on high nuclear alert in a move to deter his Soviet counterpart, Leonid Brezhnev, from military intervention in the Yom Kippur War. The conflict came to an end that day, but Heath became outraged about being left out of the loop on Washington's decision to threaten nuclear action – which he only learned about after seeing it reported in the news.

Although defined by their differences, Heath and Nixon had a lot in common when it came to the weaponisation of national security for their own political gain – and against their own people. During the Vietnam War, Nixon frequently turned to US intelligence agencies to investigate 'subversives' in the anti-war movements. Under that pretext, the CIA, FBI, and Army intelligence spied on journalists, civil-rights leaders, and members of Congress, through extensive infiltration and electronic surveillance. 'The government sought not only to investigate its critics on a massive scale, but also to expose, disrupt, and neutralize their efforts to affect public opinion,' according to an NSA report citing a Senate Select Committee investigation into US intelligence. 'The Government has often undertaken the secret surveillance of citizens on the basis of their political beliefs, even when those beliefs posed no threat of violence or illegal acts.'

In Britain, Heath had long been determined to use M15 to target industrial unions. He was paranoid that the hidden hand of Communists had played a role in masterminding industrial action to undermine his government and take over the country. In his mind, industrial strikes were acts of subversion dressed up as demonstrations for workers' rights. During his early days as Prime Minister, Heath urged MI5 to bug union meetings to try to establish what they were plotting, but the British agency refused his demand, seeing right through his political agenda. Heath renewed his pressure on the agency in the winter of 1972 after his government caved in to the demands by the National Union of Mineworkers for improved wages amid a strike that lasted almost two months. The prime minister was yet again convinced the strike had been an act of subversion, but a subsequent investigation by MI5 into the Communist Party of Great Britain, whose headquarters it had bugged, revealed that they had influence but no control over unions – much to the disappointment of Heath and his government.

In the summer of 1972, Heath promoted MI5's former deputy director, Michael Hanley, to the top job, aware that he would take strong action against the unions. He wanted Hanley to uncover links between Communists and industrial action. MI5 found increasing evidence that British Communists had been strategising with the National Union of Mineworkers with the ultimate intention of overthrowing the government. Heath weaponised MI5's intelligence for his political aspirations, using it to help shape his anti-union election message in early 1974: 'Who governs Britain?'

Despite his machinations, Heath lost the election in February 1974, six months before President Nixon was forced to resign as a result of the Watergate scandal in which people linked to his re-election campaign, including a former CIA officer, had broken into the Democratic National Committee headquarters in Washington to steal secret documents and bug the phones of his political rivals. Nixon had then asked the CIA to help stop an FBI investigation into the break-in, but his demand was refused by the agency which he had leaned on in the past for his own agenda. The illegal operations that Nixon had encouraged the CIA to conduct, including the surveillance of the anti-war movement, forced his successor Gerald Ford to commission an inquiry within weeks of being sworn in.

In addition to dealing with the CIA's mischief at home, the new White House Administration faced accusations by the Australian prime minister, Gough Whitlam, of the agency interfering in his country's politics. Whitlam's suspicion was heightened when he discovered through his staff that Richard Stallings, a CIA officer with political connections to the conservative Country Party in Australia, had been the first US chief of Pine Gap, the satellite base. This had raised questions about Langley's role in the base – despite misleading assurances from Washington that the facility had been operated by the Pentagon.

On arriving in Australia in September 1966, Richard Lee Stallings had lived multiple lives in the service of his country – the United States. He had served as an intelligence officer with the US Navy in both World War II and the Korean War, rising through the ranks to lieutenant commander, before joining the CIA in the mid-1950s. But unlike many CIA careerists who had remained strapped to their desks at Langley, Stallings, in his late thirties by then, had shown a knack for operational management while working at the agency's office of ELINT, or electronic surveillance. It was a skill that proved valuable for overseas postings. He was sent to Frankfurt to run the CIA's signals operations in Europe, liaising with both the NSA and West German Intelligence Service. And when the agency required an 'undeclared' frontman at Pine Gap, it turned to Stallings. His skills in communication interception would undoubtedly have been a factor, but his former background in the armed forces was what provided the perfect cover for overseeing a facility that, to the outside world, appeared to be a Pentagon defence project rather than a CIA intelligence mission.

The stated aims of the public agreement relating to Pine Gap, finalised between Canberra and Washington in December 1966, three months after Stallings had arrived in Australia, was that the facility was to be 'established, maintained and operated by [...] the Australian Department of Defence and the Advanced Research Projects Agency (ARPA) of the United States Department of Defense.' However, the public agreement was merely tailored for press releases and bilateral spin. It was signed in early December by a US Embassy representative and Australia's minister of external affairs, with a lifespan of ten years and the opportunity for any party to terminate it with twelve months' notice. The following month, Stallings left Canberra for Alice Springs where he remained until December 1968 – enough time to oversee the initial construction of Pine Gap in preparation for its undeclared CIA mission to intercept satellite communications. The legacy of his work at Pine Gap was supposed to have remained a closely guarded secret.

The secret risked being exposed six years later when the Australian prime minister was notified by Labor Party staff members in October 1975, that Stallings had been working for the CIA during his time as Pine Gap's operational chief. To verify the claim, Whitlam ordered his foreign affairs department to provide him with the names of all declared CIA officers who had officially served in Australia in the previous decade. Stallings's name was missing from the list, despite an understanding between Washington and Canberra that each would inform the other of the intelligence officers who were operating in their host nations. Stallings had operated so far beneath the radar, however, that even ASIO had been unaware of him. That heightened the prime minister's suspicion. He generally despised the CIA's activities, from its destabilisation, and at times overthrow, of left-wing governments, to its interactions with Australia's security service.

A year earlier, Whitlam had ordered ASIO to sever its ties with Langley but had been convinced otherwise by the agency's director-general, Peter Barbour, who had warned him of the harm that a loss of US intelligence could have on Australia's security. The prime minister softened his stance, but ASIO had been forced to limit social interactions with the CIA and maintain a strictly formal, operational relationship. The move agitated the intelligence community in Washington and coincided with the appointment of Dr Jim Cairns as deputy prime minister following Whitlam's second election victory in June 1974. Henry Kissinger, who by then was both US Secretary of State and National Security Advisor, perceived Cairns as anti-American and too enamoured by the Chinese Communist regime. His concern prompted a review of the bilateral relationship between Washington and Canberra, to weigh up the setbacks and benefits of sharing intelligence with Australia and retaining surveillance bases there, including Pine Gap, according to ASIO's official history. Although the US review ruled in favour of maintaining relations, the mutual suspicion between the two nations' leaderships remained.

By the time Whitlam had started asking questions about Stallings, Nixon had been forced out over Watergate, and his former vice-president, Gerald Ford, had been elevated to the Oval Office for just over a year. In June of 1975, a commission that had been ordered by President Ford into the CIA's misuse of power, including mass surveillance of American citizens who were opposed to US government policies, reported its findings. The Rockefeller Commission report was largely dismissed as a whitewash after merely recommending for the CIA to establish better 'oversight' of its staff and operations and for its leadership to demonstrate a finer 'judgement, courage, and independence to resist improper pressure and importuning, whether from the White House, within the Agency or elsewhere'. It also stated that the agency 'must rely on the discipline and integrity of the men and women it employs'. And it was the integrity of one such employee that had continued to intrigue Whitlam when he turned to the secretary of Australia's defence department, Arthur Tange, for answers. Tange's ministry was nominally the joint operator of Pine Gap, as outlined by the public agreement relating to the facility. He had been aware of Stallings's role as a CIA officer and that it was Langley, not the Pentagon, that ran Pine Gap. However, Tange reportedly withheld that information from Whitlam because of an alleged running dispute between the CIA and NSA about which of the two agencies should ultimately run the interception base in Australia.

The prime minister became determined to expose the truth about Pine Gap's true operator, and on a visit to Alice Spring on 2 November publicly declared, without providing evidence, that the CIA had funded the Country Party – which had been in coalition with the Liberal Party – Labor's opposition. The prime minister's claim, intended to damage both the CIA and his political opponents, may have been based on the fact that Stallings had temporarily rented a house in Canberra from the Country Party leader, Doug Anthony, in 1967. Whitlam's claim of political financing by the CIA was denied by the agency, by the US Ambassador to Australia, and also by Anthony.

Although Whitlam did not mention Stallings by name on making his accusation, an article in the Australian Financial Review newspaper the following day named Stallings as a CIA officer. The 3 November story was written by Brian Toohey, a Canberra correspondent specialising in national security, whose ability to consistently uncover Australian government secrets had become a perpetual annoyance to the intelligence community. Toohey's exposé of Stallings forced the questions about the CIA's role at Pine Gap – which until then had been largely contained to the political corridors of Canberra – into public view. The newspaper revelations would undoubtedly have played into Whitlam's hands. Baited by his political opponent, Doug Anthony, to provide evidence of Stallings's CIA background in parliament, Whitlam planned to do so on 11 November, the day parliament had been scheduled to resume. Under parliamentary privilege, Whitlam would have been entitled to reference information he had sought from his defence secretary, Tange, about Stallings's previous role at Pine Gap and his background as a CIA official.

The security crisis had been playing out against the backdrop of a political struggle between the House of Representatives, where Whitlam's government had majority control, and the Senate, where it did not. A few weeks earlier, the Senate had blocked Supply – or budgetary funds for the government to continue its day-to-day operations – and called for a new election. Whitlam refused, saying the Senate had no constitutional right to decide who should hold government. Washington had been acutely aware of the political crisis in Canberra, but it had been mostly preoccupied with the intelligence crisis. In a message received by ASIO headquarters on 9 November, the CIA expressed its concern that continued reference in Australia to its organisation could 'blow the lid off those installations in Australia [...] particularly the installation at Alice Springs' – Pine Gap.

The message was reportedly shared that same day by an Australian defence department official with Sir John Kerr, Australia's governor-general – a role in which the office holder is empowered by the Queen to execute and maintain both the Constitution and the laws passed by parliament. On 11 November, the day Whitlam had been scheduled to expose Stallings in parliament, Kerr used his powers to sack the prime minister in the most controversial decision in Australia's political history, and appointed Leader of the Opposition Malcolm Fraser as caretaker, before an election was called. Kerr's unprecedented move was ostensibly over Whitlam's refusal to 'resign or to advise an election after failing to obtain Supply,' according to a record of the event on Australia's parliament house website. However, Whitlam's government funds – the Supply – could have lasted another 19 days, according to journalist Brian Toohey, raising questions about whether Kerr's premature dismissal of the prime minister had been influenced by the CIA's fear that he was intending to expose Stallings and Pine Gap's connection to the US agency that day. Although Whitlam maintained that the CIA had a hand in his dismissal – a view shared by his allies, some media pundits and historians alike – his claims were never proven and were repeatedly denied by Langley and Kerr. Forty-five years later, in July 2020, it was revealed that Kerr had not sought the Queen's approval for Whitlam's dismissal.

Whether by conspiracy or coincidence, Whitlam's removal ushered in a Coalition government under Fraser that was more to Washington's taste, restoring intelligence relations between ASIO and the CIA. In the first half of the 1970s, Whitlam's leadership, along with Ted Heath's in Britain, became a defining power struggle within the Five Eyes, with Canberra and London both trying to independently diminish Washington's stranglehold over their respective foreign policy decisions and intelligence communities. The US had reinforced its dominance within the Five Eyes by prevailing against its two allies, but it still needed to prove its dominance to the alliance's greatest existential threat – the Soviet Union. The opportunity for a proxy war against the Kremlin presented itself shortly after President Jimmy Carter was elected to office in 1977. Washington was still reeling from its defeat at the hands of Soviet-backed forces in Vietnam in a military campaign that lasted two decades. Zbigniew Brzezinski, Carter's national security adviser, had the idea of 'giving the USSR its own Vietnam'. Instead of risking the lives of US troops in the process, Brzezinski turned to the CIA for help.

CHAPTER NINE

BAITING THE SOVIETS

ON CHRISTMAS EVE OF 1979, as millions of Americans prepared to celebrate the biggest cultural and religious holiday in the Christian calendar, US National Security Advisor Zbigniew Brzezinski was consumed by an event that was unfolding six thousand miles away – the beginning of the Soviet Union's invasion of Afghanistan. A little more than three decades into the Cold War, the Kremlin had unknowingly been drawn into a trap that Brzezinski had masterminded with the help of the CIA. Unknown to the outside, the US intelligence agency had been secretly arming, training, and financing Afghan rebels, the Mujahideen, for around six months before the Soviet invasion. Brzezinski had correctly predicted that the CIA's clandestine programme, codenamed Operation Cyclone, would not only support the insurgency but ultimately bait Moscow into a battle in Afghanistan.

Brzezinski had been in the role for almost three years at the time of the invasion, but he had proved to be a seasoned opportunist. He spotted the 'compensating factors' Afghanistan had and questioned whether it could ultimately become a 'Soviet Vietnam' by embroiling the Red Army in an unwinnable war against the Mujahideen. His assessment was made in a memorandum to US President Jimmy Carter, urging him to provide greater support to Afghan rebels, who for almost two years had been ramping up their fight to overthrow successive Soviet-backed regimes in Kabul. 'This means more money as well as arms shipments to the rebels, and some technical advice,' according to the declassified missive written by Brzezinski, dated 26 December 1979. He told the president that the US 'might be in a position to exploit' the outrage felt by Muslims towards the Soviet invasion and should 'connect with the Islamic countries in both a propaganda campaign and in a covert action campaign to help the rebels'.

Brzezinski's hatred of the Soviet Union and his ambition to aid in its destruction, had its origins in the Red Army's 1939 invasion of Poland, his country of origin, at the beginning of World War II. As the son of a Polish diplomat, Brzezinski had grown up with an acute interest in geopolitics and became devoted to studying the Soviet Union. After gaining a doctorate in political science from Harvard University in the early 1950s, he had become a US citizen and actively thrown himself into furthering the foreign policies of his adopted nation. Over the following two decades, he lectured and wrote about the threat of Soviet expansionism and advised two White House Democratic administrations in one capacity or another before being appointed National Security Advisor by President Carter in 1977.

Two years into his high-profile role – in which he held a similar sway over US intelligence agencies and global affairs as Henry Kissinger had done in the two previous White House administrations – Brzezinski became increasingly suspicious of the Soviet Union's scaled up military aid and influence drive in the late 1970s extending from South America, through Africa and the Middle East.

In January of 1979, Islamic revolutionaries in Iran overthrew the regime of Shah Mohammad Reza Pahlavi, who had been installed by a joint CIA and MI6 sponsored coup 26 years earlier. The Shah's removal eventually placed religious fundamentalists in power and robbed the US of a strategic ally in the Middle East, where it had operated monitoring sites to spy on Soviet missile activities. Two months later, a Kremlin-backed coup overthrew the government of Grenada, in the Caribbean

– and in Nicaragua, central America, socialist rebels, the Sandinistas, deposed the regime of President Anastacio Somoza, which had been closely allied with Washington. The Kremlin's growing dominance in the Third World was reinforced by its provision of military weapons to client states, including Cuba and Libya, which heightened the White House's concerns and lead to the collapse of a proposed arms-limitation treaty between Washington and Moscow following the Soviet invasion of Afghanistan.

In his memorandum to President Carter, Brzezinski said the 'Soviets are likely to act decisively' in Afghanistan – and he was right. On 27 December, less than 72 hours into the invasion, Soviet forces killed the Afghan president Hafizullah Amin, a pro-Moscow leader who had only been in power for three months. The Kremlin had feared that Amin's background, including the time he had spent in New York studying at Columbia University in the late 1950s, meant that he could ultimately turn his back on Moscow to align himself with the West. Based on this assessment, and the KGB's suspicion that he had been a CIA agent, the Soviet leader, Leonid Brezhnev, approved his assassination.

A day before Amin and some of his supporters were lined up and shot, Brzezinski had urged Carter to be firmer with Moscow, instead of issuing 'expressions of concern' over its actions in Afghanistan which would largely be disregarded by its leadership. He said America's unwillingness to meaningfully stand up to the Kremlin could backfire domestically: 'Soviet "decisiveness" will be contrasted with our restraint, which will no longer be labelled as prudent but increasingly as timid.'

Brzezinski's warning arguably became a turning point in Carter's approach to Moscow. But instead of taking unilateral action, the president turned to his closest ally in the Five Eyes – Prime Minister of the United Kingdom, Margaret Thatcher.

During a phone call with the British premier on 28 December, President Carter stated that immediate action was required in response to Soviet hostility in Afghanistan. Thatcher, who had at that point been receiving, on Carter's orders, regular updates from the CIA about the situation in Kabul, agreed with the president. She had been at Downing Street for under a year but had an unflinching determination to project her authority onto geopolitics. The idea of mobilising Britain's spies against the Kremlin's interests hardly required a second thought as it served a dual purpose for Thatcher: a chance to secretly hurt the Communist regime in Moscow and the opportunity to sate her own obsession with the art of tradecraft. Since her entry into office, the prime minister had quickly familiarised herself with the dealings of MI5, MI6 and GCHQ and had become a voracious reader of their intelligence reports, much like Winston Churchill had done during World War II.

In late January 1980, within a month of Thatcher's conversation with Carter, Lord Carrington, now Foreign Secretary, had already developed plans for covert action against the Red Army invaders involving the provision of training and arms to the Mujahideen by MI6. The British secret intelligence agency and the CIA were in pursuit of the same goal in the fight against the Soviet invasion, but they went about it in different ways and, to a large extent, independently of one another. They also played by slightly different rules. The White House had banned the US agency's personnel from entering Afghanistan for fear of being discovered by Soviet troops and ultimately sparking a war with Moscow. As a result, CIA officials conducted their business from over the border in Pakistan, liaising with the country's own intelligence service to support the Mujahideen. Such restrictions did not apply to MI6: its officers were able to travel in and out of Afghanistan.

However, the CIA and MI6 faced similar frustrations in dealing with the Mujahideen because the rebels were not a homogenous group. They were tribal and urban cells fighting alongside different warlords who had their own political agendas and territories to protect. Some were also favoured more than others by the Pakistani intelligence service, the ISI, which operated as the gateway between the fighters and the covert support that Washington and London had been providing. The Pakistanis largely controlled the distribution of aid to the 'Peshawar Seven' – the group of Mujahideen warlords leading the battle against the Red Army. The money and weapons were then redistributed by the warlords to their respective field commanders and onto their tribal fighters in regions around the landlocked country.

One of the CIA's greatest recipients of funding and arms during the conflict was Jalaluddin Haqqani, a Pashtun tribesman who formed the Haqqani Network in the early 1970s with the intention of overthrowing the communist government in Afghanistan. Having trained militants in North Waziristan, Pakistan – on the southeast border of Afghanistan – for almost a decade, Haqqani was perceived by the CIA as a safe bet, especially because of his affiliations with other militant groups, including Hizb-e-Islami, a faction of which was led by Yunis Khalis – an Islamic scholar who was fighting Soviet troops in Afghanistan.

Instead of pinning its hopes on a Pashtun warlord like the CIA had done, MI6 was drawn to one of Tajik ethnicity, Ahmad Shah Massoud, predominantly for the territory he controlled in northern Afghanistan rather than fighting ability of his group, Jamiat-i-Islami. Massoud, merely in his late twenties, was idolised by the 150,000 people who lived in the Panjshir Valley, around ninety miles northeast of Kabul, and perceived as a revolutionary. The valley under Massoud's control had become a key target for Soviet artillery, as three quarters of Moscow's supplies transported by heavy vehicles for Kabul needed to go through the Salang highway that ran through the valley. It was there that his fighters conducted gun-and-run guerrilla operations against the Soviet Union, destroying its supplies and killing its men. Their operations were reinforced with a helping hand from Britain.

On meeting with MI6 representatives shortly after the Soviet invasion, Massoud had stated that his soldiers required specialist weaponry and training to continue their resistance. The British agency officials obliged, because although they were more seasoned at agent-running than at military operations, they had access to 'the circuit'– a group of former soldiers from Her Majesty's Special Forces who were both 'born adventurers and very skilled and capable' at warfare, according to a former British military official with close knowledge of their work. The retired Special Air Service and Special Boat Service soldiers on the circuit were predominantly in their early forties with a burning sense of patriotism and a proven track record for preserving national secrets. MI6 recruited the best among them into its 'semi-military' division known as the 'increment'.

A team of eight or so MI6 and increment officers would travel to a secret location in the Panjshir Valley twice a year under false identification, and at times under the cover story of being journalists, to provide 'plausible deniability' for the British government in case they were ever caught. The British teams would spend two to three weeks on each visit providing Massoud's fighters with training that ranged from the use of sniper rifles and mortars, to the creation of improvised explosive devices. The training ultimately delivered great dividends in the eyes of Massoud's fighters, leading to the destruction of hundreds of Soviet tanks and armoured vehicles.

The CIA had its own way of projecting plausible deniability about its covert operations to prop up the Mujahideen. Instead of providing US-made weaponry, the agency would purchase Soviet-designed arms, including AK-47 rifles and SA-7 shoulder-held anti-aircraft missiles, from countries such as Egypt and China, and send them to the battlefields of Afghanistan. 'This covert purchasing process not only covered US tracks, but ensured the availability of weapons that were compatible with the kind captured by the rebels from their Soviet-supplied enemies.'

While Washington and London were closely cooperating on plotting the Soviet Union's downfall through secret intervention in Afghanistan, their views, along with others in the Five Eyes, differed when it came to other matters of foreign affairs – namely, the participation in the 1980 Moscow Olympics. President Carter's Olympic boycott was disregarded by Britain and New Zealand but observed by Canada and Australia, yet again illustrating that intelligence alignment within the alliance did not automatically translate to agreement across all government areas. Malcolm Fraser's Australian government went even further in its bans against Moscow by putting an end to Australia's engagement with the Soviet Union on matters relating to academia, culture, and science and suspended some of its commercial contracts, including the exportation of grain. But perhaps the greatest decision made by Fraser was restricting visas to Soviet diplomats with previous intelligence connections. The restriction hampered Moscow's ability to send Kremlin spies to Australia under diplomatic cover and ultimately reduced the contact between Soviet and Australian officials across all government areas. On the flipside, ASIO did notice an uplift in contact between Soviet intelligence officials and the Australian media, presumably with the intention of trying to repair Moscow's image in the press.

The Western press had become a major front in undermining the Soviet armed forces in Afghanistan, particularly for MI6 and the CIA. Intelligence officials on both sides of the Atlantic wanted to draw public support for the Mujahideen and briefed their respective press contacts accordingly. The chief of MI6, Dickie Franks, even hosted a dinner party for media editors to extol the bravery of the battle-hardened Afghan men who were resisting Soviet troops. Franks told the editors that the unconventional fighters were not rebels as Moscow had pejoratively described them, but rather 'freedom fighters' and that the Kremlin was flouting international laws. The melodic phrase, 'freedom fighters', had already gained some traction and eventually became the defining attribute of the Islamic insurgency in the eyes of the both the Western world and Muslim nations. It had lived up to Brzezinski's appeal to President Carter to reinforce the covert operations with a 'propaganda campaign'.

The Mujahideen became a vehicle for Washington and London in their attempt to defeat the Soviet Union by proxy, and the glowing media campaigns favoured the Islamic insurgents and masked their nasty side, which included their appetite for violence, subjugation of women and disregard for human rights. The manipulation of the media also related to the stated date of the CIA's intervention in Afghanistan which had given the impression that it came after, and not before, the Soviet invasion. 'According to the official version of history, CIA aid to the Mujahideen began during 1980; that is to say, after the Soviet army invaded Afghanistan on 24 December 1979,' Brzezinski recalled years later. 'But the reality [...] is completely otherwise'. While the US did not push the Russians into intervening, 'we knowingly increased the probability that they would.

That secret operation was an excellent idea,' Brzezinski said. 'The effect was to draw the Russians into the Afghan trap.'

Brzezinski's influence over the US intelligence agencies during the Soviet–Afghan War had been somewhat curtailed by President Carter's single-term presidency. But the national security adviser's robust use of covert operations against Moscow was far from disregarded on Ronald Reagan's entry into the Oval Office in 1981. The new president scaled up Washington's offensive against Moscow to defy Soviet-backed aggression through the provision of more financial and armed support to the Mujahideen in Afghanistan and resistance movements in pro-Communist regimes across the globe, including Libya in North Africa, and Nicaragua in Latin America. President Reagan's aspirations of deposing Nicaragua's leadership were shared by the head of Argentina's ruling military government, President Leopoldo Galtieri. The Argentinian leader had been embraced by the White House for providing financing and training to the Contras, the right-wing opposition rebels who had been fighting the Sandinistas in Nicaragua since the socialist militants seized control of the nation in 1979. Galtieri soon realised that his closeness to Washington did not transcend the Special Relationship with the United Kingdom when he ordered the invasion of the Falkland Islands, in the South Atlantic, on 2 April 1982.

The surprise invasion of the Falklands, which Argentina claimed should be under its sovereignty despite the archipelago's status as a British colony since the first half of the nineteenth century, exposed an intelligence oversight by GCHQ and MI6, which had failed to foresee the military incursion. It was an embarrassment that led to the resignation of Foreign Secretary Lord Carrington, who was responsible for both intelligence agencies, and raised questions within Britain's intelligence community about whether US spy agencies had withheld information from London about the planned invasion to keep Galtieri's regime on side. The White House publicly adopted a neutral stance in the interest of tempering Buenos Aires's aggression and encouraging it to withdraw its troops. Away from the public spotlight, however, the US was secretly helping the UK against

Argentina. Washington provided intelligence to Britain, including aerial photography from the CIA with accompanying reports that identified that Argentinian forces on the ground had taken 'improved defensive positions' around the Falklands capital, Stanley. 'Argentine occupation forces had constructed approximately 16 defensive/weapons positions on the southern outskirts of Stanley', stated an intelligence report dated 28 May 1982, which detailed some of the aircraft that the invading nation had in its possession, including, 'one F-28, two probable Cessna 150-type aircraft, three Chinook, and one probable UH-1 [helicopter]'.

The US intelligence reports aided Britain in the Falklands after Margaret Thatcher had rebuffed Washington's suggestion of resorting to a diplomatic settlement with Argentina. The British prime minister had rejected a peace plan proposed by the Reagan Administration by which a third country, such as the US or Canada, would handle the negotiations with Buenos Aires and ensure the withdrawal of Argentine forces.

'The Prime Minister has the bit in her teeth,' the US Secretary of State, Alexander Haig, informed President Reagan in a cable on 9 April 1982, following a five-hour meeting with Thatcher and some of her key officials, including Defence Secretary John Nott. Haig said that Thatcher and her officials had not 'thought much about the diplomatic possibilities' and that the prime minister was 'clearly prepared to use force' and 'rigid in her insistence on a return to the status quo ante, and indeed seemingly determined that any solution involve some retribution. Her defence secretary is squarely behind her, though less ideological than she. He is confident of military success.' Thatcher, Haig reflected, 'wants nothing that would impinge on British authority'.

Along with receiving intelligence from the US, Britain's counter-offensive in the Falkland Islands was predominantly supported by GCHQ's interception of Argentina's order of battle that was being communicated between the country's navy and its warships at sea. The light cruiser ARA *General Belgrano* was among the vessels in the Argentinian fleet that had had not entered a total exclusion zone declared by Britain. The zone covered a 200 nautical-mile radius from the centre of the Falklands, and although *General Belgrano* had not entered, it had been deemed a threat after GCHQ intercepted communication in which the Argentinian navy had been ordered to attack the British military task force. On 2 May, a British nuclear-powered submarine torpedoed the junta's vessel, killing 323 people on board – almost half of Argentina's total military deaths during the conflict.

The Falklands War lasted 74 days and resulted in the junta's defeat in the summer of 1982. While British and US intelligence played a significant role in the mission, New Zealand, the most junior member of the Five Eyes, also lent a hand through its newly formed spy agency, the Government Communications Security Bureau (GCSB). The organisation's NR-1 listening station, also known as Irirangi, located around 165 miles north of Wellington, had been able to intercept Argentina's naval traffic in the South Pacific to provide its British counterpart with more clarity about the invader's battle plans. Until that point, New Zealand had largely existed, both in the context of intelligence and more generally across geopolitical issues, as an obliging member of the Five Eyes – pretty much up for anything within its capabilities to support the alliance. But much like Britain and Australia had earned the wrath of Washington after attempting to stand up to the White House during the previous decades in the Cold War, New Zealand decided to play its own hand of defiance in the mid-1980s.

Politicians are notorious for disregarding campaign promises once elected into office, but David Lange challenged that cliché on becoming Prime Minister of New Zealand in 1984. The former Liberal lawyer, who had entered parliament only seven years before seizing a landslide election victory for the Labour Party, had secured his meteoric rise to power by campaigning for nuclear disarmament. At 41, he was one of the youngest premiers in the country's history. He was also of a generation that had been critical of America's role in the Vietnam War and was unflinching about standing up to the superpower. Less than a year after taking over the helm in Wellington, Lange defied President Ronald Reagan by refusing to allow a US destroyer to access New Zealand ports, in keeping with his election campaign promise to ban nuclear-armed and nuclear-powered ships from entering the country's territorial waters. 'Whatever the truth of its armaments, its arrival in New Zealand would be seen as a surrender by the government,' Lange said of his government's decision to block the proposed visit of USS *Buchanan* in February 1985 despite an assurance that the nuclear-capable vessel would not be armed. He garnered international acclaim for maintaining his stance on nuclear weapons and made international headlines for going head-to-head with the Oval Office. Those who supported his view that nuclear weapons were morally indefensible perceived him as an idealist; his critics described him as a political opportunist.

The White House was among his critics and its reprisal for his defiance was swift. During a heated meeting with a US State Department official on 27 February, Lange was told that ANZUS, the tripartite, military treaty that had existed for 34 years between his country, the US and Australia, would be terminated with immediate effect. As would joint military exercises and public exchanges and interactions between the US armed forces and their counterparts in New Zealand. Lange was resolute in his position, saying the severance of military ties with Washington was a 'price we are prepared to pay' to remain nuclear-free, in spite of the potential security implications for his country. The global press had also been misled to believe that the fallout between Washington and the Kiwi nation was extended to the intelligence agreement between them. The press had been misinformed because although it had served Washington's interests to admonish its junior partner, and ultimately relegate Wellington from its status of 'ally' to 'friend', the five-country spy alliance was far too important to break up. Lieutenant General Lincoln D. Faurer, Director of the US National Security Agency – arguably the most powerful agency in the alliance – forcefully argued against voices in Washington who had favoured removing Wellington from the Five Eyes.

Almost four decades later, Admiral Mike Rogers, NSA director between 2014 and 2018, said that 'an interesting dimension of the Five Eyes structure is in some areas you can have a cooling of relationships and in other areas you are not impacted. So, the nuclear issue for New

Zealand – that had impact from a military perspective.' He said the NSA had made its case to the White House during the fallout between Washington and Wellington 'because we get so much value out of this that the price would far exceed the benefit if you actually just said, "Hey, we want to make it four eyes on SIGINT."' Rogers said the preservation of the signals intelligence partnership with Wellington during the crisis illustrated the flexibility within the Five Eyes alliance. 'You can have different levels of comfort and access in some areas as opposed to others,' he said. 'It's not an all or nothing – there's much more flexibility, much more finesse and much more resilience. Which again is a really powerful dimension to this and one of the reasons it has lasted for so long.'

New Zealand had been a late bloomer in the spy game, in contrast to other nations within the alliance. Although its signals experts had contributed to the Central Bureau set up in Australia during WWII by US General Douglas MacArthur to intercept Japanese communications, it was not until 1955 that the New Zealand Combined Signals Organisation (NZCSO) was created – one year before the country was brought into the Five Eyes. Its creation had been recommended by a senior British official from GCHQ, who also suggested that the proposed organisation would benefit from advanced training by posting a third of its staff at any one time to British and Australian signals stations. Although set up under New Zealand's Navy Office, the NZSCO was overseen by a signals committee that operated independently of the navy. From the time it was established to the late 1970s, it regularly posted officers overseas, including Singapore, where an interception facility near the centre of the island was operated by British and Australian officials, targeting South-East Asian countries. The agency's core work, however, remained at home where it handled New Zealand's signals interception from the NR-1 listening station, north of Wellington, liaising closely with its Five Eyes partners.

New Zealand's human-intelligence capability was also late to develop, emerging a decade after WWII. It was not until November 1956, one month after the official formation of the Five Eyes, that Wellington created the New Zealand Security Intelligence Service (NZSIS) with the help, and in the operational image, of MI5. The new agency immediately embraced the Five Eyes's Cold War mission, running joint operations with its Australian and British counterparts against Soviet targets, and received training and operational advice from the CIA. Its coming of age in the early 1960s followed a joint investigation with ASIO into the First Secretary of the Soviet Embassy in Canberra, Ivan Fedorovich Skripov, who had been using his diplomatic cover to conceal his work for the KGB. By then, Australia had re-established diplomatic relations with the Kremlin following the Petrov Affair in the previous decade, even though ASIO had been aware that Soviet spies were still operating in its country. The joint investigation into Skripov exposed him as a spy and led to his expulsion from Australia in February 1963.

Alongside its counterespionage work, the NZSIS had also been focused on vetting government employees during the 1960s and 1970s to prevent the inadvertent appointment of subversives to the civil service. The country's human-intelligence organisation had become respected among its Five Eyes counterparts, but New Zealand was eager to improve and expand its signals operations. It created the Government Communications Security Bureau (GCSB) in 1977 as a successor to its post-war signals agency. The intelligence derived from the newly-formed organisation became of great importance for the NSA – so much so that the US agency was desperate to preserve the relationship, despite the fall out between the Lange Government and Reagan Administration in 1985. The GCSB had become prolific at spying on radio and satellite communications through its interception station in Tangimoana, in New Zealand's north island, targeting a range of foreign nations, including China, Vietnam, Japan, Egypt and East Germany.

Despite Wellington's remaining position in the Five Eyes, Washington reduced the intelligence it shared with the GCSB, forcing it to shoulder the burden of bridging the signals gap. The agency received more government funding to expand its workforce and capabilities, and while it continued receiving intelligence reports from within the Five Eyes on the conflict between Iran and Iraq and the ongoing Soviet–Afghan War, it failed to identify a plot to bomb Greenpeace's flagship vessel, *Rainbow*

Warrior, at the port of Auckland. The bombing in July 1985, authorised by France – an ally of New Zealand – had been intended to stop the ship from protesting a planned French nuclear test in the southern pacific, and had led to the death of a crew member. While the French government initially denied any involvement, it struggled to maintain the lie in the face of public outrage and ultimately fired its defence minister and the head of its foreign intelligence service, the DGSE, over the incident of the *Rainbow Warrior*. Diplomatic relations were expectedly strained between Wellington, which deemed the bombing a terrorist act, and Paris. Some intelligence officials in the island nation also questioned whether the NSA-operated listening station in Yakima, Washington State, had intercepted any French communication that foreshadowed the bombing and withheld it from New Zealand as a repercussion for its anti-nuclear stance.

Lange counterbalanced his dilemmas with Paris and Washington with an eagerness to be perceived as independent on foreign affairs, rather than a US-stooge. The rift with President Reagan had quickly played into Moscow's hands as it tried to increase its regional influence in the Oceanic region at the expense of Washington. But the New Zealand's prime minister saw through the Soviet cheers of his anti-nuclear policies, according to a declassified CIA report. 'The Key Soviet goal in Oceania is the reduction of Western influence, particularly the denial of US military access,' said the report, dated July 1987. 'Specific Soviet objectives are to disrupt the ANZUS relationship and to encourage the transformation of the region into a nuclear-free zone.' The CIA believed that the Kremlin would 'continue to pursue commercial relationships with the South Pacific states', but that Lange would rebuff its attempts. The prime minister, said the CIA, wanted to avoid any economic arrangements with Moscow which could be construed as 'opening the door to closer Soviet–New Zealand relations'.

The CIA's concerns about Moscow's ambition to draw Wellington closer coincided with the Kremlin's unrelenting effort to infiltrate western government agencies, including in Britain, where an MI5 officer, Michael Bettaney, had been sentenced to a 23-years' imprisonment in

1984 after trying to offer his services to the KGB. Bettaney's potential damage to British intelligence was curtailed by a tipoff from the deputy station head of the KGB in London, Oleg Gordievsky, who had been working as a spy for MI6. Gordievsky's motivation to become a double agent followed the invasion of Czechoslovakia by Soviet and Warsaw Pact troops in August 1968 – an event which like the Hungarian Revolution 12 years earlier helped Moscow reinforce its grip on the Eastern Bloc, displaced hundreds of thousands of people, and resulted in no active support from the West. Gordievsky had already been disillusioned with the Soviet regime's aggression by that point. But the Kremlin's crushing of anti-Moscow resistance by Czech protestors during the 'Prague Spring' ultimately led him to begin spying for MI6 in the early 1970s. Before defecting to Britain in 1985, Gordievsky had provided his British handlers with intelligence that the Kremlin's had misinterpreted Operation Able Archer, a military exercise between the US and its NATO allies in 1983, as preparation for a pre-emptive nuclear strike against Moscow. His intelligence was shared with the White House and CIA to help illustrate the paranoia of the Kremlin's leadership. And it was against the backdrop of that atmosphere of extreme distrust between the East and West that Langley wanted to expand its covert operations in Afghanistan where the Red Army was still locked in battle with the Mujahideen.

By the mid-1980s, the CIA was ploughing around US$700,000 a year into supporting the insurgency – more than MI6's entire agency budget. The British agency was still in the game, however. Through Pakistan's Inter-Services Intelligence, which had maintained its stranglehold on covert action in Afghanistan, MI6 was providing the Mujahideen with limpet bombs to blow up Soviet barges. It reportedly also lent a helping hand to the Pakistanis and the CIA in conducting guerrilla operations in neighbouring Uzbekistan and Tajikistan. The operations targeted Soviet troops through whom Moscow had been funnelling supplies to the Red Army in Afghanistan.

MI6 efforts in propping up the insurgency in Afghanistan had not been overlooked by the CIA, but the British agency's commitment paled in significance to that of its US counterpart. MI6 provided ineffectual 'Blowpipe', shoulder-fired surface-to-air missiles, and had only been able to supply 500,000 rounds of ammunition for imperial-vintage British rifles used by the Mujahideen, despite the CIA's request for 400 million of such bullets. A year later, in 1986, the CIA armed the Mujahideen with 'Stinger' surface-to-air missiles. It was a strategy that would change the course of the war in Afghanistan.

Ten Mujahideen from a faction of Hizb-i-Islami, a militant group that had been receiving arms and funding from the CIA, arrived at a secret training camp in Rawalpindi, northern Pakistan, in the late summer of 1986 to familiarise themselves with a new weapon. The Soviet invasion of their country had been raging for seven years, and despite their ongoing resistance, the AK47 rifles and mortars used by the Mujahideen in general were some way from overpowering the Red Army's weaponry, and in particular, its aircraft. That was about to end when the CIA introduced the ten militants to Stingers – lightweight missiles propelled by portable, shoulder-held launchers, which use an infrared sensor to lock onto the heat of an aircraft's exhaust.

Over the period of one month, the small team of Mujahideen were trained to use Stingers, learning how to balance and aim the launchers on their shoulders, and initially used dummy missiles to target objects in the distance. Only eight of the ten trainees were deemed fit to move on to real ammunition and were dispatched in two teams to Afghanistan. One unit was tasked with shooting Soviet planes carrying troops in Kabul, and the other went after Hind helicopters – heavily armoured gunships that had claimed the lives of many civilians and Mujahideen since the start of the invasion.

On the afternoon of 26 September 1986, the Afghan team in pursuit of Hind helicopters made their way into farmland on the outskirts of Jalalabad, eastern Afghanistan, to put their training to practice. Overhead, a flight of about ten Hind helicopters was making its way to an airfield, preceded by the cacophony of their propellers. One of the Afghan trainees on the ground aimed his Stinger missile at one of the helicopters which suddenly burst into flames and nosedived to land. It was a joyous moment for the Mujahideen trainees celebrating below; one that would eventually be celebrated by all Five Eyes nations. The success of the CIA's experiment encouraged it to send more than 2,000 Stingers to the Mujahideen.

In November 1987, President Reagan even invited five Mujahideen leaders for a meeting at the White House, including Yunis Khalis, head of a faction of the Hizbut-i-Islami rebel group and newly elected first chairman of the Islamic Alliance of Afghan Mujahideen. 'The support that the United States has been providing the resistance will be strengthened, rather than diminished, so that it can continue to fight effectively for freedom,' the US President told the media following his meeting. While Reagan refrained from elaborating on what 'support' he had in mind, the CIA's backing of the Mujahideen had by then grown by more than seven-hundred times – from US$700,000 annually in the mid-1980s, to US$500 million a year. The agency spent a total of around US$3 billion over the course of its covert operations in Afghanistan, but its introduction of the Stingers into the war was hailed as a key to forcing the Soviet Union's retreat. Moscow signed bilateral agreements with Islamabad, Kabul and Washington, collectively known as the Geneva Accords, and started withdrawing its 115,000 troops from Afghanistan in May 1988, with the last of them retreating the following February.

The withdrawal was the final nail in the coffin for the militarily and economically defeated Soviet Union – a fact only reinforced by the collapse in November 1989 of the Berlin Wall which had divided Communist East Germany from West Germany for 28 years. The fall of the Iron Curtain ultimately spelled the end of Communism in Eastern and Central Europe, the breakup of the Soviet Union on Christmas Day of 1991 and the resignation of its leader, Mikhail Gorbachev. It was a seismic moment, celebrated by the Mujahideen in Afghanistan. In April 1992, the rebels toppled the Kremlin-installed government of President Mohammed Najibullah and eventually killed him. A new era began in Kabul, which attracted a Saudi national who had spent time in Afghanistan in the 1980s supporting the anti-Soviet struggle by financing the airfares and accommodation costs of jihadists travelling into the country from overseas, particularly Arab nations. The Saudi man in his twenties had close links with some of the Mujahideen leaders but he had not registered on the CIA's radar, and nor had his small organisation, the Afghan Bureau Service. His name was Osama Bin Laden.

In 1988, six months before the Red Army completed its withdrawal from Afghanistan, Bin Laden had been emboldened by the insurgency's victory over the Soviet Union. He had also amassed a loyalty among Mujahideen and Arab volunteers, from countries in North Africa, Asia and the Middle East, who shared a common purpose: holy war. Bin Laden created Al Qaeda, a militant organisation with the initial aim of relocating the jihadist struggle to other countries. He identified his new target when American troops were deployed to Saudi Arabia at the invitation of the ruling in 1990. While the US military was ostensibly there to safeguard the Saudis from their hostile neighbour, Iraq – which had invaded Kuwait in August of that year – Bin Laden was opposed to America protecting the birthplace of prophet Mohammed: to him, that was a duty for Muslim fighters, not disbelievers, or 'infidels'.

He left Saudi Arabia for Sudan to coordinate the early terrorist attacks against the US, including the New York World Trade Centre bombing in 1993, after which Bin Laden returned to the safety of Afghanistan to continue his mission. The CIA's station chief in Islamabad, Bill Murray, noticed an increasing number of former Arab volunteers who no longer had a jihad to fight in Afghanistan, attending training camps in the Federally Administered Tribal Areas (FATA) in northwest Pakistan. 'They were training in FATA for this concept of universal jihad,' he said. The Arab fighters first became 'cannon fodder' in the first Chechen War against Russia in the mid 1990s. And at some point between the end of the Soviet–Afghan War and 1996, the former Mujahideen leader Jalaluddin Haqqani became one of Bin Laden's 'closest mentors', according to the US Office of the Director of National Intelligence. The Pashtun leader headed the Haqqani Network that had been a major beneficiary of CIA funding and arms during the conflict. His organisation, designated by Washington as a terrorist network years later, specialised in small-arms assaults, rocket attacks, suicide bombings and improvised explosives, among other things. Haqqani provided Bin Laden with training centres in the southeastern region of Afghanistan, where some of the Haqqani Network operations were based. It helped Al Qaeda plot its terrorist attacks against US-interests, including, in June 1996, blowing up a fuel truck at a US military complex in Saudi Arabia, killing 19 American soldiers and wounding nearly 400.

Zbigniew Brzezinski, who had long retired from his role as the White House's National Security Advisor, maintained his support for the US strategy in Afghanistan, despite the growing number of Islamist terrorist attacks around the world. In January 1998, when asked by a French publication, *Le Nouvel Observateur*, if he had any regrets about the way he had supported 'Islamic fundamentalism' during the Soviet– Afghan conflict, he said: 'What is more important in world history? The Taliban or the collapse of the Soviet empire? Some agitated Muslims or the liberation of Central Europe and the end of the Cold War?'

Seven months after the interview, one of those 'agitated Muslims', Bin Laden, orchestrated the bombing of the US embassy in Tanzania, killing more than 224 people, including twelve Americans. Three years later, the Al Qaeda leader would initiate the biggest terrorist attack on a western nation to date. The 11 September 2001 attacks on the United States – the worst on its home soil since Pearl Harbor in 1941 – killed around 3,000 people and exposed monumental failures within the country's intelligence agencies. Bin Laden had drawn the Five Eyes into a new conflict: the War on Terror.

PART THREE:
THE WAR ON TERROR

CHAPTER TEN

A POST 9/11 WORLD

ON 12 SEPTEMBER 2001, three British intelligence officials arrived at Brize Norton air force base in Oxfordshire, northwest of London, hoping to travel across the Atlantic. Their unannounced arrival caught the base commander by surprise. As did their proposed destination, the United States, which seemed like an impossible mission as the North American airspace was closed in the wake of the previous day's terrorist attacks on the US. The station commander was sceptical about who they said they were despite introducing themselves as Richard Dearlove, chief of MI6, Francis Richards, head of GCHQ, and Eliza Manningham-Buller, deputy director-general of MI5. 'The commander refused to believe who we were,' said Manningham-Buller. She had joined Dearlove and Richards on the mission that day in lieu of MI5's director-general who was required to remain in London to brief prime minister Tony Blair about the threat of Al Qaeda. Aside from her seniority and operational experience, Manningham-Buller was the most suitable MI5 representative to be included on the US trip because of the close working relationships she had established in Washington's intelligence community over the previous two decades.

Having joined MI5 in 1975 in her late twenties following a brief stint as a secondary-school teacher, she had worked on some of the agency's most secretive mission, including the successful hunt for a spy in her own service, Michael Bettaney, and the debriefing of former KGB colonel Oleg Gordievsky following his defection to the UK in 1985. Manningham-Buller had neither been deterred nor intimidated by the male-dominated intelligence community in which she existed, but turned down a job to become the agency's deputy senior liaison officer in Washington in the 1980s because she had been told that the FBI's representative in the capital 'would not deal with a woman' from MI5. She did however take up the more senior role in the subsequent decade, and by the late 1990s, had become a respected figure in the Five Eyes intelligence community and likely a future head of MI5. So it made complete sense to deploy Manningham-Buller as the face of her organisation to Washington on September 12. She and her two colleagues were delayed by more than an hour as Brize Norton's commander made inquiries about the viability of their journey which had already been authorised by Prime Minister Tony Blair and President George W. Bush.

The British delegation was flown on a VC-10 airplane which was ultimately escorted by several F-16 fighter jets to Andrews Air Force Base (Joint Base Andrews), outside Washington, DC. From there, they were taken by motorcade to the CIA headquarters at Langley. During a meeting hosted by George Tenet, the CIA's director, and attended by high-ranking officials, including NSA director-general Michael Hayden, discussed the deployment of joint capabilities against Al Qaeda. Much like President Roosevelt's emissary, William Donovan, who had travelled to Britain at the beginning of World War II to determine the support required by Prime Minister Winston Churchill, or the Sinkov Mission in 1941 which kick-started the exchange of signals intelligence between Arlington Hall and Bletchley Park, Manningham-Buller, Dearlove and Richards were to make history. The Special Relationship between London and Washington was about to be intensified and so was the information sharing and operational coordination between the Five Eyes.

The unifying threat that the alliance had faced during the Cold War had ended a decade earlier with the collapse of the Soviet Union.

While the Five Eyes remained structurally intact, the very purpose of its creation, tailored to combat the Kremlin's aggression, seemed rather outdated. Member countries of the alliance still faced threats – but not collectively. MI5 and its sister agencies in the UK, for instance, had been locked into the final stages of the Troubles that had been escalating for three decades. Also known as the Northern Ireland conflict, Protestant loyalists and unionist paramilitaries in favour of remaining part of the United Kingdom were at war with nationalists elements, including the Irish Republican Army (IRA), who were determined to end British rule in Northern Ireland. The IRA's terrorist attacks stretched beyond its paramilitary base in Northern Ireland and into England and even mainland Europe, killing many innocent civilians in their wake. In 1990, two Australian tourists were shot dead in Holland by the IRA after they had been mistaken for off-duty, British soldiers. It was a case that naturally drew the attention of the Australian security service, ASIO, which had been monitoring potential IRA plots against British interests in Australia but had been unable to find any evidence, despite identifying a source of financial support for the paramilitary organisation in the country.

The lessons learned by MI5 and its British sister agencies throughout the Troubles, from agent recruitment, to penetration and disruption of terrorism plots, provided a greater understanding of tackling Al Qaeda not only for the United Kingdom, but for the rest of the Five Eyes. 'Countering IRA terrorism is a major part of the life and history of MI5,' said Manningham-Buller. 'It also meant that we were better prepared to deal with Al Qaeda; we had protocols in place to deal with terrorist threats with the police.'

However, while the IRA's activities were globally known, its operations were predominantly domestic – often using conventional weapons such as bombs and carried out by terrorists who wanted to avoid being captured or killed in the process. In many cases, they had even provided warnings ahead of their attacks to limit the amount of carnage while still making a political point. Unlike the IRA, Al Qaeda was global in its ambition and reach. It presented the Five Eyes with a unified threat – and one that was far more difficult to predict and contain than the enemies the alliance had faced during the Cold War. Those who espoused Al Qaeda's views were often willing to die for their cause. They were everywhere but nowhere – a stateless phenomenon bound by a poisonous, religious ideology that could not be easily targeted and bombed out of existence. They wanted to cause maximum carnage. To them, anyone was fair game: Muslims and non-Muslims, military personnel and civilians. Even women and children were not spared.

Al Qaeda did not rely on sophisticated encryption methods to communicate, plot and recruit, but instead on like-minded people who had embraced a selective and warped interpretation of Islam. Its worldview was also shared by fringe preachers who perpetuated a hatred of the West and an 'Us and Them' mentality among their fanatical followers. Such behaviour had largely been dismissed as 'radical', rather than a serious national security threat by the Five Eyes before the September 11 attacks. 'After 9/11, we were suddenly dealing with a cross-border, non-state organisation with a presence in many countries and no one member of the Five Eyes was ever going to be able to combat it alone,' said a former Australian intelligence official. 'A terrorist plot or attack in the Middle East could lead to something in Melbourne, Australia, and so on. Yes, the CIA is the octopus that has tentacles everywhere, but they had suddenly been stretched beyond their capabilities.'

The CIA and MI6, which had thrived during the Soviet–Afghan War, coordinating their operations from a distance and through a proxy – the Mujahideen – suddenly found themselves on the back foot after the attacks on America, with little to no Arabic-speaking analysts within their ranks or those of their Five Eyes partners. The alliance had underestimated Al Qaeda and needed to quickly adapt. Instead of cryptographers, they required more agent-runners; instead of being predominantly focused on SIGINT, they needed to expand their HUMINT capabilities. The distinction between domestic and foreign intelligence became blurred. According to Peter Clarke, Scotland Yard's former head of counterterrorism, MI5 started working more closely with the Metropolitan Police. The intelligence gathered and assessed by MI5 became the 'lifeblood of counterterrorism work in the UK' and joint objectives and investigative strategies between the security service and the police became 'daily routine', he said.

MI5, which had historically been focused on domestic threats, also wanted to lead on all intelligence relating to Islamist terrorism, including that which had been generated overseas and that had typically been the responsibility of its sister agency, MI6. And while the relationship between the CIA and British intelligence had predominantly been handled and, some would say, monopolised by MI6 before the War on Terror, MI5 managed to establish a direct connection with Langley. The closer cooperation between London and Washington, reinforced by Manningham-Buller and her two British colleagues during their meeting with US officials, immediately expanded to include other intelligence agencies of the other Five Eyes nations.

In late 2001, counterterrorism developments started taking place in Australia where ASIO and ASIS, the domestic and foreign intelligence services respectively, set up a unit with representation from both agencies for addressing Islamist threats emerging in Indonesia, Malaysia, Thailand and the Philippines. 'We pooled information and expertise on the Asia-Pacific region and worked very closely with our Five Eyes partners, and especially the CIA and FBI,' according to the former Australian intelligence official who helped oversee the joint operations. Tradecraft secrets, tipoffs and raw intelligence were exchanged between alliance members in an attempt to get ahead of future terrorist attacks. 'Intelligence-sharing becomes a greater imperative because the terrorist threat is global,' the former official said. 'The sharing of assessments on terrorist intent and capabilities is also crucial to effective counterterrorism.'

However, intelligence assessments are not an exact science. One of the CIA's assessments of Osama Bin Laden had raised concerns about the Al Qaeda leader's intent on hijacking US aircrafts almost three years before the September 11 attacks. In a Presidential Daily Brief, dated 4 December 1998, the agency alerted President Bill Clinton to a tipoff the agency had received from British intelligence which indicated that Al Qaeda had been 'preparing for attacks in the US, including an aircraft hijacking' and that 'some of the Bin Laden network have received hijack training [...] but no group directly tied to Bin Laden's Al Qaeda organisation has ever carried out an aircraft hijacking'. While the CIA had been informed that Al Qaeda 'are moving closer to implementing anti-US attacks at unspecified locations' Langley's intelligence officials had been unable to determine that they had related to 'attacks on aircraft'.

In the summer of 2001, two months before the attacks on America, Washington informed MI5 and MI6 that Al Qaeda had been developing major terror plots but ones that would likely target foreign-based US interests, including those in Kuwait, Bahrain, Saudi Arabia and Kenya, rather than mainland America. MI5 also had its own leads on Al Qaeda's threat against the West. Its intelligence coverage indicated that Bin Laden had been planning a range of attacks, including vehicles and suicide bombs, that would most likely target US interests abroad, including those in the Gulf States or the Middle East and Turkey. But despite the intelligence assessments and the increased chatter between Al Qaeda operatives that had been intercepted in 2001 by agencies within the Five Eyes, none had been able to stop the 19 terrorists who hijacked US civilian planes and crashed them into America's most iconic cites, including the Twin Towers in New York and the Pentagon building, near the heart of the US capital.

Several hours into the crisis talks at Langley, which dragged into the late evening of 12 September 2001, Eliza Manningham-Buller and her British colleagues felt appreciated by their American hosts. Their visit, in the hour of need, helped mitigate the distress felt by Washington's intelligence community. Yet the sense of self-blame felt by CIA officers and their domestic counterparts intensified their overwhelming desire for retribution. A military response was already under consideration, not only by the US, but also Britain. Earlier that day, shortly after Manningham-Buller, Dearlove and Richards had left Brize Norton for their journey to Langley, Lieutenant General Graeme Lamb, boarded a Royal Air Force plane from the same base.

As the head of Britain's Special Forces, which include the Special

Air Service (SAS), Lamb had been sent to the US by the British prime minister to personally assess the military and intelligence reaction to the attacks. Over several days, he conducted a brief tour of America's key intelligence and military facilities, including the CIA, and Fort Bragg, North Carolina, headquarters of the Joint Special Operations Command, counterpart to Britain's Special Forces. Lamb's assessment, based on a person familiar with his findings, was that some US officials 'felt personally responsible, as though the September 11 attacks were an indication of their own failure as military or intelligence professionals. That mindset dominated their thoughts, their proposed strategies and everything in between.'

On returning to Britain, Lamb travelled to Chequers, the official country residence of the prime minister in Buckinghamshire, southeast England, to brief Tony Blair on his findings. He told Blair that every official he had met during his US visit had been 'emotionally compromised' by the terrorist attacks on their country. Lamb is said to have told the prime minister that people 'don't make good decisions when they're emotionally compromised'. He was correct. The decisions around the plan of retaliation against Al Qaeda were not made by sober military and intelligence assessments. Even worse, they were heavily influenced, and arguably, dictated, by political leaders – namely Tony Blair and George W. Bush – who always thought they knew better than the intelligence and military officials advising them. 'Whether it's the military or intelligence communities, they are made up of departments working for a political authority,' a British official said. 'Decisions made by them are inbuilt with bias towards their master's opinion.'

Neither the White House nor Downing Street had to look for too long to identify what they deemed as reliable intelligence to bolster their political mission. It was a mission far greater than simply finding Bin Laden who it emerged had been hiding in Afghanistan. Bush and Blair also wanted to take the fight to an old foe – the Iraqi dictator, Saddam Hussein. Was he in any way linked to Al Qaeda? What were his connections to Bin Laden? Surely, the dictator had stockpiled some chemical weapons which could end up in the hands of terrorists or be used by his own regime against the West? Such is the nature of intelligence-gathering that the answers to questions, including the ones that had been asked by the US Administration and British government following the 9/11 attacks, often appear in fragments – like random pieces of a jigsaw puzzle that can form a part of the picture but leave the rest of it open to interpretation.

While intelligence officials on both sides of the Atlantic were making inquiries into Saddam's weapons, the US and Britain mobilised elite members of their armed forces, along with intelligence officers, for military intervention in Afghanistan, prioritising the hunt for Bin Laden. By late September, around fifty CIA officers and three hundred US Special Forces personnel were sent to Afghanistan to target Al Qaeda and topple the Taliban – the militant, Islamic regime that had been harbouring Bin Laden and which had refused to hand him over to Washington. The US effort was initially bolstered by about 100 British Special Forces personnel, including members of the Special Boat Service, drawn from the Royal Military Commandos and specialising in highly classified, undercover raids. MI6 officers were also on hand. The British agency had already been 'conducting counter-drugs and international terrorism work on Afghanistan' and 'had established a network of contacts', which its officers were able to draw on after the British government authorised their deployment to the country on 28 September 2001 to 'support the US-led military and covert action'.

The British and American teams coordinated their ground raids with aerial strikes around the country, including Kabul, Kandahar and Jalalabad. Their efforts were also supported by the Northern Alliance, an Islamic military front that had been fighting the Taliban regime since its takeover of the country five years earlier. The Taliban stood little chance, collapsing on 13 November, around six weeks after the US and British intervention. While the swift victory generated glowing headlines in the West, and kudos for the political leaderships in Washington and London, it rang somewhat hollow because Bin Laden was nowhere to be found, despite an effort by British and US special forces who had trudged around Tora Bora, eastern Afghanistan, in search of the Al Qaeda leader.

Tora Bora was an unusual setting. It covers a section of the Spin Ghar, or White Mountains, and stretches about six miles long and as many miles wide across numerous narrow valleys and jagged peaks as high as 14,000 feet. A British Special Forces commander said the conditions at Tora Bora made the search for Bin Laden practically impossible. 'The idea that either the Brits or American had a technological handle on Bin Laden's whereabouts was unrealistic because he was not stupid,' he said. 'We did not own any of the communications infrastructure in Afghanistan. Also, he would have known not to use a mobile phone or sat phone to avoid capture. Most of his comms would have been done through word of mouth.' By late 2001, it emerged that British and American units in Tora Bora had requested reinforcement to try to close in on Al Qaeda's leader, but the Pentagon refused to commit ground troops to what it had rightly or wrongly considered a futile attempt to secure the border to Pakistan – to where Bin Laden ultimately escaped. 'The notion of blocking the borders of Tora Bora is completely mythical,' said the British commander. 'Even if you were able to get a pile of soldiers, stand them shoulder to shoulder like a Praetorian guard for the Roman Empire, Bin Laden would still have found his way out by taking a different route out.' The commander added that there was no sense of exactly where Bin Laden was, nor exactly how he had escaped – just rumours, often propagated by local warlords who were corruptible and would not have thought twice about taking a financial bribe from Bin Laden to smuggle him out of Afghanistan.

While Bin Laden managed to initially get away, one of his senior operatives, Ibn Sheik Al-Libi, who had been overseeing a militant training camp near Tora Bora, did not. He was captured by Pakistani forces after fleeing over the Afghan border. The Libyan national was turned over to the CIA in January 2002 before being 'renditioned' to Egypt – a process under which the agency was able to relocate detainees to countries with little to no regard for human rights, let alone regulations on the treatment of prisoners. Al-Libi was subjected to hours of torture, confessing to alleged plots, including one to blow up the US Embassy in Yemen, and he provided information relating to the whereabouts of some senior Al Qaeda militants. He also claimed that 'Iraq was supporting Al Qaeda and providing assistance with chemical and biological weapons'. His revelations were on par with hitting the jackpot for the CIA which at the time was still under pressure to produce evidence linking Al Qaeda to the Iraqi regime, and Saddam to biological weapons.

Al-Libi's claims helped reinforce a narrative about the ties between the terrorist organisation and the Iraqi dictator that was being perpetuated by the Bush Administration. US Vice President Dick Cheney gave credence to uncorroborated intelligence from the Czech government that Mohammed Atta, the ringleader of the 9/11 attacks, had met with an Iraqi intelligence officer in Prague before the attacks on the US. While Britain's intelligence community was generally dubious about Bin Laden's links to the Iraqi leader, Tony Blair's obsession with obtaining evidence relating to Saddam's biological weapons remained undimmed. He and President Bush stepped up the pressure on their spy chiefs to determine the threat from Baghdad. And who better to provide some insights on the dictator's alleged biological weapons than a self-proclaimed chemical engineer who had fled Iraq before the turn of the millennium to seek political asylum in Germany.

Rafid Ahmed Alwan Al-Janabi was unlike other tourists arriving at Munich International Airport in November 1999. Although travelling on a tourist visa, he had little interest in checking out the historical sites in the capital city of Bavaria, southeast of Germany. He had hoped that the visa in his passport would be a gateway to a better life. All he needed was the opportunity to tell his well-rehearsed, heart-breaking story – and he found his audience in immigration officers at the airport. He told them that he had fled his native Iraq, fearing for his life, after embezzling money from Saddam Hussein's brutal regime. In a mixture of Arabic and broken English, Al-Janabi relayed the apparently harrowing events surrounding his escape in a bid for political asylum.

The story that had been provided by the Baghdad-born asylum seeker to immigration officers resulted in his transferral to a refugee centre in Zirndorf, around 100 miles north of Munich, in preparation for a host of procedures, including interviews and identity checks. Applications for political asylum can be stressful and laborious at the best of times, but Al-Janabi, aged 31, figured out a short-cut to expedite his case. The Iraqi engineer came up with an even more compelling narrative for his escape from Baghdad – one which would draw the attention of the German Federal Intelligence Service (BND) and, eventually, the Five Eyes.

He told German intelligence officials that he had been recruited by Iraq's Military Industrial Commission in 1994 – while studying at Baghdad University's engineering school – to oversee a group of engineers building mobile biological-weapons labs. The labs, he claimed, were approximately seven trucks repurposed into warfare vehicles, fitted out with equipment to manufacture weapons of mass destruction (WMDs). Some of the equipment was even German made, he said. Al-Janabi would undoubtedly have hoped that the story he had spun would create some intrigue, even if he may not have known that it would ultimately sate the West's obsession with Saddam's biological programme, which UN weapons inspectors had been trying to expose since the end of the first Gulf War in 1991. Within a few months of his initial debriefing, the Iraqi fantasist was granted political asylum and relocated to an apartment, as German intelligence officials continued interviewing him about his story well into the summer of 2001. The Germans shared a lot of their interview findings with MI6 and the US Defense Intelligence Agency (DIA), but kept Al-Janabi's identity secret and refused to provide direct access to him. He was codenamed 'Curveball' by the Americans, but he was very much a German asset and Germany's alone. And an asset, like the intelligence they produce, is a product. The control and ownership of such a product is imperative for both the reputation of an intelligence agency and an agent handler, and the amount of operational, personal and political capital they can leverage from it.

To help maintain their hold on Curveball, the Germans even claimed he was unable to speak English and that he hated Americans. Of course the language barrier had been a minor hurdle that could easily have been navigated by a trusted interpreter, but the Germans had another agenda: they were concerned about the potential backlash that would emerge if it were discovered that Saddam's biological weapons featured German equipment, as Curveball had told them. Nonetheless, the Germans provided 100 reports from their debriefings with Curveball to the DIA which ultimately shared them with other agencies in the US intelligence community. On a technical level, Curveball's information was deemed credible by some of those who had access to it in Washington, particularly some CIA officials who were eager to assure the Bush Administration which appeared increasingly determined about going to war with Iraq. However, other US officials, and MI6 analysts, were sceptical about the veracity of Curveball's information.

One evaluation by a DIA biological-weapons analyst concluded that Curveball's accounts were inconsistent and should not be completely relied on. 'Overall, the fact that the source may be valuable and the reporting appears to be of major significance are presently compromised by the reporting inconsistencies.' A US Department of Defense detailee, the only American official to ultimately be given direct access to Curveball in the lead up to the Iraq War, stated that the Iraqi source had a 'terrible hangover' on the morning of their meeting and said that further inquiries should be made about him before relying on him as the 'backbone of one of our major findings of the existence of a continuing Iraqi BW [biological-weapons] program!'.

The concerns that had been expressed by members of the intelligence communities in Washington and London about Curveball's reliability were largely disregarded by Downing Street and the White House. On 12 September 2002, President George W. Bush addressed the UN General Assembly, declaring that the Iraqi regime was continuing to 'develop weapons of mass destruction' and that the 'first time we may be completely certain he has a nuclear weapons [sic] is when, God forbid, he uses one. We owe it to all our citizens to do everything in our power to prevent that day from coming'. In a nicely coordinated double-act, Bush's counterpart in Britain was preparing to deliver his own message about the situation in Baghdad. The evidence he was about to provide was the result of an assessment by the Joint Intelligence Committee (JIC) into the case for weapons of mass destruction in Iraq. The assessment, which became known as the 'September Dossier', or 'Iraq Dossier', was overseen by the JIC's chairman, John Scarlett, a former MI6 officer and Russia expert who had built his credentials on running Oleg Gordievsky before the KGB officer defected to the Britain 1985. Scarlett had overseen the content in the Iraq Dossier, which featured intelligence obtained by MI6, including that which had been provided by Curveball via the Germans.

On 24 September, Blair addressed parliament to outline his fears about the dossier's findings which he said had raised a 'current and serious threat to the UK national interest'. The prime minister said the dossier was 'extensive, detailed and authoritative' and it had concluded that 'Iraq has chemical and biological weapons, that Saddam has continued to produce them, that he has existing and active military plans for the use of chemical and biological weapons, which could be activated within 45 minutes, including against his own Shia population, and that he is actively trying to acquire nuclear weapons capability'. Blair also assured parliament that the threat from Saddam was 'not imagined' and that his weapons were real, not based on 'American or British propaganda'. The British leader said he was not after military conflict but rather a UN-led 'process of disarmament' and believed that the 'ending of this regime would be the cause of regret for no one other than Saddam.'

A British military official, who regularly briefed Blair on matters relating to Iraq and Afghanistan during that time, said the prime minister's determination to align London with Washington's foreign policy reinforced the fact that the UK's interest since World War II had laid in favour of America over Europe. 'We are European by proximity, but by and large Europe had been a trading space for economic purposes,' he said. 'But our value on the global interests lay in shared values and freedoms with the US. And Blair obviously recognised the crucial importance of siding with US foreign policy when it came to the issue of Iraq.'

While Blair made absolutely no mention of the alleged links between Saddam and Al Qaeda during his parliamentary address in September 2002, the following month, President Bush gave a public speech in

Cincinnati, Ohio, in which he claimed that the Iraqi dictator's regime had trained members of Bin Laden's organisation in 'bomb-making and poisons and deadly gas' and that 'Iraq could decide on any given day to provide a biological or chemical weapon to a terrorist group or individual terrorists'.

As the drums of war were sounding towards Christmas of that year, the CIA's bureau chief in Paris, Bill Murray, was working to recruit Iraq's foreign minister, Naji Sabri, who had attended all government meetings with Saddam and had also been the closest and most senior regime source that any western agency had attempted to turn. Murray had developed a significant network of contacts in his 35 years at the CIA, especially around the Middle East where he had served in countries including Saudi Arabia and Lebanon. Murray had also closely investigated the movements of the Mujahideen and their interactions with the likes of Bin Laden following the Soviet withdrawal from Afghanistan. The CIA official was a seasoned and highly respected member of the US intelligence community who was known for calling bullshit what it is. Through an intermediary, Murray had provided Sabri a set of questions relating to Saddam's weapons.

'I gave him a set of questions and he answered them and the questions related to stockpiles of weapons of mass destruction – chemical, biological and nuclear,' said Murray. 'And he responded to all those questions by indicating that there was simply nothing there.' Separately, Murray had obtained copies of purchase orders for aluminium tubes which stated that Saddam's goal for developing WMDs had never been realised. The CIA officer detailed his findings in a report which he sent to Langley and was later distributed to senior staff both at the agency and the White House. However, a National Intelligence Estimate outlining the findings of the US intelligence community failed to cite Murray's report. 'The information was never shared with NIE,' said Murray. 'I don't know who specifically decided to not share it with them.'

During the winter of 2003, Colin Powell, the US Secretary of State gave a presentation to the United Nations about Saddam's biological-weapons programme, citing information from an unnamed 'Iraqi chemical engineer' as his top source. Although he did not mention the source by name, Powell was referring to Curveball and said that his information had been 'corroborated by other sources'. The Bush Administration official claimed to have 'firsthand descriptions of biological-weapons factories on wheels'. Powell also sought to confirm the link between Saddam and Al Qaeda, saying although one was a secular dictator and the other an extremist, religious organisation, their 'ambition and hatred' were enough to unite them – 'enough so Al Qaeda could learn how to build more sophisticated bombs and learn how to forge documents, and enough so that Al Qaeda could turn to Iraq for help in acquiring expertise on weapons of mass destruction.' Some of the intelligence relating to Powell's claim about the nexus between the Iraqi regime and the terrorist organisation had come from Ibn Sheik Al-Libi who had been renditioned to Egypt a year earlier and made his confession while being subjected to torture.

Powell's proclamations coincided with about 400 UN inspections at 300 sites in Iraq at which no weapons were found. Hawkish political and intelligence officials in Washington and London dismissed the conclusions reached by UN inspectors. They deemed them as failings rather than probable indicators that the alleged WMD's were a myth. However, others took a different approach regarding the UN's conclusions, particularly some CIA officials who had generally known that while Saddam had a stockpile of chemical weapons in the lead up to the Persian Gulf War of 1991, the weapons had been destroyed. Five Eyes intelligence officials from outside of the Washington and London circles had no direct intelligence on Iraq nor Al Qaeda that could sway the thinking at the White House or Downing Street. 'There was a level of caution in the Australian intelligence community, even though intelligence from the likes of Curveball were shared by the Americans with the other four eyes,' said a former ASIO official. 'But Australia did not have any independent verification capability.'

The junior partners in the Five Eyes were unable to either stand up or discredit the intelligence relied on by London and Washington – and so the Blair Government and Bush Administration ploughed on with their mission, which was also being increasingly supported in public by the Australian prime minister, John Howard. While intelligence agency bosses in London, Washington and Canberra were unlikely to rock the boat, some of their staff members were preparing to do exactly that. In Australia, Andrew Wilkie, an unknown analyst in the Office of National Assessment, which advises the prime minister on matters including evaluations of foreign intelligence, strongly supported the view that the proposed invasion of Iraq was about US politics, rather than Saddam's alleged links to Al Qaeda or WMDs. He worried that an invasion could lead to a humanitarian disaster and inflame anti-Western views in the Middle East and, in early 2003, was prepared to put his job on the line to make that point. Around the same time, and in a completely unrelated case, Katharine Gun, a translator at Britain's GCHQ, read an email from an NSA official which had ordered a secret operation to bug the United Nations offices of six Security Council 'swing nations' whose vote could determine whether the UN approved the invasion of Iraq. Through a friend, Gun leaked the email to the *Observer* newspaper in Britain and was arrested on 5 March after she confessed to the leak. Six days later, in an unconnected case, Wilkie resigned from his job in Australia and went public, saying the 'Iraq problem is unrelated to the war on terror, it's more related to US-Iraq bilateral relations, US domestic politics, the issue of US credibility and so on.' While he agreed that Iraq was a rogue state, he said it did not pose a threat to the West because its military was weak and that an invasion of the country could 'push us all just that little bit closer to the so-called, clash of civilisations, that we've so far managed to stay well clear of'.

Wilkie's views in Australia and Gun's leaks in Britain were largely played down or disregarded by the political machine. The fabricated intelligence relied on by the US and Britain had fulfilled its purpose, and with Australia's help, the bombing campaign against Saddam's regime began on 19 March. The invasion was not approved by the UN Security Council and it was also opposed by Canada after its intelligence assessments had found no evidence of WMDs in Iraq. 'It was, in fact, the first time ever that there was a war that the Brits and the Americans were involved [in] and Canada was not there,' Canada's prime minister Jean Chretien later said, 'Unfortunately, a lot of people thought sometimes that we were the 51st state of America. It was clear that day that we were not.' New Zealand also initially refused to take part but eventually deployed armed troops and engineers to support the coalition forces following the invasion.

As tens of thousands of Iraqi civilians were displaced, wounded or killed, the GCHQ whistle-blower Katharine Gun was charged with breaching Britain's Official Secrets Act. She pleaded not guilty, citing as her defence the prevention of loss of lives in an illegal war. On 24 February 2004, Gun's case was dropped after the government refused to give evidence in court. In the same year, Curveball was discredited as a liar in a report by the US Select Committee on Intelligence which revealed that he was a 'design engineer' not a 'biological weapons expert'. He eventually went public and admitted fabricating the information he had provided on Saddam and his alleged WMD's, but said he stood by his actions. 'I tell you something when I hear anybody – not just in Iraq but in any war – [is] killed, I am very sad,' Curveball told the *Guardian* newspaper. 'But give me another solution. Can you give me another solution? Believe me, there was no other way to bring about freedom to Iraq. There were no other possibilities. Saddam did not [allow] freedom in our land. There are no other political parties. You have to believe what Saddam says, and do what Saddam wants. And I don't accept that. I have to do something for my country. So I did this and I am satisfied, because there is no dictator in Iraq any more.'

The White House refused to respond to why the report that had been generated by CIA official Bill Murray had been disregarded. And National Security Advisor Condoleezza Rice later claimed that its reliability had been questionable because it had been single-sourced – failing to see the irony that a lot of intelligence that Washington had relied on during the lead up to the invasion – including Curveball's allegations which formed the basis of the US case for war – had in fact also been single-sourced.

The information from the Czech government relied on by US Vice President Cheney was also proven to be untrue. Al-Libi, who had claimed the connection between Saddam and Al Qaeda, 'recanted the claim', saying he had only told his alleged torturers 'what he assessed they wanted to hear'. Despite the ridicule and disdain that the US and British intelligence leaderships were subjected to, for overseeing one of the worst intelligence scandals in history, John Scarlett, the chairman of Britain's Joint Intelligence Committee which produced the discredited Iraq dossier, was promoted to become the chief of MI6 in 2004 – with Blair's full blessing. Half a million Iraqis were killed and more than nine million were displaced during the Iraq War, and despite numerous inquiries by Britain and the US into the policy and intelligence failures that led to the invasion, Blair's position on it remained largely unchanged. More than a decade after the invasion, he stood by his actions, saying 'we made the right decision and the world is better and safer' and that he was 'sorry if people find that difficult to reconcile'.

Nothing has defined modern day political scandals, policy and intelligence failure like the invasion of Iraq. It raised questions about the ability of intelligence bosses – who ultimately allowed themselves to be manipulated by the White House and Downing Street – to maintain their integrity in the face of political pressure. The theme of political manoeuvrings outweighing the objectivity of intelligence did not end with the invasion of Iraq: it contaminated operational thinking of many intelligence agencies in the Five Eyes in their desperation to get 'upstream' of potential future attacks. They detained suspected terrorists – including citizens of countries within the alliance – and interrogated them for information. Among the accused was a Canadian citizen of Syrian origin who had wrongly been suspected by the Royal Canadian Mounted Police and, later on, the FBI, of being linked to Al Qaeda.

CHAPTER ELEVEN

MORE EQUAL THAN OTHERS

SURVEILLANCE OFFICERS FROM THE Royal Canadian
Mounted Police (RCMP) were immediately intrigued by Maher Arar
when he walked into a café in Ottawa on 12 October 2001 to meet with a
member of the local Muslim community whom they had been monitoring.
Arar was unknown to the undercover operatives, but the person whom he
was meeting, Abdullah Almalki, was suspected by the RCMP of being
an 'important member' of Al Qaeda and a 'procurement officer' for its
leader, Osama Bin Laden. Fearing that the terrorist organisation had
been plotting operations in Canada – following its attacks on the United
States the previous month – the RCMP stepped up its monitoring of
Almalki to gain a clearer understanding of his activities and networks. His
interaction with Arar at Mango Cafe made surveillance officers suspicious
because the pair 'appeared to be taking great pains not to be overheard'
before leaving for a stroll outside to continue their conversation in the
rain. It was unlikely that the two men had known they were being tailed as
they subsequently visited a local prayer hall for around 15 minutes before
driving in Arar's car to examine computer equipment at a shopping mall
nearby. In the three hours that Arar had spent with Almalki between the
late afternoon and early evening that Friday, he unknowingly went from

being a random guy who had stumbled into a surveillance operation to a 'person of interest'.

The RCMP started investigating Arar's background within three days of his meeting with Almalki, and quickly found common threads between them. Both were engineers of Syrian origin and, at 31, Arar was only about one year older than his friend. But unlike Almalki who had been of interest to multiple agencies, including the FBI in the United States, Arar had never emerged on the radar of any security organisation nor had he been suspected of any wrongdoing since he had arrived in the country to settle in Montreal 14 years earlier. By the time he had relocated to Ottawa from Montreal in 1998 with his wife, Dr Monia Mazigh, and their daughter, Arar had become a Canadian citizen and was on his way to landing a job as a communication engineer with The MathWorks, a tech firm headquartered south of the border in Boston, Massachusetts. He was still working as a consultant for the company when he was ensnared by the RCMP's investigation.

In Ottawa, counterterrorism officials within the RCMP and its sister agency, the Canadian Security Intelligence Service, had been overcome by the same kind of operational hysteria surrounding the threat of Al Qaeda that had plagued the judgements of organisations in other Five Eyes countries. In the name of defending western democratic values and way of life, the distinctions between legitimate terrorists and those who were suspected of aiding them was almost completely eroded as Five Eyes members followed in lockstep with the United States to disrupt and destroy enemies within – citizens with questionable allegiances – and Islamist organisations with global reach. President George W. Bush had signed into law the Patriot Act about six weeks after the 9/11 attacks on America. The Act authorised law-enforcement agencies with sweeping measures, including the expansion of their surveillance of terror suspects by wiretapping domestic and foreign communications. Other measures paved the way for raiding the properties of suspects without the use of search warrants and indefinitely detaining accused terrorists until they had been removed from the country.

The prioritisation of national security over human rights and moral values split public opinion, with some saying it was commensurate with the scale of the threat faced from Al Qaeda, and others suggesting it was unconstitutional. But such debates became footnotes in public and political discourses which did not diminish the resolve of intelligence agencies in the Five Eyes to continue their relentless pursuit of terrorists, using all methods available to them. Local mosques and Islamic prayer halls were at times operationally perceived as legitimate spaces for the recruitment of intelligence agents or accused of being hotbeds for radicalisation – or both. Counterterrorism monitoring on a whole was intensified, ranging from more airport security checks to the penetration of internet forums and other websites where emerging threats could be identified and pursued. However, the so-called War on Terror introduced unconventional security measures, including the secretive programme of 'extraordinary rendition', that would ultimately haunt the legacy of the Five Eyes. Washington took the lead in co-opting allies – especially those with less stringent protections for human rights such as Pakistan and Egypt – into outsourcing their territories for the detention and interrogation of citizens or nationals of Five Eyes countries. The unstated purpose of the rendition programme was to subject terrorism suspects to brutal methods of interrogation – and persuasion – which would be illegal in any of the Five Eyes nations. In public relations messaging and government spin, it was sold as a move to accelerate debriefing of dangerous terrorists, but ultimately became a shortcut for torture where presumption of innocence – a legal right that distinguishes democratic nations from authoritarian regimes – became one less headache for some Five Eyes intelligence agencies to deal with. As did the right to remain silent – a fundamental human right – which even by President Bush's admission, would have made it more difficult to extract urgent intelligence from suspects. Challenging Washington on the notion of rendition risked isolating members of the alliance at a time when they were desperate to keep the US intelligence taps flowing and their own countries protected.

The fear of failing to stop another Al Qaeda attack overwhelmed Five Eyes agencies, including the RCMP and its sister agency, CSIS, which had remarkably improved their cooperation following the 9/11 attacks on the US, much like the relationships between MI5 and MI6 in the London, and the FBI and the CIA in Washington. Canada's human-intelligence organisation, CSIS, barely two decades old at the beginning of the War on Terror, did not have the historical experience of its counterpart agencies in the Five Eyes. Its creation in 1984 had followed a public inquiry into some of the illegal activities by the RCMP's intelligence division in the 1970s, including unauthorised break-ins, document forgery and illegal wiretaps. The inquiry recommended the separation of policing from intelligence work, and with that, CSIS was set up to lead on issues of national security, including the collection, analysis and distribution of intelligence.

Yet in the wake of 9/11, CSIS handed the RCMP some investigations into suspicious targets whom the intelligence agency believed could be involved in criminal activities. The RCMP also created a new division, Project A-O Canada, to which around 20 officers were appointed to expand the organisation's counterterrorism inquiries. Most, if not all, of the information obtained against the targets was shared by the RCMP with the FBI in the spirit of increased cooperation among Five Eyes alliance members on matters relating to terrorism. And while Maher Arar was deemed a person of interest on whom more information was needed – rather than a 'target' on whom the RCMP was attempting to uncover evidence which could lead to charges – the Canadians still passed the information they had on him to the Americans in November 2001. The FBI launched its own investigation into him. The border between Canadian and American agencies 'came down' in the interest of working together to 'prevent further attacks from occurring anywhere around the world'. The hard-and-fast-rule to which the RCMP subscribed was that any investigative information provided to another agency within the Five Eyes was for intelligence purposes only – and not be used for prosecution without prior agreement. 'If an external agency wanted to use RCMP information for another purpose, it would have to obtain the RCMP's permission.'

As part of its background search into Arar, the RCMP had been able to establish that he had listed Almalki, the alleged Al Qaeda operative, as an 'emergency contact' on his rental application for his family home. It was a compelling development – but it did not indicate any evidence of criminality against Arar and thus was insufficient for the RCMP to obtain a search warrant for the property. Nonetheless, the Canadians passed on their new finding to the FBI. Despite the regular, in-person meetings between representatives of the FBI and the RCMP in Ottawa and Washington to discuss cross-border threats, the US organisation shared little to no information regarding its own investigation into Arar – proving the Orwellian paradox that while all agencies were equal in the Five Eyes alliance, some are more equal than others.

The FBI's interest in Arar was stepped up, and on 19 February 2002, five of its agents made an unannounced visit across the border to the offices of the RCMP's Project A-O Canada to meet with some of the unit's team members. The RCMP officials could not recall inviting the FBI officers to take part in the meeting, but 'out of courtesy, they were allowed to view materials, strictly on an intelligence basis, until a formalized request arrived'. The American visitors requested more information about Arar without providing any details as to why – and the Canadians obliged. Yet when they asked the FBI representatives about a request that had been made by the RCMP three months earlier for information about the US organisation's own investigation into Arar – on which they 'had not heard anything back'– the Americans 'promised to follow up on the issues'. They never did.

While the Americans and Canadians had placed Arar's details on a 'lookout list' – a system that helps border authorities flag anyone wanted for a variety of concerns, including those relating to weapons or terrorism – he had still been able to travel undeterred. That all changed in September 2002 following a holiday with his wife and their two children to spend time with his in-laws in Tunisia. Arar cut short his break after being contacted by MathWorks, the Boston-based tech firm, which required him to do some consultancy work. He left his family behind in Tunis to return to Canada on an indirect flight through Zurich and New York. Around one hour before he was due to transit through

New York at around 2 p.m. on 26 September, the FBI's legal attaché in Ottawa contacted the RCMP to say that Arar would be questioned upon landing and ultimately forced to return to Zurich. The Canadian officials had no idea that Arar would be transiting through New York until they had been tipped off by their American colleagues. However, they were not informed that the Canadian citizen would be detained until he was already in the FBI's custody the following day, having already endured hours of interrogation relating to his background, including his work, travel patterns and links to Almalki. He was relocated to a holding cell at the Metropolitan Detention Centre in the New York City borough of Brooklyn. Arar had been fingerprinted, photographed, draped in a fluorescent orange jumpsuit and had his wrists and ankles shackled. Despite repeatedly denying his interrogators' accusations that he was a member of Al Qaeda, they refused to believe him. The FBI subsequently assured the RCMP that the decision to take him into custody related to its own investigation rather than theirs, but did not provide the Canadians with any of its findings to justify the action taken against Arar.

On 5 October 2002, ten days into Arar's detention, the FBI finally admitted to the RCMP that it 'did not have sufficient evidence to support charges against' him, and instead, intended to have him appear before an immigration hearing to authorise his removal from the country back to Zurich, Switzerland, as had previously been planned. In search of an alternative solution, an RCMP official questioned whether it might be more operationally sound to have Arar 'dropped off at the Canada–United States border' and placed under Canadian surveillance until a clearer picture emerged about what further steps should be taken against him. An FBI official seemed receptive to the idea and suggested that it was 'more than likely' what his organisation would do so. By then, Arar had received a visit from the Canadian consulate in New York, been provided with a lawyer, and his family had been informed of his whereabouts.

But in an unanticipated move, an FBI official visited the offices of Project A-O Canada at 10.30 a.m. on 8 October to inform the RCMP that a 'removal order' had been served against Arar for a planned deportation to either Canada or Syria. The Canadian officials were bemused because although Arar was of Syrian origin, he had not lived there for 15 years – but the RCMP officials failed to 'take any steps to dissuade the Americans from doing so, nor did they register any objections'. Operationally, however, even if they had raised any objections, they would not have mattered because they had been lied to by the FBI official who had claimed that Arar was still being detained in New York. In fact, the Canadian citizen had been whisked away from the United States at 4.00 a.m. that morning on a private plane to Jordan and driven across the border to Syria. To conceal the truth of Arar's whereabouts, the FBI even gave the RCMP the impression that its officers may be able to interview him – yet by 9.04 a.m. the following morning, 9 October, an American official called the Canadians to say that the offer was no longer available to them. The FBI did not inform the Canadians of Arar's rendition to Syria until 2 p.m. – 34 hours after he had been removed from the US.

By then, Arar had been ushered by his new hosts to an unlit, windowless cell, barely large enough to lay flat, or tall enough to stand up straight in. He was beaten repeatedly by his Syrian jailers, whose choice of torture devices included a two-inch thick electric cable. Although they mainly aimed for his palms when using the cable, they sometimes missed and struck his wrists instead. The pain in his battered body was compounded by the fear he felt daily in anticipation of another torture session. At times, the fear made him lose control of his bladder and urinate on himself – and at the end of each beating, he was warned that the next day's punishment would only be worse. The only sounds he became acquainted with, aside from those of his own screams, were the screams of other people being tortured in the same facility. 'I never saw, but only heard, the agony of my fellow prisoners,' Arar later said. 'I agreed to sign any document they put before me, even those I wasn't allowed to read.' The RCMP was informed by Canadian diplomats in Damascus that a Syrian military-intelligence official had 'confirmed links between Mr Arar and al-Qaeda' and that the prisoner had 'undergone training in Afghanistan'. Under duress, Arar had admitted to anything his jailers accused of, including that he had spent time at a training camp in Afghanistan. 'I told them I had been to Afghanistan. It wasn't true, but it seemed important enough to my jailers. After a month, broken physically and mentally, I was also instructed to write these things down on a piece of paper next to the other answers to other questions that they had gone ahead and penned on my behalf.'

It is believed that the questions asked by Arar's interrogators during each session were informed or supplied by US authorities who then received reports from the Syrians on his responses. After being subjected to brutal punishment and torture and spending about one year in conditions that 'not even animals can withstand', Arar was released by Syrian security officials into the custody of the Canadian Embassy in Damascus on 5 October 2003, and flown out that evening to Ottawa, where he was reunited with his wife and two children.

Even by the admission of Syria's ambassador to the United States, Imad Moustapha, no evidence was found against Arar. 'We did our investigation,' he said. 'We traced links. We traced relations. We tried to find anything. We couldn't.' The RCMP, and its Project A-O Canada division, faced a mounting backlash in the media over the role the Canadians had played in Arar's rendition to Syria. Ironically, some of the officers involved in the bungled investigation into him expressed 'frustration' at the number of 'inquiries and insinuations' being directed at them which had suggested that 'they had somehow pushed the Americans to deport Mr Arar to Syria'. While they felt that they had to 'defend themselves at every turn', they were at least doing it from the comfort of their offices and with the guidance of lawyers – in contrast to what Arar had sustained in his fight for life in a dungeon-like cell and countless hours of torture. It was not surprising that other US agencies were determined to distance themselves from the FBI's blunder in the Arar case. Richard Fadden, who ran the Canadian Security Intelligence Service between 2009 and 2013, said that other parts of the US government argued that they had been unaware of the steps taken by the FBI to rendition Arar. 'They played on this in order to keep in our good graces,' said Fadden. 'I find that law enforcement institutions – of which the FBI is one and the

RCMP for example – are not as flexible in what they do as the intelligence agencies. When the FBI see a violation of the law, they'll move forward and deal with it ninety-nine per cent of the time. Whereas, MI6, CIA, CSIS, will not knowingly violate the law but they will take a much looser construction; they'll take their time and find ways around it. And I think in the case of Arar, the FBI decided "there is a problem here and we've gotta do something about it" and they just moved forward.'

While only Canada and the United States were embroiled in Arar's case, other Five Eyes countries were watching closely. As signatories to the 1987 United Nations Convention against Torture, the alliance had been collectively aware that it not only prohibits torture, but allows no wriggle room for it. The convention states that no 'exceptional circumstances whatsoever, whether a state of war or a threat of war, internal political instability or any other public emergency, may be invoked as a justification of torture.' It also states under Article 3, 'No State Party shall expel, return ("refouler") or extradite a person to another State where there are substantial grounds for believing that he would be in danger of being subjected to torture.' Following such conventions in an unconventional war, in which terrorists kill indiscriminately, seemed practically impossible for the Bush Administration and its intelligence chiefs. It was an attitude that ultimately dragged other Five Eyes agencies into the quagmire of CIA-run 'black sites' – secret prisons in countries around Asia and the Middle East where alleged terrorists were being held without legal recourse before, in many cases, being transferred to the US military prison in Cuba, Guantanamo Bay, for further interrogation and punishment. The Bush Administration had been quick to assert that Guantanamo was reserved for the 'worst of the worst' terrorists, but the torture of innocent civilians presented political leaders of the Five Eyes with domestic problems that threatened their popularity in the polls, especially when victims, such as Maher Arar in Canada, made public disclosures of what governments and their intelligence agencies were desperate to cover up.

Following his return to Ottawa, Arar sought to create a cautionary tale out of his case by holding to account those who had been involved in his mistreatment, including the FBI. As his team of lawyers started building their case, civil-rights movements of all Five Eyes nations demanded answers about the potential complicity of their own political leaders and spymasters regarding the use of rendition. In Australia, the government had been unapologetic about one of its citizens, David Hicks, who had been captured in Afghanistan in December 2001 before being taken into custody by the Americans and transferred to Guantanamo Bay the following year, around the same time that another Australian citizen, Mamdouh Habib, was taken there.

Although their cases had been unrelated, the pair had been accused of affiliation with Al Qaeda – and Hicks eventually became the first captive of US allied nationality to be charged with terrorism-related offences. The Australian prime minister, John Howard, said 'nothing alters the fact that by his own admission, Hicks trained with al-Qaeda, met Osama Bin Laden on several occasions – describing him as a brother. He revelled in jihad.'

In Britain, Prime Minister Tony Blair was under pressure by the public and parliament to resolve the cases of 17 British nationals and citizens who had been captured in foreign countries – including Afghanistan and Pakistan – on suspicion of terrorism-related offences and rendered to Guantanamo Bay where they were held in indefinite detention without any charges. Among them was Moazzam Begg, a British-born man of Pakistani heritage who had run an Islamic bookstore in Birmingham, in England's West Midlands, having relocated to Islamabad shortly before his arrest in February 2002. Pakistani authorities had wrongly accused him of affiliation with Al Qaeda and subsequently transferred him to a US facility in Afghanistan, where he had been held for a year before ending up in Guantanamo Bay. His detention was among the cases of British Guantanamo suspects that Downing Street was attempting to resolve with the Oval Office. Negotiations between London and Washington were intensified when a British delegation was sent across the Atlantic in early 2004 – within days of an agreement being reached between the Foreign Office and Washington to release the first five of the British detainees.

During the first of several meetings in Washington, the British delegation was provided with access to secret files that the US authorities had on the Guantanamo detainees in question. On 27 February, the British visitors, who included representatives from the Foreign Office, Cabinet Office and Scotland Yard's deputy assistant commissioner, Peter Clarke, went through the material over several hours during a meeting at Eisenhower Executive Office Building, which overlooks the White House. The secret files had been intended to convey the 'level of threat' that the detainees were said to be posing.

As the head of Scotland Yard's counterterrorism command and Britain's national coordinator for terrorist investigations, Clarke had a unique insight into raw intelligence and its likelihood to produce prosecutable evidence. The last thing he wanted was for the relocation of detainees to accelerate a new phenomenon of domestic terrorism that had emerged in Britain the previous year during Operation Crevice, an investigation by Scotland Yard and MI5. The investigation which had not been made public at the time of Clarke's meeting in Washington, ultimately led to the identification of an Al Qaeda terrorist cell operating around England, with links to extremists in Canada and the US. The cell members had plotted to target trains, pubs and nightclubs with fertiliser bombs – which had the potential to kill and injure hundreds of people in Britain – before they were subsequently arrested and convicted.

Yet, unlike the actionable intelligence that had been gathered during Operation Crevice, the information against the Guantanamo detainees was flimsy at best. 'The intelligence was not sufficient to charge the detainees with anything,' said Peter Clarke. 'None of the material they provided us with would have been admissible in court.' The US authorities even questioned, with a degree of hope, the likelihood of imprisoning the British Guantanamo detainees on their return to the UK, yet the delegation completely dismissed the idea. 'The Americans were looking for assurances that if the detainees were to be returned to the UK they would not be in a position to re-enter the battlefield and cause issues and threats to US citizens,' Clarke said. 'We had to explain repeatedly that whatever happened to the detainees on their return to the UK could only be strictly in accordance with UK law. There would be no arbitrary detention, unauthorised surveillance or extra-legal restrictions placed upon them, and we would certainly not be able to bring prosecutions on the basis of evidence gleaned by interrogations whilst they had been held in US custody. This was not because I was aware of any mistreatment, but because their interviews had not been conducted with the safeguards, legal framework and access to legal representation that would render anything they had said admissible in a UK court.'

While such assurances were being negotiated, the Blair government was still uncertain of how it would be impacted by the information that the prime minister had provided to the UK's parliamentary Security and Intelligence Committee earlier in the year. Blair had told the committee in January 2004 that MI5 and MI6 officers had 'observed the questioning' of British detainees at Guantanamo for the purposes of gathering 'information that might prove valuable to the protection of the UK and its citizens from terrorism, rather than to obtain evidence for use in criminal proceedings'. According to the parliamentary committee, MI5 representatives who had conducted interviews with some of the British detainees at the US facility in Cuba reported that 'some of the detainees were depressed and withdrawn and that their mental condition was deteriorating'. One had also 'complained about being held in solitary confinement for over a year, not seeing daylight for four months, being denied reading material and restriction of mail.' The MI5 officers immediately reported the detainees' concerns to the British government which ultimately raised them with Washington. However, none of that had been made public yet and the Blair government – still reeling from its emerging intelligence failures on the Iraq War regarding the absence of WMDs – was nervous about how the information relating to British Guantanamo detainees would play.

By and large, the negotiations between the British delegation and US authorities in Washington generated a tangible outcome for the Blair government, and on 9 March, the first five British Guantanamo detainees were flown to the UK and freed without any charges. A month later, the allegations that had generally been made by those who had been held at the facility in Cuba – and which had been repeatedly denied by the Bush Administration – took on a whole new significance after a Pentagon inquiry into another US-operated detention facility exposed the scale of torture and sexual abuse committed by American troops against alleged terrorists at Abu Ghraib prison in Iraq. The Pentagon's own findings fuelled a media storm which came against the backdrop of news stories that had emerged in the previous year about the mistreatment of Iraqis by American soldiers, and in other instances, British soldiers. During a counter-insurgency raid on a hotel in September 2003, British troops arrested a group of Iraqi men and took them to a facility in Basra, south-eastern Iraq, where they were forcefully beaten while blindfolded and handcuffed. One of the detainees, Baha Mousa, the hotel's receptionist, died after sustaining 93 injuries, including a broken nose and fractured ribs. A British serviceman was eventually dismissed from the army and jailed for one year for the inhumane treatment of civilian detainees, including Mousa.

As the British Ministry of Defence faced public outrage around Mousa's case and was ultimately forced to pay his widow and their two children compensation of £2.83 million, the Bush Administration was desperate to shape its own messaging around the mistreatment of Iraqi prisoners. White House staffers and US Secretary of Defense Donald Rumsfeld attempted to play down the Abu Ghraib prison scandal. They claimed it had been an isolated incident and attributed the humiliation and abuse of prisoners – which had included attaching wires to one detainee's 'fingers, toes, and penis to simulate electric torture' – to junior-ranking American soldiers. The official explanation had little effect. Instead of reassuring the public, it magnified suspicions of the Bush Administration and other governments within the Five Eyes which had either been condoning or tacitly supporting the mistreatment of detainees. Suddenly, there was more urgency about questions that had already been asked by the public, media, and political committees regarding mistreatment in Guantanamo.

While the Canadians were still reeling from the allegations that had been made against them by Maher Arar over the torture he had experienced in Damascus, Britain and Australia were becoming concerned about their own exposure over the abuse of Guantanamo detainees at the hand of US agencies, and especially the CIA, in the name of national security. MI5 admitted to Britain's Intelligence and Security Committee that it had not been informed by Washington about the whereabouts of some top Al Qaeda suspects in its custody and the conditions they had been held in. The US authorities, according to the British agency, were also under no obligation to 'disclose to us details of all their detainees and there would be no reason for them to do so unless there is a clear link to the UK. We have however received intelligence of the highest value from detainees, to whom we have not had access and whose location is unknown to us'. One of the detainees was Khalid Sheikh Mohammed, head of Al Qaeda's military operations, who had masterminded the 9/11 attacks on the US. The Kuwaiti-born militant, who became widely known as 'KSM' in western intelligence circles, had been captured in Pakistan in March 2003 and found to be in possession of information relating to the attacks, including computer hard drives containing background information, codenames, and photographs of the 9/11 hijackers.

He was taken to a CIA black site in northern Poland for questioning, and within a 'few minutes' of his debriefing, had been subjected to enhanced interrogation techniques, including stress positions, sleep deprivation, and rectal hydration (forced feeding), giving agency officials 'total control over the detainee'. His interrogation plan quickly incorporated waterboarding – a type of 'slow-motion drowning' in which a victim is generally laid on their back, their face covered in a cloth, before being choked with a steady stream of water that is poured over their face. KSM was waterboarded at least 183 times, confessing to alleged Al Qaeda plots, including ones relating to Heathrow Airport in London and the capital's Canary Wharf business district 'that would have killed thousands of people in the United Kingdom'. The information he provided was shared with the British intelligence community – and when senior MI5 officials quizzed the CIA about how the information had been obtained, they were told that KSM had been cooperative and 'very proud of his achievements'. Washington made no mention of his torture to London, but that alone was not going to let the British intelligence community off the hook – because agency officials had become aware of 38 cases in 2002 alone of 'officers witnessing or hearing about the mistreatment' of detainees by the US. While British agencies later argued that such cases were 'isolated incidents', it was hardly a convincing riposte, not least because when viewed collectively, such cases highlighted a systemic problem. It had also become known by then, at least within the senior circles of MI6, that the US agencies' 'gloves were off' in their pursuit of revenge for 9/11. American spymasters told MI6 in the autumn of 2001 that the 'change was coming quick and profound' and that they would 'not stop until the enemies were all dealt with'. Such posturing from the US agencies was not evidence of the forthcoming torture they would be complicit in. But it did raise questions about whether the British intelligence community had tried to gain assurances that all intelligence provided to London through the interrogation of detainees would be obtained by the US in a lawful and humane way.

The approach that had been adopted by the American intelligence community regarding the rendition of detainees was completely out of step with the other Five Eyes agencies in both its legal and ethical basis. It illustrated that violating the human rights of suspects and prisoners was not only typical to authoritarian regimes, but that even the world's most powerful democracy had the capacity to go rogue.

Eliza Manningham-Buller, who had become the head of MI5 in October 2003, informed US State Department officials of her concerns relating to the rendition of detainees and the impact it was having on public opinion in Britain. She also expressed her agency's opposition to black sites and said that while MI5 still trusted Washington's intelligence community, 'we have a better recognition that their standards, their laws, their approaches are different, and therefore we still have to work with them, but we work with them in a rather different fashion'.

A 2018 inquiry by Britain's Intelligence and Security Committee revealed that British agencies 'shared an unprecedented amount of intelligence with foreign liaison services to facilitate the capture of detainees'. The parliamentary committee accused British spy agencies of failing to 'consider whether it was appropriate to pass intelligence about a detainee to the detaining authority where mistreatment was known or reasonably suspected. This could indicate that the Agencies were deliberately turning a blind eye so as not to damage the relationship and risk the flow of intelligence; if the Agencies started raising concerns, the US could have refused UK officers access to the detainees and stopped passing on any intelligence they obtained.'

The inquiry revealed in one of its two reports that in 232 cases, British officials continued to supply questions or intelligence to other agencies despite knowledge or suspicion of mistreatment. 'We also found 198 cases where UK personnel received intelligence from liaison services which had been obtained from detainees who knew they had been mistreated – or with no indication as to how the detainee had been treated but where we consider they should have suspected mistreatment,' the inquiry concluded. But perhaps the most damning indictment against British intelligence was that MI5 or MI6 – which had repeatedly pledged ignorance about rendition operations – 'made, or offered to make, a financial contribution to a rendition operation' on three separate cases. In a further 28 cases, the agencies 'suggested, planned or agreed to rendition operations proposed by others.' And in dozens of other instances, MI6 or MI5 enabled rendition operations through the provision of intelligence or 'conspicuously failed' to take action to prevent the rendition of British suspects.

The revelations by the parliamentary inquiry came eight years after the UK government desperately tried to save its intelligence agencies from public humiliation by agreeing to settle an out-of-court deal with British Guantanamo detainees. The British government reportedly paid the 17 men £20 million in compensation. In a similar tactic, the Australian government paid an undisclosed sum to Mamdouh Habib, the Australian citizen of Egyptian origin who had been wrongly suspected of being an Al Qaeda trainer after being captured in Pakistan in 2001, being taken to an Egyptian prison, and ultimately to Guantanamo Bay, where he was tortured. The Australian intelligence agency, ASIO, denied knowledge of his torture. Habib was released without charge in 2005 and six years later, the Australian government paid him out, claiming to have acted in 'the best interests of the Commonwealth to avoid further protracted litigation and to enable our agencies to focus on their core responsibilities of protecting our national security'. In 2015, David Hicks, who had been the first citizen of a Five Eyes country to be charged with terrorism offences while at Guantanamo – offences including attending an Al Qaeda training camp in Afghanistan – had his conviction overturned by a US court on the grounds that his charge was not a war crime and should not have been heard in a military court. The Pentagon did not appeal the decision. By then, revelations about the physical and psychological torture that had been meted out against terror suspects at Guantanamo Bay had become all too familiar, thanks in no small part to the US Senators who conducted an investigation into the CIA's operations around Guantanamo detainees.

A dressing down of the CIA had been inevitable. An inquiry by the US Senate Select Committee on Intelligence into the agency's detention and interrogation programme found that detainees were subjected to cruelty, including waterboarding, wallings – slamming detainees against a wall – sleep deprivation and other brutal methods at the hands of US intelligence officials. 'The use of the CIA's enhanced interrogation techniques was not an effective means of obtaining accurate information or gaining detainee cooperation,' concluded the investigation's report in 2014. Perhaps even worse, the senate committee investigation revealed that the CIA had not learned from its mistakes leading up to 11 September. 'While being subjected to the CIA's enhanced interrogation techniques and afterwards, multiple CIA detainees fabricated information, resulting in faulty intelligence. Detainees provided fabricated information on critical intelligence issues, including the terrorist threats which the CIA identified as its highest priorities,' the report added.

The select committee's chairman, Dianne Feinstein, said 'in some cases, there was no relationship between the cited counterterrorism success and any information provided by detainees during or after the use of the CIA's enhanced interrogation techniques' and that the agency 'consistently omitted the significant amount of relevant intelligence obtained from sources other than CIA detainees who had been subjected to the CIA's enhanced interrogation techniques – leaving the false impression the CIA was acquiring unique information from the use of the techniques.'

The black sites and torture tactics embraced by Langley during the early days of the War on Terror had led the FBI to limit its 'involvement in CIA interrogation and detention activities', according to committee's report, which is somewhat ironic as the FBI had been responsible for the rendition of the Canadian citizen Maher Arar to Syria. The US law-enforcement agency, much like the CIA, had its own chequered past. Some of its greatest achievements during the Cold War, including the work by Special Agent Robert Lamphere on the Venona Project to root out atomic spies and other Russian threats, had been undermined by J. Edgar Hoover's obsession to crush Communist and other left-wing political organisations that he had deemed dissenting or subversive. Through the 15-year lifespan of the organisation's counter-intelligence programme, known as COINTELPRO – which started in 1956 and continued under four White House administrations – Hoover had authorised illegal and unconstitutional operations, including the discrediting, intimidation, and wiretapping of anti-Vietnam activists, Black civil-rights groups, and women's movements. In other cases, and in collusion with White House incumbents, the FBI was tasked to gather intelligence on political critics of President Lyndon B. Johnson, and President Richard Nixon also ordered the organisation to obtain personal information through wiretaps on critics, including a Supreme Court Justice. In 1975, a bi-partisan Senate inquiry into US domestic intelligence, including the activities of the FBI, exposed systemic misconduct. Led by Senator Frank Church, the investigation revealed that the FBI made little to no distinction between legal dissent and criminal conduct. 'What some suspected and others feared has turned out to be largely true – vigorous expression of unpopular views, association with dissenting groups, participation in peaceful protest activities, have provoked both government surveillance and retaliation,' the Church inquiry concluded. 'The FBI resorted to counterintelligence tactics in part because its chief officials believed that the existing law could not control the activities of certain dissident groups, and that court decisions had tied the hands of the intelligence community. Whatever opinion one holds about the policies of the targeted groups, many of the tactics employed by the FBI were indisputably degrading to a free society.' While the Church inquiry's recommendations ultimately limited the FBI's ability to target people without an indication of their suspected criminality, 25 years later, the events of 9/11 led to the expansion of surveillance methods under the Patriot Act, which also became vulnerable to abuse.

When it came to assessing the FBI's misconduct in Maher Arar's case, the organisation refused to testify at a Canadian public inquiry into his case. The inquiry concluded that while the Canadian intelligence and law-enforcement authorities had not been complicit in the decision to send him to Damascus, 'it is very likely that, in making the decision to detain and remove Mr Arar to Syria, the US authorities relied on information about Mr Arar provided by the RCMP'. Arar's lawsuit against the US government was dismissed on the grounds of 'state secrets' privilege, claiming that litigation would 'harm national security and foreign relations'. However, he did receive an apology from Canadian prime minister Stephen Harper in 2007 and was compensated with more than CAD$10 million. As for his friend Abdullah Almalki, who had been under investigation for alleged Al Qaeda links when Maher came to the RCMP's attention in 2001, he, too, was cleared of any wrongdoing – but only after being arrested during a family visit to Syria and detained and tortured for almost two years. Almalki and two other Canadians of Syrian origin, who had also been held and tortured in Syria, also received an apology from the Canadian government and were compensated CAD$31.25 million between them.

Up until the bungled investigations during early stages the War on Terror, public criticism of foreign policy failures had largely centred on political leaders – intelligence officials were the unsung heroes who were at times forced to do bad things by their morally bankrupt political overlords. However, the revelations of torture overturned that narrative – intelligence officers were unable to shirk accountability, even though they had tried their best to do so. They were no longer seen as the 'James Bonds' and 'Jason Bournes' in the fight against the enemy: they suddenly became villains in the eyes of the general public. It was a moral and operational disaster, which awakened the world to the shady nature of the intelligence services within the Five Eyes.

While almost 800 detainees were ultimately held at Guantanamo Bay, the majority were released without any charges. Thirty-nine detainees remain there in a constant reminder of both the human rights abuses committed by the US, and other Five Eyes officials, and the spectre of terrorism that continues to loom. Eventually, the threat posed by Al Qaeda's ideology was overtaken by Islamic State of Iraq and Syria (Isis). Along with eclipsing the evil acts and devastation that Al Qaeda had committed, Isis proved its skill at weaponising social media for the purposes of recruiting men, women, and children to its cause following its declaration of a so-called 'caliphate' in the summer of 2014. Raqqa, in Syria's northeast, became the de facto capital of the organisation's caliphate, and soon thereafter, the new home for Isis recruits. Among those who fled the west to join the barbaric organisation were three teenage girls from east London. Their journey into Syria created an operational problem, not only for British authorities, but also for an agency in another Five Eyes country – the Canadian Security Intelligence Service.

CHAPTER TWELVE

A DELAYED ADMISSION

RICHARD WALTON PRIDED HIMSELF on being a detective, especially after his takeover of SO15, the counterterrorism command at Britain's largest law-enforcement organisation, Scotland Yard. His entry into the high-profile role in 2011 made him publicly accountable for the actions and inactions, successes and failures of around 2,500 officers who had been on the frontline of investigating terrorist and espionage attacks against Britain, including the Al Qaeda-inspired London bombings in 2005 and the murder of Russian dissident Alexander Litvinenko a year later. Public accountability was not merely a concept for Commander Walton – it was a reality. He could not hide behind the veil of secrecy that legally forbids the identification of intelligence officers below the highest rank at Britain's spy agencies, including MI5 and MI6, because he was not one of them.

Nonetheless, he respected the work of spooks and had become accustomed to meeting with Five Eyes intelligence officials across a range of areas – from social functions hosted by their embassies, to discussions around mutual targets and threats. 'The vast majority of terrorist investigations have an international dimension that requires co-operation between police and intelligence organisations globally,' Walton said. 'Intelligence agencies created across the Five Eyes have no executive powers of arrest so police powers have often been called upon to assist with making arrests of foreign spies and in more recent times, the arrest of terrorists.'

On operational matters, most of Walton's interactions with intelligence officers from the alliance had been also attended by representatives from the UK's spy agencies, predominantly MI5. Which is why it seemed rather odd that officials from the Canadian Security Intelligence Service had organised to meet with him on short notice in the spring of 2015 to discuss an operational matter without inviting anyone from Britain's security services. On greeting the two CSIS officers at Scotland Yard's headquarters in central London, Walton sensed that they seemed uneasy, as if weighed down by the gravity of some contrition. Even their smiles appeared forced as they sat down with him and some of his staff members to discuss a case relating to a man whom the Canadians had recruited to infiltrate Islamic State in Syria.

At that point in early March 2015, it was an enormous coup for any of the Five Eyes to have some on-the-ground visibility of the terrorist organisation's activities, let alone to have successfully penetrated its ranks. In conventional wars, such as the invasions of Afghanistan and Iraq, intelligence agencies, including the CIA and MI6, had been able to sneak into the countries under the cover of military protection to conduct recruitment operations on the ground, turning well-positioned militants and local government officials into spies. That was not possible in Syria, because in the summer of 2013, the British parliament had voted down a proposed military intervention against the regime's use of chemical weapons. Although Washington subsequently approved military action that same year against Damascus, the use of combat troops had been forbidden. A year later, when Isis declared the creation of its Islamic state, neither Britain nor the US had any military footprint on the ground in Syria and were often forced to rely on aerial assets, including drones and spy planes, to assess the threat emerging from the country. Isis became paranoid about being watched and made infiltration of its ranks virtually impossible after shooting or beheading many people it had suspected of spying for the West, creating cautionary tales of such murders by releasing videos of them online. The gruesome videos had become part of its propaganda campaigns, largely driven by some of the hundreds of jihadists who had left Britain to join Isis fighters on the battlefields of Syria and Iraq, before urging other westerners, including those from Canada, to join their cause.

During the meeting with Walton, the two CSIS officers were aware that more young men and women from the UK had continued to slip the radars of Scotland Yard and MI5 in pursuit of their extremist ambitions in the Middle East region. The Canadian intelligence officials understood the sensitivities, the political backlash, and the public relations disaster that such investigative setbacks had generated for their British colleagues. Walton and his team had also borne the brunt of hostile media commentary relating to their inability to stop three schoolgirls, aged between 15 and 16, who had been suspected of fleeing the country for Syria in the winter of 2015. The three teenagers from east London – Shamima Begum, Amira Abase and Kadiza Sultana – had become part of a new, and rapidly growing phenomenon of young women being drawn to the battlefield not for combat, but rather as potential spouses for jihadists. While an estimated four thousand male western foreign fighters had joined Isis at that point, more than five hundred women and girls had travelled to Syria, drawn by what they wrongly perceived would be an ideological awakening and an answer for their identity crisis.

Sir Kim Darroch, Britain's National Security Adviser at the time, said that 'Isis were pretty effective at online recruiting – targeting isolated or troubled youths in British cities as potential recruits.' He said the creation of the so-called caliphate by the terrorist organisation had been transformational in elevating the status of Isis in the eye of its potential recruits.

'It meant it wasn't just another obscure terrorist organisation, operating out of who knew where,' he said. 'It had created a base – actual land for people to travel to and live in. And that was absolutely critical for Isis's appeal to this generation of young people.'

The reported escape of the three school pupils had generated global headlines and an emotional public appeal by members of their families, urging them to return home. Their disappearance had caught their families by surprise, and it was yet another wake-up call for Scotland Yard. What was not publicly known until they went missing was that the teenagers had been interviewed by Walton's detectives in December of the previous year after one of their school friends had fled to Syria earlier that month. Nothing had indicated to the detectives, however, that the three teenagers had been at risk of doing the same.

Yet, on the morning of 17 February 2015, the schoolgirls left their family homes and boarded a flight to Istanbul from London's Gatwick Airport. Walton appeared at a press conference three days later, saying that while their intended final destination was likely to be Syria, their exact whereabouts remained unknown. The counterterrorism chief also informed the media that Scotland Yard had launched an unprecedented international search for the schoolgirls and that his department had been liaising with Turkish authorities to try to locate them. 'We are extremely concerned for the safety of these young girls and would urge anyone with information to come forward and speak to police,' Walton said, unaware that the three girls had been met on their arrival at Istanbul Airport by an Isis smuggler who had subsequently accompanied them on a bus journey to Gaziantep, in Turkey's southeast, near the Syrian border. The girls' journey into Syria only became apparent after the Isis smuggler, Mohammed al-Rashed, was arrested by Turkish authorities on 28 February and found to be in possession of travel documents, including bus tickets, belonging to the British teenagers.

During the meeting at Scotland Yard in March, the Canadian intelligence officials briefed Richard Walton about the journey of the three British teenagers into Syria. At that point, it suddenly dawned on him why the CSIS officers had avoided the usual protocol of inviting other British intelligence representatives to accompany them to a meeting where operational matters were discussed. The Canadians had in fact come to confess to Walton that they knew more about the case relating to the disappearance of the teenage girls from east London than he could have possibly imagined. The person who had helped smuggle them into

Syria – Mohammed al-Rashed – had been working as an agent for the Canadian Security Intelligence Service. An agent who had been arrested by Turkish authorities the previous month but whose case had not yet been made public.

During the interrogation of Mohammed al-Rashed by Turkish intelligence officials, he claimed that his journey into human trafficking had started via a hospital he had been working at in Raqqa, north Syria. It was there that he had met a regional chief of Isis – a British fighter known by his alias, Abu Kaka – who recruited al-Rashed on the promise that the terrorist organisation had been created 'in accordance with God's will'. Abu Kaka wanted him to meet jihadists and 'jihadi brides' arriving in Turkey from countries such as Britain and organise their travel arrangements over the border into Syria. What Abu Kaka did not know was that al-Rashed was desperate to begin a new life outside of Syria, his country of birth, and had been trying to seek political asylum in Canada by submitting an application at the country's embassy in Jordan. There, Canadian intelligence representatives from CSIS had seen his asylum application as a gateway for his recruitment as an agent – and from then on, al-Rashed started documenting the details of people he had smuggled for Isis by photographing their passports on the pretext that he required proof of their identification to buy their transport tickets for domestic travel. He would then upload the passport images into his laptop and forward them to his CSIS handler at the embassy in Jordan.

Al-Rashed had entered Turkey on his Syrian passport more than thirty times for the purposes of his work for Isis and reportedly helped more than 140 people, who were largely of British origin, to reach the warzone. Following his arrest, Turkish authorities searched his laptop and found a video clip he had filmed of the three British schoolgirls, along with images of maps for Isis camps in Syria and pictures of passports for at least 20 people. His arrest provided Turkey with great public relations ammunition to offset the criticism it had faced from the west, and especially Britain, for neglecting its porous borders that had been repeatedly used by foreign fighters as a corridor into Syria.

Aware that the Turkish authorities would likely leak information about al-Rashed's arrest to the media, the Canadians tried to get ahead of it to avoid any further embarrassment around the role CSIS had played in running him as an agent. And it was in that spirit of post-operational manoeuvring that the two CSIS officers had travelled from the Canadian High Commission in London to meet with Walton – before the arrest of their agent in Turkey had been made public. The purpose of the visit had been self-serving and Walton immediately felt that. Perhaps most surprising to Walton was that the Canadian intelligence officials were not meeting with him to offer an apology over the fiasco, but rather in the hope that any ongoing investigation into the teenagers' journey to Syria would not force CSIS to be questioned or held accountable. 'The CSIS officers knew that Scotland Yard had a live investigation into the three schoolgirls and also knew that sooner or later the finger would point at them,' a Five Eyes source familiar with the case said.

At 49, Walton thought he had seen it all in a Scotland Yard career spanning almost three decades. But he suddenly faced the prospect of having to question an intelligence ally about what they knew and when, and whether they could have stopped the three teenagers from getting to Syria. Had CSIS prioritised the protection of its own informant ahead of the teenagers' safety and wellbeing? 'If you are running agents, you are acquiescing to what they are doing,' said Richard Walton. 'You are turning a blind eye to their actions because it is being trumped by a rich vein of intelligence.' The difficulty of running agents on the ground in Syria blurred the boundaries for Five Eyes agencies between legality and becoming an 'accessory' to human trafficking. As uncomfortable as it was, Walton had to weigh up the bigger picture of the potential benefits that al-Rashed's intelligence could have provided the Canadians – and in turn the Five Eyes – with the public backlash that he had continued to bear from the disappearance of the three teenagers. As a former agent-runner himself, who had been trained by British intelligence, Walton knew that spy agencies would go to great lengths to protect their 'ownership' of informants. Despite the intelligence-sharing between the Five Eyes, it is the end-product that is often shared – such as analysis –

rather than details about the exact source of information, or direct access to an informant. The relationship between a handler and informant spy is jealously protected at all times and can be leveraged by agencies in exchange for greater access from their Five Eyes partners. That much is accepted wisdom in the art of spying.

As had been anticipated, the Turkish government publicly announced its arrest of al-Rashed, saying he had been working for an intelligence agency with the US-led coalition against Isis. During a press conference on 12 March, the country's foreign minister, Mevlüt Çavuşoğlu, said the Syrian smuggler had been working for the 'intelligence services of a country in the coalition', and while he did not name the Canadians, Turkey's pro-government media outlets did. The Doğan news agency quoted al-Rashed from a statement he had given to police, in which he confessed to human trafficking. 'I would take photographs of the identity documents of the foreign fighters I met at Istanbul airport, using the excuse that I needed to buy tickets [for domestic travel], and then I would send them over the internet to the officials from the Canadian embassy,' al-Rashed said in the statement.

Al-Rashed's statement could easily have been dismissed by Canada's intelligence service as the rant of a fantasist, desperate to implicate the west in his terrorism-related activities. However, a subsequent statement from the Turkish authorities gave credence to al-Rashed's claims – and with that, the fears among CSIS officials of having their role exposed in the agent's affair suddenly came true. The statement by Turkish security services claimed that al-Rashed said, 'he worked for Canadian intelligence, travelled from time to time to Jordan with tickets purchased by the [intelligence] service and shared the information he had gathered at the Canadian Embassy in Jordan.' While the Turks had been unable to obtain any evidence of money provided by CSIS to al-Rashed, they claimed to have found text messages between him and his handler.

CSIS remained silent about the explosive allegations, taking refuge in the one thing that protects all intelligence agencies, including those within the Five Eyes, against potential embarrassment: secrecy. 'The main objective was to keep it out of the media as much as possible,' said a senior Canadian security source familiar with the matter. The notion of saying nothing and hoping for the scandal to go away worked in Canada's favour with regards to keeping the lid on how an agent for CSIS had smuggled western children and young adult volunteers into Syria while their British allies struggled to contain the flow of aspiring jihadists fleeing the UK to join Isis. CSIS largely succeeded in covering up the role it had played in the recruitment and running of al-Rashed, and the agency's deputy director was deployed to Ankara to beg forgiveness for failing to inform the Turkish authorities that they had been running a counter-intelligence operation in their territory. 'The purpose of the visit from the deputy director was to acknowledge that a mistake had been made and that it should not happen again,' the Canadian source said. 'We were there with a cap in hand.'

The Canadian government and CSIS did not publicly deny that al-Rashed had been working as a spy for their country, yet unsurprisingly, they refused to be drawn on the details of the case. But the details mattered, especially to establish when the Canadians had first learned that their agent had helped smuggle the three British schoolgirls. Al-Rashed claimed that he had informed his CSIS handler about the case on 21 February – a week before his arrest. If so, why did it take CSIS until March to inform Scotland Yard's Commander Richard Walton about it? And would the agency have informed Walton had it not suspected that the Turkish government would ultimately make the matter public? Such questions played at the back of Walton's mind during his meeting with the CSIS officers, but he equally knew that irrespective of the answers, the Canadians could not have done anything to stop the three teenagers from travelling into Syria – because by the time al-Rashed's handler had found out, the schoolgirls had already crossed the border into Isis territory.

It made no operational sense for Scotland Yard to publicise Canada's involvement in al-Rashed's case because any public verification would have reinforced Isis's ongoing paranoia and compromised any chances of infiltrating it through new informants, according to many intelligence officials interviewed by this author. It would also have inflamed the distrust between Turkey and the Five Eyes as the regime in Istanbul had rightly suspected that the alliance's intelligence agencies had not been transparent about their operations. Turkey had insisted that any agent-running activities conducted by foreign intelligence services within its country had to be made known to its own security officials. But the reality was that some Five Eyes agencies had been withholding information about agents from each other, so they were hardly going to abide by Turkey's orders.

While al-Rashed's arrest had been operationally damaging to the Canadians, it did not dent the relentless effort of some other Five Eyes agencies to penetrate Isis. Months before al-Rashed was in the custody of Turkish authorities, MI5 and FBI officers stationed in Jordan had been desperately trying to find ways to infiltrate a cell of four Isis terrorists who had abducted foreign journalists and humanitarian workers, including British and American citizens, and held them in a makeshift prison in Raqqa. Conscious that western spy agencies had been searching for the men in their captivity, the four militants had been careful to keep their identities secret by always wearing black masks around the hostages. Yet the captors betrayed a part of their own identities by speaking fluent English, leading their 15 hostages to nickname them 'The Beatles' – after the 1960s pop group – due to their British accents. When some of the hostages were released in return for ransoms in the summer of 2014, they revealed the torture to which they had been subjected by 'The Beatles' and the names of some of the people who were still being held by them, including American journalist James Foley and British humanitarian worker, David Haines. It was a shocking revelation to MI5 and the FBI, not least because British terrorists had been torturing US citizens. MI5 intensified its efforts to try to plant an agent close to the Beatles, yet its mission was aborted shortly after the cell's ringleader, known as 'Jihadi John', appeared in a video online, masked and threatening to behead Foley in August 2014. The video ended with the beheading of the American journalist, became a propaganda coup for Isis and catapulted Jihadi John into a global social media sensation for terrorism. But it also provided Commander Richard Walton's SO15 Command, along with the British signals intelligence service, GCHQ, with some very important clues about the identity of the man behind the mask.

The Isis executioner's voice had been disguised, yet within hours of his video appearing online on 19 August 2014, GCHQ analysts, using voice-recognition software, found a match. They cross-checked Jihadi John's voice against that of an Islamist extremist from northwest London, Mohammed Emwazi, who had been investigated by MI5 and Richard Walton's detectives before fleeing the UK for Syria two years earlier. Scotland Yard's investigative file on Emwazi included phone intercepts and surveillance videos which allowed intelligence analysts to make further matches between him and the Isis executioner. Jihadi John's accent; the shape and colour of his dark eyes peering from underneath a mask; the veins on his knife-wielding left hand; and his posture. They all matched those of Emwazi's.

It was a counterterrorism coup, but one that Walton and senior intelligence officials at GCHQ and MI5 wanted to keep out of the public domain and from the eyes of the media. The British authorities feared that an acknowledgement of a positive identification of Jihadi John – even one that did not mention his real name – could compromise the lives of his other hostages. 'There was public pressure to name this individual but we knew that if we were to name Emwazi there was a high risk that he would conduct more murders and more beheadings of the hostages,' said Walton. The sensitivities around the identification of Jihadi John were also understood by the FBI and its London-based liaison officers who were closely working with their British partners on the case. But the public discourse around Jihadi John made it seem like he was shaping the narrative around the international threat posed by Isis. British and US authorities – for all their resources, manpower and surveillance capabilities – seemed, at least in the eyes of the public, to have lost control and any ability to stop Jihadi John. That view had been reinforced after the Isis executioner released two more beheading videos in early and mid-September – one revealing the murder of American journalist Steven Sotloff, and the other, of British aid worker David

Haines. Later that month, sensing a need to perhaps realign the power dynamic in the authorities' favour, FBI director James Comey assured the public that Jihadi John had been positively identified but refused to be drawn on details, including his name or nationality.

A British citizen, Emwazi's journey from a shy London schoolboy to Jihadi John – the most high-profile executioner and propagandist for Isis – had baffled behavioural therapists at Scotland Yard and MI5 who specialise in assessing the mindset and violent inclinations of extremists. He had been an outsider from the beginning of his life, having been born in Kuwait to a family of 'Bidoons'– a tribe of stateless people who are persecuted in the Middle East. Aged six, he migrated with his family to London in 1993 and went on to have a fairly unremarkable childhood during his primary and secondary school years. He was a computer geek, supported Manchester United football club, enjoyed listening to pop music, was occasionally teased for having bad breath and managed to do his own share of teasing. Yet he did not seem to have a violent streak and nor did he show any criminal intentions until well into his late teens when he became close friends with Bilal al-Berjawi and Mohamed Sakr – two fellow Londoners. Emwazi's friends were around four years older than him, in their early twenties, and had Islamist connections in East Africa which had brought them to the attention of the British counterterrorism authorities. By the time Emwazi graduated from Westminster University in 2009 with an information technology degree, al-Berjawi and Sakr had travelled to Africa where they joined Al Qaeda in Somalia. Their path to jihad had inspired Emwazi to pursue a similar cause, which Scotland Yard's counterterrorism unit and MI5 had caught on to, so when Emwazi travelled from London to Tanzania in March 2009, he was stopped and questioned at Dar es Salaam airport by local authorities who had presumably been tipped off by their British counterparts. Emwazi's claim that he had travelled to the country with the intention of going on a safari tour was dismissed by the Tanzanian authorities who threw him in a cell overnight, beat him up and forced him to return to the UK the following day. British authorities rightly suspected that Emwazi had been radicalised and had developed a desire to become a jihadist like his two close friends. Like about 2,000 other British Islamists who were at risk of engaging in terrorism activities, he had been regarded as a 'subject of interest' by the authorities. But without enough evidence to arrest him for terrorism offences, Scotland Yard and MI5 sought to turn him into an informant. 'We made approaches to him [and] wanted to give him the opportunity to work for us and to desist from becoming a terrorist,' Walton said. 'There's always a risk when you make these approaches and the chances of success are, in any event, fairly minimal. On the one hand we had absolutely understood the threat he posed, but ultimately we failed because he became what he wanted to be: potentially one of the worst terrorists of all time.'

Walton questioned whether the failed attempt to recruit him had 'contributed to his further radicalisation', but Emwazi's jihadist aspirations and hatred of the west had pre-dated his brushes with the police and the security services. On the spectrum of national security threats, Emwazi had been deemed a minor player by British authorities, not the kind of high priority target requiring round-the-clock monitoring that would have involved a team of about 20 surveillance officers. As such, Emwazi managed to flee the country unhindered in early 2012. By then, dozens of young British men had left the UK to support civilian and armed struggles in the Middle East. What had started off as anti-government protests in Tunisia in January 2011 and quickly led to the fall of the authoritarian regime in the country, had created a movement by tens of millions of Arabs, fed up with the corrupt leaders of their own countries. It became known as the Arab Spring. But unlike uprisings before it in the region, the familiar methods used by dictators to crush dissent – including indiscriminately killing protesters by firing live ammunition at them during demonstrations – had failed to stop its momentum. By the end of that year, the dictatorships of Egypt, Libya and Yemen had fallen and others in the region, including Syria, looked increasingly vulnerable. A civil war was sparked between the Assad regime in Damascus and armed rebel groups, attracting foreign fighters from the west, including Britain. By the beginning of the following year, the conflict in Syria had spread to Iraq, as more foreign fighters joined the battlefields and terrorist groups, including those affiliated with Al Qaeda, joined the rebellion – but for a jihadist, rather than patriotic, cause. The Five Eyes, along with other western intelligence agencies, had failed to predict the emergence, scale, and intensity of the Arab Spring, much like the CIA had failed to foresee the Hungarian Revolution almost six decades earlier. General David Petraeus, who had led the Coalition armed forces in Iraq and Afghanistan before becoming the director of the CIA in the autumn of 2011, said the Arab Spring and its sudden ramifications could not have been predicted, however. 'You can't anticipate a spontaneous combustion of a society,' said Petraeus. 'You can have a sense of a society's enormous dissatisfaction, resentment, alienation and all the rest – but you never know what is precisely going to be the catalyst that sparks the uprising and whether that uprising will succeed.'

Intelligence agencies across the Five Eyes have often faced criticism for failing to predict threats despite the billions they receive in funding. In Britain, the intelligence agencies also failed to foresee conflicts in the Middle East, including the Arab Spring, the Libyan Crisis in 2011 and Russia's invasion of Crimea in 2014 – despite the improved communication between intelligence officials and policymakers following the creation of the National Security Council by the Cameron Government. The unforeseen events took place during David Cameron's prime ministership after he had been elected to office in 2010. 'I knew I was inheriting the tail end of the Iraq and Afghanistan conflicts,' he said. 'But the Arab Spring was unpredicted; Libya was unpredicted; Isis was unpredicted; Crimea unpredicted. Most of the things that happen on your watch as Prime Minister are unpredictable and I'm afraid to say unpredicted. That's not really to criticise the Foreign Office or the agencies. It's a big and difficult world to guess what's going to happen next. And also, we knew that there was a range of Islamist extremist problems around the world [...] and wherever there was a failed state they would pop up there. But I think, generally speaking, most of the things I was dealing with, the horizon-scanning [intelligence-gathering] exercises didn't reveal them. There were some politicians who used to make the point of saying "We're spending all this money on horizon-scanning, why do we never seem to predict those things?". I wasn't particularly of that view.'

The Arab Spring failed to depose Assad in Syria and was instead exploited by jihadists hellbent on creating their own version of an Islamic utopia in the region. Mohammed Emwazi had ended up there after fleeing the UK in early 2012. By the time British authorities realised he had gone missing, Emwazi was already on the battlefields of Syria – where, in less than three years, he went from being a seemingly insignificant enemy of the United Kingdom to one of the most wanted people in the world. Scotland Yard, MI5, and GCHQ wanted him brought to justice, but their American colleagues at the FBI, CIA and Pentagon wanted him dead. And so began the hunt for Emwazi – or in American military vernacular, the mission to 'find, fix and finish' him.

Linked to the beheadings of at least seven westerners, including American, British, and Japanese citizens, Emwazi's barbaric actions had also magnified Isis's recruitment campaign which predominately attracted men, yet also some women and children, from all Five Eyes nations to Syria – and radicalised many others to plot and ultimately conduct terrorist attacks in their own countries. He had also become the epitome of evil on one hand, and on the other, an uncomfortable reminder of failed foreign policy and intelligence decisions by the US – with the help of Britain and Australia – during the Iraq War from a decade earlier. Emwazi's brutality had been blessed by the leader of Isis, Abu Bakr al-Baghdadi, who had sown the seeds of his organisation during his incarceration at Camp Bucca – a US military facility built in southern Iraq in early 2003 to intern some of Saddam's regime officials and military commanders, along with criminals and Al Qaeda terrorists. The facility also held detainees from Abu Ghraib, who were relocated there following the revelations of human rights abuses at the hands of American soldiers. Camp Bucca was the largest US detention complex in the country and ultimately interned tens of thousands of Iraqis – the majority held for months or years without any charges.

During his time there in the early and mid-2000s, al-Baghdadi had become a respected Islamic scholar, gaining the trust of an array of people, including former Iraqi military officials and aggrieved Al Qaeda militants. 'There is a significant amount of mystery about al-Baghdadi and the circumstances of his life that ultimately resulted in him being incarcerated in Camp Bucca,' said Douglas Wise, a former CIA officer who helped oversee the agency's Middle East operations during the hunt for Emwazi, al-Baghdadi's disciple. 'Al-Baghdadi knew that the best way for him to survive in that camp was to take on the persona of a senior respected individual in the camp community by gaining the trust of the US military. He clearly understood, not being a warrior himself, that he could in fact lead and manage warriors. So, this was the laboratory in which his culture was grown.' By the time the US armed forces shut down Camp Bucca in 2009, it had effectively become a terrorist training school and recruitment platform for al-Baghdadi's vision of creating an Islamic State. Five years later, he declared its creation with the help of some former Camp Bucca detainees, and appointed himself as its leader, or Caliph. He urged young Muslims to join its jihadist mission – and Emwazi, who had already been in Syria for two years flirting with Islamist militant groups aligned with Al Qaeda, took al-Baghdadi's call to arms literally and stepped up to become the Isis leader's messenger and executioner in chief.

In February 2015, six months after American journalist James Foley appeared in Jihadi John's first video, the British and US press identified the executioner as Emwazi. The public disclosure of his identity added to the pressure on British prime minister David Cameron. He had been desperate to reclaim the narrative in the fight against Isis, and while GCHQ had already been working with the FBI and Pentagon to identify Emwazi's movements – or 'pattern of life'– in Raqqa, the prime minister wanted its mission to be stepped up. He instructed Britain's signals agency to turn Emwazi into a high priority. From that point, Emwazi was added to a kill list featuring key national security targets, including Abu Bakr Al-Baghdadi. Emwazi's self-awareness about the media profile he had generated through his heinous and murderous acts was offset by a calculated self-preservation. With no allied forces on the ground, he was also aware that the greatest military threat he faced would be from a drone strike. The use of unmanned drones by the US and UK for extrajudicial killings had generated a controversy following the deaths of innocent civilians who had been wrongly targeted in countries such as Pakistan, Yemen, Somalia and Iraq. Such 'collateral damage' – a euphemism invoked by western militaries to blur the reality of civilians killed by drone operators from thousands of miles away at air bases in Nevada, in the western US, or Waddington in northwest England – had created a public backlash and ultimately served terrorists such as Emwazi. Knowing that civilians effectively doubled as human shields, Emwazi surrounded himself with non-combatants and children, according to the Pentagon, to make a drone strike without innocent lives being lost close to impossible. Compounding that operational obstacle was Emwazi's proficiency with using computer software to conceal his location and avoid leaving digital fingerprints.

'He was an interesting case because he had studied computer science,' said Robert Hannigan, who served as the director of GCHQ during the mission to target Emwazi. 'He had clearly taught himself a lot. He understood therefore the best way to avoid surveillance and was good at it. He used a whole series of commercially available products to obscure his identity, including very strong encryption and virtual private networks. Any one of those products would have been very difficult for an agency to tackle. What he was doing was layering them on top of each other.' Emwazi also made sure that he wiped the computer after each correspondence to safeguard it from bugs. 'Any agency's ambition if they can find the machine that a terrorist is using is to put something on to it that stays there and can communicate back what a person is doing,' said Hannigan. 'What Emwazi was able to do was to ensure that every time that he switched off his machine that it was wiped of anything and everything. And that made it extremely difficult and very, very time-consuming to do anything really with his communications.'

Signals intelligence operations had countless limitations in Raqqa for closing in on specific terrorist targets. Unlike allied missions against the likes of the Taliban in Afghanistan – where agencies such as GCHQ and its American counterpart, the NSA, had been able to exploit telecommunication networks to pinpoint the whereabouts of terrorists by tracking their mobile phones – most people in Raqqa communicated through Wi-Fi, making it harder to pick out targets. 'For us at GCHQ this was a largely desk screen-based campaign,' said Hannigan. 'If you looked at a picture of Raqqa you would see these little VSat terminals – these little satellite dishes all over the roofs. And they were connecting direct to the internet and that is the way that people were communicating. They were not using telephone company GSM [global system for mobile communication] networks because they didn't trust them.'

GCHQ also had to contend with false alarms relating to the whereabouts of Emwazi that it received through contacts on the ground in Raqqa. As a signals agency, GCHQ had not, nor was it supposed to have, prioritised the recruitment of spies on the ground – but thankfully, the FBI had. The US law-enforcement agency had also made significant intelligence gains through Syrian agents in Raqqa whom it had recruited online. By using internet communication to correspond with their handlers, the agents provided key details about Emwazi's movements and social circles which had been shared with the relevant members of the British military and intelligence communities. 'I think where you have any target who is very good at communication security they are almost always made vulnerable by others that they communicate with – so by those around them,' said Hannigan. Emwazi's greatest vulnerability became the new family he had formed while in Syria after marrying a local woman and having a son with her. It had become easier to track Emwazi in correlation to his interactions with them.

On the evening of 12 November 2015, Pentagon and British military officials received intelligence about Emwazi's movements. A drone, operated from a US air base in Iraq, was dispatched to follow his car from several miles away. After 45 minutes of driving around, Emwazi emerged from the vehicle. 'Because of the conditions – it was night – we were using infrared,' said Steve Warren, former Pentagon spokesman, who had been at the operation centre watching a live feed from the drone that was positioned to strike Emwazi. 'You can't see his face but we could sort of see how he moved, the cut of his jib, so to speak. The angle of his beard, these things we could see. Eventually we were convinced that this is Jihadi John. And so the floor commander at the time orders, "Take the shot".' Emwazi was obliterated within 15 seconds of the missile being launched. Unlike the hunt and subsequent killing of Al Qaeda leader Osama Bin Laden in May 2011, which had been unilaterally conducted by the CIA and US military to the exclusion of other Five Eyes, the operation against Emwazi had been a joint and successful effort by London and Washington. Yet unlike Bin Laden's killing which had left a temporary vacuum in Al Qaeda's operations and its ability to regroup, the demise of 27-year-old Emwazi merely dented the propaganda machine and perceived invincibility of Isis, but it did not impact the organisation's military activities in Syria or overseas. The terrorist network's brutal campaign of killings lasted two more years before it was largely curtailed by the Kurdish-led Syrian Democratic Forces, an alliance backed by US air power and special forces. In late 2017, Raqqa, which had served as Isis's headquarters and capital, had been recaptured by the alliance and a secret deal had been brokered between the victors and the Isis fighters. The deal allowed convoys carrying hundreds of Isis fighters a safe passage out of the city, to save the lives of the women and children among them and restore a sense of peace in the territory. 'They made an agreement so that they literally didn't have to destroy Raqqa to save it,' said General Petraeus. 'I'm sure that was the least bad of the options. Now what you're seeing already is the remnants of these forces turning into insurgent groups. These are elusive enemies now, they are no longer wearing uniforms or flying black flags, they are hiding among the population.'

Isis leader Abu Bakr al-Baghdadi was not among those given safe passage. He remained on the run until a CIA-led counter-surveillance operation obtained intelligence detailing his whereabouts in Syria, at a hideout near the Turkish border. US Special Forces troops, backed by the aerial support of drones, fighter jets, and helicopters, raided al-Baghdadi's compound on 26 October 2019. While several militants at the compound were killed, and others were captured, al-Baghdadi fled into an underground tunnel wearing a suicide vest and accompanied by two children. There, '[He] crawled into a hole with two small children and blew himself up,' said Commander of US Central Command, General Frank McKenzie, who had overseen the operation against the Isis leader. 'So you can deduce what type of person that is based on that activity.' He said the DNA used to confirm al-Baghdadi's identity after he had killed himself and the two children had been cross-checked against samples collected during his time in detention at Camp Bucca in Iraq. The two most high-profile British disciples of al-Baghdadi – Alexanda Kotey and El Shafee Elsheikh, who, along with their ringleader Jihadi John, had been members of the terrorist cell nicknamed 'The Beatles' – were flown to United States in early 2020 to face terrorism charges, two years after they had been apprehended by Kurdish forces and transferred to the American military in Iraq. Shortly after their capture, they were stripped of their British citizenships based on a precaution by the UK government to protect its nation's security and safety. They were both accused of involvement in the murder of Jihadi John's victims, including American journalist James Foley and British aid worker David Haines. Kotey pleaded guilty to all eight charges against him and was jailed for life in a US prison in early 2022. Elsheikh was convicted of conspiracy to commit murder and hostage-taking and was expected to be sentenced in August 2022. The atrocities committed by 'The Beatles' had become a hallmark of Isis's brutality, as much as the case relating to the three east London schoolgirls who fled Britain to join the terrorist organisation had kick-started the debate about the role women play in jihad. Two of the teenagers were reportedly killed in Syria and the third, Shamima Begum, was stripped of her British citizenship on national-security grounds after she was found in a refugee camp in 2019. Her case went on to reframe the citizenship debate in all Five Eyes countries concerning western fighters – and so-called 'jihadi brides' – who wanted to return home following their time on the battlefields of Syria and Iraq.

It has become accepted wisdom in counterterrorism circles that violent ideology spawned by Isis will continue to poison the minds of many other men, women and children for generations to come. Yet the destruction of the terrorist organisation's so-called caliphate has mitigated that threat and highlighted the importance of intelligence cooperation in the absence of traditional military action. While the United States, in comparison to other Five Eyes countries, shouldered most of the heavy lifting in the fight against Isis, the overall gains had been a victory for the entire alliance and largely shifted public opinion in favour of intelligence work. It had been a much-needed win for the Five Eyes agencies after facing almost two decades of public condemnation over their failures in the Iraq War. But it was not enough to completely transform their image, which had been tarnished by yet another scandal – the mass surveillance of their own civilians, exposed by a whistle-blower from within the heart of the US signals intelligence community.

CHAPTER THIRTEEN

THE SNOWDEN AFFAIR

FIVE YEARS INTO HIS role as director of GCHQ, Sir Iain Lobban had become accustomed to late-night work calls relating to his agency's global missions across multiple time zones. Yet even so, when his home phone rang in the small hours of 6 June 2013, he knew from its timing that it must have been related to an urgent matter. During the 2 a.m. call, Lobban was informed by one of his staff members that the US National Security Agency was concerned about one of its secret surveillance programmes being exposed by the *Guardian*. The British newspaper intended to print a story imminently, he was told, and the NSA had alerted GCHQ in the hope that his organisation could prevent the story's publication. It was a strange request, despite the historic operational ties between the two agencies that had been forged by their predecessors, Bletchley Park and Arlington Hall, since the early days of World War II. Reinforcing that organisational closeness was Lobban's own connection to the US: he had created fond memories and lasting friendships in the country after spending a little more than three years in the early 1990s as a GCHQ liaison officer in Maryland where the NSA is headquartered. On becoming the leader of his organisation in 2008, Lobban understood the responsibilities that position entailed, not only for the protection of his nation against aggressors, but also for nurturing the Special Relationship between Britain and the US. However, the proposition of urging a newspaper to spike the article for the sake of the NSA seemed a step too far. It was neither the purpose of his agency nor his own to deal with the NSA's public relations. As a lifelong spook for whom secrecy was as much an operational imperative as it was a means for his personal existence, he generally felt uncomfortable around dealing with the media – and that was obvious to anyone who knew him. But he equally supported the freedom of the press, even if inconvenient truths were revealed under such a principle.

A few hours after the early morning call at his home, Lobban woke up to a front-page headline in the *Guardian* regarding the NSA obtaining the telephone records of tens of millions of Americans under a secret court order sought by the FBI on behalf of itself and the US signals agency. The order required Verizon, one of the US's largest telecoms companies, to supply the information on an 'ongoing, daily basis' to both American agencies and banned the provider from disclosing to the public or any unauthorised person the existence of the request or the court order itself. Under the order, the Foreign Intelligence Surveillance Court (FISC), which authorises electronic surveillance warrants against foreign spies or terrorists inside the US, the NSA gained indiscriminate – or bulk – access to the phone numbers of both the callers and call recipients, irrespective of whether they had been suspected of any wrongdoing. While the FBI and NSA were not entitled to access the content of conversations between callers, the agencies were able to track 'location data, call duration, unique identifiers, and the time [...] of all calls'. There was no suggestion of illegality being committed under the domestic spying programme, but in the minds of civil-rights activists it reeked of surveillance overreach at the very least.

To British intelligence officials, the *Guardian's* story may have seemed misplaced on the front page of the newspaper since Verizon did not operate in the UK. Nor was the British public generally aware about the functions of the Foreign Intelligence Surveillance Court – which had been created in 1978 following the abuse of monitoring powers by the

CIA, FBI and NSA – to keep the electronic spying operations of the agencies in check. However, what the *Guardian* knew that outsiders did not, was that its story was the first part of an avalanche of scoops. Its disclosures, spearheaded by Glenn Greenwald – an American journalist and attorney specialising in US constitutional law and civil liberties – would ignite a historic debate around what many viewed as the violation of privacy and human rights worldwide, not least of all, in the countries of the Five Eyes.

While top officials at the NSA were trying to determine how the Verizon story had leaked, a coordinated scoop emerged the following day in the British newspaper and the *Washington Post* that revealed the existence of Prism, a top-secret, US-run and owned programme to which GCHQ had been given a limited access. Through Prism, the US agencies had allegedly been able to secretly tap into the servers of nine tech companies, including Facebook, Apple, Google and Microsoft, to spy on the online communications of potentially millions of internet users. The programme allowed US eavesdroppers to obtain an individual's emails, photographs, chat records, and other social network information. Unlike other programmes which had been automatically shared by the US with GCHQ, the British signal agency had to first obtain the agreement of the NSA, FBI and CIA before applying for a legal authorisation in America to access Prism. 'We were only given a limited access to Prism and the process was very heavily governed,' said a British intelligence official. While GCHQ had been given access to Prism three years earlier in 2010, there was no evidence of it still being used by the British agency. GCHQ insisted that it had not broken any laws and that its work was 'carried out in accordance with a strict legal and policy framework which ensures that our activities are authorised, necessary and proportionate'.

Unlike the Verizon story, the implication of GCHQ's access to Prism left its top officials in a tailspin about how such a highly sensitive secret could have ended up in the press. 'We were looking at these stories thinking, "Where did they come from" – because some of the information in them was specific to us,' said a senior GCHQ official who was closely involved in investigating the newspaper revelations. 'At any one time, you may be concerned about a set of employees who may be aggrieved, or in need of finances. We were worried that one of them may have been involved or may have been part of a group that was behind the leak.' As GCHQ tried to manage the media fallout, its director was deeply concerned about the potential impact the leak would have on London's relationship with Washington if it were to be discovered that a British intelligence officer was behind it. After all, the British intelligence community had form when it came to insider threats, from the Cambridge Five during the Cold War to Katharine Gun, the GCHQ whistle-blower who a decade earlier had leaked to the press an email from an NSA official urging the British agency to monitor swing nations in the lead up to the Iraq War.

To determine the leaks to the *Guardian*, General Keith Alexander initiated a mole hunt into the NSA's own workforce, and Lobban orchestrated a separate 'security breach investigation' into his own agency. 'I asked the security division at the agency if there had been anyone of concern to them,' recalled Sir Iain Lobban. 'We needed to know whether there were any individuals with flashing-red concerns. It was not a situation of "Let's lock the building down and check everyone", but rather, "Let's try and work out who this could be". Lobban and General Alexander communicated frequently, but only one of them knew the identity of the leaker as the Prism story had emerged in the press on 7 June. However, that person gave nothing away.

It was not lost on Lobban that BRUSA, the document relating to the inter-agency partnership which led to the UKUSA Agreement, and subsequently, the Five Eyes, had been signed almost exactly 70 years earlier. 'I was definitely worried that if one of our people was behind the leak, I would be remembered as the boss who turned the lights off for UKUSA,' said Lobban of his fears that Washington would end its dealings with London over such a breach of trust. The disclosure of Prism spooked intelligence officials on both sides of the Atlantic and its timing also presented a strategic blow to President Barack Obama, who had been preparing to meet with the new Premier of China, Xi Jinping, at the Sunnylands Summit in California. While the two-day summit had been set up to discuss a range of issues, including climate change and the improvement of business ties between the two largest economies, Washington had been preparing to confront Beijing about Chinese hackers targeting American companies. However, the Prism story weakened Washington's hand because it showcased its agencies' own appetite for internet spying, and as a result, Obama's planned confrontation was tempered to general discussions around cyber-security.

Obama defended the two surveillance programs that had been exposed in the press, saying they had been authorised by Congress and had a 'whole range of safeguards in place' that were being properly observed. 'I think it's important to recognise that you can't have 100 per cent security and also then have 100 per cent privacy and zero inconvenience,' he said. 'And what I can say is that in evaluating these programs, they make a difference in our capacity to anticipate and prevent possible terrorist activity.' Obama's assurances made little impact on the public outrage that was beginning to swell around the perceived breaches of privacy, and by the weekend, as the US President rubbed shoulders with his Chinese counterpart at the summit, questions about the origins of the leaked stories were answered. Edward Snowden, a contractor for the NSA, declared to the world in a video message from Hong Kong on 9 June that he had been the source of stories. A few days shy of his 30th birthday, Snowden had arrived three weeks earlier in the one-time British colony after taking a leave of absence from Booz Allen Hamilton, the consulting firm through which he was contracted to the NSA. Asked in the video why he had decided to become a whistle-blower, he said: 'The NSA has built an infrastructure that allows it to intercept almost everything. With this capability, the vast majority of human communications are automatically ingested without targeting. If I wanted to see your emails [...] all I have to do is use intercepts. I can get your emails, passwords, phone records, credit cards. I don't want to live in a society that does these sort of things [...] I do not want to live in a world where everything I do and say is recorded. That is not something I am willing to support or live under.' Snowden immediately became a hero to human rights and civil liberty activists, and a traitor to law-enforcement and intelligence officials.

His self-disclosure had not come as a shock to the NSA. It had identified him a few days before but failed to inform GCHQ, despite the British agency's continued investigation into the leaker and fear that it could be one of its own. 'If you're the US, you're the big dog and you tell them [the rest of the Five Eyes] in your own time,' a senior British intelligence insider said. 'It was a chilling reminder of how important you are, or how important you're not. If it was GCHQ which was responsible for the leak, we would've thought about what we had to do to assure our US partners. When it comes to the US […] the US doesn't give a damn.' Another British intelligence official who had been close to the GCHQ investigation into the leak said, 'You learn pretty quickly that the US will not be accounting to you.'

On 13 June, on the eve of being charged in absentia in the US for a string of offences, including breaching the Espionage Act through his disclosures of state secrets, Snowden appeared in an interview in the *South China Morning Post* and alleged that the US had been targeting the computers of businesses, universities, and public officials in Hong Kong and China for many years. 'We hack network backbones – like huge internet routers, basically – that give us access to the communications of hundreds of thousands of computers without having to hack every single one,' Snowden told the newspaper. He said his disclosures were partly to expose the hypocrisy of the US government which claims to not target civilian infrastructure. 'Not only does it do so, but it is so afraid of this being known that it is willing to use any means, such as diplomatic intimidation, to prevent this information from becoming public.' His declaration dispelled any doubts that Snowden was waging a one-man war against the US intelligence agencies and their Five Eyes partners, as he continued releasing documents to news outlets around the world, amid a request from Washington to Hong Kong to detain him for the purpose of extradition so he could face criminal charges back home.

Regular discussions were being held between Five Eyes officials to determine the scale of the material Snowden had downloaded while working with the NSA. Were there dozens of stolen documents in his possession? Thousands? Hundreds of thousands? The intelligence exchanged between the Five Eyes signals agencies, including phone, email and satellite intercepts, are in many cases stored on shared networks for processing, analysis, and distribution. Such systems enable the alliance's SIGINT operators to work more efficiently and as one. XKeyscore, one of the systems shared between the NSA and other Five Eyes agencies, was exposed by Snowden as operating like a vast database containing internet browsing histories of millions of people, along with details of their emails and online communications. Through the database, analysts were able to run specific searches for the IP addresses, names, and telephone numbers of their targets, along with the 'real-time' interception of their internet searches and websites visited.

Signals intelligence officials in London, Canberra, Ottawa and Wellington initiated 'damage control assessments' to establish how many of the secrets they had provided the NSA – either directly or through the shared Five Eyes networks – may have ended up in Snowden's hands. 'We asked the Americans about this and they said, "It's going to take some time to figure it out",' a British official said. While the true scale of the disclosures may never be known, Snowden had downloaded and made off with around 1.5 million secret documents. According to a leak inquiry by the US House Permanent Select Committee on Intelligence, 'If printed out and stacked, these documents would create a pile more than three miles high.' The stolen documents included 160,000 NSA files, close to a million from the US Defense Intelligence Agency, more than 15,000 from Australian intelligence and about 60,000 from Britain's GCHQ. The New Zealanders and Canadians, who had historically benefited from less international scrutiny for being junior partners in the Five Eyes, had not been spared by Snowden, either. New Zealand's signals agency was accused of spying on its allies and sharing its interceptions in bulk with the NSA. Through its interception site at Waihopai, south of Wellington, New Zealand's Government Communications Security Bureau intercepted data from across the Asia-Pacific region, including trading partners and governments in countries such as Fiji, Papua New Guinea and Tonga, and passed it onto the NSA through XKeyscore, the shared database.

Like their New Zealand counterparts, the Canadians had also been targeting allies. The Communications Security Establishment, Ottawa's signals organisation, had helped the NSA spy on 'approximately 20 high-priority countries', according to a leaked document that did not identify the targeted nations by name. Another Snowden document revealed that the Canadian government had allowed the NSA to use the US Embassy in Ottawa as a command post in June 2010 to spy on the G20 summit, which had been attended by international leaders to discuss matters such as economic and financial stability. The revelation was in keeping with an earlier story that had emerged in the *Guardian* in which GCHQ was accused of spying on diplomats who had attended the G20 summit in London in 2009, including the South African and Turkish delegations. Snowden's revelations continued to dominate global headlines, partly because they were relatable to billions of everyday people whose lives revolved around the usage of electronic communications, including mobile phone and emails, and who suddenly started questioning whether they, too, were being spied on. The whistle-blower had turned cyber-spying – which had thus far been largely perceived as the domain of nations targeting other nations – into a topic of interest among the general public. It was a masterstroke that had been in the making for years.

Unlike millions of young people around the world who opposed the Iraq War in 2003, Edward Snowden had embraced the Bush Administration's mantra that 'Operation Iraq Freedom' had been in the interest of protecting America's national security against the so-called 'Axis of Evil' – state sponsors of terrorism which included the regimes in Baghdad, Iran, and North Korea. He was 19 at the time of the US-led invasion, driven by a sense of patriotism that had been shaped two years earlier by his anger at the 9/11 attacks. He enlisted in the US Army in 2004, but his hope of liberating Iraqis was derailed after he broke both of his legs in a training accident, spelling an end to his military career. Snowden had already become disillusioned by then about the real purpose of the Iraq War after witnessing army colleagues being more preoccupied with the notion of killing Arabs than freeing

Iraqis from their oppressors. But he remained committed to the idea of serving his country through some other means, much like his parents and other family members had done through their work for various federal government departments. In between dropping out of high school and his fleeting service in the US military, Snowden had become a certified systems engineer. His talent for computers landed him a job as a contractor for the CIA in 2005, and by the following year, he became a member of staff ahead of a posting to Geneva, Switzerland, to assist agency officials around Europe in dealing with cyber-security vulnerabilities, targets, and threats. Over the duration of his three-year stay in the Swiss capital, Snowden resented the behaviour of some of his colleagues who considered themselves beyond accountability and even above the law.

In late 2009, towards the end of his deployment in Geneva, Snowden had contemplated blowing the whistle but worried that leaking CIA secrets could compromise the identities – and lives – of the agency's undercover agents and spies. It made more sense to him to expose surveillance programmes which illustrated technological abuses. So he resigned from the CIA and became a contractor for Dell Corporation, a tech development firm that is also used by US government bodies, including the NSA, to provide computer services. Through that job – and the subsequent contracting role for Booz Allen Hamilton – Snowden gained access to highly confidential material, including intelligence relating to the Five Eyes, which alleged widespread – and almost limitless – spying by the government agencies on the general public. By the time he took leave from Booz Allen Hamilton and headed to Hong Kong in May 2013, Snowden had connected with American journalist Glenn Greenwald and Laura Poitras, a documentary maker, with the view to exposing documents and methods which he considered a threat to privacy. Snowden never disclosed his methods for obtaining the secret files from the NSA, but he reportedly used a 'web crawler' – a software designed to scrape and download files based on keyword searches.

After his self-disclosure, US intelligence officials – still uncertain about the scale of his document heist – attempted to play down Snowden's penetration of the NSA, claiming he had been a systems administrator with limited access to top secrets. Not only were such claims incorrect, but they also neglected the findings of an internal study commissioned by the NSA two decades earlier which had warned about an 'insider threat' from disillusioned or compromised system administrators. 'System administrators are able to read, copy, move, alter, and destroy almost every piece of classified information handled by a given agency or organisation', said the declassified NSA study, dated September 1991. 'Today's system administrators can obtain full-length copies of entire reports, including draft versions, as well as informal e-mail messages, electronic calendar appointments, and a wide variety of other data.' They were the modern-day equivalent of cryptographers during World War II and Cold War, the study added. 'Just as unbreakable US cryptography [...] pushed foreign intelligence services to target the people who control the key, so, too, will stronger network security spur increased targeting of the people who control the computers'. In the end, the greatest threat to the NSA was not from foreign intelligence agencies but from an insider with a point to prove.

Following the revelations of the NSA's secret monitoring of Verizon customers, and the Prism programme which had enabled it and its British counterpart to tap into the servers of big tech companies, yet another damaging leak emerged on 21 June 2013. GCHQ was revealed to have developed a programme codenamed Tempora, which allowed it to 'tap into and store huge volumes of data drawn from fibre optic cables for up to 30 days so that it can be sifted and analysed'. The disclosure was yet another shock to Sir Iain Lobban and his team at GCHQ. According to the *Guardian*, which broke the story, Tempora had been running for 18 months to access and process 'vast quantities of communications between entirely innocent people, as well as targeted suspects' and share its intercepted material, including calls, email messages, and Facebook entries, with the NSA. 'Documents reveal that by last year GCHQ was handling 600 million 'telephone events' each day, had tapped more than 200 fibre-optic cables and was able to process data from at least 46 of them at a time.'

While GCHQ had not broken the law, Tempora had pushed the limits of existing legislation to hoover up such a large volume of data, the newspaper claimed. Whether by sheer coincidence or design, the story about Tempora emerged on Snowden's 30th birthday and the same day that the US had announced it had charged him with espionage. Forty-eight hours later, he left Hong Kong for Moscow, where he remains to this day. There has never been any evidence that the Kremlin provided him sanctuary in return for any of his secret files. However, that question had been on the minds of the Five Eyes – yet four of the alliance member countries felt powerless to do anything about it because none could really hold the US to account for Snowden's actions.

In the summer of 2013, a meeting was held in Australia between Five Eyes intelligence officials to discuss Snowden's revelations. During the meeting, which was attended by senior representatives from all signals intelligence agencies, including the NSA, GCHQ and the Australian Signals Directorate, British officials found themselves alone in their attempt to question the US about its security failures, which had compromised the alliance's secrets as well as its own. Ahead of the meeting, GCHQ officials had been pressed for information by Britain's Intelligence and Security Committee – the parliamentary body tasked with keeping the country's spy agencies in line – about 'how the hell the leak had happened', according to a British security official. 'The committee demanded assurances from GCHQ that nothing like this could ever happen again.'

America's ability to safeguard its secrets had clearly malfunctioned. Among the challenges that the US had been facing was that about 1.5 million people in the country had top security clearances, about a third of whom were contractors, like Snowden, with access to the most sensitive government files. That represented a seemingly insurmountable vulnerability as too many outsiders had effectively boundless access to endless state secrets.

Sir Kim Darroch, who was Britain's national security adviser during the Snowden Affair, said the UK's intelligence community had been 'astonished at what Snowden had been allowed to access as a contractor'.

He said, 'People would say that that simply wasn't possible in our system – contractors inside the British system couldn't get that level of access and therefore wouldn't have been able to steal that amount of stuff.'

British intelligence officials were 'seized with the imperative', said a GCHQ source, to find out what measures had been taken to plug further insider threats. According to a Five Eyes official who was present at the meeting, Canberra's representatives seemed desperate not to call out the NSA, but rather claimed their unquestioned allegiance to Washington by invoking the memories of the cooperation between their two capitals, which dated back to World War I. 'The Aussies always wanted to make out like they were America's best friends,' the official said. The New Zealanders, having once experienced the wrath of the White House following the controversy over American nuclear submarines in the mid-1980s, were not prepared to risk their ties with Washington after having been partially cut from US intelligence for more than two decades. As for the Canadians, they feared upsetting the NSA because they shared a geographic border with the US, and also relied heavily on its intelligence community. 'Those reactions pretty much represented what everyone had known but no one had been willing to discuss,' said the security official 'and that if it is a US cock-up, the other members of the alliance have to mask their discontent and be statesman-like about it.'

Sir Kim Darroch, only the second person to hold the office of national security adviser created in 2010 by the Cameron Government to, among other things, offer personal advice on matters of security to the prime minister, said there had been no point to having any 'lengthy recriminations' with the US intelligence community over the Snowden leaks because 'there was a feeling that the US are the senior partners and had apologised for what had happened and promised to tighten up their procedures'. He added that 'the US give us more than we give them so we just have to basically get on with it [...] The other thing that is important here is that there is some unfortunate history on our side, notably the Cambridge spy ring. So there is always that hanging over us and it inhibits our being too critical about US security breaches.'

Mike Burgess, the director-general of the Australian Security

Intelligence Organisation, ASIO, said the Snowden revelations did not 'impact our inter-Agency relationships' within the Five Eyes. 'We knew that if we got cranky with the Americans because of Snowden, there could well come a time when, heaven forbid, one of us could have the same problem. We're all very good at saying, "We need to tell you the bad news right now; we need to tell you what has been compromised so you can make your own risk assessments." Because the Snowden case didn't just impact American capabilities, it impacted the Five Eyes capabilities, including Australia's but we don't judge the Americans badly for that because we all make mistakes and we all move forward [...] Snowden betrayed us all and he didn't damage the relationship. Even though some elements of the press say he was a hero and a whistle-blower, we know he wasn't. He was a traitor.'

It was not until the year after the Snowden revelations that the NSA would publicly state that he had 'probably not' been working as a spy for a foreign intelligence agency. 'Could he have? Possibly. Do I believe that's the case? Probably not,' the NSA's then newly appointed director, Admiral Mike Rogers, said in 2014.

Historically, signals intelligence agencies within the alliance had always prided themselves on a specific difference between them and human-intelligence organisations. 'One of the main reasons behind the Five Eyes agreement was to develop a seamless intelligence-sharing platform between SIGINT agencies – and "sharing" was the key word,' said a GCHQ insider. 'That distinguishes them from human-intelligence agencies who do not share, but instead "exchange" intelligence. So human-intelligence agencies are a lot more transactional in their approach to cooperating with the Five Eyes partners: if you want something from them, they would expect something in return.' The spirit of sharing was disrupted after the CIA had become a much closer operational partner with the NSA in the wake of the 9/11 attacks. The CIA did not want the intelligence it provided the NSA to be automatically passed on to other Five Eyes agencies, and as a result, had increasingly labelled it 'NOFORN' – 'not for release to foreign nationals' – to prevent its wider distribution. 'The CIA's relationship began to bear down upon some of the instinctive presumption of sharing,' the insider said. 'There was a risk that the NSA would become more transactional in its approach.' The NSA's shift in attitude had not gone unnoticed by its alliance partners. During a workplace event hosted by Iain Lobban for GCHQ staff at the agency's headquarters in Cheltenham, a visiting NSA official expressed his organisation's commitment to its British counterpart but was keen to make a point to illustrate the reality of the partnership. 'He removed a US passport from the pocket of his suit jacket, pointed it to the GCHQ staff members and said, "You don't have one of these; the people who work at the CIA do,"' said a senior GCHQ official who had been present at the event. 'The kind of "big dog" attitude which some took it as saying, "Yes you're great and we like working with you, and love your warm beer and great culture – but you're not one of us." But the additional point made by the NSA official was that his agency not only prized GCHQ's capability and reach, but also the agency's willingness to act as a soundboard, challenge and even disagree with NSA views.'

The same GCHQ official who had attended the event was also present for the Five Eyes meeting that was held in Australia following the Snowden revelations. He recalled that as much as GCHQ wanted to castigate the NSA, it neither had the backing of the junior alliance partners to do so, nor did it want to push its chances because of its countless joint operations with the US agency for which it also received funding. 'GCHQ received funding from the NSA and other signals intelligence agencies in the Five Eyes, including [from] the smaller partners like the Australians,' said the official who had direct knowledge of the funding process. 'Sometimes even smaller partners like the Australians also provided funds – and it was always for mutually beneficial projects, including intelligence collection assets such as satellites. It was all part of improving the overall operations and capabilities within the Five Eyes.'

In the summer of 2013, a series of Snowden documents revealed that the NSA had paid at least £100 million to its British counterpart since 2010 for a range of mutually beneficial projects, including £17.2 million towards one of the GCHQ's interception programmes, £15.5 million for the redevelopment of UK's listening stations in Bude, on England's southwest coast, and half the costs of running its eavesdropping site in Cyprus. One document also revealed GCHQ's eagerness to maintain a strong partnership with the NSA. 'Our key partnership is with the US,' the internal document said. 'We need to keep this relationship healthy. The relationship remains strong but is not sentimental. GCHQ must pull its weight and be seen to pull its weight.' Nine years later, a British official familiar with the leaked document said: 'The de facto position was that costs would lie where they fall and certain projects required joint funding, but it would be hugely misleading to say that GCHQ relied on funding from the NSA.'

The leaked document about the NSA's financial contribution to GCHQ did bring into question – at least in the eyes of the public – the grip the NSA had over its UK sister agency. At the time, Britain's annual intelligence budget – shared by GCHQ, MI5 and MI6 – was around £1.92 billion. It was dwarfed by the NSA's annual budget of US$56.2 billion that it was set to share with the CIA. None of the Five Eyes members could afford to fall out with Washington. Sir Geoffrey Palmer, New Zealand's deputy prime minister during the fallout between Washington and Wellington in the mid-1980s, once recalled that being part of the alliance meant there was 'always a feeling that we have to earn our stripes'. GCHQ, too, had to earn its stripes, as one of its greatest fears was Washington's perception of a diminishing partnership that could lead 'to loss of access, and/or reduction in investment [...] to the UK', as had been stated in one of its internal documents.

A membership in the Five Eyes alliance entails too many operational advantages to pass up – benefits that other nations have for years been desperate to tap into, but have only managed to remain on the periphery of. Up to thirty-three countries, including Germany, France, Italy, Singapore, Japan, India, Israel and the United Arab Emirates, are 'Tier B' partners with the United States, with whom limited intelligence-sharing exists, especially on matters relating to counterterrorism and the armed services during conflicts. Non-US members to the Five Eyes also benefit from the secondary tier partnerships through the virtually limitless cooperation between the alliance members. Unbeknown to the 'Tier B' allies, they, too, 'could not be considered to be off limits' to Five Eyes spying, according to a GCHQ insider, including from eavesdropping operations against their leaders and officials, or in the way of bulk interception which sweeps up everyday conversations of millions of their citizens. 'It is a fact of life that bulk access will have the incidental consequence of sweeping up these everyday communications which are then discarded as a matter of policy,' said Sir Iain Lobban in defence of the British agency's bulk interception. 'To describe the incidental collection as targeted is plain wrong. Think of it as a way of throwing away the hay as you search out those needles in the haystack which amount to the chit chat and command and control of terrorists living in our western societies.'

To the embarrassment of Washington and London, Snowden revealed that the NSA and GCHQ spied on allies, including Germany and its Chancellor Angela Merkel, whose mobile phone was tapped by the Five Eyes. Merkel was outraged by the discovery that her discussions with world leaders, including French President Nicolas Sarkozy and UN Secretary-General Ban Ki-moon, had also been listened to and urged an explanation from US President Barack Obama. In an attempt to defuse tensions between Washington and Berlin that threatened to damage their bilateral ties, the White House issued a carefully worded denial, saying the US 'is not monitoring and will not monitor the communications of Chancellor Merkel'. The statement made no mention, however, of whether Merkel's calls had been spied on in the past.

A document leaked to the German online magazine *Der Spiegel* labelled 'Top Secret' and marked 'USA, AUS, CAN, GBR, NZL' disclosed that the Five Eyes were targeting the communications of 122 country leaders. They ranged from 'presidents of Peru, Somalia, Guatemala and Colombia right up to Belarusian President Alexander Lukashenko', the magazine revealed. The disclosure added weight to revelations from a decade earlier by Britain's Secretary of State for International Development, Clare Short, who had accused her government of spying on the head of the United Nations, Kofi Annan, saying she had read 'transcripts' of his conversation, implying that his office had been bugged by the UK. 'These things are done,' she said. 'And in the case of Kofi's office, it has been done for a long time.' Short's claims outraged the British government, and in particular, GCHQ, at whom the finger of blame had pointed. Yet it was also claimed at that time that MI6, too, had a handful of officers in New York dedicated to spying on the UN. 'It is their entire job,' a British former official had told Britain's *Sunday Times*. 'They bug places and they have been doing it for years.'

Short's revelations in 2004 were a drop in the ocean in comparison to Snowden's disclosures, which had oversight bodies in the Five Eyes on the back-foot over how to watch the watchers and hold them to account. Britain's parliamentary watchdog, the Intelligence Security Committee, had been seeking more transparency from the heads of services for at least six months before Snowden's secrets came to light in June 2013. The ISC's proposal for a televised hearing to discuss matters of national security had received mixed responses from Sir John Sawers, chief of MI6, MI5's director-general Andrew Parker and GCHQ's director Sir Iain Lobban. As a former diplomat, Sawers had seemingly been most comfortable with the idea of appearing at a live hearing. However, Parker, who had only been in charge of his agency since April was far less easy about the proposed idea, especially because he had been an MI5 'lifer' who had spent his entire professional career in the shadows. Lobban, too, was opposed to a live hearing and had even drafted a letter of opposition which he had planned to provide to the ISC in the summer of 2013. However, Snowden's revelations put an end to Lobban's reluctance and effectively forced his hand. The GCHQ director knew that there was no way that he could legitimately send the letter because it would be deemed a reaction to the spying affair, rather than a position he held for months before Snowden's revelations. According to those who worked closely with Lobban, he decided to go public despite a 'massive discomfort'.

GCHQ's workplace in central London was located opposite one of the busiest tube stations in the capital, but few outside of the intelligence community were aware of its existence. The Palmer Street site was a nondescript, red-brick building that looked like a disused adjunct to St James's Park Underground Station – unlike the agency's headquarters in Cheltenham, southwest England, which is a signposted, circular building with the imposing presence of an Olympic stadium. GCHQ's London base was virtually invisible, except for two unmarked front steel doors with as many security cameras above them. It had been commandeered by the organisation in 1953 to scale up its Cold War activities, be within earshot of its political masters in Westminster – Britain's political heartbeat – and run joint operations with its sister agencies, MI5 and MI6. The 'Palmer Street hub' had also been the setting for countering various national security targets, including Kremlin spies, IRA and Al Qaeda terrorists. Yet exactly six decades after its creation, the hub unexpectedly became the setting for countering a reputational, rather than, security threat.

It was there that Lobban showed up on the morning of 7 November 2013, in preparation for 'war-gaming' his scheduled appearance before a parliamentary hearing later that day. GCHQ's director entered the building with a takeaway coffee in hand, walked into his office and took the unusual step of closing the door behind him. He removed a mound of paper files and documents from his desk, making room for about 25 cue cards, which contained his thoughts from the night before. With a pen in hand, Lobban amended some of the cards, refined his thoughts, until four of his top advisers walked into the office and provided him with a briefing pack that included legal notes relating to GCHQ's past surveillance operations. Lobban spent the morning being quizzed by his advisers, who assumed an interrogative role to prepare him for the showdown. 'Iain's major concern was that the parliamentary hearing would be turned into a gladiatorial session where he and his lifetime organisation would become the main target,' said an intelligence official who worked closely with Lobban. 'Because the disclosures that had been made by Edward Snowden about Britain very much pointed the finger at GCHQ, along with its programmes and methods of operation.' With that in mind, Lobban spent the rest of the morning with his advisers honing his messages – it was his chance to hit back and protect the image and work of his organisation's 6,000 employees. He anticipated punches to be slung his way, but wanted to make the point that his organisation had behaved lawfully and had received authorisations from a secretary of state level, including the foreign secretary, to conduct its surveillance activities.

In the afternoon, as he appeared at the televised parliamentary hearing alongside his two counterparts, MI5's Andrew Parker and John Sawers of MI6, Lobban was ready to reclaim some grounds in favour of his organisation which had been effectively thrashed in the media for the five months following Snowden's first leak. The GCHQ director said documents stolen and released into the public by Snowden had compromised Britain's security as they had alerted terrorists groups in Afghanistan, the Middle East, and South Asia, on how to avoid interception. Terrorists had even assessed the 'communication packages they wish to move to', Lobban told the hearing, 'to avoid what they now perceive to be vulnerable communications methods'. He insisted that GCHQ did not conduct mass surveillance of ordinary citizens, despite collecting huge volumes of mobile and internet data. Another point Lobban had been keen to make had been suggested to him by one of his advisers: it was that 'I don't think secret means sinister'. The phrase succeeded in being widely quoted by the international press, but it also summed up Lobban's view that secrecy was an absolute requirement for intelligence agencies to identify, track, and evaluate the threat of their targets without tipping them off in the process. It was part and parcel of spying: 'It feels strange to say: we have nothing to hide, given that we work within that ring of secrecy, but that ring of secrecy has the oversight mechanism, has the safeguards [...] to actually exercise that on behalf of the British public.'

During the ninety-minute hearing, held before a nine-member panel of the Intelligence and Security Committee in parliament, Lobban was being closely watched by GCHQ's employees at the agency's headquarters in Cheltenham, known as 'The Doughnut' because of the building's circular shape. 'At The Doughnut, there were people going into conference rooms to watch if their director was going to say something useful or end up as roadkill,' a GCHQ insider said. 'At least one person even brought popcorn along.' The consensus among agency officials was that their boss had put up a robust defence of their work at a time when they had all been struggling to deal with the villainous image that they perceived had been attributed to them by the mainstream media and champions of civil rights. Although Lobban felt satisfied in the representations he had made on behalf of GCHQ, he did not feel there was anything to celebrate. He turned down an offer for a post-hearing drink from the heads of his sister agencies and made his way home.

The ISC's hearing succeeded in partially humanising the bosses of Britain's three intelligence agencies, because until then, the public had barely been exposed to pictures of them, let alone seen them appear on television. Yet that was not enough to overturn Snowden's anti-surveillance narrative. He had won the public relations debate in the eyes of the general public – not only in the UK, but right across the Five Eyes and beyond. Snowden had been able to demonstrate an overreach by the NSA and GCHQ that brought into question the adequacy of their oversight and their operational methods, regardless of whether or not it was legal or proportionate.

The disclosures eroded public trust in the intelligence community yet again, after the Five Eyes had continued to suffer from their post-9/11 spy scandals surrounding the rendition and torture of Guantanamo detainees by the CIA. In June 2015, almost two years to the day following Snowden's first disclosure, the US Senate passed a bill – the USA Freedom Act – which ended the NSA's program for the bulk collection of millions of Americans' phone records. In September 2020, the US Court of Appeals for the Ninth Circuit – the largest of its kind in the country – stated that the telephone metadata programme may have been unconstitutional. The following year, the European Court of Human Rights (ECtHR) ruled that GCHQ's bulk interception of online communications 'was in principle compatible with human rights law, but that gaps in the pre-2016 supervisory regime meant that the rights to privacy and freedom of expression had been violated', said David Anderson, QC, who served as Britain's Independent Reviewer of Terrorism Legislation during the Snowden Affair, and authored two reports in 2015 and 2016 that resulted in new legislation to improve the democratic oversight of government surveillance.

The ECtHR ruling states: 'In order to minimise the risk of the bulk interception power being abused, the Court considers that the process must be subject to "end-to-end safeguards", meaning that, at the domestic level, an assessment should be made at each stage of the process of the necessity and proportionality of the measures being taken; that bulk interception should be subject to independent authorisation at the outset, when the object and scope of the operation are being defined; and that the operation should be subject to supervision and independent ex post facto [retrospective] review.'

The Snowden revelations played a great part in exposing the reach of spy agencies, but how much of a difference did they really make in forcing them to change their methods? 'Snowden did the world a service by revealing to the public the cutting-edge surveillance methods that were used under the loosely-drafted surveillance laws of the Five Eyes,' Anderson said. 'This caused a short-term blow to public trust, and to the cooperation that governments received from the private sector. But in the longer term, the Snowden revelations have resulted not in the rolling back of surveillance powers but in laws providing for improved transparency and oversight – the essential basis for public trust. Snowden's legacy has not been to end the use of bulk powers, but to precipitate the democratic consent mechanisms on which their continued use depends.'

The 2021 ECtHR ruling around GCHQ's bulk interception was hailed as a victory for civil liberties, yet by the time it emerged, the Five Eyes intelligence community had rehabilitated its image in the eyes of the public, thanks in part to the election of a US Presidential candidate who had effectively invited Russia to spy on the communications of his campaign rival.

PART FOUR: UNCONVENTIONAL BATTLEFIELDS

CHAPTER FOURTEEN

AUSTRALIAN INTERVENTION

IN THE SPRING OF 2016, as Donald Trump's popularity among American voters continued to defy domestic and international expectations, Alexander Downer, Australia's most senior diplomat in Britain, had become curious about the presidential candidate's outlook on the historical ties between Washington and Canberra. Downer's responsibilities as his country's London-based High Commissioner were specific to the diplomatic relationship with the United Kingdom – not the United States – but his seemingly insatiable appetite for global affairs, which was a hangover from his previous role as Australia's longest serving foreign minister, had reinforced his intrigue in Trump. So when the opportunity came up to be introduced to a member of his team in early May, Downer leapt at it. He accompanied Erika Thompson, a counsellor from the Australian High Commission, to the meeting she had organised with George Papadopoulos, a foreign policy adviser on Trump's campaign.

The adviser had been recruited to the campaign only two months earlier while he had been working as an energy consultant in London –

and despite his lack of experience in foreign policy, he had been described by Trump as 'an excellent guy'. It was unclear whether the presidential candidate's praise for the 28-year-old from Chicago, Illinois, related to his personality or ability – or both. But it had been enough to place him on the map as player: a person who appeared close to a potential future president of the United States. Papadopoulos's confidence resembled that of a Silicon Valley entrepreneur, and he was unafraid of flexing whatever authority he thought he had in the face of world leaders. In a newspaper interview on 4 May 2016, he lambasted David Cameron after the British prime minister described Trump's proposal to ban Muslims from the US as 'divisive, stupid and wrong'. Papadopoulos did not hold back in his admonishment: 'It's unfortunate that Prime Minister Cameron was one of the most outspoken critics of Mr Trump,' he told *The Times*. 'Not even the Chinese premier came out with negative statements, or other European leaders. To see Mr Cameron come out as the most vocal opponent was uncalled for. Considering that we believe that the UK–US relationship should be a cornerstone not just of NATO policy but elsewhere, it would be wise for him to reach out in a more positive manner to Mr Trump.'

Within days of the story's publication, Downer and Thompson met with Papadopoulos at the Kensington Wine Room in west London for an after-work drink. Downer brought up *The Times* article and told the young adviser that his approach of attacking the British prime minister in the media 'was not a good idea' for relationship building. It was more of an avuncular piece of advice, rather than an admonishment, from a geopolitical heavyweight who had been at the forefront of cultivating diplomatic relationships with the Democrats under the Clinton Administration and the Republicans under George W. Bush. If Papadopoulos felt castigated in any way at the time, he certainly did not let on, but instead talked about what Trump's foreign policy vision would be if he were elected to the White House. It was a cordial discussion. 'Australia had such little insight into what Trump's policy would be if he won the election,' Downer said. 'We had no idea whether Trump would be successful or not.'

But there was hardly anything counterintuitive about most of Papadopoulos's spiel, including a prediction that Trump would win the election, maintain America's commitment to NATO and take a hard-line approach against China. However, during the hour-long meeting, he made a casual admission that piqued Downer's interest. Papadopoulos claimed the Russian government was said to have obtained material on Hillary Clinton, Trump's main rival in the Democratic camp, and indicated that it could release it anonymously to damage her campaign. 'It sounded bad, but my attitude at the time was who would know whether this was even true,' Downer said. Yet his curiosity outweighed his scepticism, and since it is customary for the head of a diplomatic mission to report back to their government matters of geopolitical interest, Downer authorised a cable to Canberra which summarised his meeting with Papadopoulos, including Russia's intentions against Clinton. And that was supposed to be that.

A separate matter relating to Moscow's interest in the US election had come to GCHQ's notice that spring. One of its analysts identified Kremlin's cyber-spies attempting to compromise the computer networks of the Democratic Congressional Campaign Committee and the Democratic National Committee. The analyst translated the code, or 'raw intelligence', relating to what appeared to be a 'spear phishing email' urging unsuspecting users to click on a link which would allow hackers to steal their login and password details. The details of the attack were outlined in an internal report which GCHQ provided to its closest American partner, the NSA. The British agency's leadership understood the political sensitivities around any Russian interference in the US election, but it provided the report as part of its ongoing intelligence-sharing rather than a politically motivated act.

Although it was not publicly known at the time, Russian hackers working on behalf of the country's military-intelligence organisation, the GRU, had secretly infiltrated the IT networks of Democratic officials in the United States, including some of Hillary Clinton's most senior advisers. The hackers had stolen thousands of emails relating to communication between DCCC and DNC members, including passwords and research on the Republican Party. Hackers also targeted the networks with X-Agent, malware which tracks each keystroke typed on its victim's device, and is able to take screenshots and gather other data about their infected computer.

Moscow was well-known for meddling in international politics, having propped up anti-Western leaders in countries including Egypt, Hungary and Afghanistan during the Cold War, but the cyber-attack against US Democratic officials was yet another forward leap in the Kremlin's arsenal of disruptive behaviour. Russia had planned to undermine the western political process in what it had hoped would be a deniable cyber-attack. It was part of a long-running cyber-war that Moscow had been waging against the West, a war it had started two decades before its interference in the US election with a more traditional, and less ambitious, purpose – good old-fashioned espionage.

In the second half of the 1990s, about five years after the collapse of the Soviet Union, the Kremlin's Cold War nuclear posturing had given way to a less obvious tactic to compete with the West: computer hacking. In one of the first major cyber espionage campaigns ever recorded, Russian hackers reportedly targeted government institutions in countries including the US, Britain, and Canada, to steal information relating to military, technological, and scientific research. The new and unanticipated threat caught the Five Eyes flatfooted and it was not until about three years into the network intrusions campaign that the FBI twigged on. It launched a series of investigations in 1999 codenamed Moonlight Maze. The investigations revealed that the hackers had targeted 'military systems, as well as various governmental, commercial, and educational computer systems in the United States', including the Pentagon and the National Aeronautics and Space Administration (NASA). Los Alamos National Laboratory, New Mexico – home to the Manhattan Project where the atomic bomb was built during WWII – had also been targeted by the cyber-spies as the facility was at the forefront of research relating to national security, including countermeasures to biological terrorist threats. The FBI's investigation found that the network attacks had predominantly targeted thousands of sensitive, yet unclassified documents, including maps of military installations and hardware designs.

Moonlight Maze led to the deployment of FBI special agents to Moscow to try to identify the source of the hack. According to a declassified FBI document, dated 15 April 1999, other law-enforcement authorities in the Five Eyes, including Britain's Scotland Yard, also assisted the US law-enforcement organisation in its inquiries. Despite such measures, the FBI had been unable to find out whether the network hacking campaign was sponsored by the Kremlin, even though all the clues pointed in that direction. That year, John Hamre, the US Deputy Secretary of Defense, who oversaw security matters relating to the Pentagon's computer systems, confirmed that 'officials believe some of the most sophisticated attacks are coming from Russia.' He said investigators had detected 'probes and attacks on US military search and technology systems – including the nuclear weapons laboratories run by the Department of Energy.' The scale of the online heists was unparalleled. Moonlight Maze ultimately found that the stolen documents, if printed and piled up, would stand more than 1,650 feet tall – three times the height of the Washington Monument in the US capital. In response, agencies within the Five Eyes, including the NSA, MI5, GCHQ and Australia's domestic security service, ASIO, formed a cyber working group to assess Russia's online threat, according to a British intelligence official familiar with the initiative.

In the lead up to the new millennium, the Kremlin was still picking itself off the floor following its military defeat in Afghanistan, economic collapse at home, and the failure of Communism as an ideology. The command and control within Russia's security services, which had accompanied Boris Yeltsin's leadership in the early 1990s, had collapsed. The British and US spy agencies, including MI5, MI6 and the CIA were enjoying an 'open season' of intelligence leaks from KGB officers who were either desperate for relevance or money, or in other cases, ideologically driven to expose the former crimes of the Kremlin. One of the greatest intelligence coups for the Five Eyes followed the defection of Vasili Nikitich Mitrokhin, an archivist for the KGB. His attempt to defect to America after walking into the US Embassy in Riga, Latvia, in March 1992, had been turned down by the CIA because the documents he had offered were long-hand transcripts of files – rather than the originals – to which he had access during his 28-year service for the KGB. He then tried his luck at the British Embassy and he and his family were ultimately whisked to Britain by MI6, and given a safe house and a new identity. MI6 had in some way redeemed itself for turning down Fritz Kolbe – Hitler's foreign office official during World War II who had offered to spy for the British service – only to be recruited by the CIA instead.

Mitrokhin directed MI6 to 11,000 pages of his handwritten documents buried in the garden of his country house in Russia. They became known as the 'Mitrokhin Archives', revealing the KGB's secret operational history, including the identities of some of its spies, its provision of weapons to Palestinian militants and the Irish Republican Army, and a plot it had developed in the 1960s and 1970s to target power supplies in some US states in the event of a war with the country. Mitrokhin provided details about the penetration of the Australian intelligence agency, ASIO, by Soviet spies in the 1970s and 1980s. The Australian government commissioned an inquiry in the 1990s into the scale of the penetration, but it remains secret to this day. However, it is claimed that at least four ASIO officers had been spying for Moscow and were quietly retired with no action taken against them to protect the organisation's reputation.

Mitrokhin's defection was kept secret by Britain for seven years until a book he co-authored about the KGB was released in 1999. Its revelations were unsurprisingly played down by the Kremlin – and while it highlighted the ongoing distrust between Moscow and the West – it did not openly impact diplomatic relations. Even when Vladimir Putin became president in 2000, the Five Eyes felt that the former superpower's military threat had been neutralised and its espionage capabilities severely diminished. The new Russian leader, who had served as an intelligence officer with the KGB for 15 years during the Cold War before becoming the director of its successor organisation, the FSB, had not been known for his love of the West. But during a press interview shortly after he became president, Putin stated that he would not rule out joining NATO 'if and when Russia's views are taken into account as those of an equal partner'. He said, 'Russia is part of the European culture. And I cannot imagine my own country in isolation from Europe and what we often call the civilised world.' He had even won over many sceptics in Britain's intelligence community after claiming that he wanted his intelligence services to cultivate a working relationship with the UK. In late 2000, shortly after becoming president, he deployed Nikolai Patrushev, the head of the FSB, to London to meet with MI5 officials. And by the following year, there was even optimism within the Five Eyes that their intelligence agencies would be able to engage with the Kremlin to defeat a mutual threat – Islamist extremism – following the 11 September attacks on the United States. By 2002, Russia was facing its own Islamist threat on home soil as armed Chechen rebels seized a crowded theatre in Moscow. They demanded the withdrawal of Russian troops in Chechnya – who had invaded the country two years earlier – in return for releasing the 900 theatre hostages. Russian security forces eventually forced their way into the theatre in a botched rescue mission that killed 170 people, including 130 hostages.

By that point, Australia's intelligence services had effectively shut down their counter-Russia operations to focus on the Islamist terrorism. However, at MI5, officials opposed the attempted closure of the agency's Russia desk and instead favoured keeping a smaller number of analysts focused on the counterintelligence threat, in case the Kremlin was ever to reactivate its hostile operations. The agency's instincts would prove to be on the right side of history after Russia's residual paranoia from the Cold War began to dominate its foreign policy decisions. Putin blamed Western intelligence agencies, including the CIA, for fomenting popular uprisings in former Soviet states – including Georgia in 2003, Ukraine the following year, and Kyrgyzstan in 2005 – which became known as the 'colour revolution' and resulted in the removal of Kremlin-aligned, authoritarian regimes.

* * *

Vladimir Putin maintained his nation's diplomatic ties with the West despite his suspicions of its intelligence agencies and its political leaders. The Russian leader arrived in London in the autumn of 2005 to meet with British Prime Minister Tony Blair. According to a statement by Kremlin, published on 5 October, shortly after the meeting at Number 10 Downing Street, the two leaders discussed cooperation in a range of areas, including 'joint efforts in counterterrorism'. It was Putin's second trip to the country in as many years, after an historic state visit in June 2003 that marked the first such occasion by a Russian leader since Tsar Alexander II in 1874.

During his October 2005 visit, Putin was also briefed by Eliza Manningham-Buller, director-general of MI5, who had been dealing with the aftermath of the London bombings – a series of coordinated suicide attacks by home-grown terrorists which had killed 52 innocent people and injured almost 800 three months earlier. The meeting had been arranged at Blair's request and held at the Cabinet Office's Briefing Room 'A', or COBRA, which is usually reserved for the British government's emergency-response committee to convene during a national crisis. 'It was during the autumn after the London terrorist attacks and at that stage we were really trying to be friends,' said Manningham-Buller of her meeting with the Russian leader and her agency's attempt to maintain a cordial working relationship with its counterparts in Moscow. However, Putin seemed to show little sensitivity over what London had been through and, instead, criticised MI5 over the deadly attack. 'He said, "It is the duty of the security service officer to put themselves between the terrorist and the victim",' Manningham-Buller recalled. 'The implication there was that we failed in our job – which to some degree was true – but it was a hostile statement for him to make.'

Britain's cooperation with Russia on counterterrorism continued nonetheless. In early 2006, a team of British intelligence officials travelled to Moscow to meet with the SVR, Russia's external intelligence service, to discuss issues relating to Afghanistan, Iran and Al Qaeda. During the bilateral talks, which focused on intelligence assessments and judgements – rather than sharing or exchanging secrets – the SVR warned Britain

Above: As New Zealand's Prime Minister between 1984–9, David Lange attracted international acclaim for standing up to Washington in favour of his government's anti-nuclear position. His defiance resulted in Wellington being partially cut from the Five Eyes for more than twenty years.

Right: In his first public speech as the director-general of MI5, Jonathan Evans warned in 2007 that Russia had been spending 'considerable time and energy trying to steal our sensitive technology [...] and trying to obtain political and economic intelligence at our expense.'

The World Trade Centre buildings in New York were among the targets of coordinated terrorist attacks by Al Qaeda on the United States on 11 September 2001 which killed almost 3,000 people.

Above: On 12 September 2001, a day after the terrorist attacks on America, Eliza Manningham-Buller was deployed to Washington to meet with US intelligence officials. The following year, she was promoted to lead MI5 through some of the greatest security challenges in the agency's history.

Below: Alleged terrorism suspects at Guatanamo Bay, some of whom were subjected to torture such as 'waterboarding'. Of almost 800 detainees held at the US military prison in Cuba, the majority were released without any charges.

Above: Richard Fadden, who led Canada's intelligence agency, CSIS, between 2009–13, said it is the way that spy agencies handle the fallout from security breaches that 'determines whether or not you're taken seriously'. Fadden also served as his country's national security adviser in the Five Eyes' battle against Islamic State-inspired terrorism.

Below: Under Malcolm Turnbull's government, Australia banned the Chinese tech firm, Huawei, in a move that was eventually followed by other partners in the alliance. 'In terms of Huawei, we were the leaders of the Five Eyes in banning it from involvement in our 5G network,' said the former prime minister.

Left: Richard Walton, who ran Scotland Yard's counterterrorism division during the rise of ISIS, was shocked to hear that an agent of the Canadian intelligence service, CSIS, helped facilitate the entry of aspiring British jihadists into Syria.

Below: Shamima Begum, Amira Abase and Kadiza Sultana at a bus station in Turkey before they were smuggled into Syria by a Canadian Security Intelligence Service agent in February, 2015.

© PA/PA Archive/PA Images

Above/below: Sir Iain Lobban, director of GCHQ during the international controversy that followed Edward Snowden's revelations, gave evidence at the first televised Intelligence and Security Committee hearing in Parliament on 7 November 2013.

The hearing was also attended by Sir John Sawers, head of MI6, and the director-general of MI5, Andrew Parker.

© Barton Gellman/Getty

© PA/PA Archive/PA Images

Above: The NSA contractor Edward Snowden, whose theft of about 1.5 million secret documents in a security breach that exposed the global spying operations of the Five Eyes led to a historic debate on civil liberties, and triggered multiple investigations into surveillance programmes.

Top left: As the chief of GCHQ's National Cyber Security Centre, Ciaran Martin clashed with US officials over differences of opinion regarding Huawei. He also defended GCHQ against allegations of 'wiretapping'.

Right: Former British Prime Minister Theresa May said her government had to adjust to a more 'volatile' environment during President Donald Trump's term in office. '[T]here had always been an assumption of smooth running relationships.'

Below: Kim Darroch served as Britain's national security adviser and the country's ambassador to the United States, gaining a unique insight into the transatlantic Special Relationship on matters relating to intelligence.

Above: President Barack Obama is joined by Joe Biden, Hillary Clinton, and security officials in the White House Situation Room, watching a live feed of the operation to kill Al Qaeda leader Osama Bin Laden in May 2011. The Americans did not inform their Five Eyes partners of the operation beforehand.

The Russian invasion of Ukraine in February 2022 was correctly foreseen by the Five Eyes.

about its involvement in Afghanistan, which had been ongoing for almost five years. 'They spoke about their own experience in Afghanistan in the 1980s and told us that we were unlikely to defeat the Taliban,' said a British intelligence official who was on the visit. 'They said, "Even when you think you've driven the insurgency away, they'll eventually come back – and that will continue happening time and again."' The SVR's advice was somewhat prophetic, for the Taliban would return to rule Afghanistan 15 years later in 2021 – despite a 20-year military campaign by the US and its allies to keep the militants away.

After the talks in Moscow in early 2020, the British officials invited their hosts to repay the visit, with the view to welcoming them to the UK later in the year. But the invitation was effectively torn up once the Russian state proved its disregard for British sovereignty by killing one of its dissidents, Alexander Litvinenko, in London. The former FSB officer had sought political asylum in Britain in 2000 after fleeing Russia with his wife and son. Despite fearing retribution, he continued to publicly criticise the FSB of widespread corruption, including connections to the mafia and orchestrating bombings in Russia in 1999 to create a pretext for the Putin regime's war against Chechnya. Litvinenko's knowledge of the FSB gained him a role as a paid consultant to MI6. In November 2006, a few weeks after he and his family had become naturalised as British citizens, Litvinenko was killed by two FSB assassins who had laced his tea with polonium-210, an invisible and almost virtually undetectable radioactive substance. Although Putin denied Russia's involvement in his killing, a counterterrorism team from Britain's Scotland Yard uncovered insurmountable evidence which tracked the assassins back to Moscow. 'To take the risk of carrying out such an attack in the UK suggested that they had trialled the method successfully elsewhere and were given approval to hit Litvinenko on that basis,' said Eliza Manningham-Buller. The killing of Litvinenko severed all intelligence cooperation between London and Moscow and led to a public inquiry in Britain which found 'strong circumstantial evidence of Russian state responsibility' and concluded that the dissident's murder had been 'probably approved by Mr Patrushev [head of the FSB] and also by President Putin'.

Scotland Yard's investigation into Litvinenko's murder had been partly assisted by the FBI: the US law-enforcement agency invited a small team of British authorities, including a member of the UK's Atomic Weapon's Establishment – whose scientists had identified the radioactive substance during Litvinenko's post mortem – to visit Los Alamos Labs in New Mexico. The British delegation were provided with insights about the polonium-210, including that it had most likely originated from Russia's nuclear research centre in Sarov – the same place Stalin's atomic bomb had been developed during World War II.

While cooperation among Five Eyes agencies on matters relating to Russia was stepped up behind closed doors, in 2007, the incoming director-general of MI5, Jonathan Evans, publicly criticised the Kremlin's hostility towards Britain and warned about the 'undeclared Russian intelligence officers in the UK – at the Russian Embassy and associated organisations conducting covert activity in this country'. In fact, a little more than four decades after MI5 had expelled 105 Soviet spies from the Soviet Embassy in London, Moscow had slowly been able to reinstate approximately 100 undeclared intelligence officers at its embassy. In his first public speech in November 2007, Evans also warned that Britain's adversaries, with the Putin regime at the top of the list, devoted 'considerable time and energy trying to steal our sensitive technology on civilian and military projects, and trying to obtain political and economic intelligence at our expense.' Neither MI5 nor any other agency in the Five Eyes had known that, in the summer of that year – four months before Evans's public speech – a Canadian navy analyst with access to some of the most sensitive intelligence in his country's possession had walked into the Russian Embassy in Ottawa and offered to spy for the Kremlin. Jeffrey Paul Delisle's offer to sell secrets had been enthusiastically received by the GRU, Moscow's military-intelligence organisation, which immediately recruited him for espionage work in July 2007. The sub-lieutenant had a top-level clearance, with wide-ranging access to secrets, including those that belonged to the Canadian Security Intelligence Service and other agencies in the Five Eyes. The Canadian authorities eventually discovered that Delisle had 'robust access to all source intelligence from our partners [...] Australia, Canada, Great Britain, and the United States'.

Three years into Delisle's espionage mission for Moscow, the Five Eyes made a breakthrough on a separate case. A joint investigation by MI5, the CIA, FBI and Canadian intelligence officials took down a Kremlin espionage ring operating undercover in the US. Anna Chapman, a 28-year-old Russian spy also known as Anya Kushchenko, was among the ten Russian spies who pleaded guilty in a New York courtroom to 'conspiracy to act as an unregistered agent of a foreign country'. Chapman, who had made her home in London between 2004 and 2006 and obtained British citizenship after marrying a local man, was working for Russia's external intelligence service, the SVR. Two other spies who pleaded guilty, Elena Vavilova and Andrey Bezrukov, were a husband-and-wife team who had cemented their deep cover in the early 1990s in Canada. Their cover story as the owners of a nappy delivery service had been so convincing that even their son had no idea that they were SVR agents. The joint operation by the Five Eyes agencies against the Russian spies led to a Cold War-style prisoner swap, with Moscow's foreign ministry announcing the 'return to Russia of 10 Russian citizens accused in the United States, along with the simultaneous transfer to the United States of four individuals previously condemned in Russia'. Among the prisoners released by Moscow was Sergei Skripal, a former military-intelligence officer with the GRU, who had been imprisoned for working as a double agent for MI6.

The embarrassing operation exposing the Russian espionage cell in the US did not deter the Kremlin's hostility towards the West – and as for one of its greatest recruits in Canada, Jeffrey Delisle, it was not until two years later that he was busted for his crimes. The delay in his arrest to the winter of 2012 was the result of a failure by the Canadian Security Intelligence Service to act on an FBI tip from the previous year. CSIS feared that Ottawa's secrets could be exposed in the event of open court proceedings should a case be brought against Delisle. The refusal by CSIS to act frustrated the FBI, which was at the time under the leadership of

Robert S. Mueller III, and as a result, the US law-enforcement agency alerted the Royal Canadian Military Police, who finally arrested Delisle on 13 January 2012. It was impossible to determine the volume of secrets that he had provided to Russia in return for US$110,000 over more than four-and-a-half years. Delisle pleaded guilty to his crimes and admitted that it was not just 'Canadian stuff' he had targeted: 'There was American stuff, there was some British stuff, Australian stuff – it was everybody's stuff.' Before being handed a 20-year prison sentence, Delisle attempted to justify his action, telling police: 'We spy on everybody. Everybody spies.' He said the majority of the information he had stolen related to electronic eavesdropping rather than intelligence obtained by human agents. 'There's no human assets listed on our machines [...] It's SIGINT really.' General David Petraeus, who was director of the CIA during the Delisle affair, said the Canadian's recruitment by the GRU had been one of the biggest infiltrations by Russia into a Five Eyes intelligence service since the end of the Cold War. 'I remember at the time how big a deal this was,' he said. 'It was a big penetration.' But he said despite the breach, Washington's intelligence relationships with Ottawa were not affected because the Canadians are 'high quality people' and 'great partners who did not need to be scolded. They would have scolded themselves sufficiently over what had happened.'

As the chief of Canada's intelligence service – CSIS – at the time, Richard Fadden recalled the concerns the Delisle case had generated among Five Eyes partners who looked to Ottawa for an explanation. Some intelligence officials were outraged by the breach but could do little about it. 'All the Five Eyes raised, reasonably enough, these concerns with us,' he said. 'But, we pointed out that these breaches happened to everyone. Not entirely happily, this view had to be accepted. We told the allies quickly and we started a damage analysis which we shared very broadly. I think the allies were satisfied with how we handled the fallout which goes back to my point that it's how you handle the fallout that determines whether or not you're taken seriously.'

Even after being exposed twice in as many years for its spy operations in Five Eyes countries, the Kremlin remained unflinching in its eagerness to pursue its aggressive foreign policy agenda. A decade after Litvinenko's murder, the Kremlin had maintained its campaign of disregard for the sovereignty of nation states, annexing Crimea from Ukraine in 2014 before deploying its cyber warriors to target the US presidential election two years later. It became publicly known by the summer of 2016 that Russian cyber-spies had accessed thousands of emails by hacking the computer networks of the Democratic Congressional Campaign Committee and the Democratic National Committee. The stolen emails had been strategically released to various online platforms, including *Wikileaks*, by 'Guccifer 2.0' – a moniker purporting to be a Romanian hacker who the FBI rightly suspected to be front for the Russian military's intelligence arm, the GRU. Five Eyes intelligence officials were hardly shocked when the Putin regime denied its role in the hacking campaign against the US Democrats. Their shock emerged eight days after Donald Trump had been officially confirmed as the Republican Party's nominee when he publicly urged Russia to hack into the email accounts of his Democratic rival, Hillary Clinton.

'Russia, if you're listening,' Donald Trump declared during a press conference in Doral, Florida, 'I hope you're able to find the 30,000 emails that are missing. I think you will be rewarded mightily by our press.' His appeal on 27 July 2016 was in reference to emails from Hillary Clinton's time as Secretary of State during the first term of the Obama Administration. The emails had become a focal point following an investigation into a terrorist attack in 2012 on a US diplomatic compound in Benghazi, Libya, in which four Americans were killed, including the ambassador to the north African country. In the course of the FBI investigation, it had emerged that Clinton's team had deleted 33,000 emails which had been deemed as 'personal and private'– unrelated to her work. According to the FBI's director, James Comey, no evidence of 'evil intent and intent to obstruct justice' had been found by his organisation's inquiry. Yet that did not matter to Trump, who wanted to weaponise the past issue for the sake of undermining his Democratic presidential rival. The day he urged Russia to find the emails – a proposition he later characterised as a joke – the Kremlin's hackers secretly launched an attack against the email accounts of Clinton's personal staff members. That same day, the Republic presidential nominee's words also provoked the Australian High Commissioner to Britain, Alexander Downer, to contact the US Embassy in London with a view to disclosing details relating to his meeting with the Trump campaign adviser, George Papadopoulos, that had taken place two months earlier.

With the US Ambassador on vacation, his deputy, Elizabeth Dibble, who had been left in charge of the embassy, was briefed by Downer on 28 July about his meeting with Papadopoulos. Within hours of Downer's briefing, a select few people at the FBI headquarters in Washington, DC, were provided with the Australian High Commissioner's account by email. Among them was Peter Strzok, deputy director of the organisation's counterintelligence division, who was immediately intrigued by the timing of the meeting that had taken place between Downer and Papadopoulos. The fact it had been in May 2016 suggested that Trump's adviser had been aware of Russia's planned election interference one month before the issue had become publicly known. It also suggested that he had been aware of the proposed meddling into Clinton's campaign even before the FBI did.

The political sensitivity of Downer's briefing meant that the FBI had to act with urgency but also ensure that only a handful of its officials were briefed on the case to prevent any potential leaks. A seasoned investigator with 20 years of experience at the FBI, Strzok was tasked with probing the Trump campaign's ties to Moscow. By the time he flew from Virginia to London with a colleague to interview Downer on 2 August, he had initiated the investigation into Russian meddling, code-naming it 'Crossfire Hurricane'. It was a reference to a song by the Rolling Stones, 'Jumpin' Jack Flash', which opens with the line: 'I was born in a crossfire hurricane.' It was a prescient codename for what would become a major political storm in US history.

Downer's tipoff to the Americans had been shrouded in so much secrecy that even the Australian prime minister, Malcolm Turnbull, had no idea that the High Commissioner had informed the US Embassy about it – let alone agreed to a meeting with the FBI – until Strzok had landed in London. Turnbull was uniquely positioned as a national leader in the Five Eyes: he was a shrewd political operator who understood the importance of cultivating Australia's historical connection with the United States, but also understood the nuances of intelligence matters and the potential they had for backfiring if not delicately handled. As a former lawyer in the 1980s, Turnbull had defeated the British government's attempt to stop the Australian publication of a book revealing embarrassing secrets about MI5, including the uncorroborated claim that one of the agency's former directors-general, Roger Hollis, had been a KGB agent. While *Spycatcher*, the memoirs of former MI5 officer Peter Wright, had already been banned in the UK, the Thatcher government failed to achieve the same result in Australia – in large part due to Turnbull's courtroom battles – and ultimately lifted its ban in Britain. So Turnbull knew a thing or two about dealing with sensitive cases, and while he appreciated that the information that Downer had provided the US was 'important', he questioned the manner in which it had been handed over.

The Australian prime minister was outraged by the High Commissioner's behaviour, saying he had 'acted without any authority' and that he should have provided the information to Washington through Australia's intelligence officials at ASIO, and not directly as he had done. 'Downer's information, which he had reported to Canberra and our Washington Embassy in May, should only have been passed onto the Americans via the most discreet intelligence community channels,' Turnbull said. 'Blundering into the American Embassy in London, blurting out political gossip of the most intense political sensitivity was the worst possible way to do it.' Turnbull even accused Downer of being reckless. 'What he did would have got any other ambassador sacked,' the former prime minister said. 'It was reckless and self-indulgent and put the Australian government in a very awkward position.' Asked why Downer had not been fired, Mr Turnbull said: 'Alexander was a good friend of mine and the Foreign Minister, Julie Bishop. He is our longest serving Foreign Minister, a former leader of the Liberal Party. And at the time we learned of his foolish behaviour we had every interest in keeping it confidential.'

Turnbull said he had only heard about Mr Downer's approach to the Americans after the High Commissioner contacted Canberra to inform the government that the FBI had been preparing to interview him. 'The first we knew about it was when the FBI arrived in London and asked to interview him,' he said. 'At that point, he did have the common sense to tell Canberra what had happened. In the circumstances we could hardly refuse to allow him to speak to the FBI but great care was taken to ensure that his evidence would be kept confidential. That worked until it didn't, and, in December 2017, Downer's role was revealed in the *New York Times*.' Turnbull said Downer's actions had brought into 'question the discipline and professionalism of our foreign service' and had also given Donald Trump 'every reason to believe' that the FBI's investigation into Russia 'was instigated by the Australian government'. Turnbull was forced to intervene to preserve Australia's relationship with the Trump Administration. 'As a consequence we had to explain that Downer had acted on his own, without authority,' he said.

There is no way to properly determine the extent to which Downer's tipoff to the FBI influenced Trump's impression of Australia. In January 2017, Trump opposed an immigration deal that had been struck between his predecessor, President Obama, and Turnbull to resettle more than 1,200 asylum seekers from countries including Iraq and Afghanistan, who had been refused entry by Australia. During a telephone discussion on 27 January 2017, Trump told Turnbull that a phone call from earlier that day with Russian president Vladimir Putin had been 'more pleasant' than the one with the Australian prime minister. If that was not bad enough, Trump's team then allegedly leaked the transcript of the phone call with Turnbull to the press, hoping to embarrass the Australian leader and please Trump's support base by showcasing the president's tough stand on asylum seekers. However, the leak backfired: it exposed Trump's petulance in contrast to Turnbull's statesmanship and the US administration was forced to accept the immigration deal in favour of Australia. It also revealed Trump's abhorrence for accountability – as his intelligence community, along with other agencies in the Five Eyes, would soon discover.

Donald Trump's contempt for political rivals, the media and anyone else who opposed his worldview, was matched by a good dose of hatred for his country's intelligence and law-enforcement agencies, especially the CIA and FBI, which he considered part of the 'deep state' – evil conspirators who had colluded to try to block his path to the Oval Office. As someone who had never relied on facts, let alone evidence, to back up spurious claims, the 45th President of the United States had likened the US intelligence community to 'Nazi Germany' nine days before his inauguration over a leaked dossier that made numerous – and largely unsubstantiated – claims, including Trump's alleged links to the Kremlin and that he was liable to blackmail by the Putin regime, which had compromising material against him. The so-called 'Steele Dossier' had been prepared by Christopher Steele, a former MI6 officer, on behalf of Trump's political opponents, including the presidential campaign of Hillary Clinton.

Long before Steele admitted that 'not everything in the dossier is 100% accurate', Trump was criticised by the CIA's outgoing director, John Brennan, for likening his intelligence officers to Nazis over the leaking of the dossier to the online newspaper *Buzzfeed*, which published an article about it on 10 January 2017. 'What I do find outrageous, is equating an intelligence community with Nazi Germany,' Brennan told Fox News. 'I do take great umbrage at that, and there is no basis for Mr Trump to point fingers at the intelligence community for leaking information that was already available publicly.' Trump's hostility towards the US spy agencies over allegations of Russia's interference in the presidential campaign, had been intensified after the US Office of the Director of National Intelligence (ODNI) revealed its findings several days earlier on 6 January. Drawing on intelligence gathered by the FBI, CIA and NSA, the ODNI stated with 'high confidence' that Putin had 'ordered an influence campaign in 2016 aimed at the US presidential election' and that together with his government 'aspired to help President-elect Trump's election chances when possible by discrediting Secretary Clinton and publicly contrasting her unfavourably to him'. Moscow's goals were to 'undermine public faith in the US democratic process, denigrate Secretary Clinton, and harm her electability and potential presidency'.

Trump completely rejected the ODNI's assessment and targeted senior national security officials in what appeared to be a vendetta against his critics. Three months into his presidency, he fired the FBI's director, James Comey – whom he labelled 'a real nut job'. The disparaging language was consistent with Trump's tone for US authorities, as he had also previously called CIA officials 'clowns'. Trump initially claimed that he had dismissed the FBI director over his handling of an investigation into the deletion of emails from Hillary Clinton's private server. His stated reasoning made little sense to Five Eyes officials because the media storm surrounding the thousands of missing emails had politically benefited Trump, who, during the presidential campaign, had even praised Comey for pursuing his Democratic rival. Intelligence chiefs in London, Canberra, Ottawa and Wellington considered Trump's justification for firing Comey a mere smokescreen to take down an incorruptible FBI boss who wanted to preserve his organisation's independence from the White House and continue his investigation into Russian interference. Trump's disruption of the FBI investigation somewhat paralleled President Nixon's attempt to stop an inquiry by the law-enforcement organisation into the Watergate break-in. Much like Nixon's request for the CIA to block the FBI investigation into his administration had been rebuffed, Trump's sacking of Comey backfired. On 17 May 2017, the week after Comey's departure, Robert Mueller III, former director of the FBI, was appointed as a special counsel by the US deputy attorney general to investigate whether there had been any links between the Kremlin and Trump's presidential campaign. Peter Strzok, the FBI investigator who had been told by the Australian High Commissioner Alexander Downer about potential Russian interference, joined Mueller's team. As the investigation carried on, Russia struck again – but this time, against Britain.

* * *

On 4 March 2018, the Kremlin dispatched two GRU assassins to kill Sergei Skripal, one of its former officers, who had been relocated to Salisbury, southern England, following the spy swap with Moscow eight years earlier. Skripal and his daughter, Yulia, survived the Novichok nerve agent attack, but a police officer who had tended to their rescue suffered major health complications from exposure to the poison – and a British woman later died after she coincidentally discovered, eight miles from Salisbury, a fake perfume bottle containing Novichok, which had reportedly been discarded there by the GRU assassins. Britain's Five Eyes partners and its international allies, including NATO members, joined in condemning the Putin regime over the nerve-agent attack, and followed the UK's lead in expelling Russian spies from their embassies. A total of 153 Russian intelligence officers were expelled, including 23 from Britain, 60 from the US and 35 from the European Union. Another two Russians working under diplomatic cover in Australia were forced to return to Moscow, and Canada also expelled four Kremlin spies. It was the biggest expulsion of Russian spies since Britain's Operation Foot in 1971.

In the wake of the Salisbury attack, Britain's Prime Minister Theresa May knew she needed to make a persuasive argument to other national leaders, hoping they would follow the UK's retaliatory measures against the Kremlin. Her argument, she said, had been bolstered by the British intelligence services' evidence against the alleged assassins – evidence shared beyond the Five Eyes. 'I suppose when you go into those things you're never a hundred per cent confident that you are going to get the answer you want, but you have to persuade,' May said. 'And it's not just about the leader to leader call, it's about the work that is done by the intelligence services and that is where the sharing of intelligence is important. Because that then gave the evidence on which other leaders were able to be advised and to take their decisions. So how it came about is there were certain ones [leaders] that I spoke to and then of course for some of the countries, members of the European Union, I actually sat around the European Union council table and to talk at that level – talk to a number of them all together rather than speaking to everyone individually.' May said the ability to share intelligence 'and to be public about what we had and why we believed it was Russia was very important in that whole process of others feeling that "Yes, we should do something about this". And because it was so egregious – the use of a chemical weapon.'

The expulsions following the Salisbury attack appeared to be a successful campaign for the Five Eyes intelligence agencies against Russian aggression, even though there was a lot of uncertainty in Britain over the Trump Administration's feelings towards the Putin regime.

Theresa May said her government had to adjust to a more 'volatile' environment at the White House. 'We were learning to adjust to operating in a more volatile environment in the United States than we had been used to previously,' said the former British prime minister. 'With a more volatile environment in the United States – and probably [...] not everybody necessarily in position, and some churning of people in senior positions in the intelligence world exacerbated that sense of volatility.' The churning of people was in reference to the turnover of national security advisers by the Trump Administration. Within 15 months of being in office, Trump had turned over four of them, including one who had served in an acting capacity – an unprecedented number by any US President during their first term. The unpredictability of events in Washington had even brought into question the historic relationships between Britain and the US. Theresa May was candid when asked by this author what it had been like to adjust to the White House volatility: 'It would be helpful not to have to adjust to something like that but in a sense we had to start to think about the relationships. The relationships had been going on for so long and there had always been an assumption of smooth running relationships.'

The fallout from the Skripal affair – including the way it had exposed the Kremlin's disregard for international laws and global order – was all but ignored by Trump when he appeared alongside Putin at a meeting in Finland in July 2018. The US president denied that Russia had tampered with the 2016 election – undermining, yet again, the US intelligence community's assessment. 'They said they think it's Russia; I have

President Putin; he just said it's not Russia,' Trump told reporters. 'I will say this: I don't see any reason why it would be [...] So I have great confidence in my intelligence people, but I will tell you that President Putin was extremely strong and powerful in his denial today.'

Trump's claim about his 'confidence' in his intelligence agencies was an exaggeration at best – because if he had faith in their findings, he would have believed their unanimous verdict from a year earlier in which they had concluded that Russia did meddle in the 2016 election. By publicly expressing his faith in Putin, over and above his own intelligence community, Trump effectively gave the Russian president the green light to continue his electoral interference and assassination plots.

Trump's willingness to politicise and divulge intelligence at the expense of his spy agencies was 'in a league of its own', said Martin Green, Canada's coordinator of intelligence assessments. The president's denigration of US intelligence services even brought into question the 'exchange of intelligence between the Five Eyes as there were worries that critical collection, tradecraft, and analysis would be compromised,' he said. Despite such concerns, agencies within the alliance put up a united front, and were of the view that 'there was never a more important time for the Five Eyes to stick together [...] there is a strength in numbers'. Even though Trump 'purged several senior career IC [intelligence community] officials and replaced them with inexperienced and unqualified loyalists,' US agencies 'continued to privilege Five Eyes intelligence analysis and sharing,' said Green. 'In effect, we all benefit from being able to tell our senior leaders and clients that this is how the other[s] are assessing various situations or events. Even though it may not impact a final decision, the US IC could draw on the assessments of other members to say this is the take of others on a certain issue. It is the prerogative of our elected leaders to use intelligence as they wish. In Trump's case it is pretty evident that on some issues he ignored analysis – notable would be Russian interference in the 2016 US elections.'

Theresa May said there was a 'fine line to be drawn' by political leaders when questioning intelligence. 'Leaders have to be very careful that yes they are challenging the agencies and of course you question them and you want to be as certain as you can be in what they are saying to you, but you can't interfere in operational matters. It's like dealing with the police [...] there's very clear operational independence.'

Donald Trump even disregarded Mueller's investigation, which resulted in three Russian companies and 34 people, including twelve Kremlin spies, being indicted for criminal offences. Among those indicted was George Papadopoulos who had lied to the FBI about the timing of his discovery that the Russians had planned to release damaging material on Hillary Clinton. He pleaded guilty and was sentenced to 14 days in prison. While the report of Mueller's inquiry, published in a redacted version in April 2019, did not establish that Trump's campaign had conspired with the Kremlin to influence the election, Mueller later stated that if his team 'had confidence that the president clearly did not commit a crime, we would have said so'. Through the duration of the Mueller inquiry – and even leading up to it – Trump's continued swipes at the intelligence community had been engineered to foment public distrust towards them. And he had not limited his accusations of wrongdoing to domestic agencies only; he had even been prepared to trample on the Special Relationship and accuse Britain's GCHQ of spying on him.

CHAPTER FIFTEEN

DISRUPTION: THE SPECIAL RELATIONSHIP

DURING A PRIVATE CONVERSATION on the sidelines of a cyber conference, Ciaran Martin, a senior official at GCHQ, was focused on a far more pressing matter than the event that his organisation was hosting in Liverpool, northwest of England. As he stood in front of his boss, Robert Hannigan – away from hundreds of people who had gathered at CyberUK 2017 – Martin sensed a hint of urgency in the voice of GCHQ's director. Known for his unshakable calm, Hannigan was concerned about a Fox News Channel item in which his organisation had been accused of bugging Donald Trump's New York residence during the 2016 presidential campaign.

The accusation by Andrew Napolitano, a former Superior Court judge working as a senior legal analyst at Fox, cited three unnamed intelligence sources to state that the GCHQ 'wiretap' had been initiated on the order of Trump's predecessor, President Barack Obama. 'He didn't use the NSA, he didn't use the CIA, he didn't use the FBI and he didn't use the Department of Justice – he used GCHQ,' Napolitano had declared on 14 March 2017 during a segment of *Fox & Friends*, Trump's favourite morning talk show. 'What the heck is that? That's the initials for the British spying agency. They have 24/7 access to the NSA database.' On the spectrum of 'fake news', Napolitano's claims were a box-office hit. But left unchallenged, they threatened to damage the reputation of GCHQ.

Hannigan had taken over the reins at the British agency in November 2014 when it was still smouldering in the blaze of the post-Snowden Affair. His elevation to spymaster during a civil service career spanning almost two decades was a departure from the earlier path he had taken as a seminarian – and despite not entering priesthood, Hannigan still invoked the self-composure of the devout. After cutting his teeth many years earlier as a director of communications at the British government's Northern Ireland Office, he had understood the importance of 'comms' and, upon taking over the agency, immediately expanded GCHQ's press team to demonstrate that even a secret organisation needed to be publicly accountable, transparent, and proactive in humanising the stories and missions of its staff members. Part of his transparency mission culminated in the creation of a public-facing agency, the National Cyber Security Centre, which he based in London to, among many other things, use 'industry and academic expertise to nurture the UK's cyber security capability'. His achievements at GCHQ were self-evident and fairly well publicised, but they risked being tarnished by Napolitano's allegation on Fox News.

Despite Martin's assurances that the former judge's ramblings were unlikely to be followed up by other media, or given oxygen by anyone reasonable, Hannigan remained concerned. The last thing Hannigan wanted was a scandal on the eve of his farewell from GCHQ after he had unexpectedly tendered his resignation in January, citing family-related reasons. The outgoing director had only a few more days to go in his role and wanted to keep his legacy intact at a time when concerns about his departure were gathering momentum in the Five Eyes intelligence communities. After all, his predecessor, Sir Iain Lobban, had spent a six-year term at the helm of the agency – double the time that Hannigan had served.

Within a few hours of his conversation with Hannigan, Ciaran

Martin wrapped up the third and final day of the cyber conference at the Arena and Conference Centre in Liverpool and was picked up by his driver. He was halfway through a four-hour drive back to his home, catching up on unread emails, when his mobile phone rang. It was Hannigan calling to inform him that, only moments earlier, President Trump's spokesman, Sean Spicer, had quoted Napolitano during a press conference at the White House. The allegation against GCHQ could no longer be dismissed as a meaningless ramble; it had suddenly been given legitimacy by the world's most powerful office.

Spicer was known for his aggressive, no-nonsense approach. The former US Navy reservist would often walk into the James S. Brady Press Briefing Room at the West Wing as if appearing at a pre-fight weigh-in. He was caricatured for being Trump's mouthpiece in every way and even seemed to share the hatred felt by the president for the mainstream media. Just like Trump, he never liked either his own authority or his own facts being questioned. By the time he had parroted Napolitano's claims relating to GCHQ, Spicer had become a minor celebrity as a one-man spin machine, especially after he had massively exaggerated the turnout of 'Make America Great Again' fans at Trump's presidential inauguration two months earlier. It seemed that Spicer and his team had not even bothered to check the veracity of Napolitano's allegation relating to GCHQ's so-called 'wiretap'. Instead, they embraced it as an opportunity to validate a series of unsubstantiated claims made by the US President himself against his predecessor two weeks earlier on Twitter, including one that stated: 'Terrible! Just found out that Obama had my "wires tapped" in Trump Tower just before the victory. Nothing found. This is McCarthyism!' The tweets on 4 March 2017 had been intended to detract from an intelligence assessment by US agencies, including the CIA and FBI, which had revealed with 'high confidence' that Russia had orchestrated an influence campaign of cyber-attacks and fake news stories planted on social media during the 2016 presidential challenge.

Spicer's validation of Napolitano's wiretap claim outraged Martin, Hannigan and other British government officials, including senior figures at Downing Street. Britain's Ambassador to Washington, Sir

Kim Darroch, approached Spicer directly to have him withdraw his statement, and the prime minister's national security adviser, Sir Mark Lyall Grant, contacted his counterpart General H.R. McMaster to express his concerns – all in the interest of tempering what was fast becoming a major diplomatic showdown between the US and its closest ally. 'We even went to Sean Spicer directly through our embassy officials in Washington asking him to retract the allegations he repeated earlier that day and he didn't,' said a British intelligence official who was involved in the discussions. 'At the time Britain had voted for Brexit and there were obvious concerns about what impact that would have on our relationship with the US, in terms of trade agreements. But none of that was part of the calculation of GCHQ's response. The only thing that came into play was the potential impact their response could have on the intelligence relationship between the UK and US. And thankfully, our other partners in the Five Eyes – especially Australia, who were initially chummy with the Trump administration – were very sympathetic to us. So we felt confident about taking a tough stand.'

Senior officials at the National Security Agency (NSA) assured their counterparts at GCHQ that the allegation should be viewed as a political misjudgement which would have no impact on their intelligence-sharing. Admiral Mike Rogers, the NSA's director, told Hannigan that he supported whatever decision he wanted to take against the 'baseless allegation'. A US official familiar with the exchange, said, 'Mike told him, "You have to do what's right for you, what's right for your organisation, for the demands of your government and for the citizens you serve."' The prevailing view within the NSA was the allegation against GCHQ was 'BS' and they felt confident that it would not 'impact our relationship with our British colleagues'.

Rogers wanted the issue resolved and was prepared to take it up with the Oval Office. As that played out in Washington, Ciaran Martin, still in the car on his way home from the cyber event, started drafting a statement on his laptop – a riposte to target the White House and its incumbent. The 'neither confirm nor deny' policy that GCHQ had historically ascribed to on all intelligence-related matters to avoid being drawn into media commentary or political scandals was about to be breached in an unprecedented manner. Martin knew that to let the White House's repetition of the accusation go unchallenged was to risk sparking a controversy akin to that which had embroiled the British government of John Major in 1992 when his Conservative Party was tasked with digging up dirt on US Democratic Presidential candidate Bill Clinton. At the time, the Republicans had been attempting to discredit Clinton by trying to establish whether he had ever applied for British citizenship during his time as a student at Oxford University in the late 1960s to avoid being drafted by the US Army to serve in Vietnam. The controversy forced Major to apologise and strained relations between Downing Street and the White House until the Conservative Party leader was unseated by Tony Blair at the 1997 election. A significant difference between the Major government's political interference in Clinton's campaign and the White House's allegation against GCHQ almost two decades later was that Britain was morally unimpeachable in the latter.

Both Hannigan and Martin agreed that Napolitano's allegation against their agency was 'utterly ridiculous' and wanted that phrase reflected in their statement, which they refined during their phone conversation before emailing it to Downing Street for approval. 'They came up with the "utterly ridiculous" phrase and Hannigan recommended it to Downing Street,' said one insider. The prime minister's office made no changes to the statement written by Hannigan and Martin. 'Out of courtesy they may have given the White House a warning of a maximum of one hour that GCHQ was going to reject this claim made by Spicer in the strongest possible terms,' the insider said. The statement asserted the authority of an agency against a president testing the waters of the Special Relationship, even though it did not name him directly. 'Recent allegations made by media commentator Judge Andrew Napolitano about GCHQ being asked to conduct "wiretapping" against the then President Elect are nonsense,' the agency's statement said. 'They are utterly ridiculous and should be ignored.' Before it hit the headlines on the evening of 16 March 2016, journalists took to Twitter – Trump's cherished platform – to post it. The GCHQ statement demonstrated typical British restraint, but in everyday terms, it was the equivalent of saying the allegation was rubbish.

After the statement's release, a spokesman for Theresa May, the British Prime Minister, was asked whether the conversations between US and British officials had been heated. He referenced GCHQ's unprecedented rebuke, saying 'you can draw your conclusions from there'. May had been the prime minister for only eight months at the time of the wiretapping allegations, and her government had already been forced to deal with the controversy surrounding the 'Steele Dossier', which had made several unsubstantiated claims linking Donald Trump to the Kremlin. 'The important thing to remember is that around that time there were various stories going around and suggestions being made about involvement of British intelligence around the American scene,' said May in regards to the backdrop against which the GCHQ wiretapping allegations had been made. The prime minister recalled that the decision to discredit the wiretap claim publicly was in the interest of the Special Relationship between Britain and the United States. 'There was a different approach taken here because normally these sorts of things you neither confirm nor deny but I think it was important given the context of the relationship between the UK and US that there was a point that we were willing to say "No".' She said maintaining the relationship between London and Washington 'at all levels' was crucial: 'It was at the early stages of a relationship with an incumbent president,' said May. 'There is a key, important relationship between the US and UK. You're talking about the Five Eyes in this book, but obviously at the centre of the Five Eyes is that very strong security and defence relationship between the US and UK [...] So ensuring that there was nothing that was being said erroneously that could lead to jeopardising that relationship is important.'

On the same day that GCHQ issued its statement labelling the wiretap claims 'nonsense', the White House issued a statement through a spokesman, but more to quell the transatlantic tension than to apologise. 'Ambassador Kim Darroch and Sir Mark Lyall Grant expressed their concerns to Sean Spicer and Gen McMaster,' said the White House statement. 'Mr Spicer and Gen McMaster explained that Mr Spicer was simply pointing to public reports, not endorsing any specific story.' Fox was also forced to distance itself from Napolitano's remarks. 'Fox News cannot confirm Judge Napolitano's commentary,' the anchor Shepard Smith said on air. 'Fox News knows of no evidence of any kind that the now-president of the United States was surveilled at any time, any way. Full stop.' The news channel also temporarily pulled Napolitano off air – but not even that reaction or GCHQ's statement were going to stop Trump from pursuing his allegations.

At a press conference the following day, on Friday 17 March, the president appeared with German Chancellor Angela Merkel, who was visiting the White House. Her visit had been scheduled earlier in the week but a snowstorm had delayed her arrival. Despite dodging the meteorological hazard, Merkel found herself in the eye of a different storm when Trump leveraged her appearance alongside him on the podium to push his own agenda. When asked by a journalist about the now-discredited wiretapping allegation against GCHQ, the president cited historical revelations during the Snowden Affair which detailed how America's own NSA had spied on Merkel's phone calls, and her advisers', over several years during the Obama administration.

'As far as wiretapping, I guess, well, you know, by this past administration […]' Trump signalled to Merkel standing to his right on the podium '[…] at least we have something in common, perhaps.' His comment generated laughter among the press pack, which he acknowledged with a wry smile. His reaction illustrated that Spicer's citation of Napolitano's claim the previous day was not some sort of freelance act delivered without any consideration: it seemed to have had the president's blessing. During the press conference alongside Merkel, Trump continued deflecting responsibility for the Napolitano allegation, saying, 'All we did was quote a certain, very talented, legal mind who was the one responsible for saying that on television.' Shortly afterwards, Spicer held up a similar defence, telling reporters: 'We just reiterated the fact that we were just simply reading media accounts. That's it.' When asked if he regretted repeating the allegation, he said,

'I don't think we regret anything. We literally listed a litany of media reports that are in the public domain.'

The episode became a turning point in the attitudes held by intelligence officials in the Five Eyes towards the greatest and most well-resourced contributor to the alliance – the United States. Officers from the NSA, CIA and FBI felt the need to repeatedly assure all their colleagues within the 'members club' that their historical relationship should not be shaken by politics, and particularly, by the sitting President. Rick Ledgett, the NSA's deputy director, publicly supported GCHQ in an interview with the BBC, branding the claims against the British agency as 'arrant nonsense'. Ledgett said: 'Of course they [GCHQ] wouldn't do it. It would be epically stupid,' adding that Napolitano's claim had shown 'a complete lack of understanding in how the relationship works.' Ledgett's boss, Admiral Mike Rogers, who had already given his assurances to his counterpart at GCHQ that the NSA would publicly dismiss the wiretap claim, also issued a public denial, saying the allegation 'clearly frustrates a key ally of ours'. But in private, Rogers had been more forthright in his opposition to the allegation. 'Mike told the White House that he would publicly testify that this is total BS,' according to intelligence officials familiar with the case. 'Mike also told the president himself: "Sir, this is not the way this relationship works. This is not the way the Five Eyes work. Such activity is prohibited under the Five Eyes agreement and culturally we would not do that."' Trump's reluctance to take any responsibility or apologise for the Napolitano affair reflected the disdain he harboured for his own intelligence community with whom he was clearly at war. GCHQ, the organisation that his nation had worked closely with since Britain's cryptographers had broken Hitler's Enigma in 1941, was in his mind, merely guilty by association.

Douglas Wise, a former deputy director of the US Defense Intelligence Agency who also served as the CIA's bureau chief in Baghdad during the 2003 invasion of Iraq, said that Trump had been acting in his own self-interest when he elected to war with his intelligence agencies and others in the Five Eyes. 'The Five Eyes is an enterprise which only exists because we, as its members, recognise strength is in unity, collaboration and mutual support,' he said. The personal relationships within the alliance are beyond the signed intelligence-sharing agreement between their countries, Wise added. 'It is unqualified, unquestioning trust which binds each member to the others by sharing the risk and bearing an equal burden to fight a common enemy for a common purpose. However, the minute that trust is eroded or the minute that any member thinks one member, through words or actions such as those by Donald Trump, is not acting in the best interests of all, then the enterprise is screwed. But thankfully, the Five Eyes agencies had been able to see beyond Trump's claims and self-serving agenda.'

Trump's takeover in Washington had quickly united the intelligence communities within the Five Eyes against the misinformation emerging from the White House. The assurances given by US agencies to their counterparts across the alliance proved, to a large extent at least, that the preservation of intelligence-sharing should be safeguarded from politics. It was a laudable effort, until the CIA and NSA sided with White House officials on matters relating to Huawei – a Chinese tech firm with links to the Communist party in Beijing, which Britain was determined to engage with, based on a recommendation made by Ciaran Martin.

A White House delegation arrived in London in the spring 2019 on a policy disruption mission. Their brief was to oppose a British government plan that would allow Huawei limited access to help build the country's next-generation cellular data network, known as 5G. As the head of GCHQ's National Cyber Security Centre, Ciaran Martin had anticipated a debate with the American visitors because he had become familiar with Washington's warnings to the Five Eyes regarding the risks associated with Chinese technology. The other reason he had predicted a showdown was because the Trump Administration had already expressed its disapproval of the British government's plan after its details – which should not have been made public for almost another year – were leaked to the press two weeks earlier by Theresa May's defence secretary, Gavin Williamson. He was fired from his job, despite repeatedly denying the allegation that he had tipped off the *Daily Telegraph* newspaper for the article dated 24 April. Williamson was among a vocal group of Conservative members of parliament who vehemently opposed any involvement from Huawei in the creation of Britain's 5G network. And the press leak had been engineered to compromise the plan relating to Huawei – a plan recommended to the Prime Minister by Martin himself based on a series of detailed intelligence and technology assessments by his team.

Within minutes of the White House delegation's arrival at the Cabinet Office in May 2019, Martin and other senior British officials, including the deputy national security adviser Madeleine Alessandri, were effectively shouted at by one of their guests for around five hours. That guest was Matthew Pottinger, a former US Marines intelligence officer parachuted into the White House in early 2017 to become the National Security Council's senior director for Asia. He was known for his distrust of China's authoritarian regime. It was a sentiment shaped during his previous life as a foreign correspondent for the *Wall Street Journal* in Beijing, where he had been subjected to surveillance, and even physically attacked by the regime's authorities. On taking up his role in the Trump Administration, Pottinger's influence on US foreign policy towards China was immediate. He was described by Steve Bannon, the former White House chief strategist, as 'one of the most significant people in the entire US government'. One year into his role, Pottinger had played a major role in the White House's decision to impose tariffs on US$200bn of Chinese goods. The US President had already declared that 'trade wars are good, and easy to win' when he had decided to punish China's Communist regime for the theft of intellectual property and the loss of what he considered American jobs to China's cheaper workforce. Beijing retaliated with its own tariffs on US products in a tit-for-tat that had formed the backdrop to the Trump Administration's opposition to Huawei.

While Matthew Pottinger and Ciaran Martin were both in their mid-forties, and equally influential within their respective governments, that was pretty much where any of their similarities ended. Martin and his team were determined to work with their opposite numbers in the US to counter China's tech ambitions on a strategic level. 'We were keen to work with the US to counter those ambitions,' Martin recalled. 'The problem was: on our side we didn't think Huawei's limited involvement in UK 5G was the most important thing in a much wider strategic challenge. Whereas the US were only interested in that part of the problem, for reasons we couldn't fathom.'

Although well aware of Beijing's appetite for cyber-hacking members of the Five Eyes to steal their research and military secrets, Martin was confident in the NCSC's technical abilities to manage China's relationship with the UK through risk analysis and network defences. His judgement, although supported by Prime Minister Theresa May, polarised cabinet ministers in the UK, including Defence Secretary Gavin Williamson, long before he had been dismissed for the leak. The international reverberations surrounding the leak had coincided with the opening day of CyberUK 2019, hosted by Martin and attended by officials from the Five Eyes, including Rob Joyce from the NSA, who had immediately made his opposition to the UK's decision on Huawei known to his host. Martin despised the US accusation that Britain had defied the Five Eyes by unilaterally planning to give Huawei the thumbs-up. 'The whole thing about Britain breaking the Five Eyes unity was ridiculous, because Australia had made its own decision on Huawei unilaterally,' said a British security official. Australia's ban against Huawei in August 2018 had been the result of a series of intelligence assessments by the Turnbull Government, including investigations by the Australian Signals Directorate, the NSA's counterpart in Canberra.

In the lead up to banning Huawei in Australia, Prime Minister Malcolm Turnbull had familiarised himself with the technology of 5G networks and ordered Australia's intelligence community to try to determine whether there was a way to utilise Huawei's services without compromising his nation's security. 'I was trying to find a way to mitigate the risk – and I did not want to ban the vendor if I could manage it,' he said. During a series of discussions with his top intelligence officials, including Mike

Burgess, then director-general of Australia's signals organisation, ASD, Turnbull concluded that there was no way to safeguard against the risk that Huawei presented. 'It was obvious that they [Huawei] had both a legal and a political obligation to comply with the wishes of the Chinese Communist Party,' said Turnbull. 'We were identifying a loaded gun, not a smoking one.' The prime minister then informed Trump and other Five Eyes partners that Australia had identified technical problems with Huawei's kit. Turnbull said that 5G was very different. 'The old techniques of restricting high-risk vendors to the edge of the network and away from the core was no longer viable. I had raised this issue with the Americans, including President Trump, from 2017. The provider of a nation's 5G network, or much of it, had considerable capability for disruption, interference and espionage.'

While there were varying views in Washington about whether the Chinese tech firm should be allowed to operate in the US, Admiral Mike Rogers, director of the NSA, was among those who supported Turnbull's views on the potential national security risks that Huawei presented. During a visit to Canberra ahead of the Australian ban, Rogers had been invited by Burgess and Turnbull to express his views on the Chinese telecoms firm. While the US had not yet formed a policy on Huawei's potential involvement in the development of 5G networks, Rogers shared the national security concerns held by Turnbull and Burgess. The Australian prime minister wanted to form his decision on the basis of technical assessments rather than political agenda. 'In terms of Huawei, we were the leaders of the Five Eyes in banning it from involvement in our 5G network,' said Turnbull.

Mike Burgess, who left Australia's signals directorate to become the director-general of the country's domestic intelligence agency, ASIO, in 2019, said his country had been 'pursuing the defence of our own national interest' when it banned Huawei. 'Australia recognised this problem early because we recognised that mature 5G would be about much more than faster phones for your kids to watch cat videos on,' he said. 'We knew that mature 5G would be like a nervous system for the economy – it would enable and connect critical functions in a way that made it a critical function, too. Of course we also understood the threats faced by our region where we'd seen China change over the last ten years.'

Among those changes in China were its technological developments which had been largely driven by a huge demand from western liberal democracies, desperate for cheaper products. Such desperation had been part of the reason why Five Eyes nations had not developed their own technology to avoid having to rely on the likes of Huawei in the first place. 'Governments used to invest in research and development during the Cold War but that stopped and everything was privatised,' said an Australian intelligence official. 'And the private sector is really good at making a profit, and how do you make a profit – you drive cost out of your business [...] And we've adopted services industries and we're quite happy to buy technology from the cheapest manufacturing base. At the same time, there was wholesale intellectual property theft going on which saw the rise of companies like Huawei and others. That's how it happened. It was a by-product of something that was good but in hindsight we overlooked some things.'

The UK's perspective on Huawei differed to Australia's – and senior ministers within the Turnbull government, including the prime minister himself, remained unconvinced by Britain's intelligence assessments relating to the Chinese firm. The Australians were highly doubtful that their British counterparts could mitigate the risks associated with Huawei. They also felt that the British intelligence community had been 'saying what the politicians wanted to hear'.

While that sentiment was shared by Washington, the British felt that the opposite was true. Theresa May hit back at the accusation that her government's plan to use Huawei had somehow placed politics ahead of technical expertise. 'Any decision taken by a politician can by definition be described as a political decision, but this was not a decision based on politics,' she said. 'It was based on the fact that we believed that [...] we had the capability of ensuring that we could protect what needed to be protected.' The May Government's proposed plan to use Huawei had been based on what was available – and while there were other options, namely through Scandinavian tech firms Nokia and Ericsson – the

Chinese telecoms company had been the cheapest by far. 'I think the context was looking at the marketplace – and again, that's where the West slightly took its eye off the ball,' said May. 'But many were quite happy to go with the Chinese kit because it was cheaper. Yes, there's a couple of other Scandinavian countries but the West didn't have the competitor to Huawei and that's where the issue was. So the question was less about China's economic place in the world and more about nationally when you looked at developing 5G and so forth, how would you do that if you were not going with what was one of the major providers. And I think the UK was – and we were in a position of feeling that we were able to protect our systems. So we were perhaps in a different position than others.'

US intelligence agencies and White House officials had repeatedly lobbied all members of the Five Eyes to ban Huawei on 'national security' grounds. While New Zealand had followed Australia and banned the Chinese telecoms company in November 2018, Canada was still considering its options (and would not announce its intention to ban Huawei until May 2022). The US Secretary of State Mike Pompeo – a former director of the CIA during the early days of the Trump Administration who championed hawkish foreign policies on China – had declared in February 2019 that countries using Huawei equipment were a 'risk' to the US, in a thinly veiled warning to Britain. Staff from his office were also using backchannels to remind their counterparts in Britain that they were risking their place in the Five Eyes should the UK decide to approve Huawei.

Washington's suspicion of Huawei pre-dated the Trump Administration and could be traced back to 2012, when an investigation by the US House Intelligence Committee concluded that the firm was a national security threat, because it was unwilling to 'provide sufficient evidence' regarding its 'relationships or regulatory interaction with Chinese authorities' in Beijing. Following the intelligence committee's findings, and with prior fears that Huawei equipment could potentially be used to spy on American companies and individuals, the Obama Administration banned Huawei, and another Chinese firm, ZTE, from bidding for

US government contracts. Five years later, the Trump Administration warned that China's 2017 National Intelligence Law, which states that organisations must 'support, assist and cooperate with state intelligence work', could force Huawei to snoop on countries it was operating in on behalf of Beijing.

Two years later, in May 2019 – the same month Matthew Pottinger had flown over with the US delegation for the meeting at the British Cabinet Office – the US president signed an executive order (EO) to prohibit Chinese companies, including Huawei, from selling any equipment in America because of the 'undue risk of sabotage' and 'catastrophic effects' on the country's communications systems and infrastructure. The US Department of Commerce also placed Huawei and sixty-eight of its affiliates on a trade blacklist for 'activities contrary to the national security or foreign policy interests of the United States'.

Such hardline measures had defined Pottinger's thinking and very much shaped his declarations during the meeting at the Cabinet Office between his team and British officials, including Ciaran Martin. 'Pottinger just shouted and was entirely uninterested in the UK's analysis,' said a British intelligence official who was at the meeting. 'The message was, "We don't want you to do this [accept Huawei], you have no idea how evil China is". It was five hours of shouting with a prepared, angry and weirdly non-threatening script. We tried to offer a policy discussion but Pottinger didn't care. We even said that we didn't contest the analysis of the Chinese threat and explained our technicalities, but the US officials weren't interested in that. Pottinger was continuously and repeatedly obnoxious.'

Martin even gave Pottinger assurances that Huawei's work on the country's 5G network would neither compromise the UK's intelligence-sharing channels with the Five Eyes, government systems, nor nuclear facilities, as such sensitive areas were linked to computer networks that would be inaccessible to Huawei. But even such guarantees were not enough to appease Britain's counterparts during – or after – their meeting in London.

Kim Darroch, who had previously served as Britain's national security adviser before becoming the UK's ambassador to the US in January 2016, said the Trump administration had sent a technical team to Britain to discuss matters relating to Huawei but 'they didn't really have any compelling technical arguments that undermined the GCHQ case. I remember GCHQ seeming pretty unimpressed. The encounter exposed that the US case was really political not technical. So GCHQ stuck to their guns, and initially so did the prime minister.'

The unshakable position on Huawei held by the US officials was particularly insulting to their British colleagues, because GCHQ had spotted a technical threat in the Chinese company's products two years before the company had been banned by the White House in May 2019. In fact, GCHQ had created an oversight facility in Banbury, southeast England, to identify any risks associated with Huawei's products. The only reason for not excluding the Chinese company altogether was because its products were significantly cheaper than those of its competitors, Nokia and Ericsson.

Britain had historically shared America's suspicion of China – and for decades, its colony of Hong Kong had given the Five Eyes a key operational advantage for eavesdropping on the Communist state. In 1957, one year after the formation of the Five Eyes, the UK had built a base on Tai Mo Shan, the highest coastal peak in Southern China, run by the Royal Air Force's 117 Signals Unit and Australia's Defence Signals Directorate (DSD). It was through that base that the intelligence alliance discovered China's first nuclear weapons test in 1964. The base was shut down following the handover of Hong Kong to China in 1997 and GCHQ relocated equipment from there to Kojarena, a DSD site in Western Australia, to maintain its eavesdropping on Beijing.

The military threat that China had once posed pivoted to cyberspace, and around 2010, China expanded its cyber-warfare operations and began indiscriminately targeting everything from government departments to educational institutions in western countries. Beijing's hostility towards the Five Eyes included an attack on Australia's intelligence service ASIO in 2013, targeting the blueprints of the agency's new headquarters in

Canberra. Chinese hackers also attacked Canada's national research and technology organisation in 2014. In 2015, the regime's hackers targeted the US Office of Personnel Management (OPM), the agency that handles security clearances of US government employee records, in a data breach that compromised the personal details of at least 22.1 million federal employees along with their families and friends. China, as expected, denied any responsibility for the hack.

The Communist Party in China has been historically undeterred by accusations levelled at it by the Five Eyes, and much like Moscow, always denied any involvement in cyber-hacking against western nations. In 2015, after the OPM hack, US President Barack Obama warned Beijing over its industrial espionage in cyberspace, saying such hostility threatened to 'put significant strains on a bilateral relationship if not resolved and [...] we are prepared to take some countervailing actions'.

The Five Eyes had already been fighting back against Beijing's aggression, not only through defensive operations and diplomatic channels, but with aggressive cyber operations of their own. In 2015, it was revealed that New Zealand's Government Communications Security Bureau (GCSB) had teamed up with the NSA to hack into the diplomatic communications of the Chinese Ministry of Foreign Affairs. The cyber-espionage mission had been running while New Zealand's then prime minister, John Key, was negotiating a trade deal with Beijing worth more than £10 billion. When the hack was exposed in the media, it embarrassed the GCSB and the NSA, which had often publicly attacked China for targeting the networks of the Five Eyes.

In Britain, the intelligence community was all too familiar with Beijing's cyber espionage, yet it had not anticipated a move by the CIA to try to discredit the UK's position on Huawei in the eyes of their European allies. By that point in early 2019, the European Commission Vice President, Andrus Ansip, had already warned during a press conference in Brussels of the Chinese firm having to 'cooperate' with Beijing's intelligence services. CIA officers from the agency's Belgium station met with their counterparts in the French, German, Italian and Norwegian intelligence services, among others, to express their concerns about the UK's misjudgement on Huawei. British intelligence officials were outraged by what they described as a 'black-ops' mission facilitated by the CIA – some even calling it a betrayal of friendship. Yet again, the Special Relationship between London and Washington had been strained and risked being permanently disrupted by the CIA, not only in the eyes of Britain's intelligence community, but also in the minds of their European partners.

On 14 July 2019, two months after his team clashed with Pottinger in London, Ciaran Martin travelled to Washington with Britain's national security adviser, Sir Mark Sedwill, to meet with US officials at the White House. The meeting had been specifically organised to discuss Huawei, and among those present was Pottinger once more, along with Sedwill's counterpart, John Bolton. Notably missing was Britain's ambassador, Kim Darroch, who had been handling the crisis behind the scenes, but had been forced to resign a few days earlier after leaked emails revealed he had described Trump as 'incompetent', 'insecure' and 'inept' in cables he had sent to London shortly after the president had been elected to office.

During the hour-long meeting at the White House, Bolton reassured Martin and Sedwill that he was sympathetic to the UK's assurances and said he would task members of his own security council to devise a plan that would help resolve their differences over Huawei. Pottinger seemed largely deferential to Bolton during the meeting, and the aggression he had showcased a month earlier in London had all but disappeared. Perhaps it was because he knew that the US had a trick up its sleeve that would ultimately force Britain to back down. The UK's newly elected prime minister, Boris Johnson, had supported Ciaran Martin's recommendations on dealing with the Chinese telecommunications giant – as had Johnson's predecessor, Theresa May.

In January 2020, Johnson approved Huawei to build the 5G network, but with more limitations, excluding Huawei from any access to military and nuclear sites and Britain's national infrastructure. The limited approval would only allow Huawei to build parts of the network that would connect devices and equipment to mobile-phone masts. Britain's defiance to press on with its plans for Huawei against Washington's wishes was met with the ultimate checkmate. Trump introduced further sanctions in May 2020 that banned Huawei from using semiconductors reliant on US technology. As a result, Martin could no longer guarantee the security of Huawei's products, and two months later, in a remarkable public U-turn, Johnson finally banned Huawei from operating in Britain. His move would delay the country's 5G rollout by up to three years and cost Britain at least £2 billion to remove all existing Huawei 5G equipment from its networks by 2027.

US Secretary of State Mike Pompeo welcomed Johnson's decision: 'The UK joins a growing list of countries from around the world that are standing up for their national security by prohibiting the use of untrusted, high-risk vendors,' he said. Pottinger must have also been cheering. Not only had his opposition to Huawei's role in Britain come to fruition, but by the time it did, Trump had already promoted him to Deputy National Security Advisor.

Lord Darroch said while the decision to ban Huawei in Britain had been made after his departure from the British foreign service, 'the pressure from the US was starting while I was there'. During his time as the UK's ambassador to the United States, Darroch said H.R. McMaster, Trump's national security adviser between February 2017 and April 2018, would raise with him the matter relating to the Chinese tech company and 'explain why they thought we should ban Huawei'. The pressure from Washington was stepped up after Darroch left his role in December 2019, he said.

'There was a lot of media speculation and Parliamentary interest in whether we would ban Huawei or not,' said Darroch. 'In my time, GCHQ had led on detailed analysis about the risk from Huawei kit on the communications network and had concluded that, provided it was not at the core of the network, it was okay. This analysis was a central part of the discussion at the national security council and key to the then agreed outcome that Huawei equipment could be used in certain parts of the network. It was basically driven by the analysis of GCHQ.' Darroch said during his time as ambassador 'the Americans had no compelling technical arguments for banning Huawei. This doesn't mean it shouldn't have happened – it would be legitimate to do it for political reasons, or because it was so important to the Americans, or as an expression of Five Eyes solidarity, or whatever. But it shouldn't be dressed up as technical.'

Ciaran Martin stepped down from his role as the head of GCHQ's National Cyber Security Centre in September 2020 to become a professor at Oxford University. Reflecting on Britain's unsuccessful plan for Huawei to help build the country's 5G network, he said his confidence in the plan had always been underpinned by technical assessments and he had been under no illusions about the potential risks that Huawei posed. 'In reality, anyone can have a go at hacking anything,' he said. 'We in the UK, thanks to the US sanctions, are now entirely dependent on Nokia and Ericsson. For sure, we trust their boards of directors. But are we seriously saying that just because they're not Chinese, they can't be hacked? By neighbouring Russia, for example? Or China?'

Almost two years after the UK's ban of Huawei, when Theresa May was asked whether she had any regrets that Britain had not been able to exploit the Chinese company's technology because it had to fall in line with Australia and the US, she said: 'That happened because of action taken by the US – sanctions which meant that it wasn't going to be available. So actually if we'd gone down the route, ultimately we would have been in a difficult position. So it was perforce that the market place was changed. I think the interesting question for now is how can the Five Eyes if you like come together and try and ensure that we're not in that position again in the future as we look to the next generation and the generation after that.'

THE FUTURE OF THE FIVE EYES

THERE IS NO OTHER spy network with the same round-the-clock geographical reach and capabilities as the Five Eyes, where intelligence, analysis, technology, tradecraft and even personnel are shared between like-minded organisations in the interest of a common purpose. Unlike other alliances, including NATO, which have expanded their membership base over time, the Five Eyes has maintained its exclusivity since its creation. Another point of difference is its very existence is not legally binding, but instead built on a framework of institutional and individual trust, secrecy, information assurance, and friendships. Successive leaders of intelligence agencies have had to work on maintaining the role and reliance of their organisations in the Five Eyes club, from attending annual gatherings to discuss areas of mutual interest and concern, to gaining a better personal understanding of their counterparts at other partner organisations. Sir John Sawers, who served as a senior diplomat, including as Britain's ambassador to the United Nations before leading MI6 for five years, said such events were necessary for maintaining the close collaboration between agencies. 'We used to have and still do have annual gatherings of the Five Eyes agencies and it's very striking there that the heads of the CIA and the FBI and the NSA would be equals with the heads of the services of New Zealand and Canada as well as the heads from the UK and Australia,' he said. 'That leads to a level of personal engagement at top level which feeds down – not that it was hugely needed – but it helped solidify and give top cover to the very close collaboration that was taking place at operational level.'

The Five Eyes rely on their close cooperation to advance their understanding of their opponents and respond more effectively, especially with regard to borderless and non-geographic threats such as terrorism and cyber-hacking from the likes of Russia, said Lord Jonathan Evans, a former director-general of the British security service, MI5. 'Shared information on cyber issues, including from Russia over the last 25 years, gave MI5 some early warning of developing threats,' he said. 'We are all subject to similar information and interference threats. The techniques our opponents use are the same and how to recognise and counter them is a joint endeavour.'

Sir Iain Lobban, former director of GCHQ, agrees. 'If you're seeking to discover and disrupt extremist or terrorist activity, it's very rare that such activity has its genesis solely within your own national borders,' he said. 'Sharing raw data collected, workshopping analysis, exchanging thematic or threat reporting is all very well. But ultimately, with trusted partners [...] counterterrorism brought about a thrust to share the underpinning collection and processing "capabilities" with partners beyond the Five Eyes.'

Intelligence-sharing between the Five Eyes, along with the joint operations that bind them, has made them increasingly dependent on each other, despite the autonomous nature of the spy agencies within the alliance. However, there are instances where partners within the alliance would designate the intelligence they generate as 'not for release to foreign nationals' – NOFORN – to withhold it from anyone, including the Five Eyes. And in some cases intelligence shared by some member nations with the US would be reclassified by the recipient agency in

Washington. 'It was very common for the intelligence we provided to the US to disappear into the American machine and classified as NOFORN,' said General Sir Richard Barrons, the former head of Britain's Strategic Command, who oversaw military, intelligence and cyber operations that required joint capabilities. 'This is just a reflection of how the US system works, particularly in the relationships between perhaps 18 agencies.' It is, however, the US's unparalleled intelligence capabilities that make the other four member countries more secure in their existence and the state of their national security. 'We are so much more secure from the benefit of sitting in the privileged club because of US intelligence,' said Barrons.

The business of intelligence-sharing is never a free-for-all, even among Five Eyes members. Sharing among HUMINT agencies is not as seamless as it is among their SIGINT partners because there is a fear among spy handlers of the impact their provided information could have on the identification of secret informants, which could potentially result in their arrest or death. 'In SIGINT, we are a technically focused endeavour, in which access is routinely gained and lost for a variety of reasons,' said Admiral Mike Rogers, who ran the NSA during parts of the Obama and Trump administrations. 'But we're generally able to regain access over time, a fair amount of the time. So generally there is a view in SIGINT where you say 'I may have lost the ability to access right now, but if I work hard, there's a good chance I could get back'. It doesn't mean you always do. And there's no real human price [to] losing access, so to speak. On the HUMINT side, it is a human-based endeavour and there is a human price to pay when you lose access, when you lose a source, when it is outed.'

While HUMINT agencies are not bound by an equivalent official agreement to the one that binds the signals organisations within the Five Eyes, they do share a classification system largely based on trust, according to the FBI. 'There is a Five Eyes designation built into our networks to be able to share information readily,' said Michael J. Driscoll, assistant director of the FBI who is responsible for its New York field office. 'This applies to all types of intelligence, including HUMINT, so we don't need to create a specific path to ensure the information is shareable with those partners; it's part of our system.' He said while the Five Eyes all have robust intelligence capabilities, that capability is naturally bolstered when it is pooled. 'What we've realised is that together, our resources are significantly stronger,' said Driscoll. 'And in a way, that has created a new dependency.' Such is the nature of partnerships that successes are shared collectively, but so are the failures to a great extent. Almost every agency within the Five Eyes has been infiltrated either directly or indirectly over the last seven decades. British officials, and especially those within MI5 and MI6, continue to wince about the Cold War KGB penetration of their agencies through the Cambridge Five. The Canadian naval officer Jeffrey Delisle compromised the Five Eyes by selling alliance secrets to the Russians. Several ASIO officers in Australia were said to have passed on secrets to the Kremlin. And the American NSA contractor Edward Snowden exposed the surveillance overreach by signals intelligence agencies within the alliance. Such big breaches forced a rethink by the Five Eye agencies of their internal security procedures – especially in the wake of the Snowden revelations.

Sir Iain Lobban, who led GCHQ in the lead up to and during the Snowden Affair, said there was a parallel between 'cyber intrusions on networks' and organisations being compromised by rogue insiders. 'Lots of effort goes into building a really strong defensive perimeter in cyber security, but the reality is that cyber actors will find a way past that, often laterally,' he said. 'In the same way, considerable attention is paid to recruits to intelligence and security organisations. Yes, there are regular follow-up security processes, but insiders can wittingly or unwittingly do enormous damage to the host institution. And given people are the lifeblood of an organisation, it's really important to treat them with respect and to build mutual trust, not monitor your workforce in some insidious "Big Brother" way. Increasingly the answer for both assumed cyber penetration and insider trust is to use sophisticated anonymised analytics that throw up anomalies to be investigated.'

For almost a decade, agencies have increased scrutiny of their staff members, with vetting procedures, including background checks, interviews and polygraphs, being conducted more frequently. Richard Fadden, former director of the CSIS – Canadian Security Intelligence Service – said insider threats were an ongoing challenge for spy agencies that had previously been exacerbated by officials who are protective of their colleagues. 'I don't think anybody ever passes up dealing with an obvious case, but if there's a grey area, and I mean this for all of the Five Eyes, sometimes they get a pass when they shouldn't,' he said. 'And I know that dealing with such matters is now stricter than it used to be.' He said with increasing threats from China and Russia, 'all of us will be compelled to increase the scrutiny of this potential problem more seriously than we have done in the past.'

At the FBI, there is a constant vigilance about insider threats, said Michael Driscoll, and there is a constant evaluation of staff members who are granted trusted access to secrets. 'So that if somebody is downloading thousands of documents that they shouldn't have access to, there has to be a system in place to prevent that from happening or at least monitor it so that you know it is happening,' he said. 'We're constantly looking at our systems, our networks, our people, to make sure we understand the threats we are inheriting by offering trust to these individuals.' The fear of inheriting threats is among several reasons why the Five Eyes has not been expanded since its creation to include other nations. France, Germany, Japan and South Korea are among the nations that have declared their interest in the joining the ranks of the alliance, with some critics accusing it of being elitist and inferring that race has played a part in keeping non-white and non-English-speaking countries out.

Throughout his six-year term as British prime minister, David Cameron became acutely aware of the 'professional jealousy' among the UK's allies towards membership of the Five Eyes. That feeling had existed despite numerous bilateral deals that had been signed by individual Five Eyes' partners with nations outside of alliance, including the 2010 Lancaster House Treaties between the UK and France which strengthened their defence and security cooperation. While Cameron had been aware of the Five Eyes during his time as Leader of the Opposition, it was only after he was elected prime minister that he discovered the extent of the intelligence relationship within the alliance. 'It's only as Prime Minister that you see the power of the relationship, the extent of the sharing between not just SIGINT but HUMINT,' he said. 'I think you also see a bit of professional jealousy amongst European partners that there is this incredibly close relationship. We do have a close relationship with the French and with the Germans and others, and I hope I played a part in that with things like the Lancaster House agreement with the French, and with the Germans on understanding Islamism and Russia. Chancellor Merkel and I had a joint seminar with our intelligence chiefs at Chequers on that [in 2015]. But there was definitely a sense from our European allies that the Five Eyes was something special that we had created.'

Most of the countries wanting membership have been seen among the Five Eyes as being more motivated by what they could gain in the way of capabilities, knowledge, and insights, rather than what they would offer in return. The reality is that between them, the Five Eyes agencies pretty much have what they need in terms of its global surveillance reach, and the view among their spy chiefs is that if ever they require further operational support, they can provide temporary invitations into the circle of trust on a case-by-case basis if it is in the best interest of the alliance.

Numerous intelligence-led operations following the War on Terror required Five Eyes agencies to form partnerships with counterparts in countries such as Iraq, Afghanistan, and Pakistan. 'A lot of the work that we did in Afghanistan, for instance, would not have been successful if we did not share information about active terrorism cells with Pakistan,' said Driscoll. 'If you look at a lot of the work we did in Africa to address Isis and Al Qaeda threats, that doesn't succeed if we're not in lockstep with our partners in African countries. So we've taken the lessons of the Five Eyes model and learned to be better partners and better collaborators.'

The former deputy director of the US Defense Intelligence Agency, Douglas H. Wise, said that while friendly countries have long campaigned to be inducted into the Five Eyes, there is always a 'duality of benefits and risks' associated with intelligence relationships. 'The default relationship is bilateral because the benefits and risks of more than two partners increases the counterintelligence risks and with three or more partners, it is much more difficult to have equal measures of trust and significantly more challenges in reaching consensus on extremely sensitive matters,' he said. 'The Five Eyes alliance members would be the first to acknowledge this as they went through their own learning and trusting process over the last 80 years. While this trust is certainly the coin of the realm for the alliance, having a common world view and shared assessment of the threats and solutions is necessary as well to achieve unity of action.' Wise said the common language, cultural values and, to an extent, legal, oversight, and political systems, have helped the Five Eyes create a cultural foundation among its agencies for how intelligence frames views and views frame intelligence. 'At this dangerous and unsettled geopolitical period in history, the alliance needs to be at its most efficient and function at its greatest effectiveness. This is not the time to be distracted by organisational challenges and stress, brought on by on-boarding new members and taking another eighty years to get where we are today.'

While the Five Eyes are not purely defined by the number of agencies that exist within each member country, such numbers do present a slanted picture in favour of America – even when accounting for the variations in the way that each nation defines which agencies are part of its intelligence community. For instance, the FBI is part of Washington's spy community according to the US Office of the Director of Intelligence (ODI), while Scotland Yard in Britain – which also handles intelligence and serves as its country's federal police force – is not deemed an intelligence agency by the UK. And while America, Britain, and Australia have separate domestic and foreign human-intelligence agencies, Canada and New Zealand do not.

The two founding countries of the Five Eyes, the US and Britain, have the largest number of personnel – and budgets – in the alliance, but the difference between them is stark. Contractors and paid informants aside, the CIA, NSA and FBI, have around 100,000 staff members between them, a number more than six times greater than the 16,500 or so personnel at their British counterpart agencies, MI6, GCHQ and

MI5. As for the US's intelligence budget, it was US$84.1 billion in 2021, compared to Britain's £3.75 billion (around US$4.6 billion) that year – a difference of more than 18 times in size. The discrepancies in numbers, important as they are, convey only a small part of the overall intelligence picture of the Five Eyes' founding countries. Sir John Sawers, former chief of MI6, said Britain's contribution to the alliance is 'partly geography, partly skills, partly access', and in the world of intelligence having assets across the world matters. 'One of the things that the UK brings to the US is parts of our old colonial heritage: Diego Garcia, Ascension Island, are two obvious examples. Cyprus is another one,' he said. 'Intelligence collection is a global business and you can't do it all from the mainland United States and so there is a strong geographical addition that the UK and other Five Eyes partners bring, and also a difference in culture and perspective. We also had a long tradition of running secret agents in hostile environments which was valued by other Five Eyes partners.'

As with British prime ministers before him, and ones who followed, David Cameron is adamant about the UK's contribution to the intelligence alliance and the way that feeds into the Special Relationship between London and Washington. 'I do not hold a sort of romantic view about the capabilities of the UK,' he said. 'I think not only about the resourcing, but also the GCHQ expertise we have and the assets of the UK around the world, which are important. And then you've got the respect for the UK's human intelligence [capabilities] and the uplift that it got, particularly with respect to countering Islamist extremism. And then there are the separate intelligence partnerships. Obviously, the Americans have strong partnerships with the Saudis and others – as we do. But there are some countries, like Oman, where our partnership is stronger than the Americans. So I don't think it's Britain just pretending that we bring something to the Special Relationship, I think it is genuinely appreciated. And I can think of specific incidents, really quite important ones, including perhaps the one you made a programme about [the Jihadi John case] where there was a very important input from British intelligence.'

To illustrate the intelligence ties between Washington and London, Cameron said his first national security adviser, Peter Ricketts, had become so close to his US counterpart, Thomas Donilon, that President Obama often joked they were one person. 'The relationship is very tight between the UK National Security Adviser and the US National Security Advisor,' he said. 'In fact, President Obama used to joke that for a while that he thought Ricketts-Donilon was one person – because Peter Ricketts and Thomas Donilon were so close. "Let's leave that to Ricketts-Donilon", he used to say.'

There has never been any doubt about London's closeness to Washington, but when it comes to scale and reach, the US eclipses the four other member nations on budgets and labour-force. In some ways, Britain, Australia, Canada, and New Zealand are much like talented backup vocalists in a band: they are there to provide the lead singer with vocal harmony. But intelligence coups are not always defined by the size of the agency responsible for it. 'The five members don't have the same size, they don't have the same level of assessment, they don't have the same sets of capabilities, they don't have the same relationships,' said Admiral Mike Rogers. 'One may be stronger in a different part of the world, a different area – not just geography, but a topic or subject or a skill or expertise [...] It's about this idea of "Can you bring value?" and by bringing value you also receive value.' Rogers said the value that each country brings to the alliance can also evolve over time. 'The Five Eyes is not just about value today, it's about potential value in the future,' he said. 'So, for example, take New Zealand – a small island in the South Pacific. How would they be in an alliance in which all members aren't all on the same level, in part because you're thinking "Look, I may not know what's going to be important in ten years from now, and it may be an area that New Zealand has access to or an insight they have access to. Ten years from now it is really going to be important in a way that it isn't now". You always think of the long game with the Five Eyes structure. It is the one thing that has sustained this alliance structure that has such a broad disparity in size.'

Value is also defined by the quality of intelligence brought in by each service and the extent to which it can be validated. And while a healthy rivalry exists between member countries – and even on an inter-agency level – no one is left behind. 'We all have clever people who operate in that slim area between the difficult and the impossible to do things our adversaries think cannot be done,' said Mike Burgess, who ran the Australian Signals Directorate before becoming the head of ASIO in 2019. 'Yes, size, reach and scale do matter, but they are not the only things that deliver value in a partnership as mature and sophisticated as the Five Eyes.' Burgess said the agencies in the alliance also function at different speeds: 'We don't move at the pace of the five, we move at the pace of the fastest. That means two or three of us might join up on something but the other two don't fret because they know they're still trusted and deep in the Five Eyes and they don't need to worry about the competition because you do need to move quickly.' By way of example, an Australian intelligence official said: 'Typically you might see a SIGINT organisation hooking up with the might of the CIA and doing some amazing stuff. I make that up but you get my drift. It's driven by pure selfish national and agency interest[s] and where those things overlap brilliant things happen.'

A growing challenge for human-intelligence – or HUMINT – agencies within the Five Eyes, including the FBI, Britain's MI6 and ASIO (the Australian Security Intelligence Organisation) is the recruitment of well-positioned informants who are either at the heart of terrorist organisations or within the governments or diplomatic services of adversarial nations such as Russia, China and Iran.

While source recruitment for such agencies is the centrepiece of their work, adversarial powers have become increasingly adept at hunting informants – and then either killing them or turning them into double agents. Lost informants are typically bad for recruitment campaigns, and those who are turned can compromise the intelligence analysis and policy decisions of the countries they target by feeding misinformation to their handlers. In some instances, the eagerness to recruiting sources in operational missions has overridden vetting procedures, leading to fatal outcomes. An example of 'mission over security' in 2009 led to the deaths of seven CIA officers at a US base in Khost, Afghanistan, when a Jordanian doctor who had been recruited by the agency to infiltrate Al Qaeda was turned against his handlers and blew himself up in a suicide attack. It was a wake-up call for all Five Eyes agencies in the midst of the so called 'War on Terror', much like another cautionary tale linked to the CIA in which the agency's classified communication system was compromised, exposing the organisation's network in China and Iran. Informants were executed in both cases. About 20 CIA sources who had been rounded up between 2010 and 2012 had either been killed or imprisoned by the Chinese alone.

The challenge of recruiting human sources was highlighted at the start of 2022, following Russia's invasion of Ukraine, which had been correctly foreseen by the Five Eyes. The Russian leader's unpredictability was increasingly preoccupying the Five Eyes – and amidst the humanitarian disaster in Ukraine, where tens of thousands were being killed or wounded and millions were fleeing, the alliance partners were eager for an intelligence breakthrough by exploiting western sanctions against Moscow's economy and leadership, hoping that the anti-war sentiment in Russia would ultimately lead to voluntary defections from Putin's inner circle. Spy chiefs naturally wanted to understand Putin's intent to inform their own counter-operations and their policymakers – and such an understanding was not going to emerge from the interception of communication between his troops on the battlefield. The Five Eyes' pursuit of voluntary defectors, or 'walk-ins' as they are known in intelligence circles, became paramount.

Spy chiefs and world leaders who had been familiar with Putin's increasingly dictatorial posturing were shocked that he placed his nuclear forces on alert shortly after the invasion. The crisis in Ukraine reinforced the gulf between the Five Eyes' ambition to predict his next move and its inability to infiltrate his inner circle. Questions were even being raised about the state of Putin's mental health and whether the isolation that resulted from the covid pandemic had rendered him delusional. The Russian leader had rarely allowed anyone into his orbit – and even world leaders who had met with him could barely recognise the person he had morphed into. Among them was Julia Gillard, who met the Russian leader twice during her time as Prime Minister of Australia between 2010 and 2013. While she had never considered him a political leader who 'shares our values', she had once thought of him as a 'rational actor in self-interest' who was somewhat predictable. 'The benefit of rational actors in self-interest is that you can normally kind of figure out what they are going to do next,' she said. 'The most frightening thing on the political stage is someone who does not seem to be rational in self-interest. And I think the intelligence issue now with Putin is whether there's something about covid isolation or some other contemporary factor that has led him to such dictatorial delusions that he is no longer as predictable as perhaps he would have been.'

Lord (Kim) Darroch, who had access to Britain's top secrets for almost a decade during his roles as a national security adviser and UK Ambassador to the United States, said understanding the Russian leader's motives was the 'gold dust' that the Five Eyes were desperate to attain. 'On Russia, the real gold dust would be anyone who could give us insights on what Putin and his immediate, very small entourage, are saying to each other, including instructions from Putin to the military and so on,' he said. 'And whether we can obtain that really depends on whether we have any source right at the centre – someone who would be personally in an extremely dangerous position. In the past there have been such individuals.'

Throughout the Cold War, major intelligence breakthroughs by agencies of the Five Eyes were provided by voluntary Russian defectors, including: Igor Gouzenko in Ottawa, who revealed Stalin's ambition for nuclear supremacy following World War II; Oleg Penkovsky, who flagged up the Kremlin's intent ahead of the Cuban Missile Crisis in the early 1960s; Oleg Lyalin, who unmasked the extent of the Soviet spy network in Britain and US in 1971; and Vasili Mitrokhin, who exposed the KGB's operations, including those in the US and Australia in the 1992. The defectors had been driven by an ideological belief that they were acting in the greater interest of their motherland to expose the corruption and treachery of the Kremlin.

More than three decades after the Cold War had officially ended, the FBI wanted to tempt history – not wait for it to repeat itself. The US law-enforcement agency set out to exploit the resentment within Moscow's diplomatic service towards the invasion of Ukraine by leveraging social-media platforms – Facebook, Twitter, and Google – to target an advertisement at mobile phones located either inside or outside the Russian Embassy in Washington. The ad appeared in Russian text, accompanied by a picture of Putin chastising Sergey Naryshkin, head of his country's foreign intelligence service, or SVR, during a Security Council meeting in the lead up to the invasion. The ad included the words 'Speak plainly, Sergey', in reference to the humiliation to which Putin had subjected his spy chief during the publicised meeting. Using Putin's own words to make its appeal, the FBI ad, which bore the organisation's logo, stated in Russian text: 'Speak plainly [...] We're ready to listen.' While the ad had been specifically targeted at Russia's mission at the US capital, it was hardly a secret given that it featured a link to an FBI website connecting prospective recruits with representatives from the organisation. At worst, the FBI ploy heightened the level of paranoia among embassy officials about the prospect of people defecting, with the Russian ambassador, Anatoly Anatov, describing it as a 'ridiculous' attempt to 'sow confusion and organise desertion among the staff'. Yet from a counterintelligence perspective, sowing confusion and encouraging desertion in the spy-versus-spy game can easily be seen as success by an organisation like the FBI, or any other human-intelligence organisation within the Five Eyes.

Michael J. Driscoll said it was very likely that Russian defectors would come to his organisation's aid in the interest of Ukrainians. 'History has shown us that that kind of thing happens all of the time,' he said. 'We've experienced it, as have the Russians, and other countries have experienced it. And in moments like this when you're dealing with a significant conflict and there is apparently clear disagreement among Russian citizens, and you can see that from protests on the streets of

Russia, then the possibility that somebody might be willing to have a conversation with us about that and seek to perhaps to do the right thing for the sake of the greater good I think is very likely.'

Technological leaps, including facial recognition and biometric scans have been exploited by Russian, Chinese, and Iranian spy agencies to identify the movements of agent runners in the Five Eyes and to expose their informants. Martin Green, Canada's coordinator of intelligence assessments, said technology has made human-intelligence operations, or HUMINT, more challenging. 'HUMINT will be harder to sustain going forward because of advances in technology,' he said. 'It is much easier to track individuals nowadays through a variety of means including biometrics. Having clandestine agents with networks of contacts will not be easy going forward.' Green said technological breakthroughs were becoming 'mixed blessings' for the Five Eyes as their intelligence agencies try to balance the uptake of new developments against the security risk they pose.

Much like the arms race between the Five Eyes countries and the Soviet Union in the wake of World War II, the intelligence alliance is now part of a race for technological dominance, including in the area of quantum computing. Quantum computers could have a processing ability that outstrips the world's fastest supercomputers by millions of times. Intelligence officials across both the signals and human-intelligence communities in the Five Eyes are closely monitoring the impact such quantum computers, which are still at a developmental stage, could have on encrypted communications. Hacking into encrypted communications, which has long been a priority of intelligence agencies to identify the inner workings of terrorist organisations, crime rings, and rival spy services, could enormously benefit the Five Eyes if one of their nations is the first to develop the technology. But what if an adversarial nation wins the race in weaponising quantum computing to attack Five Eyes communications? Martin Green said quantum computing 'could provide intelligence agencies with more secure communications and faster access to encrypted communications used by threat actors – in parallel it will also afford the bad guys secure communications and the ability to compromise others' IT.' And the technology itself could become the target of hostile states, said the FBI's Michael Driscoll. 'I am confident that quantum computing, because it is a cutting edge technology, will be the target of hostile nation states, China being a primary concern,' he said. 'I know some experts theorise that quantum computing may render many of our current encryption techniques obsolete but I have also seen reporting that some of the newer encryption algorithms and techniques may already be "quantum resistant".'

The uncertainty surrounding quantum computing is somewhat symbolic of the ever-changing domain that the Five Eyes are operating in – where authoritarian nations are constantly pushing the boundaries of cyber-hacking, misinformation, economic warfare, and the theft of intellectual property including scientific research, to gain tactical or strategic objectives or damage their adversaries. There is a risk to a growing list of threats faced by the Five Eyes, said Martin. 'Climate change and pandemics have also entered our lines of business and there's clearly elements of both that have major security implications,' he said. 'Social media itself is being used by adversaries both state and non-state as part of toolkit to push propaganda and provide antithetical narratives to liberal democracies.'

The game of spying is not a level playing field. Countries such as Russia, China, Iran, and North Korea have shown a complete disregard for international laws, let alone human rights and civil liberties, when it comes to weaponising their intelligence services both domestically and against foreign countries such as the Five Eyes. Moscow and Beijing have become widely known for excelling in 'grey zone' operations that constitute activities that fall below the threshold of armed conflict and include the outsourcing of cyber-attacks and assassination hits to criminals. Admiral Mike Rogers said the Five Eyes need to excel and generate insider knowledge in areas relating to grey zone operations. 'That gets into things like information, misinformation, cyber, influence, use of surrogates, relationships created as cut-outs, so to speak, so that nations have some sort of plausible deniability,' he said. 'Nation states working with criminal gangs – you have to be able to deal with this grey zone which increasingly nations are using as a vehicle to create an advantage for themselves and to create disadvantage for others.' While it has become accepted wisdom that rogue states have a no-holds-barred policy in their fight against their opponents, this is counterbalanced by the strength of partnership that exists within the Five Eyes, said Mike Burgess. 'Authoritarian states can operate in ways that are effectively unconstrained by law, budgets and oversight,' he said. 'How do we counter that? We have something they do not – the power of partnerships. That's our advantage.'

While Five Eyes members have historically sought a level of comfort and confidence in their unique set-up over almost seven decades, at the beginning of 2022, spy chiefs within the alliance became nervous about what appeared to be an aggressive pact between Vladimir Putin and his Chinese counterpart, Xi Jinping, in which the two autocratic leaders declared in a public statement that the unity between their nations had 'no limits' and contained 'no "forbidden" areas of cooperation'. With each one of those nations being such a resource-intensive challenge for the Five Eyes, how would the alliance manage if the pair were to pool their intelligence and military capabilities? Three weeks after the joint statement between Moscow and Beijing, Five Eyes officials had been able to breathe a sigh of relief when China abstained on the UN Security Council resolution condemning the Russian invasion of Ukraine. Beijing's move was hardly a show of 'limitless' support from Xi to Putin, undermining the very nature of their publicised pact.

Sir John Sawers said China is 'the long-term, generational challenge' for the Five Eyes, and Theresa May, the former British prime minister, expressed concerns over Beijing's attempt to pursue strategic alliances. 'I think we have seen China reach out to other countries in a way that is exerting their influence across the world.' Australia and New Zealand were outraged in early 2022 when the Solomon Islands signed a security pact with Beijing, ostensibly to 'maintain order' in the Pacific nation which had been experiencing social unrest. However, Canberra and

Wellington fear that the pact could allow China to build a naval base on the islands, threatening the balance of power in the region.

Having served at the helm of MI6 during the first four years of David Cameron's premiership, Sawers said the Cameron government was more focused on the economic dimension that Beijing provided. 'Ultimately, that's a political balancing act. And you can argue that under the David Cameron and George Osborne [Chancellor of the Exchequer] era, we didn't get that balance right. We emphasised the economic dimension, the Golden Era and so on. The economic opportunities were taking precedence over the security challenges and that involved things like Chinese involvement in our national infrastructure.'

Cameron explained that his government's approach to China had been 'properly debated with the intelligence agencies being in the room – so there was no naivety about what the Chinese got up to'. The former prime minister said under his leadership Britain had 'quite a positive engagement programme with the Chinese, which I would defend because we were trying to build a relationship with them that was load bearing'. Theresa May, who served as Cameron's Home Secretary for six years before succeeding him as prime minister, said, 'China can't be ignored because it is such a significant player in the global economy, but I'm not sure if any of us have quite yet found the absolute way to be ensuring that the global economy can benefit from China's position and so forth while at the same time reining back some of the other aspects, the more worrying aspects of China's activities.'

The many successes that the Five Eyes has been responsible for over the last six decades or so, including the defeat of the Soviet Union, assassination of Osama Bin Laden, the destruction of Isis's so-called caliphate, are very much part of the alliance's legacy – but so are the failures, including the botched intelligence assessment in the lead up to the Iraq War and the Guantanamo Bay scandal. And while some of the victories and defeats of the Five Eyes may not become public for years – if ever – its organisations have become a little more transparent over time, and not always by choice. Very often their transparency has been forced by court action, civil-rights campaigns, bad press, and oversight committees. Government inquiries, too, have played a key role in making spy agencies more open – from those in the 1970s that exposed the illegalities committed by the CIA and FBI in the United States, and the Royal Canadian Military Police (RCMP) in Canada, right through to the post-9/11 Commission (the National Commission on Terrorist Attacks Upon the United States) and the transatlantic inquiries into surveillance overreach which were conducted following the disclosures made by Edward Snowden in 2013. Even though intelligence officials were outraged by the actions taken by NSA whistle-blower Snowden, they grudgingly agree that his revelations forced Five Eyes agencies to become more transparent on an unparalleled scale.

The 11 September terrorist attacks on the United States in 2001 gave the Five Eyes a common purpose to pursue Al Qaeda and its subsequent iterations. Two decades on, a former enemy has re-emerged to help re-energise the alliance – Russia. Putin's miscalculations on his invasion of Ukraine have – at the point of going to press – backfired: instead of preventing the growth of NATO, he has sparked its potential expansion; instead of crushing the Ukrainian resistance, he has triggered worldwide support for the country in both humanitarian and military aid. Another unintended outcome of the invasion by Moscow has been the way it has mobilised Five Eyes countries in their mission to combat the Kremlin. 'When you get new crises emerging such as the Ukraine war that we're going through now, that hasn't just revitalised NATO and the transatlantic relationship, it has also given a new purpose and a new focus – and an immediate one – to the intelligence agencies as well,' Sir John Sawers said.

The creation of the Five Eyes took place in much simpler times than today, where conflicts were taking place in nations far from the alliance's member countries and where the tussle between democracy and autocracy was largely played out through proxy military interventions, including the Korean, Vietnam and Soviet–Afghan Wars. There was a marked shift in western military interventions in the wake of the Cold War where invasions, including those of Iraq and Afghanistan, were conducted in the name of combating terrorism and with a timeline dictated by those leading the intervention – namely, the United States. While there was some blowback in the way of individual terrorist attacks against Five Eyes nations, which the likes of Al Qaeda and Isis described as revenge for foreign military interventions, the alliance never felt like it was under a real existential threat. 'That is completely unlike the situation that we are moving into, in that the fight becomes more existential,' said General Sir Richard Barrons. 'In a digital age, not only is the risk to the West and Five Eyes elevated but the way in which confrontation is executed is changing. Things that we need to sustain our daily lives – food, internet, communication, banking – all of those rely on technology and are vulnerable to cyber-attacks.' That merely compounds the other challenges facing the Five Eyes, including China's aggressive quest for global supremacy and Russia's nuclear posturing as it continues to wage its war against Ukraine.

'So many things are unthinkable until they happen,' said Julia Gillard. 'If we all got back in a time machine and went wandering around telling people "planes are going to hit the World Trade Center, and then there will be a war in Iraq, and then it will be seen to be based on false intelligence and then there will be a decade of controversy around a place called Gitmo [Guantanamo Bay detention camp], the torture of prisoners under the banner of enhance interrogation techniques", people would have gone, "Can we assist you to the nearest healthcare facility which can help you work through these delusions?"'

It has been an unpredictable, protracted, and at times divided journey for the Five Eyes which is perhaps inevitable for an alliance of such magnitude that has grown out of an arrangement between member countries desperate to protect their own national interests, including the security of their citizens. Since its formation, the Five Eyes has been occasionally mired by the personal agenda of some of the political leaders of its member countries – including Richard Nixon, George W. Bush, Tony Blair and Donald Trump – and the unaccountability and rogue practices by some of the spy chiefs at its intelligence agencies. But should contemporary agency officials within the Five Eyes be judged by the failures of their predecessors?

As the Five Eyes grapple with an increasingly unpredictable world and shoulder a responsibility for matters of national security that have expanded recently to include the likes of climate change, pandemics and social-media arenas being used by rogue countries to push propaganda and hostile narratives against liberal democracies, the alliance remains vital in attempting to foresee and combat future threats.

NOTES AND SOURCES

Abbreviations:

GLD: Guy Liddell Diaries

TNA: The National Archives

GWUNSA: George Washington University National Security Archive

Online reports: In cases where a byline did not accompany an article online, the term 'online report' is used instead.

Other citations: Details of the books featured in the notes are provided in full in the initial citation, and then in a shortened form thereafter. The same applies for the National Archives cited. In many cases, the documents contained in TNA files are individually dated. The author has cited dates where they are available; undated documents appear without dates. TNA files obtained online were split into multiple parts to accommodate their data sizes. The author has identified the part number in correlation to the files to aid their identification.

References cited as 'Private information' relate to material obtained by the author from either serving or former Five Eyes intelligence officials who requested anonymity.

CHAPTER ONE

'live in peace': The National Archives, Kew (TNA), Security Service, File KV2/193, p. 27

'Jewish blood in her veins': Ibid., p. 25

'things were easily done if one had a head': Ibid., pp. 116–17

'To test this information': Ibid.

'Inside the bag, she discovered a clue': Ibid., p. 111

'Ernst had worked as a hairdresser': Christopher Andrew, The Defence of the Realm: The Authorized History of MI5, Penguin Group 2009, p. 38

'Liddell anticipated a growing threat': Ibid., p. 209

'feeble attempt at espionage': TNA, Security Service, File KV2/ 3534, p. 8

'Approximately a month later': TNA, Security Service, File KV2/193, p. 79

'Yet more compelling were the traces': Ibid., p. 82

'a German "shadow" scheme': Ibid., p. 79

'secret plans relating to the defence': Ibid., p. 95

'medium build, dark brown hair': TNA, Security Service, File KV2/ 3421, p. 13

'Abwehr received Rumrich's letter': Rhodri Jeffreys-Jones, Ring of Spies: How MI5 and the FBI Brought Down the Nazis in America, History Press, 2020, p. 61

'every effort will be made to leave clues': TNA, Security Service, File KV2/193, p. 95

'one of ten aliases': Ibid., File KV2/3421, p. 13

'initiate a funnel of information sharing': 'The FBI and the Royal Canadian Mounted Police', https://www.fbi.gov/news/stories/100-years-of-fbi-rcmp-partnership-112219

'Dundee Police raided Jessie': TNA, Security Service, File KV2/193, p. 38

'he was a gifted musician': Nigel West, MI5: British Security Service Operations 1909–1945, Triad Panther, 1983, pp. 50–1

'anxious to have an exchange of information': TNA, Security Service, File KV2/3533, p. 83

'wan crooking of the lips': Ibid., File KV2/193, p. 49

'fair, plump, and over 50': Ibid., p. 42

'admitted making the pencil annotations': Ibid., p. 44

'relative to coastguard station': Ibid., p. 38

'The position seems to be: Ibid., p. 44

'if I had not missed a boat': Ibid., p 54

CHAPTER TWO

'His business portfolio eventually became global': William Stephenson, A Man Called Intrepid, Macmillan, 1976, p. 26

'steel plants had been ordered by Hitler': H. Montgomery Hyde, Room 3603: The Story of the British Intelligence Centre in New York during World War II, Farrar, Straus, 1963, pp. 14–17 (accessed online at http://ia802804.us.archive.org/22/items/room363001951mbp/room363001951mbp.pdf)

'he turned to the private sector for information': Ibid., p. 16

'humiliating and damaging': Gill Bennett, *The Records of the Permanent Under-Secretary's department: Liaison between the Foreign Office and British Secret Intelligence, 1873–1939*, Foreign and Commonwealth Office, March 2005, p.67. MI6's wrong information about an imminent attack on Holland was deemed 'highly sensational and highly disturbing' by Sir George Mounsey, Secretary designate to the British Ministry of Economic Warfare.

'During the interview with Stephenson': Gill Bennett, *Churchill's Man of Mystery: Desmond Morton and the World of Intelligence*, Routledge, 2007, pp. 190–3

'reversed a previous policy of sharing': William Stephenson, *A Man Called Intrepid*, p. 80

'meeting on April 16, 1940': Raymond J. Batvinis, *Hoover's Secret War Against Axis Nazis*, University Press of Kansas, 2014, p. 25

'creating the British Security Coordination': Bennett, *Churchill's Man of Mystery: Desmond Morton and the World of Intelligence*, p. 253

'Gentlemen do not read each other's mail': Evan Thomas, 'Spymaster General: The Adventures of Wild Bill Donovan and the "Oh So Social" OSS', *Vanity Fair*, 3 March 2011 (via https://www.vanityfair.com/culture/2011/03/wild-bill-donovan201103)

'met with senior statesmen, including Benito Mussolini': Douglas Waller, *Wild Bill Donovan: The Spy Who Created the OSS and Modern American Espionage*, Free Press, 2011, p. 52

'one secret Donovan would not have been made aware of': John Whiteclay Chambers II,

'OSS Training in the National Parks and Service Abroad in World War II', National Park Service', 2008, https://www.nps.gov/parkhistory/online_books/oss/index.htm

'Donovan briefed his superiors about his British mission': David J. Sherman, 'United States Cryptologic History: The First Americans: The 1941 US Codebreaking Mission to Bletchley Park', US Center for Cryptologic History (CCH), Special Series, Vol. 12, 2016, p. 6. Donovan joined President Roosevelt and Secretary Knox on a visit to Boston and Portsmouth, New Hampshire, to inspect the navy yards there. Donovan briefed the two statesmen about his British mission in a series of conversations during that journey, including one which took place on the presidential yacht as it ferried them between the two ports.

'qualify for "cash and carry"': Office of the Historian, 'The Neutrality Acts, 1930s', US Department of State, Milestones: 1921–1936, (at history.state.gov). On 27 September 1940, Germany's Third Reich signed the Tripartite Pact, a mutual defence military alliance with Italy and Japan. The three nations formed the basis of the Axis Powers and were later joined by other countries, including Finland, in their fight against the Allies.

'another intelligence-gathering journey to Britain': Bennett, *Churchill's Man of Mystery: Desmond Morton and the World of Intelligence*, p. 259

"a series of high-level briefings': Guy Liddell Diaries, TNA, Security Service, File KV4/187, entry 11 December 1940, p. 697 (via fbistudies. com). Liddell later reflected on the FBI's desperation to develop its counterespionage capabilities, because it was still reeling from its failure over the Rumrich case that Leon Turrou botched. 'I lunched with Clegg and Hince and had a long talk with Clegg,' according to Liddell's diary entry of 11 December 1940. 'They have an enormous programme which covers everything from SIS [MI6] to the Fire Brigade. They were desperately anxious to wipe out the impression left by the Turrou incident.'

'tactics, techniques, wartime policing': Raymond Batvinis, 'C-SPAN Video of Ray Batvinis Speech', 8 November 2007 (via fbistudies.com)

'to give you full details of any equipment or devices': Philip Henry Kerr, National Security Agency, Early Papers, 1940–44 series, 8 July 1940, pp. 9–10 of pdf

'opposition is based on a fear': Ibid., 4 October 1940, p. 23 of pdf

'We were all on diplomatic passports': Interview of Dr Abraham Sinkov featured in the NSA's Oral History series, May 1979, pp. 20–1

'There are going to be four Americans': GCHQ press release, 'GCHQ marks 75th anniversary of the UKUSA agreement', March 2021

'It was far from simple': Gordon Corera, Intercept: The Secret History of Computers and Spies, Weidenfeld & Nicolson, 2016, p. 24. Desperate to understand Germany's military intentions, Britain, France and Poland collaborated to break the Enigma code. In the early 1930s, a French military-intelligence official had obtained the manuals and settings for the machine through a spy he had recruited in Germany. The officials then shared the material with British code breakers – who were predominantly classicists and linguists – and their Polish counterparts who were mathematicians.

'material connected with Italian systems': Sinkov, NSA's Oral History series, May 1979, p. 2

'they had made little to no progress': Ibid., p. 17

'We were unaware at this time of the special interest': Ibid., p. 4

'Denniston did not provide his American guest with any hardware': Sinclair McKay, The Secret Life of Bletchley Park: The WWII Codebreaking Centre and the Men and Women Who Worked There, Aurum Press ,2011, p. 205. Denniston was a Scotsman who understood the value of intelligence cooperation with allied countries, having developed a working relationship with French spies during the Paris Peace Conference in 1919, ahead of the Treaty of Versailles that June. But it has been suggested that his unwillingness to provide a sample of the Enigma or bombe hardware to the Sinkov Mission was less about the preservation of Bletchley's cryptological supremacy over its allies, and more because he feared the technology could be stolen by Nazi agents from the USA. Denniston's fears may have been warranted because the Axis cryptographers would often rearrange the code and ciphers settings of machines suspected to have been exploited by the Allies – and by that point the Germans had done that on numerous occasions.

'But when that Enigma information is added': Interview of Dr Abraham Sinkov featured in the NSA's Oral History series, May 1979, p. 10

'feared the technology could have been compromised': McKay, *The Secret Life of Bletchley Park*, p. 205

'organisation's secret division at the Rockefeller headquarters': 'History of SIS Division', Federal Bureau of Investigation, vault.fbi, 1947, p. 118. The Rockefeller Center was already a landmark sight in midtown Manhattan when a business firm ostensibly specialising in foreign trade took up residence in the skyscraper in August 1940. The 'Importers and Exporters Service Company' was a front for the FBI's Special Intelligence Service (SIS) in New York, created two months earlier to run counterespionage operations against Nazi activities in Latin America and the Caribbean. But soon after the fictitious firm began operating out of Room 4332 of the building, it became 'more of a nuisance and detriment than an advantage' to the FBI after attracting a 'constant stream of salesmen' and unwitting lawyers looking for work. By the time Arthur McCaslin Thurston was promoted to the SIS in the winter of 1942, it had shut its bogus company and relocated to another area of the building – but it had also rapidly expanded , from a handful of undercover operatives to around two hundred and fifty on its books.

'Thurston was appointed as Hoover's driver': Raymond Batvinis, 'A Thoroughly Competent Operator: Former SA Arthur Thurston (1938–1944)' *The Grapevine*, October/November 2017, p. 36

'It had an estimated 1,000 agents': Henry Hemming, 'The Secret Persuader: How brilliant British spymaster Sir William Stephenson, who invented 007's martini, used twenty-first-century spin and fake news to lure America into World War 2', mailonline, 1 September 2019,

'prima donna type': GLD, TNA, Security Service, File KV4/190, entry 16 June 1942, p. 614

'Hoover hates Donovan's guts': Ibid., p.

'he had never left his country of birth': Batvinis, 'A Thoroughly Competent Operator', p. 36

'poor management and planning': 'Sir David Petrie (Director-General 1941–46)', Security Service, Who We Are series, MI5 website

'control the movements of its double agents': FBI history, 'A Byte Out of History: A Most Helpful Ostrich: Using Ultra Intelligence in World War II', FBI website, October 2011

'Thurston had created the FBI's first bureau in Britain': Batvinis, 'A Thoroughly Competent Operator', p. 36

CHAPTER THREE

'My aunt was very beautiful and intelligent': Interview by author of Gene Knight, April 2021

'ninety per cent of the code breakers:' Liza Mundy, 'The Women Code Breakers Who Unmasked Soviet Spies', Smithsonian Magazine, September 2018

'a man of considerable moral courage': Interview of Frank Rowlett featured in the NSA's Oral History series, 1976, p. 33

'*intercepted by listening posts in areas as remote as Alaska and Ethiopia*': Matthew Aid, *The Secret Sentry: The Untold Story of the National Security Agency*, Bloomsbury, 2009, p. 3

'*Clarke* particularly distrusted the Soviet Union'. Clarke's distrust of Stalin dated back to the Molotov–Ribbentrop pact, named after the Soviet and German foreign ministers who signed it on 23 August 1939, an agreement between the two countries to partition Poland, with the east going to Stalin, and the west to Hitler. Under the deal, the Soviet Union provided raw material, including oil and grain to Germany, in return for military and civilian equipment.

'*a well-established practice and rule*': Statement by A. P. Rosengoltz, Chargé d'Affaires of the USSR in Britain, regarding the Arcos raid, 1927, University of Warwick, Modern Records Centre, undated, p. 2. Liddell and MI5 had suspected ARCOS officials of spying after monitoring their links with the Communist Party of Great Britain, but they did not have enough evidence on which to act. That changed when a disgruntled former staff member of ARCOS told MI5 that the Soviet body had obtained and copied a classified British military signals training manual, in breach of the UK's Official Secrets Act.

'*a virtually unbreakable system*': Christopher Andrew, *The Defence of the Realm*, pp. 154–6

'*Make no mistakes; record all findings*': Theodore M. Hannah, 'Frank B. Rowlett: A Personal Profile' (via NSA website) Cryptologic Spectrum, based on material copyrighted by Frank B. Rowlett, Sr, and Frank B. Rowlett, Jr, 1980, p. 18

'*no obvious ways to break into five-digit code groups:*' Robert J. Hanyok, 'Eavesdropping on Hell: Historical Guide to Western Communications Intelligence and the Holocaust, 1939–1945', Center for Cryptological History, NSA, 2005, second edition, p. 6

'*We would read everything*': Rowlett, NSA's Oral History series, 1976, p. 34

'*Did we stop? We did not.*': Ibid., pp. 35–6

'*all devices, instruments, or systems in use*': NSA, Early Papers, 1940–1944 series, 4 November 1940, p. 25 of pdf

'*Around 500 ships were sunk*': Imperial War Museum, 'What You Need To Know About The Battle of the Atlantic', iwm.org.uk/history

'*Bletchley discovered that Naval Cipher 3*': *Independent* Online, 'Revealed: the careless mistake by Bletchley's Enigma code-crackers that cost Allied lives', July 2002

'*Turing's showdown with the port authorities*': Dr Alan Turing, 'Report on Cryptographic Machinery', TNA, File HW57/10, November 1942, p. 2

'*contrary to the spirit of existing agreements*': NSA, Early Papers, 1940–1944 series, 7 January 1943, pp. 91–2 of pdf.

'*refuse to permit the 'exploitation' of these secret devices*': Ibid., 9 January 1943, p. 94; see also p. 213 – the US War Department even considered obtaining British intelligence by force. 'I think we should immediately send to London six of the ablest and most aggressive officers that we can find,' said a letter from an unnamed department official dated 16 April 1943. 'These officers would go into the Air Ministry, Foreign Office [...] and devote their entire time to discovering and transmitting to us all possible intelligence. At the same time, Arlington Hall can be doing the same thing at Bletchley Park.'

'*I think we should immediately send to London*': Ibid., 16 April 1943, p. 213

'*exchange personnel and develop joint regulations*': GCHQ Online 'A Brief History of the UKUSA agreement', GCHQ website, March 2021

'*all information concerning the detection*': NSA, Early Papers, 1940–1944 series, 17 May 1943, p. 218 of pdf

'had around 5,000 people working for it': Chambers, 'OSS Training
in the National Parks and Service Abroad in World War II', 2008.
Throughout his time as a decorated fighter pilot during WWI, whose
daring personality had earned him the name 'Wild Bill', Donovan
became very familiar with military culture. But he was unfazed about
upsetting the US Army in his ambition to build the OSS – and even
headhunted some of the most capable members of the armed forces to
work for his organisation.

'Donovan sent around a dozen officers there': Ibid.

'Nazi plans to penetrate American and British operations': Greg Bradsher,
'A Time to Act: The Beginning of the Fritz Kolbe Story, 1900–1943,
Part 3', The [US] National Archives and Records Administration,
Vol. 34, No. 1, Spring 2002

'the creation of the Central Bureau in Australia': David Horner, *The Spy
Catchers: The Official History of ASIO 1949–1963*, Allen & Unwin, 2015,
p. 24

'MacArthur was forced to relocate': Samuel Milner, *Victory in Papua*,
United States Army Center of Military History (CMH), 1989,
p. 18. In a move to prevent a propaganda victory for the Axis powers,
Washington and Melbourne claimed in a joint press statement that
MacArthur's relocation to Australia had occurred at the request of
the Australian government. However, MacArthur needed more than
political spin and public relations coups to land a victory against the
Japanese in the Pacific.

'there was a problem of its one-time chart': Sinkov, NSA's Oral History
series, May 1979, p. 31

'A steel trunk containing accompanying cryptographic material': Edward
J. Drea, *MacArthur's Ultra: Codebreaking and the War Against Japan,
1942–1945*, University Press of Kansas, 1992, pp. 92–3

'The books were water-soaked': Sinkov, NSA's Oral History series, May 1979, p. 33.

In 1988, Sinkov and his team were honoured for their achievements with a typically brief public acknowledgement. A brass plaque on the wall of their former signals base in Brisbane reads: 'Central Bureau, an organisation comprising service personnel of Australia, USA, Britain, Canada and New Zealand, both men and women, functioned in this house from 1942 till 1945. From intercepted enemy radio messages, the organisation provided intelligence which made a decisive contribution to the Allied victory in the Pacific.'

CHAPTER FOUR

'regime of violence and suppression of all freedom': Igor Gouzenko, 'Statement', TNA, KV2/1428, 1945, p. 16

'highly agitated and in a disturbed state': Ibid., 'Introduction', p. 15

'the official title of "civilian employee"': The Report of the Royal Commission, Section One, Privy Council Office, Ottawa, 27 June 1946, p. 11

'everything in the manner despatches and messages': TNA, KV2/1428, 1945, p. 19

'robbed some money belonging to the Embassy': Report of the Royal Commission, Section Ten, p. 645

'whether he should be thoroughly searched and frightened': GLD, TNA, KV4/466, 11 September 1945, p. 196

'We felt on balance that it was better for May to come': Ibid., p. 201

'At Waterloo Dr May engaged a taxi': TNA, KV2/2209, File 2, 18 September 1945, p. 5

'the RCMP would welcome direct communications': GLD, TNA, KV4/466, September 18, 1945, p. 210

'everything that he does or does not do': Ibid., 25 September 1945, p. 235

'without corroboration this would not support a charge:' TNA, KV2/2209, Alan Nunn May, File 1, 19 September 1945, p. 42

'the cover name of 'Walter Thomas': GLD, TNA, KV4/185, 20 January 1940, p. 95

'deal finally settled on £2,000:' Ibid., 14 February 1940, p. 142

'documents and microfilms that contained secrets:' Robert J. Lamphere and Tom Shachtman, *The FBI–KGB War: A Special Agent's Story*, Mercer University Press, 1995, pp. 38–9

'Stalin wanted to be informed about American intelligence': CIA, 'Venona: Soviet Espionage and The American Response 1939–1957', 1996, p. 3

'providing the Soviets with one of Scotland Yard's instruction manuals': Lamphere and Shachtman, *The FBI–KGB War*, p. 38

'said to have handed over a long report': GLD, TNA, KV4/467, 20 November 1945, p. 6

'He had supplied him with a report:' Ibid., 20 February 1946, p. 114

'details of the scientific features': 'Soviet Espionage in Canada', Royal Canadian Mounted Police Intelligence Branch, Ottawa, TNA, KV2/1428, File 1, November 1945, p. 55

'he praised the 'special relationship': Winston Churchill, 'I Sinews of Peace' (post-war speeches, including the 'Iron Curtain Speech'), International Churchill Society, 5 March 1946

'procedures, practices and equipment': 'British US Communication Intelligence Agreement', NSA.gov, 5 March 1946, p. 5 (While the

Agreement was initially called BRUSA, it was retroactively renamed UKUSA in 1952, as 'Britain' is used only with Commonwealth countries, and 'United Kingdom' with all others, cse-cst.gc.ca)

'merely a deniable and non-binding memorandum': John Ferris, *Behind the Enigma: The Authorised History of GCHQ, Britain's Secret Cyber-Intelligence Agency*, Bloomsbury, 2020, p. 345

'Because Gouzenko worked with communications': US Center for Cryptologic History, *American Cryptology during the Cold War; 1945–1989*, Book I: *The Struggle for Centralization 1945–1960*, NSA, 1995, p. 161

CHAPTER FIVE

'more apparent confidence in himself': Freedom of Information Act Document: FOIA: FBI Employees: Lamphere, Robert J., file 1, p. 96

'initiative, resourcefulness and aggressiveness': Ibid., p. 347

'He made several breakthroughs by Christmas of 1946': Robert L. Benson, 'The Venona Story', NSA US Center for Cryptologic History, undated, p. 10

'purchase Soviet cipher material from them': Lamphere and Shachtman, *The FBI–KGB War*, p. 84 / Howard Blum, *In the Enemy's House: The Secret Saga of the FBI Agent and the Code Breaker Who Caught The Russian Spies*, HarperCollins 2018, p. 97. Robert Lamphere played a pioneering role in developing investigative cooperation between the human intelligence and signals intelligence communities in the US. 'He was definitely at the forefront of [cooperation between HUMINT and SIGINT] and part of it was a sign of the times,' said Michael J. Driscoll. 'It was that necessity to address what was an ever-growing threat against democracy – and because of that, they were willing to try new things. And perhaps sharing more than they had ever shared before. He was in the right place at the right time to be the vessel for that exchange. It is of no surprise to me that he came from the New York office because of the nature of the work that we do here frequently [...] on all threats and absolutely on CI [counter intelligence].'

'brought into the loop by Arlington Hall in 1945': Richard J. Aldrich, *GCHQ: The uncensored story of Britain's most secret intelligence agency*, HarperPress, 2019, p. 74

'determined to reform Australia's intelligence:' Horner, *The Spy Catchers: The Official History of ASIO 1949–1963*, p. 42

'far better idea about Australian security': GLD, TNA, KV4/169, 25 November 1947, p. 139

'Sillitoe and Hollis changed their cover story': Horner, *The Spy Catchers: The Official History of ASIO 1949–1963*, p. 59

'boasted that he had a number of informants': GLD, TNA, KV4/470, 16 February 1948, P. 31

'interception of one telegram from Australia': Ibid., 1 July 1948, p. 126

'Attlee referred to multiple telegrams': Horner, *The Spy Catchers: The Official History of ASIO1949–1963*, p. 68

'US had downgraded Australia's security clearance': Ibid., p. 69

'no choice but to overhaul his country's intelligence standards': Ibid., p. 78

'decrypted telegrams relating to Australia': Ibid., p. 91

'against espionage, sabotage and subversion': ASIO History, 'The Establishment of Asio', asio.gov.au

'Canada was finally granted an 'equal partnership'': Communications Security Establishment, 'CANUSA', cse-cst.gc.ca/, 28 June 2019

'As a last resort, MI5 sent its chief interrogator': Lamphere and Shachtman, *The FBI–KGB War*, pp. 133–46

'purely as a token payment': GLD, TNA, KV4/472, 25 January 1950, p. 24

'One of his reasoning for ceasing to pass information': Ibid., p. 25

'representative of a foreign power': Ibid., 28 April 1950, p. 70

'quite capable of reducing our liaison': Ibid., 27 March 1950, p. 65

'joined by Skardon who helped break the ice': Lamphere and Shachtman, *The FBI–KGB War*, pp. 147–8

'Milner defected to Czechoslovakia': Horner, *The Spy Catchers: The Official History of ASIO 1949–1963*, pp. 142–4

'He spoke with a stutter': Interview with Robert Lamphere, 'Red Files: Secret Victories of the KGB', pbs.org, 1999

'he was 'untrustworthy and unreliable'': GLD, TNA, K4/473, 13 June 1951, p. 89

'The two British agencies had made a formal request': Lamphere and Shachtman, *The FBI – KGB War*, p. 130

'Burgess strolled into the room while Kim was not there': GLD, TNA, K4/473, 12 June 1951, p. 88

'kidnapped by the Russians': Ibid.

'sought information about Petrov from MI5': Horner, *The Spy Catchers: The Official History of ASIO 1949–1963*, p. 318

CHAPTER SIX

'under the influence of alcohol': TNA, KV2/3439, 17 March 1953, p. 89

'immoral pursuits, in search of wine': Ibid., 18 June 1953, pp. 76 and 78

'disrupt the activities of Soviet expatriate organisations': TNA, KV2/3460, Part 1, 30 September 1954, p. 72

'work of recruitment should be carried out boldly': Ibid., Part 2, undated, p. 32

'strong MVD representation in Australia was necessary': Ibid., p. 35

'strong MVD representation in Australia was necessary': Ibid., p. 36

'cannot hope to get information unless they are given greater freedom': GLD, TNA, KV4/475, 1 January 1953, p. 12

'suffering from 'neurological-retinitis': TNA, KV2/3439, 18 June 1953, p. 81

'Lifanov's hostility toward Petrov': Robert Manne, The Petrov Affair: Politics and Espionage, Pergamon ,1987, p. 30

'The present Russian government wishes to consolidate': GLD, TNA, KV4/475, 7 April 1953, p. 82

'repeated cancellation of Petrov's travel plans': TNA, KV2/3439, 18 June 1953, p. 81

'after the appointment of a new Soviet ambassador': Horner, The Spy Catchers: The Official History of ASIO 1949–1963, pp. 329–30

'He worked his way up the ranks': Frank Cain, 'Richards, George Ronald (Ron) (1905–1985)', Australian Dictionary of Biography, Vol. 18, 2012, via https://adb.anu.edu.au

'Richards told Bialoguski to encourage him': Horner, *The Spy Catchers: The Official History of ASIO 1949–1963*, p. 330

'no time should be lost in encouraging Petrov': TNA, KV2/3439, 4 February 1954, p. 18

'cautious not to overplay its hand with ASIO': GLD, TNA, KV4/475, 2 March 1953, p. 53

'a guarantee that he would be given £5,000': Horner, *The Spy Catchers: The Official History of ASIO 1949–1963*, p. 338

'Spry strongly supports PM': TNA, KV2/3440, Part 2, 12 April 1954, p. 50

'utmost to ensure intelligence benefits': Ibid., pp. 50–71

'When we stopped the car near to the airport': Evdokia Petrov, 'Soviet defector Evdokia's statement on Mascot Airport incident', National Archives of Australia, 22 April 1945

'The weaponising of intelligence': Interview by author with Julia Gillard, March 2022

'Petrov case has now definitely put the ASIO on the map': TNA, KV2/3445, Part 3, 3 August 1954, p. 35

'ciphers of countries of the Anglo-American bloc': TNA, KV2/3460, Part 3, p. 20

'agent personnel, methods of recruitments': Ibid., p. 46

'5079 photographs and names': Horner, *The Spy Catchers: The Official History of ASIO 1949–1963*, p. 380

'direct access to the Petrovs': TNA, KV2/3445, Part 3, August 1954, p. 33

'following a trip there in 1955': Manne, *The Petrov Affair: Politics and Espionage*, p. 220

'significant in the way it helped bring us closer together': Interview by author with Mike Burgess, director-general of ASIO, February 2022

'from west of the Urals and Africa': Duncan Campbell, 'The Eavesdroppers', *Time Out*, 21–27 May 1976

CHAPTER SEVEN

'Katona walked around, observing other parts of the capital': Geza Katona, interviewed by Zsolt Csalog, 'A Major Oversight on Our Part', *Hungarian Quarterly*, Issue 182, 2006, p. 113

'methods short of war': CIA Historical Staff, 'Hungary Volume II, External Operations: 1946–1965', May 1972, p. 2 (obtained online via GWUNSA)

'intervene if an overthrow of the Government': Ibid., p. 4

'He mailed letters, purchased stamps': CIA Historical Staff, 'Hungary Volume I, External Operations:1946–1965', p. 2

'He went there by the seat of his pants': Interview by author with Susan De Rosa, August 2021

'we would send a digest': Katona and Csalog, p. 116

'we must restrict ourselves to information collection': CIA, 'The Hungarian Revolution and the Planning for the Future, 23 October–4 November 1956', Vol. I, January 1958, p. 91

'the staging of civil unrest': Tim Weiner, *Legacy of Ashes: The History of the CIA*, Penguin. 2008, p. 159

'buying up the loyalties of Egypt and Syria': Yair Even, 'Syria's 1956 Request for Soviet Military Intervention', Wilson Center, February 2016, wilsoncenter.org '*monitor the growing Soviet influence*': US Center for Cryptologic History, 'The Suez Crisis: A Brief Comint History', US National Archives (archives.gov/), National Security Agency/Central Security Service, Archives and History, 1988, pp. 24–7

'*form its own bilateral intelligence contacts:*' Horner, *The Spy Catchers: The Official History of ASIO 1949–1963*, p. 523

'*CIA's distrust of the Anglo-French intentions*': 'The Suez Crisis: A Brief Comint History', p. 14

'*form a clear-cut view of the situation*': Katona and Csalog, p. 119

'*Dulles's objective was to sabotage Nagi's leadership*': Weiner, *Legacy of Ashes: The History of the CIA*, pp. 151–2

'*should have been mistaken for an intelligence operation*': CIA, 'The Hungarian Revolution and the Planning for the Future', p. 82

'*We did not have the kind of information on which quick deft moves*': Ibid., p. 106

'*They sat idly by as Hungarian blood was being shed*': Katona and Csalog, p. 124

'*reinterviewed those whose stories did not add up*': Horner, *The Spy Catchers: The Official History of ASIO 1949–1963*, pp. 514–16

'*fully resolved to use force to crush the aggressors*': 'The Suez Crisis: A Brief Comint History', p. 23

'*ordered the CIA to send U-2 spy planes over Syria*': Ibid.

'*a gateway to feed misinformation*': Peter Wright with Paul Greengrass, *Spy Catcher: The Candid Autobiography of a Senior Intelligence Officer*, Heinemann 1988, p. 86

'seized control of a British military site in Habbaniya': Aldrich, *GCHQ*, pp. 151–4

'expelled Stone from the country': Weiner, *Legacy of Ashes: The History of the CIA*, p. 160

'Cuban exiles were captured': JFK Presidential Library, 'The Bay of Pigs', jfklibrary.org

'high-level tiff': 'The Suez Crisis: A Brief Comint History', p. 30; see also Ferris, *Behind the Enigma*, p. 379

CHAPTER EIGHT

'not after political asylum': FBI, 'Oleg Lyalin Biography', File 2, Section 2.pdf, pp. 11–14

'an investigation going into Abdoolcader': Andrew, *The Defence of the Realm*, p. 571

'penetrated the Ministry of Defence': Richard J. Aldrich and Rory Cormac, *The Black Door: Spies, Secret Intelligence and British Prime Ministers*, HarperCollins 2016, p. 298

'potential trade and international relations damage': Andrew, *The Defence of the Realm*, p. 567

'from SIGINT sites around Asia': Aldrich, *GCHQ*, p. 263

'more than more than 60,000 troops': Online report, 'The Vietnam War', National Archives of Australia

'communications channels simultaneously': Duncan Campbell, 'Development of Surveillance Technology and Risk of Abuse of Economic Information', European Parliament, October 1999, p. 4

'funded most of the infrastructure and the technology': Aldrich, *GCHQ*. p. 323

'benefits reaped by Britain': Ibid., p 268

'efforts to obtain military and industrial secrets': FBI, Oleg Gouzenko, File 1, Section 1A.pdf, 1971

'forced to ask Soviet Bloc and Cuban agencies': Christopher Andrew, 'Introduction to the Cold War', MI5, MI5.gov.uk

'new KGB officers in the NY area': FBI, 'Oleg Lyalin Biography', File 1, Section 3, p. 22

'security measures around defence sites': John Blaxland, *The Protest Years: The Official History of ASIO 1963–1975*, Allen & Unwin, 2015, p. 264

'stripped of diplomatic immunity': FBI, 'Oleg Lyalin Biography', File 1, Section 1A.pdf, October 1971, p. 73

'cornerstone of Australian foreign policy': CIA, 'The President's Daily Brief', 4 December 1972, p. 4

'covert operations in Chile': Peter Kornbluh, 'Australian Spies Aided and Abetted CIA in Chile', 2021 (online via the GWUNSA); see also Rory Cormac, *How to Stage a Coup: And Ten Other Lessons From the World of Secret Statecraft*, Atlantic Books, 2022, p. 154-6

'agency's files on Croatian extremists': Brian Toohey, *Secret: The Making of Australia's Security State*, Melbourne University Press, 2019, p. 119

'three-thousand pages of secret material': Blaxland, *The Protest Years*, p. 343

"most of the information shared': Aldrich, *GCHQ*, p. 270

'I'm cutting them off from intelligence': TELCON, 'The President/HAK', transcript of telephone call between President Richard Nixon and Secretary of State Henry Kissinger, University of Warwick, 9 August 1973, p. 2

'*hamper its own operations*': Aldrich, *GCHQ*, p. 274

'*CIA immediately cancelled all contact*': Ibid., p. 277.

'*secret surveillance of citizens*': Richard A. Clarke, Michael J. Morell, Geoffrey R. Stone, Cass R. Sunstein, Peter Swire, *Liberty and Security in a Changing World*, Princeton University Press, December 2013, p. 55

'*Who governs Britain*': Aldrich and Cormac, *The Black Door*, pp. 304–6

'*served as a naval intelligence officer*': Desmond Ball, Bill Robinson and Richard Tanter, 'Management of Operations at Pine Gap', NAPS Special Report, 25 November 2015, nautilus.org

'*established, maintained and operated*': Australian Treaty Series, 'Agreement between the Government of the Commonwealth of Australia and the Government of the United States of America relating to the Establishment of a Joint Defence Space Research Facility [Pine Gap, NT]', Department of External Affairs, Canberra, 1966

'*Stallings left Canberra for Alice Springs*': Ball et al., 'Management of Operations at Pine Gap', nautilus.org

'*even ASIO had been unaware of him*': Blaxland, *The Protest Years*, p. 446

'*perceived Cairns as anti-American*': Ibid., p. 438

'*judgement, courage, and independence*': Nelson A. Rockefeller et al., 'Report to the President by the Commission on CIA Activities Within the United States', 6 June 1975, p. 17 (online via https://www.ojp.gov/ncjrs/virtual-library/abstracts/report-president-commission-cia-central-intelligence-agency)

'*blow the lid off those installations*': Blaxland, *The Protest Years*, p. 447

'*powers to sack the prime minister*': Toohey, *Secret*, p. 83

CHAPTER NINE

'Soviet Vietnam': Memorandum for The President from Zbigniew Brzezinski, 'Reflections on Soviet Intervention in Afghanistan', 26 December 1979, p. 2 (online via GWUNSA: https://nsarchive. gwu.edu)

'client states, including Cuba and Libya': Robert Vickers, 'The History of CIA's Office of Strategic Research, 1967–81', Center for the Study of Intelligence (CSI), 2019, p. 132

'expressions of concern': Brzezinski, 'Reflections on Soviet Intervention in Afghanistan', p. 3

'reader of their intelligence reports': Aldrich and Cormac, *The Black Door*, p. 353

'the circuit': Private information, 2021

'cover story of being journalists': Gordon Corera, *MI6: Life and Death in the British Secret Service*, Phoenix, 2012, pp. 296–7

'covert purchasing process': Steve Galster, 'Afghanistan: The Making of US Foreign Policy, 1973–1990' (online via the GWUNSA)

'academia, culture and science': John Blaxland and Rhys Crawley, *The Secret Cold War: The Official History of ASIO 1975–1989*, Allen & Unwin, 2017, p. 198

'reality [...] is completely otherwise': Interviewer Vincent Jauvert, 'The Brzezinski Interview', *Le Nouvel Observateur*, 15–21 January 1998, via University of Arizona, translated from the French by William Blum and David N. Gibbs

'we knowingly increased the probability': AFP, 'CIA helped Afghan mujahedeen before 1979 Soviet intervention: Brzezinski', Agence France Press, 13 January 1998

'*Argentine occupation forces had constructed*': CIA, 'Increased Defensive Measures: Port Stanley Area, Falkland Islands', p. 3 (online via the GWUNSA)

'*has the bit in her teeth*': Secretary of State Alexander Haig, 'White House, Top Secret Situation Room flash cable', 9 April 1982, p. 1 (online via the GWUNSA)

'*NR-1 listening station*': Jeffrey T. Richelson and Desmond Ball, *The Ties that Bind: Intelligence Cooperation between the UKUSA Countries*, Allen & Unwin, 1985, p. 77

'*intercept Argentina's naval traffic*': Nicky Hager, *Secret Power: New Zealand's Role in the International Spy Network*, Potton & Burton (NZ), 1996, p. 81

'*terminated with immediate effect*': Ibid., p. 23

'*price we are prepared to pay*': New Zealand History, 'Nuclear-free New Zealand', p. 4, nzhistory.govt.nz

'*press had been misinformed:*' Hager, *Secret Power*, p. 23

'*the price would far exceed the benefit*': Interview by author with Admiral Mike Rogers, February 2022

'*overseas, including Singapore*': David Filer, 'Signals Intelligence in New Zealand during the Cold War', Security and Surveillance History Series, January 2019, p. 4

'*operational advice from the CIA*': Richelson and Ball, *The Ties That Bind*, p. 238

'*intercepted any French communication*': Hager, *Secret Power*, p. 154

'*Key Soviet goal in Oceania*': CIA, 'Soviet Relations with Oceania: An Intelligence Assessment', July 1987, pp: 4–8

'$700,000 a year': Aldrich and Cormac, *The Black Door*, p. 362

'400 million of such bullets': Rory Cormac, *Disrupt and Deny: Spies, Special Forces and the Secret Pursuit of British Foreign Policy*, Oxford University Press, 2021, p. 223

'aimed his Stinger missile': Michael M. Phillips, 'Launching the Missile That Made History; Three former mujahedeen recall the day when they started to beat the Soviets', *Wall Street Journal*, 1 October 2001, wsj.com

'to $500 million a year': David B. Ottaway, 'Afghan Rebels Assured of More Support', *Washington Post*, 13 November 1987, washingtonpost. com

'closest mentors': National Counterterrorism Center, 'Haqqani Network: Background', Director of National Intelligence, (accessed online via https://www.dni.gov/nctc/groups/haqqani_network.html)

'small-arms assaults': Reuters, 'Timeline – Major attacks by al Qaeda' reuters.com

CHAPTER TEN

'refused to believe who we were': Interview by author with Baroness (Eliza) Manningham-Buller, July 2021

'monitoring potential IRA plots': Blaxland and Crawley, *The Secret Cold War*, p. 360

'lifeblood of counterterrorism work': Peter Clarke, 'Learning from experience: Counter Terrorism in the UK since 9/11', Policy Exchange, the inaugural Colin Cramphorn Memorial Lecture, 2007

'received hijack training': Thomas H. Kean et al., *The 9/11 Commission Report*, official Government edition, 22 July 2004, p. 129

'rather than mainland America': Andrew, *The Defence of the Realm*, p. 809

'felt personally responsible': Private information

'established a network of contacts': Ann Taylor, MP, et al., 'Intelligence and Security Committee [of Parliament], The Handling of Detainees by UK Intelligence Personnel in Afghanistan, Guantanamo Bay and Iraq', 1 March 2005, p. 11

'completely mythical': Private information

'captured by Pakistani forces': Dana Priest, 'CIA Puts Harsh Tactics on Hold: Memo on Methods of Interrogation Had Wide Review', *Washington Post*, 27 June 2004, washingtonpost.com

'chemical and biological weapons': Dianne Feinstein, 'Senate Select Committee on Intelligence: Committee Study of the Central Intelligence Agency's Detention and Interrogation Program', 3 December 2014, p. 141

'embezzling money': Bob Drogin and John Goetz, 'How US Fell Under the Spell of "Curveball"', *Los Angeles Times*, 20 November 2005, latimes.com

'provided 100 reports': Corera, *MI6*, p. 374

'backbone of one of our major findings': Pat Roberts et al., 'Report on the US Intelligence Community's Prewar Intelligence Assessments on Iraq', US Senate, Select Committee on Intelligence, 7 July 2004, p. 155

'ending of this regime': Tony Blair, House of Commons, 'Iraq and Weapons of Mass Destruction', 24 September 2002, Hansard, Sixth Series, Vol. 390, parliament.uk

'European by proximity': Private information

'poisons and deadly gas': Remarks by President George W. Bush, 'President Bush Outlines Iraqi Threat', The White House, 7 October 2002

'questions related to stockpiles': Interview by author with Bill Murray, November 2021

'Al Qaeda could turn to Iraq for help': Secretary of State Colin Powell's speech, 'US secretary of state's address to the United Nations security council', *Guardian*, 5 February 2003, theguardian.com

'400 UN inspections': Corera, *MI6*, p. 377

'intelligence from the likes of Curveball': Private information

'related to US–Iraq bilateral relations': Catherine McGrath, 'Senior Intelligence Officer, Andrew Wilkie, Resigns in Protest', 12 March 2003, abc.net.au

'It was clear that day': CTVNews.ca Staff, 'Saying "no" to Iraq War was 'important' decision for Canada: Chretien', CTV News, 12 March 2013

'design engineer': Roberts et al, p. 156

'give me another solution': Martin Chulov and Helen Pidd, 'Curveball: How US was duped by Iraqi fantasist looking to topple Saddam', *Guardian*, 15 February 2011, theguardian.com

'Single-sourced': Online report, 'Ex-CIA official: WMD evidence ignored', CNN, 24 April 2006, https://edition.cnn.com/2006/US/04/23/cia.iraq

'recanted the claim': Feinstein, p. 141

'sorry if people find that difficult to reconcile': Online report, 'Chilcot Inquiry: Former British PM Tony Blair fights for reputation in wake of report's release', 7 July 2016, abc.net.au

CHAPTER ELEVEN

'*great pains not to be overheard*': Commissioner Dennis R. O'Connor, 'Report of the Events Relating to Maher Arar: Factual Background, Volume I', September 2006, p. 53

'*difficult to extract urgent intelligence*': Chris McGreal, 'Bush on torture: Waterboarding helped prevent attacks on London', *Guardian*, 9 November 2010, theguardian.com

'*have to obtain the RCMP's permission*': O'Conner, Vol. I, p. 49

'*emergency contact*': Ibid., p. 55

'*strictly on an intelligence basis*': Ibid., p. 88

'*promised to follow up*': Ibid., p. 89

'*did not have sufficient evidence*': Ibid., p. 168

'*steps to dissuade the Americans*' Ibid., p. 176

'*undergone training in Afghanistan*': O'Conner, Vol. II, p. 499

'*I was also instructed to write these things*': Maher Arar, 'Delivered Into Hell by U.S. War on Terror', *Los Angeles Times*, 10 December 2003, latimes.com

'*supplied by US authorities*': Center for Constitutional Rights, 'The Story of Maher Arar: Retention to Torture', p. 4

'*not even animals can withstand*': Jane Mayer, 'The secret history of America's 'extraordinary rendition' program', *New Yorker*, 6 February 2005, newyorker.com

'*defend themselves at every turn*': O'Conner, Vol. II, p. 506

'*They played on this*': Interview by author with Richard Fadden, March 2022

'No State Party shall expel, return': General Assembly resolution 39/46, 'Convention against Torture and Other Cruel, Inhuman or Degrading Treatment or Punishment', United Nations, Article 3, 10 December 1984

'nothing alters the fact': Online report, 'Australian David Hicks "relieved" after terror conviction quashed', BBC, 19 February 2015, bbc.co.uk

'British Guantanamo suspects': Taylor, MP, et al., p. 18

'intelligence was not sufficient': Private information

'information that might prove valuable': Taylor, MP, et al., p. 3

'to simulate electric torture': Major-General Antonio M. Taguba, 'Article 15-16 Investigation of the 800th Military Police Brigade', March 2004, p. 17

'location is unknown to us': Taylor, MP, et al, p. 20

'total control over the detainee': Feinstein, p. 82

'would have killed thousands': Ibid., p. 297

'gloves were coming off': Dominic Grieve, QC, MP, 'Intelligence and Security Committee of Parliament, Detainee Mistreatment and Rendition: 2001–2010', House of Commons, 28 June 2018, p. 30

'their approaches are different': Paul Murphy, MP, 'Intelligence and Security Committee: Rendition', 2007

'services to facilitate the capture of detainees': Grieve, p. 51

'suggested, planned or agreed to rendition': Ibid., p. 3

'the best interests of the Commonwealth': Dylan Welch, 'Secret sum settles Habib torture compensation case', 8 January 2011, smh.com.au

'omitted the significant amount': Feinstein, p. xii

government surveillance and retaliation': Senator Frank Church, 'Intelligence Activities and the Rights of Americans, Book II, Final Report,' Select Committee to Study Government Operations, 26 April 1976, p. 291

'decision to detain and remove': Press release, 'Arar Commission releases its findings on the handling of the Maher Arar case', 18 September 2006, p. 2

'compensated': Monique Scotti, 'Trudeau: Canadians rightfully angry after Ottawa pays $31.25M to men falsely imprisoned in Syria', *Global News*, 26 October 2017, globalnews.ca

CHAPTER TWELVE

'international dimension': Interview by author with Richard Walton, February 2022

'Isis were pretty effective at online recruiting': Interview by author with Lord (Kim) Darroch, May 2022

'extremely concerned': Josh Halliday, Aisha Gani and Vikram Dodd, 'UK police launch hunt for London schoolgirls feared to have fled to Syria', *Guardian*, 20 February 2015, theguardian.com

'CSIS officers knew': Private information

'If you are running agents': Interview by author with Richard Walton, June 2022

'intelligence services of a country in the coalition': Matthew Taylor and agencies, 'Man suspected of helping British schoolgirls join Isis arrested in Turkey', *Guardian*, 12 March 2015, theguardian.com

'using the excuse': Dipesh Gadher and Hala Jaber, 'British Isis recruits unmasked by double agent', *Sunday Times*, 15 March 2015, thetimes.co.uk

'*The main objective was to keep it out of the media*': Private information

'*The purpose of the visit*': Ibid.

'*he worked for Canadian intelligence*': Nil Koksal, 'Witness statement from Turkish Intelligence', *Power and Politics*: Rosemary Barton, 1:50 of video report, CBC News, cbc.ca

'*We made approaches to him*': Richard Kerbaj, 'The inside story of killing Jihadi John: How technology became the Isis beheader's undoing', *Sunday Times*, 12 May 2019, thetimes.co.uk

'*spontaneous combustion*': Interview by author with General David Petraeus, February 2021

'*inheriting the tail end of the Iraq and Afghanistan conflicts*': Interview by author with David Cameron, June 2022

'*Camp Bucca*': Michael Christie, 'US military shuts largest detainee camp in Iraq', Reuters, 17 September 2009, reuters.com

'*significant amount of mystery*': Kerbaj, 'The inside story of killing Jihadi John', thetimes.co.uk

'*the best way to avoid surveillance*': Ibid.

'*we were using infrared*': Ibid.

'*the least bad of the options*': Ibid.

'*you can deduce*': Zachary Cohen, Barbara Starr and Ryan Browne, 'Pentagon releases first images from raid that killed ISIS leader', 31 October 2019, cnn.com

CHAPTER THIRTEEN

'the 2am call': Private information

'call duration, unique identifiers': Glenn Greenwald, 'NSA collecting phone records of millions of Verizon customers daily', *Guardian*, 6 June 2013, theguardian.com

'only given a limited access': Private information

'specific to us': Ibid.

'Iain asked the security division': Interview by author with Sir Iain Lobban, June 2022

'I was definitely worried': Ibid.

'lights off for UKUSA': Ibid.

'Obama's planned confrontation': Corera, *Intercept*, p. 352

'prevent possible terrorist activity': President Barack Obama, 'Statement by the President', White House, Office of the Press Secretary, 7 June 2013

'intercept almost everything': Ewen MacAskill, 'Edward Snowden, NSA files source: "If they want to get you, in time they will"', *Guardian*, 10 June 2013, theguardian.com

'you're the big dog': Private information

'We hack network backbones': Lana Lam, 'Edward Snowden: US government has been hacking Hong Kong and China for years', *South China Morning Post*, 13 June 2003, scmp.com

'XKeyscore': Glenn Greenwald, 'XKeyscore: NSA tool collects 'nearly everything a user does on the internet', *Guardian*, 31 July 2013, theguardian.com

'We asked the Americans': Private information

'If printed out and stacked'': House of Representatives, Permanent Select

Committee on Intelligence, 'Review of the Unauthorised Disclosures of Former National Security Agency Contractor Edward Snowden', 23 December 2016, pp. 20–1

across the Asia-Pacific region': Ryan Gallagher and Nicky Hager, 'New Zealand Spies on Neighbours in Secret "Five Eyes" Global Surveillance', *Intercept*, 4 March 2015, theintercept.com

approximately 20 high-priority countries': Greg Weston, 'Snowden document shows Canada set up spy posts for NSA', CBC News, 9 December 2013, cbc.ca

contractor for the CIA in 2005': Glenn Greenwald, *No Place to Hide: Edward Snowden, the NSA & the Surveillance State*, Penguin, 2015, pp. 40–4

read, copy, move, alter': National Security Agency internal report, 'Out of Control', *Cryptologic Quarterly*, 3 September 1991, p. 1 (declassified by the NSA on 27 September 2012)

600 million "telephone events" each day': Ewen MacAskill, Julian Borger, Nick Hopkins, Nick Davies and James Ball, 'GCHQ taps fibre-optic cables for secret access to world's communications', *Guardian*, 21 June 2013, theguardian.com

how the hell the leak had happened': Private information

that simply wasn't possible in our system': Interview by author with Lord Darroch, May 2022

seized with the imperative': Private information

the US give us more than we give': Interview by author with Lord Darroch, May 2022

Do I believe that's the case?': Spencer Ackerman, 'NSA chief Michael Rogers: Edward Snowden "probably not" a foreign spy', *Guardian*, 3 June 2014, theguardian.com *'more transactional':* Private information

'Australians also provided funds': Ibid.

'GCHQ must pull its weight': Nick Hopkins and Julian Borger, 'Exclusive: NSA pays £100m in secret funding for GCHQ', *Guardian*, 1 August 2013, theguardian.com

'It is a fact of life that bulk access': Interview by author with Sir Iain Lobban, June 2022

'The de facto position': Private information

'US$56.2 billion': Barton Gellman and Greg Miller, 'Black budget' summary details US spy network's successes, failures and objectives', *Washington Post*, 29 August 2013, washingtonpost.com

'earn our stripes': Guyon Espiner, 'NZ's independence from Five Eyes has –slipped – Helen Clark', Radio New Zealand, 10 June 2020, rnz.co.nz

'incidental consequence of sweeping up': Interview by author with Sir Iain Lobban, June 2022

'not monitoring and will not monitor': Von Jacob Appelbaum, Holger Stark, Marcel Rosenbach and Jörg Schindler, 'Did US Tap Chancellor Merkel's Mobile Phone?', *Der Spiegel*, 23 October 2013, spiegel.de

'presidents of Peru, Somalia, Guatemala': Laura Poitras, Marcel Rosenbach and Holger Stark, 'GCHQ and NSA Targeted Private German Companies and Merkel', *Der Spiegel*, 29 March 2014, spiegel.de

'These things are done': Transcript, Clare Short interview, BBC, 26 February 2004, bbc.co.uk

'They bug places': Jonathon Carr-Brown and Jack Grimston, 'Speak up Kofi: What's that about spies?', *Sunday Times*, 29 February 2004, p. 16

'Iain's major concern': Private information

'packages that they wish to move to': Transcript, 'Evidence given by Sir Iain Lobban, Andrew Parker and Sir John Sawers', Intelligence and Security Committee of Parliament, 7 November 2013, p. 17

'privacy and freedom of expression had been violated': Interview by author with Lord (David) Anderson of Ipswich QC, June 2022

'In order to minimise the risk of the bulk interception': Judgement, 'Case of Big Brother Watch and other v. The United Kingdom', European Court of Human Rights (ECtHR), 25 May 2021, paragraph 350

CHAPTER FOURTEEN

'an excellent guy': Post Opinions Staff, 'A transcript of Donald Trump's meeting with the *Washington Post* editorial board', *Washington Post*, 21 March 2016, washingtonpost.com

'Not even the Chinese premier': Francis Elliott, 'Say sorry to Trump or risk special relationship, Cameron told', *The Times*, 4 May 2016, thetimes.co.uk

'Australia had such little insight': Interview by author with Alexander Downer, January 2022

'raw intelligence': Private information

'X-Agent': Special Counsel Robert S. Mueller, III, 'Report on the Investigation into Russian Interference in he 2016 Presidential Election', US Department of Justice, March 2019, Vol. I, p. 38

'governmental, commercial and educational': FBI, 'Moonlight Maze: Recent Developments', 15 April 1999, p. 2 (online via the GWUNSA)

'most sophisticated attacks': Ibid., p. 9

'Washington Monument': Ted Bridis, 'Net espionage stirs Cold-War tensions', ZDNet, 27 June 2001, zdnet.com

'an archivist for the KGB': Patricia Sullivan, 'KGB Archivist, Defector Vasili Mitrokhin, 81', *Washington Post*, 30 January 2004, washingtonpost.com

'11,000 pages': Blaxland and Crawley, *The Secret Cold War*, p. 421

'an equal partner': Jennifer Rankin, 'Ex-NATO head says Putin wanted to join alliance early on in his rule', *Guardian*, 4 November 2021, theguardian.com

'killed 170 people': Adam Taylor, 'The recent history of terrorist attacks in Russia', *Washington Post*, 3 April 2017, washingtonpost.com

'a hostile statement': Author interview, Lady Manningham-Buller, July 2021

'they'll eventually come back': Private information

'trialled the method successfully': Author interview, Lady Manningham-Buller, July 2021

'probably approved': Sir Robert Owen, 'The Litvinenko Inquiry: Report into the death of Alexander Litvinenko', January 2016, p. 244, assets. publishing.service.gov.uk

'small team of British authorities': Private information

'steal our sensitive technology': Jonathan Evans, 'Address to the Society of Editors by the Director-General of the Security Service', 5 November 2007, mi5.gov.uk

'access to all source intelligence': Colin Freeze and Jane Taber, 'Russian mole had access to wealth of CSIS, RCMP, Privy Council files', *Globe and Mail*, 22 October 2012, globeandmail.com

'previously condemned in Russia': Online report, 'Russian spy Anna Chapman is stripped of UK citizenship', BBC, 13 July 2010, bbc.co.uk

'no human assets listed': Freeze and Taber, 22 October 2012

'high quality people': Interview by author with General David Petraeus, February 2022

'All the Five Eyes raised': Interview by author with Richard Fadden, March 2022

'evil intent': Mike Levine, 'Why Hillary Clinton Deleted 33,000 Emails on Her Private Email Server', ABC News, 27 September 2016, abcnews.go.com

'Russia, if you're listening': Ivan Levingston, 'Trump: I hope Russia finds "the 30,000 emails that are missing"', CNBC, 27 July 2016, cnbc.com

'Crossfire Hurricane': Peter Strzok, *Compromised: Counterintelligence and the Threat of Donald J. Trump*, Houghton Mifflin Harcourt, 2020, pp. 110–23; and Private information

'acted without any authority': Interview by author with Malcolm Turnbull, January 2022

'Nazi Germany': Ayesha Rascoe, 'Trump accuses US spy agencies of Nazi practices over "phony" Russia dossier', Reuters, 11 January 2017, reuters.com

'not everything in the dossier is 100% accurate': Online report, 'Trump–Russia Steele dossier analyst charged with lying to FBI', BBC, 5 November 2021, bbc.co.uk

'I do take great umbrage': Eli Watkins, 'Donald Trump slams CIA Director Brennan over plea for "appreciation" of intel community', CNN, 16 January 2017, edition.cnn.com

'ordered an influence campaign': Intelligence Assessment, 'Background to "Assessing Russian Activities and Intentions in Recent US Elections": The Analytic Process and Cyber Incident Attribution', Office of the Director of National Intelligence, 6 January 2017, p. 1, (online via https://www.dni.gov/files/documents/ICA_2017_01)

'a real nut job': Matt Apuzzo, Maggie Haberman and Matthew

Rosenberg, 'Trump Told Russians That Firing "Nut Job" Comey Eased Pressure From Investigation', *New York Times*, 19 March 2017, nytimes.com

'153 Russian intelligence officers': Alia Chughtai and Mariya Petkova, 'Skripal case diplomatic expulsions in numbers', Al Jazeera, 3 April 2018, aljazeera.com

'I suppose when you go into those things': Interview by author with Theresa May, June 2022

'We were learning to adjust': Ibid.

'powerful in his denial': Chris Cillizza, 'The 21 most disturbing lines from Donald Trump's press conference with Vladimir Putin', CNN, 17 July 2018, editioncnn.com

'in a league of its own': Interview by author with Martin Green, March 2022

'fine line to be drawn': Interview by author with Theresa May, June 2022

'we would have said so': Amber Phillips, 'Mueller's statement, annotated', *Washington Post*, 29 May 2019, washingtonpost.com

CHAPTER FIFTEEN

'he used GCHQ': Chris York, 'Did Barack Obama Wiretap Donald Trump? According To Fox News, GCHQ Did It For Him', *Huffington Post*, 14 March 2017

'very sympathetic to us': Private information

'do what's right for you': Ibid.

'forced Major to apologise': Caroline Davies and Owen Bowcott, 'Major apologised to Bill Clinton over draft-dodging suspicions', *Guardian*, 28 December 2018, theguardian.com

'Out of courtesy': Private information

'you can draw your conclusions': Ben Westcott, Dan Merica and Jim Sciutto, 'White House: No apology to British government over spying claims', CNN, 18 March 2017, edition.cnn.com

'The important thing to remember': Interview by author with Theresa May, June 2022

'As far as wiretapping': Julian Borger, Patrick Wintour, Jessica Elgot, 'Trump stands by unsubstantiated claim that British intelligence spied on him', Guardian, 17 March 2017, theguardian.com

'arrant nonsense': Gordon Corera, 'Claims GCHQ wiretapped Trump "nonsense" – NSA's Ledgett', BBC, 18 March 2017, bbc.co.uk

'this is total BS': Private information

'unqualified, unquestioning trust': Interview by author with Douglas H. Wise, February 2022

'policy disruption mission': Private information

'one of the most significant people: Michael Crowley, 'The White House Official Trump Says Doesn't Exist', Politico, 30 May 2018, politico.com

'trade wars are good': Reuters staff, 'Trump tweets: "Trade wars are good, and easy to win"', Reuters, 2 March 2018, reuters.com; see also Reuters Staff, 'Factbox: Tariff wars – duties imposed by Trump and U.S. trading partners', Reuters, 13 May 2019, reuters.com

'We were keen to work with the US': Interview by author with Ciaran Martin, June 2022

'a way to mitigate the risk': Interview by author with Malcolm Turnbull, January 2022

'everything was privatised': Private information

'saying what the politicians wanted to hear': Private information

'Any decision taken by a politician': Interview by author with Theresa May, June 2022

'undue risk of sabotage': Eric Geller, 'Trump signs order setting stage to ban Huawei from US', Politico, 15 May 2019, politico.com

'foreign policy interests': Huawei ban, 'Temporary General License final rule', Bureau of Industry and Security, 20 May 2019

'shouted and was entirely uninterested': Private information

'US case was really political': Interview by author with Lord Darroch, March 2022

'built a base on Tai Mo Shan': Aldrich, *GCHQ*, p. 144

'22.1 million federal employees': Ellen Nakashima, 'Hacks of OPM databases compromised 22.1 million people, federal authorities say', *Washington Post*, 9 July 2015, washingtonpost.com

'some countervailing actions': Roberta Rampton and Lisa Lambert, 'Obama warns China on cyber spying ahead of Xi visit', Reuters, 16 September 2015, reuters.com

'embarrassed the GCSB': Ryan Gallagher and Nicky Hager, 'New Zealand Plotted Hack on China with NSA', *Intercept*, 18 April 2015, theintercept.com; David Fisher, 'Leaked papers reveal NZ plan to spy on China for US', *Herald on Sunday*, 19 April 2015, nzherald.co.nz

'Martin travelled to Washington': Private information

'Incompetent, insecure': Isabel Oakshott, 'Britain's man in the US says Trump is "inept": Leaked secret cables from ambassador say the President is "uniquely dysfunctional and his career could end in disgrace"', *Mail on Sunday*, 6 July 2019, dailymail.co.uk

'cost Britain at least £2 billion': Leo Kelion, 'Huawei 5G kit must be removed from UK by 2027', BBC, 14 July 2020, bbc.co.uk

'the pressure from the US was starting while I was there': Interview by author with Lord Darroch, March 2022

'In reality, anyone can have a go at hacking anything': Interview by author with Ciaran Martin, June 2022

'That happened because of action taken by the US': Interview by author with Theresa May

CONCLUSION

'like minded organisations': Author's note: The alliance partners are part of the Five Eyes Intelligence Oversight and Review Council, which, according to the US Office of the Director of National Intelligence, was created in 2016 to exchange views on matters of 'mutual interest and concern; compare best practices in review and oversight methodology; explore areas where cooperation on reviews and the sharing of results is permitted where appropriate; encourage transparency to the largest extent possible to enhance public trust; and maintain contact with political offices, oversight and review committees, and non-Five Eyes countries as appropriate' – dni.gov

'a level of personal engagement': Interview by author with Sir John Sawers, March 2022

'warning of developing threats': Interview by author with Lord (Jonathan) Evans of Weardale, February 2022

'If you're seeking to discover and disrupt': Interview by author with Sir Iain Lobban, May 2022

'disappear into the American machine': Interview by author with General Sir Richard Barrons, February 2022

'technically focused endeavour': Interview by author with Admiral Mike Rogers, February 2022

'there is a Five Eyes designation': Interview by author with Michael J. Driscoll, April 2022

'cyber intrusions on networks': Interview by author with Sir Iain Lobban, May 2022

'they get a pass when they shouldn't': Interview by author with Richard Fadden, March 2022

'It's only as Prime Minister that you see': Interview by author with David Cameron, June 2022

'duality of benefits and risks': Interview by author with Douglas H. Wise, February 2022

'US$84.1bn in 2021': Total Appropriated, 'US Intelligence Community Budget', Office of the Director of National Intelligence, dni.gov; 'Security and Intelligence Agencies: Financial Statement 2020–21', House of Commons, 16 December 2021. The quoted figure for the British intelligence community budget is based on £3.75 billion, converted to US dollars. Figures relating to the number of staff at MI5, MI6 and GCHQ are based on private information obtained by the author and the 'Intelligence and Security Committee of Parliament, Annual Report 2019–2021', pp. 30–6

The 2021 budgets for other intelligence agencies in the alliance are as follows: Australia's ASIO, ASIS, and ASD (2.120bn); Canada's CSE and CSIS (1.466bn); New Zealand's NZSIS and GCSB (257.3m). All of the figures supplied here are in their respective country's currency, obtained from publicly available annual reports.

'partly geography, partly skills, partly access': Interview by author with Sir John Sawers, March 2022

'I do not hold a sort of romantic view': Interview by author with David Cameron, June 2022

'the difficult and the impossible': Interview by author with Mike Burgess, February 2022

'mission over security': Mark Mazzetti, Adam Goldman, Michael S. Schmidt and Matt Apuzzo, 'Killing C.I.A. Informants, China Crippled US Spying Operations', *New York Times*, 20 May 2017, nytimes.com

'rational actor in self-interest': Interview by author with Julia Gillard, March 2022

'HUMINT will be harder to sustain': Interview by author with Martin Green, March 2022

'the real gold dust': Interview by author with Lord Darroch, March 2022

'We're ready to listen: Devlin Barrett, 'Want to talk? FBI trolls Russian Embassy for disgruntled would-be spies', *Washington Post*, 23 March 2022, washingtonpost.com

'History has shown us': Interview by author with Michael J. Driscoll

'no 'forbidden' areas of cooperation': Simone McCarthy, 'As the West condemns Russia over Ukraine, Beijing strikes a different tone', CNN, February 2022, edition.cnn.com

The reaction by members of the Five Eyes towards China's involvement in the Solomon Islands would undoubtedly have satisfied Beijing, which had condemned a tripartite pact announced by Australia, Britain and US – known as AUKUS – in late 2021. Under AUKUS, the United States and Britain will help Australia build its first nuclear submarines. While the deal is security-related, 'it does not impact the Five Eyes', according to a senior Australian intelligence official. 'Of course there are security aspects around it and there will be intelligence that feeds into that, but the intelligence bit isn't three eyes, it's Five Eyes. And we're very conscious that our Five Eyes friends, Canada and New Zealand, don't get their nose out of joint because it's about subs and only subs in that context.'

TIMELINE

(Historical events, including the formation of organisations that ultimately helped or hindered the Five Eyes)

1873: Formation of the Royal Canadian Mounted Police (RCMP) – commonly referred to as the Mounties – Canada's federal and national police service.

1908: Creation of the Bureau of Investigation (BOI), America's predecessor to the FBI.

1909: Britain's founding of the Secret Service Bureau, which subsequently became the Security Service, commonly known as MI5 (Military Intelligence, Section 5), which deals with the UK's domestic counterintelligence) and the Secret Intelligence Service (SIS), commonly known as MI6, which handles foreign intelligence.

1914: Room 40 (also known as 40 O.B.) was the cryptanalysis section of the British Admiralty during World War I.

1917: Russian Revolution.
— Establishment of the Cheka – All-Russian Extraordinary Commission

(VChk) – the first Bolshevik secret police and forerunner of the KGB.

1919: Established following World War I, the Government Code and Cypher School (GC&CS), Britain's code-breaking agency, was the predecessor to GCHQ.

1919–29: Black Chamber, US cryptanalysis organisation

1930: Signal Intelligence Service, the US Army's code-breaking agency comes into being.

1935: Federal Bureau of Investigation (FBI), the domestic intelligence, security service and federal law-enforcement agency of the United States is established.

1938: MI5 informs the FBI of a Nazi espionage ring in the US

1939: World War II begins

1940: British Security Coordination (BSC) operated as a covert organisation in New York City.

1941: America's Sinkov Mission to Bletchley Park in the UK.

1942: General Douglas MacArthur establishes the Central Bureau, a joint US–Australian signals intelligence (SIGINT); also brought on board code breakers from Britain, Canada and New Zealand.

1943: The Venona Project, a US counter-Soviet programme, begins. The Britain and United States of America Agreement (BRUSA) on signals intelligence is signed between Bletchley Park and Arlington Hall.

1945: Allied Victory achieved in World War II.
— Igor Gouzenko, a Russian cipher clerk, defects to Canada.
— The Cold War begins.

1946: The UKUSA Agreement – formally the United Kingdom–United States of America Agreement originally known as BRUSA – a multilateral agreement for cooperation in signals intelligence (SIGINT) between Britain and America. Australia, Canada and New Zealand were not parties to the agreement, but according to its terms could still benefit from it.
— GC&CS becomes GCHQ (Government Communications Headquarters), the UK's intelligence and security organisation.
— Communications Branch of the National Research Council (NRC), Canada's cryptological agency, comes into existence.

1947: The US National Security Act (1947) leads to the establishment of the Central Intelligence Agency (CIA), the US federal government's civilian foreign intelligence service.
— Defence Signals Bureau (DSB), Australia's predecessor the Australian Signals Directorate (ASD) is created.

1949: ASIO, the Australian Security Intelligence Organisation, is created.
— The formation of the North Atlantic Treaty Organisation (NATO).
— First Soviet Union atomic-bomb test. The USSR detonates its first atomic bomb at the Semipalatinsk Test Site (STS), Kazakhstan.

1952: ASIS, the Australian Secret Intelligence Service, is established.
— The national-level intelligence organisation the National Security Agency (NSA) is established.

1954: Active US involvement in the Vietnam War begins.

1955: The Warsaw Pact (a collective defence treaty formally known as the Treaty of Friendship, Cooperation and Mutual Assistance) is signed between the Soviet Union and its satellites.
— The New Zealand Combined Signals Organisation (NZCSO), later renamed GCSB, is created

1956: UKUSA is officially expanded to form the Five Eyes.
— The New Zealand Security Intelligence Service (NZSIS) is formed.

1961: A Soviet intelligence officer, Oleg Penkovsky, passes secrets to the US and UK ahead of the Cuban Missile Crisis.

1971: MI5's Operation Foot leads to the expulsion of 105 Soviet spies from UK.

1973: The US temporarily stops sharing intelligence with Britain.

1975: Australian Prime Minister Gough Whitlam is sacked amid claims of CIA interference.
— Canada's cryptological agency, the Communications Branch of the National Research Council becomes Communications Security Establishment (CSE).

1976: The Church Committee report into intelligence abuses by CIA, FBI and NSA is published.

1979: Soviet Invasion of Afghanistan.

1984: Canada's primary national intelligence agency, the Canadian Security Intelligence Service (CSIS) is created, replacing the security brief previously held by the RCMP.

1985: New Zealand is partially excluded from the Five Eyes after defying the US.
— Oleg Gordievsky defects to Britain.

1988: The Soviet Union begins its withdrawal from Afghanistan.

1989: The fall of the Berlin Wall.

1991: The Soviet Union collapses.
1999: The United States instigates Moonlight Maze, an investigation into the Russian cyber-attack on the US, UK, and Canada.
— Prime Minister Vladimir Putin appointed Acting President of the Russian Federation.

2000: Vladimir Putin is elected President of Russia.

2001: 'War on Terror' begins following the 9/11 attacks on the United States.
— The US-led invasion of Afghanistan.

2002: Guantanamo Bay detention camp is opened by the US to house suspected terrorists.

2003: The United States leads an invasion of Iraq based on faulty intelligence.

2006: Kremlin agents kill the Russian dissident Alexander Litvinenko.

2010: A Russian spy ring operating in the US and Canada is busted.

2011: Instability in the Middle East becomes the Arab Spring – a series of anti-government protests, uprisings, and armed rebellions.
— Operation Neptune Spear, a US special-ops leads to the killing of Al Qaeda leader Osama bin Laden.

2012: The Canadian naval analyst Jeffrey Delisle is arrested for being a Russian spy.

2013: The NSA whistle-blower Edward Snowden exposes abuses by the Five Eyes

2014: Isis (Islamic State of Iraq and Sham) declares its so-called caliphate.

2015: Jihadi John, the Isis executioner, is killed in a joint US–UK mission.
— China is accused of hacking the US Office of Personnel Management (OPM), compromising the personal details of more than 22 million people.

2016: Russia identified as interfering in the US presidential election.

2018: Following the attempted murder in London of Sergei Skripal – a former Russian military officer and double agent – and his daughter Yulia, 153 Kremlin intelligence officers are expelled from several countries, including those of the Five Eyes.

2019: The Mueller Report into Russian interference in the 2016 US presidential election is published.
— Isis leader Abu Bakr al-Baghdadi is killed.

2020: A US court rules that the NSA's bulk collection of telephone metadata may have been unconstitutional.

2021: European Court of Human Rights (ECtHR) rules that GCHQ's bulk interception of online communications violated freedom of expression .
— The trilateral AUKUS security pact between Australia, Britain, and the United States is announced.

2022: Russia invades Ukraine.

GLOSSARY

ASD: Australian Signals Directorate (previously, Defence Signals Directorate, DSD)

ASIO: Australian Security Intelligence Organisation

ASIS: Australian Secret Intelligence Service

BND: Bundesnachrichtendienst – foreign intelligence service of the Federal Republic of Germany

BRUSA: Britain and United States of America Agreement on signals intelligence, 1943 (*see also* UKUSA)

BSC: British Security Coordination

CIA: Central Intelligence Agency (US)

COMINT: communications intelligence – a subset of signals intelligence such as diplomatic and military intelligence gathered through the interception of wire and radio communications

CSE: Communications Security Establishment (Canada)

CSIS: Canadian Security Intelligence Service

DIA: Defence Intelligence Agency (US)

ECHELON: codename for the surveillance programme initially set up to eavesdrop on diplomatic and military communications

FBI: Federal Bureau of Investigation (US)

FSB: Federal Security Service (Russia)

FVEY: Five Eyes

GC&CS: Government Code and Cypher School (UK)

GCHQ: Government Communications Headquarters (UK)

GCSB: Government Communications Security Bureau (NZ)

GRU: foreign military-intelligence agency of the General Staff of the Armed Forces of the Russian Federation

HUMINT: human intelligence – military intelligence gained from human sources

INTELSAT: International Telecommunications Satellite Organization

ISIS: Islamic State of Iraq and Syria (usually rendered as Isis)

JIC: Joint Intelligence Committee (UK)

KGB: the main intelligence service of the Soviet Union (previously,

Cheka, GPU, NKGB, NKVD, OGPU and MGB)

MI5: Britain's Security Service (Military Intelligence, Section 5)

MI6: Britain's Secret Intelligence Service (SIS)

NATO: North Atlantic Treaty Organization

NCSC: National Cyber Security Centre (UK)

NOFORN: 'not for release to foreign nationals', a designation used by Five Eyes agencies to withhold information from other nations, including in some cases, those in the alliance

NSA: National Security Agency (US)

NZSIS: New Zealand Security Intelligence Service

ODNI: Office of the Director of National Intelligence (US)

OP-20-G: Office of Chief Of Naval Operations, 20th Division of the Office of Naval Communications, G Section / Communications Security

OSS: Office of Strategic Services (US)

RCMP: Royal Canadian Mounted Police

SIGINT: signals intelligence – intelligence gathered through the interception of transmission signals

SALT: Strategic Arms Limitations Talks – bilateral talks (and corresponding international treaties) between the US and USSR during the Cold War

SOE: Special Operations Executive (UK)

SVR RF: Foreign Intelligence Service of the Russian Federation

UKUSA: UK–USA Signals Intelligence Agreement 1946 (see also BRUSA)

SOME OF THE CHARACTERS FEATURED

Maher Arar: a Canadian engineer wrongly accused of terrorist links whose case exposed multiple intelligence failings by agencies within the Five Eyes.

Dr Michael Bialoguski: a Polish doctor in Sydney who moonlighted as a spy for ASIO and helped the Australian agency recruit a top Soviet officer.

Zbigniew Brzezinski: US National Security Advisor during the Carter Administration who wanted to draw the Soviet Union into an unwinnable war in Afghanistan.

Mike Burgess: the director-general of Australia's domestic intelligence agency, ASIO, who also ran his country's SIGINT organisation.

William Donovan: An adviser to President Franklin D. Roosevelt who created the Office of Strategic Services (OSS), the forerunner to the CIA.

Alexander Downer: Australia's High Commissioner to Britain whose tipoff to the FBI triggered an investigation by the US agency into electoral interference by Russia during the 2016 US presidential election.

Michael J. Driscoll: director of the FBI's New York office who has played a key role in his organisation's attempt to foresee – and exploit – the counterintelligence threats spawned by Russia's invasion of Ukraine.

Allen Dulles: a former US diplomat-turned-intelligence operative with the Office of Strategic Service (OSS) who ultimately became one of the most controversial directors of the CIA.

Lord Jonathan Evans: MI5's director-general who oversaw the British agency's operations during the rise of domestic extremism and a growing threat of post-Cold War espionage by Kremlin agents.

Richard Fadden: a former director of Canada's intelligence agency, CSIS, who also served as the country's national security adviser during the rise of Islamic State-inspired terrorism.

Klaus Fuchs: a German nuclear physicist working on the Manhattan Project who leaked atomic secrets to Moscow.

Igor Gouzenko: a Soviet cipher clerk at the Soviet Embassy in Ottawa whose defection to Canada helped expose atomic spies of British and US origin.

Gene Grabeel: co-founder of the Venona Project, the US decryption programme that ultimately identified Soviet spies, including those operating in the US, Britain and Australia.

J. Edgar Hoover: The longest-serving FBI director, who oversaw the organisation's victories and disasters from the 1920s and into the Cold War until his death in 1972.

Jessie Jordan: A Scottish hairdresser who worked as a Nazi agent, using her salon in Scotland as a shop front for spying missions.

Geza Katona: a CIA officer stationed in Budapest who had been recruited as part of the agency's mission to undermine Soviet influence in Hungary.

Robert Lamphere: An FBI counterintelligence officer who helped pioneer cooperation between the disciplines of HUMINT and SIGINT during the early days of the Cold War.

David Lange: New Zealand's Prime Minister during the 1980s who defied the White House with his anti-nuclear stance in a move that compromised his country's relationship with the Five Eyes.

Guy Liddell: A senior official at the British Security Service, MI5, who played a key role in overseeing counterespionage operations and helped form the bilateral relationship between his agency and the FBI – a bedrock of the Five Eyes.

Sir Iain Lobban: the director of GCHQ who guided the British signals intelligence agency through the international public backlash that followed Edward Snowden's revelations.

Oleg Lyalin: a London-based KGB officer with a complicated love life and drinking habit whose behaviour concerned the Kremlin and intrigued MI5.

Eliza Manningham-Buller: An MI5 director-general who oversaw the British agency during the most turbulent years that followed the 9/11 attacks on the United States.

Ciaran Martin: a senior GCHQ official who defended his organisation against the claim that it had 'wiretapped' Donald Trump's New York office during the 2016 US presidential election.

Vladimir Petrov: a Russian intelligence officer in Australia who became the subject of a recruitment campaign by the Australian spy agency, ASIO.

Ron Richards: an Australian spymaster of British heritage who oversaw one of ASIO's greatest achievements during the Cold War, helping to rehabilitate Canberra's intelligence capabilities in the eyes of Washington, DC.

Admiral Mike Rogers: took control of the US National Security Agency (NSA) after its surveillance programmes had been exposed by Edward Snowden.

Frank Rowlett: a US code breaker and talent-spotter who helped break Japan's secret diplomatic communications during World War II before overseeing the operations of the Venona Project.

Dr Abraham Sinkov: a US Army code breaker who helped build the foundational relationships between Arlington Hall and Bletchley Park before leading a team of cryptographers from all Five Eyes countries in Australia.

Edward Snowden: the NSA contractor who exposed the global spying operations of the Five Eyes, forcing a historic debate on personal privacy and multiple investigations into government surveillance programmes.

William Stephenson: A Canadian entrepreneur with links to the British establishment and the White House who helped MI6 create a propaganda agency in the US during World War II.

Arthur Thurston: An FBI Special Agent who liaised with MI5 and MI6 in Britain, serving as Hoover's right-hand man in London before creating his organisation's first bureau in the British capital.

Malcolm Turnbull: the Australian prime minister whose decision to ban the Chinese tech firm Huawei from operating in Australia led the way for the other Five Eyes countries to follow suit.

Richard Walton: Scotland Yard's counterterrorism chief whose mission to stop British jihadists travelling to the battlefields of Syria was disrupted by a Canadian intelligence blunder.

Gough Whitlam: Australia's Labor Prime Minister in the early 1970s who felt misled about the CIA's secret involvement in a joint US–Australian defence facility.

ACKNOWLEDGEMENTS

I knew very little about the Five Eyes before the Snowden Affair – but in 2018, my interest in researching the alliance was intensified during the filming of a documentary for HBO and Channel 4, *The Hunt for Jihadi John*. I was fortunate to interview top intelligence officials in London and Washington about the transatlantic mission to 'find, fix and finish' the ISIS terrorist. Their revelations about the joint British–US case exposed the subtle differences that play out in operational partnerships – even when both sides are in pursuit of a mutual goal.

With that in mind, I began searching for the points of difference within the Five Eyes as the world went into lockdown – and suddenly, everyone was a Zoom call away, thrilled to discuss anything but coronavirus. As an outsider, I needed to rely on those with lived experience to provide me with an inside perspective – and the generosity afforded to me by Five Eyes security professionals was a blessing.

This book could not have been written without the help and guidance of Sir Iain Lobban, Ciaran Martin, Lord Evans, Richard Walton, Douglas Wise, General David Petraeus, Mike Burgess, Michael J. Driscoll, Lord Anderson, Peter Clarke, Richard Fadden, David Irvine, Lord Darroch, Baroness Manningham-Buller, Lord Richards, Timothy Dowse, Alexander Downer, Sir Richard Barrons, Sir John Sawers, Admiral Mike Rogers, Bill Murray, Simon McKay, Kris Patina, Kurt Pipal, Meredith

Woodruff, David Irvine, Alan Rock, Wesley Wark, Martin Green, Greg Fyffe, Vincent Rigby, Joe Burton, Bill Robinson, and Paul Buchanan. Many others whom I was privileged to learn from wanted to remain anonymous, because, in some cases, they are still in active roles.

I am humbled to have been given an audience by world leaders, including Julia Gillard, Theresa May, Malcolm Turnbull and David Cameron. I am also indebted to the historians who shared their wisdom with me, including David Oakley, Gill Bennett, Dr John Fox, Gordon Corera, Brian Toohey, Richard Aldrich, Rory Cormac, Rhodri Jeffreys-Jones, Dan Lomas, Tim Weiner, Nicky Hager and Robert Manne – and also Gene Cole Knight and Susan De Rosa for sharing the stories of their loved ones with me.

The journey from idea to book was made easier by Richard Pike, my literary agent, who helped me shape the manuscript proposal (often saying, 'You just need a few more pages'), and Luke Speed, my TV agent – the first to champion my idea. Toby Buchan, my editor at Bonnier, was a delight to work with, especially when discussing the Cold War, about which he knows far more than I.

I am very privileged to have learned so much over the years from journalists including Peter Wilson, Jon Ungoed-Thomas, Tim Shipman, Oliver Shah, and Mark Hookham, and to have received the help of Ray Wells, Baroness Sanderson, Julia Atherley, Tony Farag, Tom Butler-Roberts, Angela Bell, Amy Thoreson, J. G. Debray, Juliette Debray (who at least once accessed academic journals for me while queuing outside a nightclub) and Ciara Lloyd, Isabel Smith, Ellie Carr and the team at Bonnier. Thank you also to Richard Brown and Kevin Plunkett.

I owe a great deal to Benjamin Sheehan, Rowena Stretton, the first editor to publish me, Christopher Dore, the first to give me a staff job on a newspaper, and to Greg Sheridan who told me to pursue the premier league.

To my parents, Souad and Salim, parents-in-law, Isabelle and Pierre, siblings and siblings-in-law: thanks for pretending to be enthralled each time I tell spy stories. And finally, to those whose unconditional belief in me has helped me finish this project: my wife Marine, son Leo, and my great life advisers – Dominic Kennedy and John Dauth.

INDEX